PASSPORT
TO
JEWISH MUSIC

Recent Titles in
Contributions to the Study of Music and Dance

Philosophy and the Analysis of Music: Bridges to Musical
Sound, Form, and Reference
Lawrence Ferrara

Alfred Einstein on Music: Selected Music Criticisms
Catherine Dower

Salsiology: Afro-Cuban Music and the Evolution of Salsa in New York City
Vernon W. Boggs

Dancing Till Dawn: A Century of Exhibition Ballroom Dance
Julie Malnig

Mainstream Music of Early Twentieth Century America: The Composers, Their Times,
and Their Works
Nicholas E. Tawa

Televising the Performing Arts: Interviews with Merrill Brockway, Kirk Browning,
and Roger Englander
Brian Rose

Johann Sebastian: A Tercentenary Celebration
Seymour L. Benstock, editor

An Outward Show: Music for Shakespeare on the London Stage, 1660–1830
Randy L. Neighbarger

The Musical Image: A Theory of Content
Laurence D. Berman

Opera Odyssey: Toward a History of Opera in Nineteenth-Century America
June C. Ottenberg

PASSPORT TO JEWISH MUSIC

Its History, Traditions, and Culture

Irene Heskes

Contributions to the Study of Music and Dance,
Number 33

GREENWOOD PRESS
Westport, Connecticut • London

Library of Congress Cataloging-in-Publication Data

Heskes, Irene.
    Passport to Jewish music : its history, traditions, and culture /
Irene Heskes.
       p. cm.—(Contributions to the study of music and dance,
ISSN 0193–9041 ; no. 33)
    Includes bibliographical references and index.
    ISBN 0–313–28035–5 (alk. paper)
    1. Jews—Music—History and criticism. I. Title. II. Series.
ML3776.H47   1994
780′.89924—dc20   93–35835

British Library Cataloguing in Publication Data is available.

Library of Congress Catalog Card Number: 93–35835
ISBN: 0–313–28035–5
ISSN: 0193–9041

First published in 1994

Greenwood Press, 88 Post Road West, Westport, CT 06881
An imprint of Greenwood Publishing Group, Inc.

Printed in the United States of America

∞™

The paper used in this book complies with the
Permanent Paper Standard issued by the National
Information Standards Organization (Z39.48–1984).

10 9 8 7 6 5 4 3 2 1

Contents

Part IX: Composers and Compositions

X. Women

Preface

History belongs to those who leave behind a clear record. As mankind approaches the twenty-first century, various mischievous denials have emerged: denials that the Holocaust ever happened; denials of Jewish cultural and intellectual achievements, and denials as to Judaism's companionable place alongside Christianity, Islam, and the other world religions. I am a historian of music, and the purpose of this book is to present a survey of Jewish music in order to illuminate its special role as a mirror of history, traditions, and cultural heritage. This volume, therefore, is a purposeful documentary record presenting a survey of a particular form of individual and collective artistic expression, as created and practiced over millennia. The arts interpret life and celebrate human existence, and it is a function of those arts to serve historical memory.

The contents are based upon the author's lectures and writings, products of several decades of dedicated study and scholarly labors in the field of Jewish music. Sectioned into ten different part headings, are thirty-four chapters placed in a modified chronological order to present a historical sweep of musical developments. A wide range of subject matter has been treated in each of those chapters. Part I opens with a first chapter highlighting significant contributions by collectors of Jewish music as well as some important repositories of unique collections. Chapter two details the valuable achievements of two leading figures in Jewish musicological research and publication (Abraham Zvi Idelsohn and Gershon Ephros), noting the influence of their warm personal friendship on their activities. Indeed, many other mutually encouraging relationships between leading scholars and musicians appear to have resulted in valuable endeavors on behalf of Jewish music; examples are cited throughout this book. In the third chapter, six such leaders are discussed: Henry G. Farmer, Curt Sachs, Alfred Sendrey, Egon Wellesz, Eric Werner, and Joseph Yasser.

The next four chapters, as Part II, cover a substantial range of music directly related to Jewish religious expression. Within the subject area of the biblical heritage, attention is drawn to studies made by Carl H. Cornill, Carl Engel, Carl

H. Kraeling, Solomon Rosowsky, and Jacob Beimel; also included are discussions of biblical cantillation and possible explanations for the term *selah*. Then there is a bibliographic survey of eastern European liturgical anthologies published before 1900. This is followed by a historical consideration of the cantorial art: its rise and development, musical styles, and artistry. That section is rounded out with a seventh chapter detailing the musical literature for the entire Jewish liturgical calendar. Special musical traditions are described for each of the following religious observances: High Holy Days (*Rosh Hashanah, Yom Kippur*, the *shofar* [ram's horn], and *kol nidrey* chant); *Sukkoth* (Booths), *Pesakh* (Passover) and *seder* (ritual meal), and *Shevuoth* (Weeks); *Hanukkah* (Feast of Lights) and *Purim* (Feast of Lots); the weekly Sabbath celebration; life cycle events; and such special hymns as *eyn keloheynu* and *yigdal*.

The five chapters in Part III focus on music traditions in the heritage of Sephardic and Oriental Jewry, and highlight important resource collections of those materials. Then Part IV provides some perspectives on music that is reflective of Jewish mysticism. Its three chapters range in history from the liturgical poet-bards of the medieval and later Renaissance eras to the eighteenth-century rise and nineteenth-century flowering of Hasidism (Jewish pietism) with its particular melodic custom of the *nigun* (spiritual tune); attention also is drawn to some recently published collections of this music as it is performed in more current times.

Yiddish musical expression is the core subject of Part V. One chapter is devoted to the origins and flowering of Yiddish entertainment artistry, and to the life and works of Abraham Goldfaden, founding father of the Yiddish theater. In a chapter on Russian nationalism and Jewish music, there is discussion of the important contributions of Joel Engel and the St. Petersburg Society for Jewish Folk Music, and the subsequent influences beyond Russia to America and Israel. Part VI is devoted to music reflective of the Holocaust era, commencing with the infamous tracts of Richard Wagner. The role of music in the rise and rule of Nazism is outlined, and there is a discussion of music as expressive of resistance and survival in the ghettos and concentration camps. References are made to collections of the Holocaust songs and of the topical inspiration to post-war compositions.

Part VII presents a detailed survey of three centuries of Jewish musical expression in America. The wide range of subject matter includes: pre-Colonial years to American Independence; the nineteenth century before and after the Civil War; a roster of Jewish hymnodists, including Alois Kaiser, William Sparger, Max Spicker, Sigmund Schlesinger, Frederick Emil Kitziger, and Edward Stark; American Jewish hymnals and various editions of the Reform Union Hymnal; Yiddish minstrelsy and the particular contributions of song writers David Meyerowitz, Solomon Smulewitz, Joseph Rumshinsky, Sholom Secunda, and Abraham Ellstein; the story of the song-hymn *Eili, Eili*; the emergence of distinctive American liturgical music and cantorial artistry; and a notable roster of educators, scholars, organizations, and publications. This section concludes with consideration of some developments in Canada and other areas of North America.

The next four chapters as Part VIII are devoted to the musical expression of Zionism and the emergent State of Israel. First there is a study of the life and writings of Naphtali Herz Imber, the poet of the Jewish national anthem *Hatikvah*. Then, folk song creativity is viewed in terms of Zionist *aliyah* (immigration), with attention to Chaim Nachman Bialik, Nahum Nardi, among other creative figures. The matter of serious composition reflective of Israel is viewed, with particular note of composer Paul Ben-Haim. Part IX consists of chapters on several notable composers who happen to have been of Jewish lineage, and presents biographical perspectives on their individual careers, highlighting the Judaic elements in their lives and works. That section concludes with a roster of biblical text settings by non-Jewish as well as Jewish composers

The book is rounded out with Part X, a chapter devoted to a historical view of musical expression on the part of Jewish women, and then concludes with a brief Afterword of summary remarks. Finally, an Index of Personalities provides a portal access to the book's contents, as well as a dynamic view of the multitude of individuals who have been involved in some form or manner with Jewish music over the centuries.

Concluding each of the thirty-four chapters are extensive reference notes, appended to clarify the text materials and to provide information regarding other available sources of material on a particular topic. Particular attention has been given to citations of other authors and of their published works (books, monographs, articles, and music collections), often with annotations about the contents and the relevance to Jewish music. I greatly value and deeply respect the contributions of those other cited authors, and I hope that readers of my book will wish to seek out their informative works. In many respects, this book is a partner resource to my earlier work, *The Resource Book of Jewish Music* (Greenwood Press, 1985). That previously issued volume is an annotated bibliographic compilation of the many publications in this field: reference works, books and monographs, articles, periodicals, pedagogical materials, anthologies, hymnals, and song books.

Some clarifications must be added. Biographical dates have been given only if a necrology has been verified, and those dates often are repeated from chapter to chapter to suit the substance of the text. In several cases, in order to avoid duplication or repetition, a reference note is added citing materials covered in another chapter of the book. Occasionally, however, information has been restated because it appears to fit the flow of the historical narrative or else is significant to the topical nature of more than one chapter. Transliteration (romanization) of Hebrew, Yiddish, and other non-English words may vary according to specific titles or particular idiomatic usage. Unless otherwise indicated, all translations from Hebrew, Yiddish, and other languages are my own.

Materials from my previously written articles have been taken from these publications: *Acta Musicologica: Musica Antiqua Europae* (International Musicological Society); *Congress Bi-Weekly* (American Jewish Congress); *Handbook of Holocaust Literature* (Saul Friedman, ed.; Greenwood Press); *Jewish Frontier, Judaisme Sephardi* and *Kol Sepharad* (World Sephardi Foundation); *Music in North America* (Charles Hamm, ed.; Smithsonian Institute Press and UNESCO); *Notes* (Music Library Association); *The Reconstructionist* (Jewish Reconstructionist Foundation); and two music score collections, *The Music of Abraham Goldfaden* and *The Golden Age of Cantors* (Tara Music Publications). Detailed acknowledgments have been given in the various chapter notes. I remain extremely grateful to those editors, publications, and publishers.

I also much appreciate the important assistance rendered to me in the preparation of this work by the staffs at these facilities of the New York Public Library: Central Research Library and Reading Room, Jewish Division, and Music Division of the Lincoln Center for the Performing Arts. They were all unfailingly supportive and informative, and that entire library complex is one of the joys of my life. I am thankful to Greenwood Press and editor Peter Coveney and his staff for helping bring this book into publication. Lastly, I acknowledge my indebtedness to my husband, Jacob Heskes, for his encouraging support and technical aid, and I affectionately dedicate this work to my children—Deborah and Alan Kraut, Walter and Lisa Heskes—and to my granddaughter, Julia Rose Kraut.

Music is central to the human spirit. It is the most universal and yet most personal of godly gifts. It is our continuity from past to present, and into the timeless future.

Part I

Documenting the Heritage

1

A Duty of Preservation and Continuity: Collectors and Collections of Jewish Music in America

The Book of *Koheleth* (Ecclesiastes) concludes with the admonition: "Of making many books there is no end, and much study is a weariness of the flesh." Such counsel certainly has never been heeded by bibliographers and book collectors, nor by librarians. All of them also appear to have declined the advice of the Roman stoic emperor Marcus Aurelius, we should free ourselves from the thirst for books.

Apparently, since those ancient times, many people have succumbed to an overwhelming desire not only to read and write, but to search out and acquire written materials related to a favored topic. Such passion could shape an entire lifetime of activity, the bibliographer compiling documentations and the collector gathering, sorting, and saving. Often the work of collecting has been combined with that of bibliography, and thereby that act of collection also has become a service of verification: an item was once written and then set into some form of public distribution; it has been found and preserved, and so here it is, ready for examination. In this context, collection has been, and continues to be, an instrument of history. One cannot, therefore, overlook the dynamic influence of collectors upon the actual direction and content of scholarly works. Often there have been symbiotic interactions among collectors, bibliographers, and scholars, with the collector serving less as passive conserver and more as active catalyst for a field of study.

Insofar as Jewish music is concerned, there have been some fascinating constellations of dynamic and influential relationships, some of which I hope to make clear by highlighting one significant music collector, Eric Mandell. By particularizing this collector's achievements and placing his dedicated work within the frame of other collections in the field of Jewish music, I seek to underscore the very important contributions and influences that such devoted labors have had upon the growth and enrichment of our musical heritage. In this case, the collector's objectives were dual: to advance the systematic study of Jewish music, and to provide sources of information that place this music within the aggregate of all musical expression.

Eric Mandell (Erich Mendel) was born in 1902 in Gronai, Westphalia, where he sang in a synagogue boy-choir and then as a young man prepared himself for a career as cantor and teacher in Jewish schools. He studied music in Berlin and Munich, and from 1922 to 1939 served as cantor and educator for the synagogue in Bochum, Westphalia. He first began to collect music books and scores in his youth, and by 1939 had accumulated a substantial number of items, a collection remarkable in scope and quantity for the personal library of a young man of very moderate means. Among his items were significant general music materials as well as Judaica.

Shortly before he fled to England in 1939, Mandell shipped his collection to Holland for safekeeping there, but all of it was irretrievably lost. In 1941, he came to the United States and soon took on the post of music director at Har Zion Temple in Philadelphia, where he served until his retirement. Settled in America, Mandell resumed his work of collecting, at first in the hope that his missing European materials would someday be found. His zeal for Jewish music combined with an ardent appreciation of his newly adopted country, and so he particularly sought out American items.

When all efforts to recover his European collection failed, Mandell decided to rebuild by salvaging whatever might be found of any musical Judaica left on the continent in ruined synagogues or among unclaimed personal belongings of Jewish musicians. This became a mission of dedication; he searched tirelessly at great financial sacrifice, and was remarkably innovative and venturesome in making his contacts abroad. He sought out book dealers, publishers, musicians, community leaders, and public figures, and traced all manner of leads. In America, his activities as a professional synagogue musician brought him in touch with many others in this field who either had important holdings to offer him or were able to direct him towards available items. He became especially skillful and sensitive in approaching Holocaust survivors for their music, and they also helped him to locate estates of the deceased.

Mandell was truly imaginative and instinctive in undertaking his many European negotiations, never finding himself in competition with the libraries of governments or educational institutions. He simply was singularly interested in this material, and the labor was in finding, securing, and transporting it back to his location in America. Indeed, he developed an uncanny aptitude for discovery, and by these extraordinary efforts put together a treasury that literally filled the rooms of his Philadelphia brownstone house.

By 1947, Mandell's collection had already attracted local community interest, and during that year three hundred examples of literature, scores, and manuscripts were exhibited for two months at the Free Library of Philadelphia. The following year, a display was presented at the Jewish Museum in New York City. Then, for the 1954 celebration of the tercentenary of Jewish settlement in

America, the Smithsonian Institution showed a number of Mandell's unique acquisitions. Also in Washington, D.C., in 1961 a special exhibition filled the main hall of the national office of the B'nai B'rith Organization. For each of these shows, Mandell prepared a concise guide to the origins, publication styles, and iconography of the materials.[1]

In 1965, I first visited him to see his collection and was fascinated by its size and scope, and deeply impressed with this man's devotion to his "labor of love." He knew all his acquisitions and carefully protected them. By this time, however, Parkinson's disease had slowed Mandell's energies, and soon he was compelled to curtail his professional work and became confined to home. It was about this time that a wonderful opportunity to transfer the collection developed, and since 1970 the Eric Mandell Collection of Jewish Music has been housed as the focal section of the Schreiber Music Library at the Gratz College of Jewish Studies in the Philadelphia area. Mandell was alive at the time of the earlier publication of this chapter, an off print of which he graciously acknowledged by letter to this author. He died in 1984.

Gratz College was constituted in 1895 under final provisions of a deed of trust originally executed in 1856 by Hyman Gratz (1776–1857), member of a historic Jewish family of Philadelphia. Regular instruction began in the assembly rooms of the old Mikveh Israel Synagogue on Arch Street. In 1928, Gratz College was greatly expanded to serve the general Jewish education needs of Greater Philadelphia, and by 1962 was located at a site on Tenth Street and Tabor Road. Two decades later, it was moved to a larger academic facility on a suburban campus at Old York Road in Melrose Park, Pennsylvania.

While study of hymnology and folk music had always been included in the curriculum, strengthened emphasis on Jewish music commenced with the appointment of Shalom Altman (1911-1986) as music director in 1945. Expanded and restructured in 1958, the Tyson Music Department of Gratz College has provided three main services: (1) courses of study in Jewish music for educators and scholars in an academic program, accredited by the Middle States Association of Colleges and Secondary Schools for the B.A. and M.A. degrees; (2) community wide consultation and programming activities; and, (3) the Schreiber Music Library, constituted as a central resource for Jewish music—literature, scores, recordings, and media materials—for which the Eric Mandell Collection was acquired, largely as a result of the special efforts of Shalom Altman.

During the first years of acquisition, Eric Mandell was able to serve as consultant-curator and advise on the appropriate arrangements to house his collection at the already excellent library facilities, that included a grand piano, all types of audio equipment, and many different educational aids. Over the ensuing years, the Mandell Collection has been extensively used for scholarly studies as well as performances. Consisting of some 15,000 items, it includes books, articles, clippings, catalogues, anthologies, sheet music, vocal and instrumental compilations, and a variety of manuscripts. The holdings are approximately 70 percent music and 30 percent literature, and may be divided into five distinct categories:

1. Americana, consisting of Jewish and non-Jewish materials from the early nineteenth century and comprising a broad range of hymnology and other liturgical music as well as a wide variety of secular music—folk, art, and theatrical-popular.

2. European synagogue and cantorial music, including liturgical items from the eighteenth century onward and anthologies for most of the leading synagogue music figures of the past two centuries.

3. European secular Jewish music—folk and art song compilations and manuscript scores in many languages.

4. Collected articles, clippings from newspapers and journals, and other printed matter, all treating a great variety of subjects within the frame of worldwide Jewish music.

5. An array of 350 books, of which 115 date from 1705 to 1900. For several years after this acquisition, Warner Victor (1905-1990), an archivist-researcher and accomplished German and Hebrew linguist, assisted in the preparation of annotated catalogues for these rare printed volumes.

With the installation of the Mandell Collection, the music library at Gratz College has become one of the leading sources for unique and rare materials on Jewish music. In America, it probably ranks second in scholarly significance only to the holdings at the Klau Library of Hebrew Union College–Jewish Institute of Religion on its Cincinnati campus. Klau Library houses the remarkable and monumental Eduard Birnbaum Collection of Jewish Music, also fruits of the lifelong labor of acquisition by one individual collector. No great collection can really stand alone, as the interrelationship of these great collectors amply demonstrates.

In 1875, Hebrew Union College was founded in Cincinnati by Rabbi Isaac Mayer Wise (1819–1900), considered the father of organized Reform Judaism in the United States.[2] A library was immediately begun with donations of private holdings, and by 1881 this already constituted the country's largest repository of Judaica. In 1907, Adolph S. Oko (1883-1944), who had worked in the cataloguing department of the New York Public Library, became the first professional librarian at the school. Until he left in 1933, Oko developed the library through fine acquisitions, expansion of the facilities, and catalogue organization. After World War I, he traveled in Europe on behalf of the library, seeking and purchasing many valuable items. Among Oko's triumphs was securing in 1923, by transaction with family heirs, the personal library and collection of Eduard Birnbaum: a treasury of books, manuscripts and study documents, research papers, scores and sheet music, cantorial compilations, and synagogue compositions. In this important endeavor, Oko was fortunate to have the active support of the Synagogue Music Committee of the Central Conference of American Rabbis.[3]

In 1925, Abraham Z. Idelsohn (1882–1938) was invited to join the staff of the Klau Library, and subsequently also the college faculty, serving as archival consultant and curator for the Birnbaum Collection as well as other music holdings. Unfortunately, failing health forced his premature retirement in 1934 from those positions. However, during the years that Idelsohn spent at the library and school, he completed his monumental ten-volume *Thesaurus of Oriental Hebrew Melodies*,[4] basing the contents of volumes 6, 7, and 8 upon examination of Birnbaum's studies and manuscript papers, and in particular upon his extensive thematic catalogue of traditional synagogue melodies of the period 1700 to 1900. Subsequently, Eric Werner (1901–1988) joined the Cincinnati faculty in 1939, moving to the New York campus in 1948, and his own significant scholarship over the ensuing years was nourished by direct contact with the Birnbaum Collection.[5]

Cantor Eduard Birnbaum (1855–1920) was born into family of notable rabbis and scholars, and combined his scholastic inclinations with a fine musical aptitude applied to a life of liturgical service and musicological study. For over forty-five years, despite modest financial means, Birnbaum accumulated an enormous collection of eighteenth- and nineteenth-century European synagogue music. He was also an enthusiastic teacher and maintained wide-ranging intellectual contacts.[6] Much respected by his colleagues, he soon became a sort of role model for many younger Jewish musicians. Of Birnbaum's own teacher-mentors, Cantor Salomon Sulzer (1804–1890), the celebrated music leader at a great synagogue in Vienna generally known as the Seitenstettengasse Shul, was especially influential.[7] Sulzer collected, arranged, composed, and published liturgical music, and he commissioned religious works from such notable non-Jewish composers as Franz Schubert and Ignaz Moscheles. During the years of his study with Sulzer, Eduard Birnbaum began his own collection by copying many old manuscripts from Sulzer's personal materials. Decades later, for a tribute marking the date of Sulzer's hundredth birthday, Birnbaum wrote a series of biographical and bibliographical studies treating the life and work of Salomon Sulzer.[8]

Although the Birnbaum Collection in the Klau Library at Cincinnati contains those copied Sulzer materials, many of the actual items from Sulzer's synagogue —rare scores and old choir books—may now be found only in the Mandell Collection at Gratz College. This music was acquired by Eric Mandell from the estate holdings of Heinrich Fischer (d. 1943), the last cantor at Sulzer's Vienna congregation, serving until its desecration by the Nazis in 1938. Moreover, the Gratz music library also has unique scores and papers of Eduard Birnbaum himself. These materials came by way of Mandell's acquisition of the music estate of another avid collector, Arno Nadel (1878–1943), who had been a pupil and devoted protégé of Birnbaum. In turn, Nadel had been the mentor and dear friend of Eric Mandell, and the two had shared their interests in the collection of Jewish music. Indeed, the legacy of Arno Nadel is a significant component of the collection at Gratz.

Arno Nadel came from his home in Vilna to Koenigsberg to sing in Cantor Birnbaum's boy-choir, and stayed on as his cantorial student. Nadel saved all of his music from those years, including Birnbaum's handwritten scores and inscribed manuscripts. He took them with him to Berlin, where he settled as an educator and choirmaster for the Kottbuser Ufer Shul. There, Nadel began to develop his own extensive music library. In 1923, the Berlin Congregational Community commissioned Nadel to compile an anthology of synagogue music, which he finally completed in 1938. This was intended for publication as an encyclopedia in seven folios to be used for musicological research. Arno Nadel perished in Auschwitz, but before he was taken away he left his entire library with a neighbor who managed to save a good part of the material; after the war the neighbor returned it to Nadel's estate. Eric Mandell located Nadel's widow and purchased the music from her.

Over the years, Mandell had much active and fruitful contact with other musicians, scholars, and collectors in this country. For a time he was a member of the Jewish Music Forum, a society that flourished from 1939 to 1960, sponsoring lectures and concerts in New York City. Among the other society members were: Abraham W. Binder (1895–1966), Lazare Saminsky (1882–1959), Curt Sachs (1881–1959), Joseph Yasser (1893–1981), Paul Nettl (1889–1972), Stefan Wolpe (1902–1972), Gershon Ephros (1890–1978), and Alfred Sendrey (1884–1976). In those years, Sendrey was completing his monumental bibliography of Jewish music literature and scores,[9] and Ephros, who in Jerusalem had been a young protégé of Abraham Z. Idelsohn, had launched his own work on a multivolume anthological collection of traditional cantorial music.[10]

Those years of meetings and interactions among so many gifted musicians were stimulating and fruitful, producing a multitude of projects that shaped an arena of international leadership in America for the advancement of Jewish music study, composition, performance, publication, and education. Not the least of those accomplishments was the development of excellent training schools for the cantorate. Indeed, a historical overview of the fifty-year period in American Jewish music from 1915 to 1965 would document the process by which Jewish music leadership passed over into America, and incidentally enriched the general musical climate of the country. From 1945 onward, Eric Mandell was a part of that milieu as a synagogue musician and collector.

There are some extensive collections of musical Judaica at libraries in England, France, Russia, Ukraine, and the Vatican. In the State of Israel, much material has been gathered and continues to be collected for university archives, libraries, and museums there. Especially noteworthy are the resources at the Jewish Music Research Centre of the National Library at Hebrew University in Jerusalem. Also of interest are holdings at the Haifa Music Museum and AMLI

(Americans for a Library in Israel) library as well as at the comprehensive library of Tel Aviv University.

In the United States, Jewish music scores and topical literature may be found in the libraries of universities and religious seminaries, at the Library of Congress, as well as in public libraries. There are fine materials at the New York Public Library, Jewish Division. The Music Division of the Performing Arts Research Center at Lincoln Center has a collection of literature and music materials that was acquired in 1941 from the organizational holdings of the *Mailamm*-American Palestine Music Association (1932–1939). The two sources that afford extraordinary scholarly advantages, however, remain the collection of Eduard Birnbaum at the Klau Library in Cincinnati and that of Eric Mandell at Gratz College. The essential focus of the Birnbaum materials is upon European liturgy, while the Mandell archives provide not only European materials but also an important selection of Americana. Both collections were products of the lifelong labors of two dedicated collectors whose legacies should sustain   generations of scholars far into the twenty-first century.

In the 1963 volume of *Fontes Artis Musicae* vol. 10, nos. 1/2 (Kassel: IAML, 1963), Eric Mandell contributed a brief article, "A Collector's Random Notes on the Bibliography of Jewish Music" (pp. 34–42). In it he remarked that "the true collector is an eternal student." Perhaps Mandel was too modest. Others might rather consider the collector as a devoted caretaker of continuity, as someone who serves the future. Some individuals seem by nature to be dedicated collectors. Like Mandell and Birnbaum, they combine scholarly musicality with a sense of history. Directing their energies and resources towards goals of conservation, they have gone about that mission with educated selectivity, almost limitless attentiveness, and a healthy respect for the luck of a fortuitous discovery. In this manner, those collectors influence the trend of scholarship. For better, and one hopes seldom for worse, our educated society is dependent upon their collections.

There is a mystique to the work of the inspired collector, part idealistic philanthropy and sometimes impractical occupation. Simple possession may be one objective; devotion to certain traditions or topics may be another motivation. Still another may relate to the convenience of having various research materials at hand for personal study. The collector may also wish to connect tangibly with others in the same field of interest, across time and place. To some extent, many of us are music collectors, and we may even have acquired some unique things. By these acts of conservation and preservation, we too are sustaining a continuity. We are choosing whatever we happen to value in this art, and what seems to reflect our own particular purposeful endeavors. In saving, we are passing ourselves along with those items into the uncharted time ahead.

NOTES

Following its presentation as a paper at a joint session of the Music Library Association and the Sonneck Society for American Music held in Philadelphia in March 1983, this chapter was published in the quarterly journal *Music Library Association Notes*, vol. 40, no. 2 (December 1983). It was a by-product of the author's work at the time on *The Resource Book of Jewish Music: A Bibliographical and Topical Guide to the Book and Journal Literature and Program Materials*, published by Greenwood Press in 1985. For this edition, new background materials and footnote information have been added in order to update and supplement the original text.

1. Copies of these guides are among the catalogues in the Mandell Collection.
2. For a detailed history, see Samuel E. Karff, ed., *Hebrew Union College–Jewish Institute of Religion: One Hundred Years* (Cincinnati: Hebrew Union College -Jewish Institute of Religion [HUC-JIR], 1976).
3. "Committees' Reports," in Central Conference of American Rabbis [CCAR] *Yearbook*, vols. 32 and 33 (Cincinnati: CCAR, 1922 and 1925).
Unlike Gratz College, which established a separate music library facility, Hebrew Union College has always integrated its music holdings into the main library. In 1931, a campus building was erected in Cincinnati to house what by then constituted a major resource, and an even larger structure was dedicated there in 1962 as the Klau Library. In New York City in 1922, Rabbi Stephen Wise (1874–1949) had created another school for the training of rabbis in the Reform movement, the Jewish Institute of Religion. Here, a library was created by Joshua Bloch (1890–1957) before he left in 1923 to become librarian of the Jewish Division of the New York Public Library. The two schools merged commencing in 1948. By 1980 there were four campuses of the Hebrew Union College–Jewish Institute of Religion (HUC-JIR): Cincinnati, New York, Los Angeles, and Jerusalem. All have libraries to serve students and faculty and are maintained under unified policies and practices. Inasmuch as HUC-JIR established a School of Sacred Music in 1948 on its New York City campus, there is an extensive selection of music materials at that branch library, consisting of literature, scores, and recordings, all integrated into the catalogue.
The major library at Cincinnati constitutes a chief repository for scholarly resources and houses a great array of materials, from which the other branches may draw loans while building up their own collections. The Birnbaum Music Collection is maintained at Klau Library in Cincinnati, kept in a secure area for rare books, and is accessible for examination only at that location. There is no interlibrary loan of the Birnbaum materials. Cataloguing is complete, with a fourteen-leaf inventory for reference use, and finding aids have been placed on microfilm.
4. Abraham Z. Idelsohn, *Hebraeish-Orientalisher Melodienschatz*. Editions of the ten volumes were originally published between 1922 and 1933 in Berlin, Leipzig, Vienna, and Jerusalem by publishers Breitkopf u. Haertel and Benjamin Harz. In 1973, a

photo-reproduced edition was issued in four volumes in New York by Ktav Publishing Company.

5. Eric Werner, "Manuscripts of Jewish Music in the Eduard Birnbaum Collection of the Hebrew Union College Library," in *Hebrew Union College Annual*, vol. 18 (Cincinnati: HUC-JIR, 1943/44), pp. 397–428.

6. In his memoirs, Abraham Z. Idelsohn reported that he visited Eduard Birnbaum in Koenigsberg (ca. 1899). From that account it appears that no relationship was established and the encounter at best was casual.

7. The information was derived from an article by Eric Mandell, "Salomon Sulzer," in *The Jews of Austria*, ed. Josef Fraenkel (London: Valentine, Mitchell, 1966), pp. 221-29.

8. Among those studies by Eduard Birnbaum was an essay, "Franz Schubert as a Composer of Synagogue Music," detailing Sulzer's role in the commissioning of this music. Birnbaum's article was reprinted in *Contributions to a Historical Study of Jewish Music*, ed. Eric Werner (New York: Ktav, 1976).

9. Alfred Sendrey, *Bibliography of Jewish Music* (New York: Columbia University Press, 1951).

10. Gershon Ephros, *The Cantorial Anthology: Traditional and Modern Synagogue Music*, six vols. (New York: Bloch, 1929–1975).

2

Abraham Z. Idelsohn and Gershon Ephros: Creative Connection

When the first book of the six-volume *Cantorial Anthology* compiled by Cantor Gershon Ephros was published in 1929,[1] a preface by Abraham Z. Idelsohn introduced Ephros and his unique new collection project to the musical world with these remarks: "In both his selection and arrangements, he [Ephros] shows a profound insight into the traditional Hebrew liturgy. Like precious gems, these sacred songs were picked from the treasure house of Jewish melody and arranged in the form of a complete service in the genuine spirit of Hebrew music." (vol. 1, full text pp. ix-x)

Ephros, in his own preface to that initial work in his magnum opus, stated: "Last, but not least, my profound gratitude and sincere appreciation go out to Professor Abraham Zvi Idelsohn, my dear friend and teacher in *hazzanut* [cantorial music] and harmony. His teaching has had a lasting influence on me." (full text pp. xi-xii) Indeed, in the preface to the second volume of his anthological collection, Ephros remarked: "Some years ago, Professor Idelsohn indicated the biblical cantillations as the melodic sources of our *nusakh ha-tefiloh* [melody of prayer]. My own research work in this field confirms the correctness of Professor Idelsohn's view." (vol. 2, full text pp. iv-v) In the subsequent volumes and later revised editions of his anthological collection, Ephros, as his mentor Idelsohn had done before him, probed the terminal essence of the *nusakh,* assembling the finest of liturgical materials from the twelfth century to the twentieth century, and paying special tribute to the contributions of the *paytanim-hazzanim* (poet-precentors) of earlier times as well as to the masters of unaccompanied recitative and cantorial improvisation in more recent times.

This interrelationship of two masters in Jewish music study and collection was a fortuitous blessing. Indeed, if there truly has been a chain of cultural and intellectual continuity throughout history, its links have been forged by active associations between dedicated individuals. In view of the tragic events over the centuries of Jewish history, this process of "connecting up" has constituted a vital survival force. This has been especially true for Jewish liturgical chant, which for so long a time was by tradition an orally transmitted musical art.

As cantorial successor to the noted cantor, composer, and concert violinist Hirsch Weintraub (1811–1882),[2] Eduard Birnbaum (1855–1920) based his early scholarly research and great collection of music upon materials assembled and preserved by his predecessors. He then began to consult the works of other musicians, especially the leading Jewish liturgists of his time. Birnbaum's studies of the works of Salomone Rossi (ca.1565–ca.1628) were based upon the writings of Samuel Naumbourg (1815–1880), and he gathered many music materials while studying in Vienna with Cantor Salomon Sulzer (1804–1890) and singing in his synagogue choir. In the late nineteenth century, the beginning of a "modern era" in Jewish music history was heralded with the growing awareness among cantors of the necessity for formalized cantorial training and technical musical education, as well as study of the different elements and customs of traditional synagogue music. In 1880, Moritz Deutsch (1818–1894), cantor of the leading synagogue in Breslau, founded a briefly active music institute for cantors and teachers, for which he also published an annotated collection of cantorial chants. In 1894, Rabbi Aron Ackermann (1867–1912), a former pupil of Louis Lewandowski (1821–1894), published a study on the history of synagogue music.[3] While many cantors, notably Abraham Baer (1834–1894),[4] began to collect and publish editions of the various liturgical services for the use of their colleagues, Eduard Birnbaum placed these materials into a broader musicological and historical perspective.

Abraham Z. Idelsohn, as a systematic researcher and collector of painstaking dedication, took off from those earlier beginnings and built upon the work of those who had preceded him in the field. In his turn, Idelsohn vastly widened the entire scope of synagogue music studies, as well as the range of religious and secular folksong, in terms of all three Jewish traditional branches: Ashkenazic-European, Sephardic-Spaniolic, and Oriental-Near Eastern. Moreover, through his work and personal relationships, he personally influenced as role model and mentor several notable figures, among them Gershon Ephros.

Idelsohn was born in Filzburg near Libau, Kurland (now Latvia), on July 1, 1882. His father, Azriel, was a cantor and *shokhet* (ritual slaughterer of chickens and cattle) for the community. As a child he was a *cheder* (religious school) student and choir singer, and subsequently he pursued cantorial studies at several locations. During his peregrinations as a young man, he came to Koenigsberg in 1899, where he had a very brief encounter with Birnbaum and became aware of his musical scholarship and collections of cantorial music. Soon afterwards, a trip to London proved almost disastrous, and Idelsohn was assisted financially by the writer Israel Zangwill (1864–1926) for return passage to Libau. There, he studied with an itinerant cantor named Abraham Mordechai Rabinowitz and sang in his choir. In 1901, Idelsohn went to Berlin and entered the Stern Conservatory, soon leaving for the Leipzig Conservatory. In that city, he came under the tutelage of his subsequent father-in-law, Cantor Zevi Schneider (fl. 19th cent.), who also taught him the skills of *shekhitah* (ritual slaughtering).

At the time, Idelsohn had a rather robust tenor voice of dry quality but accurate pitch. In 1903, he assumed a cantorial position in Regensburg, Bavaria, and commenced in earnest upon his own research in Jewish liturgical music. The following year, he went to Johannesburg, South Africa, to join his parents. Then, feeling strongly that his musical research could best be pursued in Jerusalem, he settled there in 1906. He began his study and collection work with the Yemenite Jews, among whom he developed many cordial relationships. A first article by Idelsohn on his studies appeared in 1907 in *Luakh Luntz*, an annotated Hebrew calendar published in Jerusalem. That Hebrew article (English trans., "The Jews of Yemen and Their Songs") drew much interest among other scholars in the community and was reprinted separately. Abroad, it impressed Russian Jewish musicians then forming the St. Petersburg Society for Jewish Folk Music. For them, Idelsohn's pioneer collection of Yemenite materials was a revelation.

In 1909, Gershon Ephros came to Jerusalem, where he began a very fruitful and fond lifelong relationship with Idelsohn. Much of the information bearing upon their association has been based upon the personal recollections of Cantor Ephros as told to this writer.

Ephros was born on January 15, 1890, in Serotzk near Warsaw. His stepfather was a cantor named Moses Fromberg (fl. 19th cent.), in whose choir he sang as a child. At the age of seventeen, Ephros joined a synagogue choir as singer and leader in the town of Sgersh. Then in 1909, he went to Palestine to join a brother, where he remained until leaving for the United States in 1911. When he arrived in Jerusalem, young Ephros had a letter of introduction to Idelsohn, who at the time was serving as officiating cantor and music teacher for several education institutions—a children's school, a teachers' academy, and a trade school— all supported by the Ezra German-Jewish philanthropic society (*Hilfsverein der Jueden in Deutschland*—Aid Society of the Jews in Germany). Ephros became Idelsohn's choir leader and assistant cantor. The religious services were attended by many of the leading intellectual figures of Jerusalem. One boy alto in the choir was Moshe Nathanson (1899–1981), who subsequently came to New York City and served as cantor and music teacher for the Jewish Reconstructionist Foundation congregation of Rabbi Mordecai Kaplan (1881–1983). The liturgical music for those Idelsohn-Ephros services was traditional eastern European Ashkenazic of the Polish-Lithuanian *minhag* (custom), but chanted in the broadest of style and incorporating other liturgical elements. This afforded Ephros a unique opportunity to study and perform much varied melodic prayer chant. At the same time, he observed at close range Idelsohn's eclectic tastes in liturgy and his particular methods of research and collection among the different groups of Jews in the area.

In 1910, Idelsohn formed an Institute of Jewish Music (in Hebrew, *Makhon L'shirath Yisrael*), for which he was helped by the Ezra organization, and

Ephros became a teacher there. The institute was open to students of all Jewish sects, and though it appears to have had some registration, did not survive for long. That year, with the assistance of several scholars in Jerusalem and members of the Ezra Society in Europe, Idelsohn received a financial aid grant from the Academy of Arts and Science in Vienna to begin his recordings of Jewish music in Palestine. His only equipment was a set of primitive recording cylinders (likely the Thomas Alva Edison "hill-and-dale" type) together with transcription notebooks, and of course a passionate zeal for the music. Ephros went along to help on "collection visits" among the various Jewish communities. Idelsohn was interested in the customs and literature of those Jews as well as their music. A robust, fine-looking man, he was well liked by the Oriental Jews and especially charmed their children with songs and stories.

For one Sabbath at that time, Idelsohn organized a service combining the liturgical traditions of many different communities, as a diasporic ingathering (*kibbutz galuyoth*). It was the first time that different groups had attempted to join together in a unified service, with each Jewish sect contributing some of its characteristic chants. Though hours-long and unintegrated for the most part, the event was a historic first for such a Jewish musical convocation, and set the way for many such ventures over the following decades. Indeed, there can hardly be a more exciting musical experience in the State of Israel than a session of comparative performances of liturgical texts by different Judaic traditions. Often in more recent years, the cognate chants of Christian and Moslem groups have also joined in these presentations with extraordinary aesthetic and spiritual effects.

During those years, Idelsohn and Eliezer Ben Yehudah (1858–1922), known as the father of modern Hebrew, were neighbors on Abyssinian Street (*Rehov Kh'bashen*) in Jerusalem. Indeed, Idelsohn even notated the music lines for his early songs right to left so as to accommodate the Hebrew print text.[5] Through Idelsohn, Ephros met Ben Yehudah and thereby strengthened his own devotion to the Hebrew language. It was Eliezer Ben Yehudah who encouraged Idelsohn in his musical research and helped him with the Aramaic and Arabic, as well as Hebrew, so necessary for communication among the Oriental Jews. For a while, Idelsohn even changed his name to Abraham Zvi Ben Yehudah (a Hebraic version of the Yiddish name Idelsohn), signing his first song collections with that name. As a result, for a while the two neighbors often had their mail and messages confused. Ephros recalled that one time when Eliezer Ben Yehudah was excommunicated by the Orthodox community because of his work on behalf of the popular secular use of the Hebrew holy tongue, Idelsohn reverted to his old European profession of *shokhet*, enabling Ben Yehudah's family to have a *kosher* chicken for their Sabbath meals.

Idelsohn became actively involved with Ben Yehudah and the other Hebraist leaders in their struggle with the Germanists over the language to be taught to all the students at the Ezra school and teachers' academy. Though Idelsohn was completely dependent for his livelihood upon a salary from those pro-German institutions, he became totally dedicated to the advancement of the Hebrew language as the modern tongue of Zion. Ultimately, the Hebraists were victorious, but not until the end of World War I.

Abraham Z. Idelsohn was especially drawn to the works of Hebrew poets, in particular Chayim Nachman Bialik (1873–1934), some of whose poems he set to music. Though not a skillful composer, Idelsohn was a rather good melodist and a sensitive musician who chose some very moving texts for his songs. He compiled a first songster in order to bring good Jewish music into the schools, adapting for educational use many Jewish folk melodies, one of which he renamed as *Hava Nagilah* (Let us be merry). It was derived from a Hasidic *nigun* (tune) sung by the followers of the celebrated Hasidic leader Rabbi Yisroel (1797–1850) of Sadigora (Krilovitz), also known as the Rizhiner *rebbe* (rabbi).

In Idelsohn's prefatory materials annotating the consecutively numbered selections collected for Volume 9 (*Folksongs of the East European Jews*) of his *Thesaurus*, he writes (p. xxiv):

No. 716 is the same Hasidic tune as no. 155 in Volume 10. This song may serve as an example of how a song becomes a popular folksong, and particularly how a song becomes Palestinian. The tune originated at the court in Sadigora [Bukowina] and was brought to Jerusalem. In 1915 I wrote it down. In 1918 I needed a popular tune for a performance of my mixed choir in Jerusalem. My choice fell upon this tune which I arranged in four parts, and for which I wrote a Hebrew text. The choir sang it and it apparently caught the imagination of the people, for the next day men and women were singing the song throughout Jerusalem. In no time it spread throughout the country, and thence throughout the Jewish world. In 1921, I printed the song in my arrangement, in my Hebrew song book, *Sefer Hashirim* on pages 164–165. Since then it has been printed in several songsters as Palestinian.

It is interesting that for the music line of no. 716 (Vol. 9, p. 200), the Hebrew text by Idelsohn is given, and the musical notation is the same as the generally known version of *Hava Nagilah*. Idelsohn's prefatory notes for Volume 10 of his *Thesaurus* point out the connection of no. 155 with the no. 716 of Volume 9. However, the melody of no. 155 (p. 43) is given without any text and in more Hasidic free-style, likely as the originally notated tune from Sadigora. Comparison between the two versions shows how Idelsohn creatively converted a Hasidic *nigun* (tune) into a popular song. Unfortunately, he did not apply for any copyright proprietorship in the United States or abroad, and so *Hava Nagilah* never earned him any money,   nor indeed is it generally known that essentially it was his musical idea.

When Gershon Ephros had left for America in 1911, he arrived with a strong liturgical and Hebraic background and good skills at music education. He was engaged by Dr. Samson Benderly (1876–1944), then Director of the Bureau of Jewish Education in New York City, to teach music to young Hebrew students.

At the start, Ephros introduced the ideas of Idelsohn, using the pioneer two-volume *Shirey Yeladim* (Songs for children) which Idelsohn had compiled for his school classes in Jerusalem. As Idelsohn had been doing in Jerusalem, Ephros began to advance the use of music in religious schools by organizing children's services, for which the youngsters learned the traditional liturgical chants and led their own groups. Ephros subsequently also embarked upon an active career as cantor, first for the religious services conducted by Rabbi Mordecai Kaplan at the YM-YWHA in New York. After several other positions, he became cantor for the congregation Beth Mordechai in Perth Amboy, New Jersey, where he remained until his retirement in 1960. Ephros began his own cantorial research and collection soon after he arrived in America. He sought out many well-known European *hazzanim* (cantors) who had emigrated and were serving at congregations in and around the northeastern part of the country. As a result, very many of their works were edited and included in his *Anthology*, thereby bridging European traditions with twentieth-century American styles.

Meanwhile, Idelsohn had become a bandmaster in the Turkish army during World War I, and then in 1919 tried unsuccessfully to reestablish his school of Jewish music in Jerusalem. By 1921, publication work in Berlin and Leipzig had begun on the first volumes of what was to become his monumental ten-volume *Thesaurus of Oriental Hebrew Melodies*.[6] With this great work, published between 1922 and 1933 in Germany and Jerusalem and made available in the United States, he began to be known as the father of Jewish musicology. Not only had Idelsohn collected and transcribed a vast and varied treasury of Jewish music, he also had zealously prepared introductory musical and liturgical analyses, together with much other significant historical information, as guidance to the contents of each volume. His masterful introduction to Volume 2, for example, provides a remarkable section of comparative notation for biblical cantillation among a dozen different Jewish liturgical traditions. Those introductory texts were variously presented in Hebrew, German, and English. Into the twenty-first century, Idelsohn's *Thesaurus* remains uniquely significant for its musical scope, topical range, dedicated scholarship, and pioneering ethnological exploration.

While visiting in Europe in 1921, Idelsohn attended the Zionist Congress being held in Carlsbad, where he discussed with Chayim Nachman Bialik his project to write a history of Jewish music. Late in 1922, Idelsohn came to the United States to lecture in several cities about his music collection then beginning to be published, and while he was in the New York area, the friendship between him and Ephros was renewed and strengthened. In 1924, Idelsohn was appointed cataloguer and curator of the Eduard Birnbaum Collection at Hebrew Union College in Cincinnati, where he soon also became the school's professor of Jewish music and liturgy.[7]

During his busy lifetime as scholar, collector, cataloguer, educator, and cantor, Abraham Z. Idelsohn also was a prolific writer and composer-arranger whose output was continuous from the first publication of his *Shirey Zion* (Songs of Zion) in 1908. As the *Thesaurus* was being completed, his history of Jewish music was published in the United States in 1929.[8] The first draft had originally been published in Hebrew (Tel Aviv, 1923) as the three-volume work *Toldoth Ha-neginah Ivrit*. In 1932, Idelsohn's book on Jewish liturgy, based on the texts used in his classes at the Hebrew Union College, was published.[9] It is still a widely used educational resource. In addition, he wrote numerous articles on a wide range of topics relating to the history and traditions of Jewish music, very many of whose topics stimulated subsequent studies by other scholars. He contributed essays to various Jewish publications as well as general journals, including ones on Jewish folksong for *Music Teachers National Conference* [MENC] *Monthly*, and *Musical Quarterly*. His articles for the *Hebrew Union College* [HUC] *Annual*, notably "Song and Singers of the Synagogue in the Eighteenth Century, with Special Reference to the Birnbaum Collection" (vol. 2 [1925], pp. 397–424), and "The Kol Nidre Tune" (vols. 8/9 [1931/32], pp. 493–509) attracted wide interest and much professional response. The bibliographic listings of his works constitute valuable resources of Jewish music information.[10] Among Idelsohn's last published studies was an article for *Acta Musicologica*, journal of the International Musicological Society [IMS], treating a topic upon which he had begun to focus his prodigious energies, "Parallels Between the Old-French and the Jewish Song" (vol. 5/6 [1933/1934], pp. 162–68/pp. 15–22). He also was examining the music of Italian Jewry, and the *HUC Annual* (vol. 2 [1936], pp. 569–91) featured a preliminary study, "Traditional Songs of the German Tedesco Jews in Italy."

Gershon Ephros frequently credited his own tireless work habits—composing, collecting, editing, teaching, and writing, in addition to congregational cantorial duties—to patterns instilled in him by Idelsohn over the years of their friendship. A letter to Ephros from Cincinnati during the early winter of 1935 reveals the deep sadness caused by a series of debilitating strokes that curtailed the very productive life of Idelsohn in his middle years. He writes:

My dear one: It has been a long time since I heard from you. At last I have received your New Year's blessing. My very dear friend Professor Samuel Cohon has promised me to try to see you when he visits his family in Perth Amboy this month. My family is well, but I am in the category of a *lo yitzlakh*, a man who is a failure. As it appears, my time is over and there is nothing left for me but to meditate and examine my past life and its incomplete work. I cannot do anything more but to think only of the past. With my blessings to you for a good New Year, your friend Abraham Zevi.[11]

Finally, by August 1937, he could no longer write his letters by hand and with one finger painfully typed this note to Ephros:

Dear friend: Although my lingering illness has made correspondence practically impossible, you have frequently been in my thoughts. I trust that you are well and happy. I expect to leave for South Africa October first, accompanied by Mrs. Idelsohn and our daughter. I shall probably go on board the S.S. *New York* of the America-South Africa Lines in Brooklyn. I plan my arrival in New York on Tuesday afternoon September 28th, giving me time until sailing Friday at 4 p.m. to see certain of my friends. It would give me particular pleasure to receive a visit from you. Looking forward to seeing you and with kind regards, Abraham Zvi.

Upon receipt of this letter, Ephros informed the membership of the *Hazzanim Farband* (Cantors-Ministers Association) in New York, and a group including Jacob Beimel (1880–1944), Moshe Nathanson (1899–1981), and Max Wohlberg accompanied Gershon Ephros to the pier to see Idelsohn off to South Africa. Though his illness had so progressed that he was speechless, this tender reunion was deeply appreciated by the ailing man. Some months after his arrival in Johannesburg, Idelsohn died on August 14, 1938.

Several months later, on the evening of Wednesday, January 25, 1939, the Cantors-Ministers Cultural Organization Association held a memorial meeting in honor of Abraham Z. Idelsohn. It was held in the sanctuary hall of the Society for the Advancement of Judaism, the congregational synagogue of the Reconstructionist Foundation, headed by Rabbi Mordecai Kaplan with Moshe Nathanson as cantor. The following was the order of that program, whose participants included some of the leading cantorial figures of the day:

> Introductory Remarks: Adolph Katchko (1886–1958)
>
> Opening Address: Leib Glantz (1898–1964)
>
> Chanting of Psalm I *Ashrey ha-ish:* Zeidel Rovner (Jacob Samuel Margowsky, 1856–1943)
>
> Address—"The Personality of Idelsohn": Gershon Ephros
>
> Choir conducted by Zavel Zilberts (1881–1949): *Enosh k'khozir*, liturgical work composed by Louis Lewandowski (1821–1894)
>
> Discussion—"Representative Works of Idelsohn": Max Wohlberg
>
> Quartet of Cantors: *Hayadu halvavoth*, the musical setting by Abraham Zevi Idelsohn of a poem by Yehuda Halevi (ca.1085–1145)
>
> Address—"Idelsohn as Musicologist": Jacob Beimel (1880–1944)
>
> Choir: *Habeyt mi-shomayim*, a traditional chant arranged by Zilberts
>
> Memorial Prayer for Idelsohn *Eyl Moley Rakhamim:* chanted by Zawel Kwartin (1874–1952)

The meeting was open to the public and extremely well attended. While no written texts remain for the talks given that evening, Ephros himself recalled that he had spoken there of the strong human ties that Idelsohn had created over his lifetime, inspiring and assisting so many of his colleagues. Other speakers paid tribute to the life's work of the man who had proved the existence of Jewish music, defined many of its distinctive characteristics, and presented it for the first time in its sweep of historical context. As cantors themselves, they all underscored their gratitude and respect to Idelsohn for having brought Jewish liturgical music rightfully into the mainstream of significant world liturgical expression.

Despite his own serious illnesses late in life, Gershon Ephros, until his death on June 28, 1978, maintained a busy schedule of composing, writing, and teaching. He composed secular works for instruments and voice as well as liturgical services, arrangements of religious chants, and revised augmented publications of his *Cantorial Anthology*. A teacher of cantorial music to several generations of students, Ephros had served on the faculty of the School of Sacred Music since its formation in New York City in 1948. Of his recollections concerning Idelsohn, in a last conversation with this author Ephros said: "He showed me a path. He showed us all, and the world. He was our greatest."

NOTES

This chapter is based upon oral history materials gathered by the author during the years 1966 to 1978, in the belief that the linkage between Abraham Zvi Idelsohn (1882–1938) and Gershon Ephros (1890–1978) constitutes a prime example of dynamic continuity between two significant scholars of Jewish music.

1. Gershon Ephros, *The Cantorial Anthology: Traditional and Modern Synagogue Music*, 6 Volumes (New York: Bloch Publishing), music and text. Vol. 1, *Rosh Hashanah* (New Year); orig. ed. 1929, 2nd ed. 1948; Vol. 2, *Yom Kippur* (Day of Atonement), 1940; Vol. 3, *Sholosh R'golim* (Three Festivals: *Sukkot*-Tabernacles, *Pesakh*-Passover, *Shavuot*-Weeks), orig. ed. 1948, 2nd ed. 1975; Vol. 4, *Shabbat* (Sabbath), orig. ed. 1953, 2nd ed. 1976; Vol. 5, *Y'mot Hakhol* (Weekday services and special occasions), 1957; Vol. 6, The Recitative for *Rosh Hashanah* (Supplement to Vol. 1), 1969. The final page of this last volume in the *Anthology* concludes with the musical setting of a "triple amen" as fitting postscript by Ephros to his substantial compilation of Jewish liturgical music.

2. He was the famous son of an equally celebrated cantor, Salomon Kashtan Weintraub (1781–1829).

3. Aron Ackermann, *Der Synagog Gesang in Seiner Historischen Entwickelung* (The synagogue chant in its historic development), Berlin: 1896. Although Rabbi Ackermann (1867–1912) issued this tract separately, he noted its having originally appeared in another privately issued book, *Di Jueden: Literatur* (The Jews: Literature), Berlin: undated, pp. 477–529.

4. Abraham Baer, *Ba'al Tefillah, oder Der Praktische Vorbeter* (Master of prayer, or the practical precentor), (Leipzig/Gothenburg: 1871/1877; repub. ed., New York: HUC-JIR, 1953). This book has been used as a standard text for cantorial study at the

School of Sacred Music (HUC-JIR) and the Cantors Institute of the Jewish Theological Seminary of America (JTSA).

5. A brief biographical piece about Idelsohn in the Israeli music annual *Tatzlil/The Chord* (Hebrew language publication of the Haifa Music Museum and Library, 1973), which provides an overview of Idelsohn's years in Jerusalem, includes two photographs: Idelsohn with a group of Jerusalem Hebraists, among them Eliezer Ben Yehuda (p. 122), and Idelsohn with young teachers in his music education seminar (p. 124). Also reproduced in *Tatzlil* (p. 123) is music from Idelsohn's early *Sefer Hashirim* (Book of songs). Given as song no. 27, it is his setting of the poem *Hala Yardeyn* (Flow on, Jordan) by Naphtali Herz Imber (1856–1897), poet of the Jewish anthem *Hatikvah* (The hope). The music lines were written from right to left, accommodating the Hebrew text, and on this music Idelsohn indicated his name as "Abraham Zvi Ben Yehudah."

Among the materials in the Eric Mandell Collection housed at the music library of Gratz College are copies of those early songs, including the *Sefer Hashirim*, with that reverse musical notation. Mandell contributed a feature article, "Abraham Zvi Idelsohn: Founder of the Science of Jewish Music" to the October 1, 1948, special Jewish New Year celebration issue of the *Jewish Exponent*, published in Philadelphia, which included a reprint of some of the music lines.

6. Abraham Z. Idelsohn, *Hebraeish-Orientalisher Melodienschatz*—Thesaurus of Oriental Hebrew Melodies, 10 Volumes (Berlin, Leipzig, Vienna, Jerusalem: Breitkopf u. Haertel and Benjamin Harz, 1922–1933; reprinted ed. as four books, New York: Ktav, 1964). Vol. 1, Songs of the Yemenite Jews; Vol. 2, Songs of the Babylonian Jews; Vol. 3, Songs of the Jews of Persia, Bukhara, and Daghestan; Vol. 4, Songs of the Oriental Sephardim; Vol. 5, Songs of the Moroccan Jews; Vol. 6, Synagogue Songs of German Jews in the 18th Century—According to Manuscripts; Vol. 7, Traditional Songs of the South German Jews; Vol. 8, Synagogue Songs of the East European Jews; Vol. 9, Folksongs of the East European Jews; Vol. 10, Songs of the Hassidim.

7. Among Idelsohn's colleagues in Cincinnati at the Hebrew Union College were his close personal friends Professor Samuel S. Cohon (1888–1958) and his wife Angie Irma Cohon (1890–1981). The Cohon couple had been instrumental in assisting Idelsohn to secure his appointment at the college. They remained deeply attached to him, both extolling Idelsohn's work years after he had died. Mrs. Cohon was especially interested in Jewish music, having written a pamphlet-monograph, *An Introduction to Jewish Music in Eight Illustrated Lectures*, which was published by the National Council of Jewish Women (Chicago, 1923). She served as Idelsohn's personal secretary and translator-editor during his years in Cincinnati. With her son Rabbi Baruch Joseph Cohon, in 1951 she prepared and privately issued a new edition of Idelsohn's *Jewish Song Book for Synagogue, School and Home* (Cincinnati: Bloch Publishing, 1928 and 1929).

8. Abraham Z. Idelsohn, *Jewish Music in Its Historical Development* (New York: Henry Holt, 1929; latest reprint ed., Westport, Conn.: Greenwood Press, 1981).

9. Abraham Z. Idelsohn, *Jewish Liturgy and Its Development* (New York: Rinehart and Winston, 1932; reprint ed., New York: Schocken Press, 1966).

10. Bibliographic listings of Idelsohn's works may be found in the following publications:

Alfred Sendrey, *Bibliography of Jewish Music* (New York: Columbia University Press, 1951; reprint ed., Millwood, N. Y.: Kraus Reprint, 1969). Numerous scattered entries.

Irene Heskes, *The Resource Book of Jewish Music* (Westport, Conn.: Greenwood Press, 1985). See various annotated entries among the book's topical listings.

Israel Adler, Bathja Bayer, Eliyahu Schleifer, and Lea Shalem, eds., *The Abraham Zvi Idelsohn Memorial Volume*, Yuval Volume V (Jerusalem: Magnes Press/Hebrew University, 1986). Two extensive bibliographic essays, with detailed annotative listings in English by Eliyahu Schleifer and in Hebrew by Shlomo Hofman.

11. Sources for this section are from the personal papers of Gershon Ephros given to the author, as well as personal conversations with Cantor Ephros late in his life.

3

Builders of Sacred Bridges: Scholars and Studies in Jewish Music

In 1930, Abraham Zvi Idelsohn wrote: "The day on which every Jew will come to realize that there cannot be a Jewish renascence without a revival of Jewish music—for just as it is impossible for a man to live without a heart, so it is impossible for a people to live without its folk music—on that day will the renascence become a reality."[1] At the time of Idelsohn's death in 1938, a monograph by Hebrew scholar Menashe Ravina (1899–1968) honoring his pioneering work in Jewish music was published by *Renanim* (Songs of jubilation), journal of the Tel Aviv/Palestinian Music Educators.[2] Almost fifty years later, the Jewish Music research Centre at Hebrew University in Jerusalem issued a volume dedicated to the memory of Idelsohn's life and work, and it constitutes a living testimony to this father of modern Jewish musicology.[3] Shaped in the form of both bio-bibliography and *festschrift* (collection of special essays), the contents amply underscore Idelsohn's legacy as a role model. Among the scholarly studies in the section appropriately titled "In Idelsohn's Footsteps" is a contribution by Eric Werner (1901–1988).[4]

Although Werner titled his own magnum opus, *The Sacred Bridge*,[5] it is apparent that a dynamic "bridge" connected his life's work with that of his predecessor at Hebrew Union College, Abraham Zvi Idelsohn. Moreover, their published legacies have "bridged" Jewish music from its singular and sacred past to its worldwide creative future. Significantly, neither man functioned in isolation, their interests having been stimulated and nourished by Jewish leaders of the *haskalah* (auto-emancipation, or quest for learning) movement in late nineteenth-century Europe. Those ideas of Judaic self-recognition—spiritual revival, intellectual renascence, and cultural creativity—found their way not only to the emergent Zionist homeland in Palestine but importantly to the American shores with the great immigration of eastern European Jews around the beginning of the twentieth century. In 1908, a group of young Jewish musicians and writers had petitioned the Russian government for permission to form the St. Petersburg

Society for Jewish Folk Music, which soon after established a branch in Moscow
and then began to communicate with groups in other eastern European cities.
The objectives were to collect, arrange, publish, and perform Jewish songs, and
even to compose new works in that genre. Following the Bolshevik Revolution
of 1917 and World War I, those musical groups dispersed and many of the
members migrated to other areas of Europe and to Palestine, but most of them
came to the United States.

An important successor to that St. Petersburg group was the Jewish Music
Forum, an organization that flourished in New York City from 1939 to 1963. It
had evolved from an earlier New York based society known by its abbreviated
Hebrew name, *Mailamm* (The American-Palestine Music Association), formed
in 1932 for the purposes of furthering musical activities in Palestine and America.
A branch group in Los Angeles, led by Joseph Achron 1886–1943), was also
active for a brief time. Arnold Schoenberg (1874–1951) was one of the many
refugee musicians welcomed to America by *Mailamm*. In 1939, spurred by
Abraham W. Binder (1895–1966), that society was reconstituted as the Jewish
Music Forum, beginning its activities at a time of growing peril to Jewish life in
Europe. For the next quarter of a century, the group was vigorously productive
on behalf of Jewish music preservation and creativity in America and abroad.
Scholars were encouraged to talk about their studies in progress; composers presented their new works; projects in music education and cantorial training were
explored; abstracts and reports were published in an annual newsletter. At the
regularly scheduled public meetings, diverse interests and activities of leading
scholars, educators, composers, conductors, liturgists, singers, and instrumentalists were brought together productively through lectures, open discussions, and
musical performances.[6]

Over the years, influenced to a marked degree by members of the forum, the
field of Jewish music was advanced in a wide variety of ways. This was apparent
in the proliferation of published materials of several types: historical monographs, topical studies in periodicals and books, annotated music collections,
textbooks and resource works, biographies, and critical reviews. Of particularly
productive consequence, following World War II, was the formation of schools
for formalized cantorial study and the training of music leader-educators for each
of the three branches of Jewish religious life in America: Orthodox, Conservative, and Reform. To serve those purposes, cantorial collections, liturgical
arrangements, hymnals, and songbooks were compiled and published. Moreover, important European works, most of which might otherwise have been lost,
were saved and made available in new reprint editions for study and performance.

In the December 1942 issue of the *Jewish Music Forum Bulletin* (vol. 3, no.
1) Alfred Sendrey (1884–1976) reports on his work in progress for a comprehensive "Jewish Music Bibliography." Introducing his project, he writes (p. 13):

For the music historian it is important to have a source of reference while planning and pursuing his work and to know where to find his literary tools. This is the prerequisite for all scientific work. Strangely enough, however, it seems not to have been applied so far to Jewish musicological research. Here, bibliography, this most important helper of all scientific research, is almost completely non-existent... Even the libraries of the Jewish Theological Seminary in New York and the Hebrew Union College in Cincinnati, the last working place of Idelsohn, the noted Jewish musicologist, have no scientifically arranged music bibliography worthy of the name... The domain and method of scientific music bibliography has been discussed in a number of special treatises, but these treatises know nothing about the great literature concerning Jewish music.

Sendrey then presents an overview of his method for classification, detailing various categories for literature and musical works and indicating his prodigious efforts to afford a comprehensive sweep of the entire field.[7]

When Sendrey's *Bibliography of Jewish Music* was published in 1951,[8] its 10,000 entries only covered published materials and manuscripts up to the year 1945. Nevertheless, that volume constitutes an awesome research achievement and remains an indispensable aid to scholars. It documents musical scores and literature that might otherwise have been lost with the destruction of libraries, museums, synagogues, and private archives during the Holocaust era. In a foreword contributed to that 404-page magnum opus, musicologist Curt Sachs (1881–1959), who like Sendrey had fled the Nazis, wrote that this substantial listing is "a dignified monument to the past. . . also a symbol of our will to survive and to contribute to man's endeavor, art, and knowledge to the full limits of our power." (p. v.) Sendrey's own introductory exposition and historical survey of Jewish music preface the book with excellent background information. In subsequent years, Alfred Sendrey drew upon the wealth of bibliographic materials that he had gathered and wrote three books treating the history of Jewish music in ancient Israel, antiquity, and European diasporic life.[9]

At the April 12, 1943 meeting of the Jewish Music Forum, Curt Sachs, Joseph Yasser (1893–1981), and Eric Werner participated in an open discussion regarding possibilities for a descriptive definition of Jewish music. They and the others at the well-attended session sought the means by which to identify representative Judaic musical expression. Like so many scholars at that time (and even now at the threshold of the twenty-first century), they examined issues of religious identity, cultural history, ethnic traditions, and societal relationships. Whether any measure of satisfactory conclusion was reached that night remains moot, for the distinctive qualities of Jewish music—such as they may be—remain highly subjective and to an extent elusive.

Joseph Yasser chaired the session, and in opening remarks said: "Scholarly discussions are not held to reach definite and unchallengable conclusions... Their primary purpose is to stimulate thinking in a certain direction, to broaden horizons, and to remove prejudices and misconceptions."[10] While denying there can be any clear definition of Jewish music, Curt Sachs divided Jewish musical expression into three major historical periods: biblical, ghetto (Diaspora), and "emancipated" (modern). Interestingly, he said that in antiquity, women were the essential carriers of music. Though unable to attend that meeting, Eric Werner, then on the faculty of Hebrew Union College in Cincinnati as successor to Abraham Zvi Idelsohn, had sent along a paper that was read by Yasser. Werner concluded that:

It is irrelevant whether the ancient melodies of the Jews are lost or not. We know that some of them still exist. Yet this preservation has no influence upon the fact that all Jewish groups possess their own songs. It matters little that many folksongs are of non-Jewish origin. This, as we know, is true of all European and much of Asiatic folksong. The decisive fact is that the songs which are generally classified as typically Jewish are being sung at present by Jews exclusively. Even when borrowed, these songs are often reshaped in a really creative way and fused with original elements into an organic reality.

As a practicing musician and music theoretician with a particular penchant for organizations, Joseph Yasser had helped implant the ideals of the Russian Jewish groups in St. Petersburg and Moscow on American shores. He was born in Lodz, Poland in 1893, and at the age of six went to Moscow to study piano, organ, and music history. After graduating from the Moscow Conservatory of Music, he taught there and was chief organist for the State Grand Opera as well as the Moscow Art Theater. In 1923, he came to the United States, performed in concerts, and was organist for several New York synagogues, settling at Temple Rodeph Sholom, where he remained until retirement. Over the years, he lectured widely, did musicological research, wrote articles and books, taught at various institutions, and actively participated in Jewish music activities. In 1932, he was a founding member of *Mailamm*, in association with others of the earlier Russian group who had emigrated to America: Joseph Achron (1886–1943), Lazare Saminsky (1882–1959), Jacob Weinberg (1879–1956), and Solomon Rosowsky (1878–1962). In 1939, Yasser worked with Abraham W. Binder to establish the Jewish Music Forum. He was also active with the American Musicological Society, the American Guild of Organists, the Jewish Academy of Arts and Sciences, and the American Academy for Jewish Research. In 1944, he was one of the founders of the National Jewish Music Council, and then promoted a nationwide annual celebration of Jewish music. Yasser also helped establish the Cantors Institute of the Jewish Theological Seminary, for which he served as a faculty member. He published on tonality, quartal harmony, pentatonics, and other theoretical topics. Among his studies on various aspects of Jewish music, articles linking Russian medieval ballads to Jewish folk song and on instrumentation in the Herodian Temple particularly drew much scholarly response.[11]

Curt Sachs was born in 1881 in Berlin, where he was educated. He began a career there as museum curator, before fleeing the Nazis in 1937. Arriving in the United States, he joined the graduate music faculty of New York University and was a music consultant to the New York Public Library. Over the years, he lectured at many educational institutions and served as chairman of the advisory council to the School for Sacred Music, established in 1948 by the Hebrew Union College-Jewish Institute of Religion. A year before his death in New York City in 1959, Sachs participated, along with Eric Werner and scholars from Israel and Europe, in a conference on Jewish music, which was held in Paris under the auspices of the World Jewish Congress. At that time, Sachs was named honorary president of the International Society of Jewish Music, a group then in formation but soon disbanded. During more than twenty years spent in America as an exceptional scholar and dedicated teacher, Curt Sachs published numerous studies and books on musical instruments, art, the dance, and music history. Late in life, he was increasingly interested in the field of musical folklore, which he called "ethnomusicology," and his last projects treated the music of non-European cultures, including aspects of Jewish music, such as *kol nidrey* chant, Babylonian liturgy, and Hasidic melodies.[12] Sachs was a skillful writer who could convey vast amounts of information in an interesting manner. His work ranged over very many different musical cultures, treating each with rare understanding and underscoring intriguing parallels in man's music making that have transcended time and geography.

A tribute volume in memory of Curt Sachs, published in 1965, included twenty-three essays by his devoted colleagues in world musicology.[13] Among those contributors were Eric Werner (1901–1988), with his article "Greek Ideas on Music in Judeo-Arabic Literature," and the Israeli scholar Edith Gerson-Kiwi, whose study on Jewish women's songs collected from the Yemenite settlers in Israel flowed productively from the earlier pioneer collection labors in Jerusalem by Abraham Zvi Idelsohn.

Often in lectures and writings, Eric Werner referred to a particular occupation with the concept of a "sacred bridge" spanning the gulf between Judaism and Christianity and his ardent advocacy on behalf of the common origins and lingering mutuality of those two liturgical music traditions. Werner's focus upon this subject area, along with a broad range of other interests in Jewish music, had evolved over five decades of dedicated association with the Hebrew Union College-Jewish Institute of Religion (HUC-JIR). Early on, his scholarly commitment was bonded to the two founding figures of modern Jewish musicology, Abraham Zvi Idelsohn (1882–1938) and Eduard Birnbaum (1855–1920). Idelsohn had been Werner's predecessor at the college campus in Cincinnati, and it was Birnbaum's monumental music collection, housed in the library there, that had brought both Idelsohn and Werner to that faculty. Moreover, Werner in himself constituted a special "human bridge," because during a long and fruitful life, he made dynamic contacts with the leading musicological scholars of the twentieth century. He produced numerous studies, articles, books, and public lectures, the sum total of which amplified the scope of general music history, enlightened the world about areas of Jewish music, and inspired several generations of scholars in America, Israel, and Europe.

Eric Werner was born in 1901 in Vienna, and began his education in piano, organ, and music theory there. Further musical studies took him to Prague and Berlin. Among his teachers in Europe were Ferruccio Busoni and Guido Adler. Earliest contacts with Curt Sachs were during those student days. Werner completed an advanced musicological degree in Strasbourg and then began teaching in several German cities, including Breslau, at its rabbinical seminary. In 1937, he fled the Nazis, emigrating to America. The following year, he was invited to teach at the Hebrew Union College in Cincinnati. When the School of Sacred Music was established in 1948 by HUC-JIR in New York City, he joined that faculty and shaped its curriculum. In later years, Werner also helped found, then chaired from 1967 to 1971, the musicology department at Tel Aviv University in Israel. In 1968, the Jewish Music Research Centre of Hebrew University in Jerusalem dedicated the first edition of its scholarly yearbook, *Yuval*, in his honor. Werner died in New York City in 1988. His legacy of published materials numbers almost two hundred entries, covering a great range of studies in comparative liturgies, ethnomusicology, and music history, as well as a detailed biography of the composer Felix Mendelssohn (1809–1847).[14]

Scholarly relationships were a highly significant part of Werner's life, and appear to have nourished his work. He had been a pupil of Curt Sachs in Berlin, and that close relationship continued in America. A study, "Music Aspects of the Dead Sea Scrolls," that Werner contributed to *Musical Quarterly* vol. 43, no. 1 (1957, pp. 21–37) was dedicated "For Curt Sachs on his 75th birthday."

For an issue of *The Reconstructionist*, vol. 29, no. 3 (1963), Eric Werner contributed a critique of Abraham Zvi Idelsohn's legacy, concluding with the remarks (p. 17):

And this is, in general, the value of the *Thesaurus* today. It constitutes an almost comprehensive collection of Jewish folklore, reasonably, not systematically ordered, fairly reliably transcribed, and at least in part well analyzed and interpreted... And it is in this very idea of ethnology where his work has proved a never-ceasing source of original ideas and suggestions. It is here that he deviates most radically from the ideas and values of his teacher [*sic*: role model, never actual teacher] Eduard Birnbaum, for this fine scholar confined himself to the world of books, of literary or musical sources, of European synagogues and their chant, and of rabbinical documents. With all this learned equipment he was much more critical of the style and value of European synagogue chant than Idelsohn. Birnbaum's historical understanding was deeper and more critical than Idelsohn's, but he relied on it exclusively. Idelsohn, on the other hand, was the first serious musicologist to come to grips with the living world of Oriental Jewry, its environment, its songs, its mores, and its daily activities. As a matter of course, his collection of songs and musical traditions was bound to be of greater value than any merely literary or even musical written source, no matter how refined. Here lies Idelsohn's main merit, here also his importance for musical scholarship in general.

In 1950, Eric Werner was invited to the International Congress on Catholic Church Music, as the first scholar of Jewish music to address an assemblage at the Vatican. While there, he met Msgr. Higinio Angles (1888–1969), a notable authority on Catholic church music, thereupon beginning a warm personal and professional relationship that lasted to the end of their lives. Msgr. Angles participated with Werner at the International Congress of Jewish Music held in Paris in 1957. At that 1950 lecture in Rome, Werner renewed contact with a former teacher, Egon Wellesz (1885–1974), the preeminent authority on Byzantine music. Wellesz, who had been the first private composition pupil of Arnold Schoenberg, had fled the Nazis to England in 1936, where he remained in residence until his death.

Egon Wellesz had studied in Vienna with musicologist Guido Adler (1855–1941), who encouraged his students to look into the music materials of the Near East, as sources for church chant. In 1913, Abraham Zvi Idelsohn's study on the elements of Arabian music had been published in Vienna, as an early report concerning the results of his funded studies in Jerusalem.[15] That year, Wellesz began his own lifelong investigations of Byzantine-Eastern Orthodox chants, commencing with studies of Armenian, Coptic, Syrian, and other Near East liturgies. In an article entitled "Egon Wellesz and the Study of Byzantine chant,"[16] Milos Velimirovic notes that his mentor and colleague Wellesz early on discovered a formulaic principle in the Serbian chant: "This principle was closely related, as Wellesz saw, to the use of *maqams* in Arabic music that Idelsohn had studied." (p. 270)

Until 1936, Wellesz taught in Vienna, where he established a section on Byzantine music at the Austrian National Library. After the Nazi *Anschluss*, he fled first to Holland and then went to England, where he was appointed a fellow of Lincoln College at Oxford. There, he resumed his scholarly work and writings, and also composed a number of vocal and instrumental works, generally in the atonal genre of his friend Schoenberg, about whom he also wrote. In his moving recollection of Wellesz, Velimirovic remarks with some irony that for more than thirty years, the Greek church outright refused to accept Wellesz's work, claiming that is was "impossible for anyone not a Greek to study and understand a body of music which was not a part of a person's own culture and national tradition." (p. 276)

Eric Werner's worldwide contacts over the years also included Henry George Farmer (1882–1965), the Christian scholar of Arabic-Moorish music who wrote about the attitudes towards music of Sa'adyah Gaon, Maimonides, and other medieval Jewish writers. Farmer's scholarly pursuits had led him to those writings as early source materials, but a privately prepared listing of his bibliography shows that late in his life, he was considering other topics in Jewish music, including the nature of a Second Commonwealth Temple instrument known as the *magrepha*. This was likely in response to the article by Joseph Yasser, and to contacts with Werner at that time (ca.1961). A photocopy of the cover page manuscript for Farmer's "Original Introduction to Sa'adyah Gaon on the Influence of Music" has the following in his handwriting: "This was written before the article on 'The Philosophy and Theory of Music in Judeo-Arabic Literature' was published by Eric Werner and Isaiah Sonne in the *Hebrew Union College Annual* vols. xvi–xvii, 1941/43." Farmer has drawn a line through the title of his study (London: Arthur Probsthain, 1943), and has written "Early Jewish Music Theory." Typed on the bottom of this page and initialed by Farmer himself is the following: "My original typescript contained this Introduction, but when it was accepted for publication by the Royal Asiatic Society in its Monograph Series, they asked that, owing to paper shortage and other requirements of war conditions, I should curtail my work. It necessitated the cancellation of this Introduction and the shortening of many other parts of the book. When I finally sought another publisher, I did not trouble to re-establish the original text."[17]

Scholars by nature and training are inclined to cite references to other works treating the same topics. Many enterprises have been spawned out of those publications, in a sense as literary progeny. The contributions of Idelsohn and Werner have bred such productivity in America as well as Europe, and in particular among a notable array of Israeli musicologists.[18] It is axiomatic that scholarship cannot flourish in a vacuum.

For example, in the critique of a book by the Italian musicologist Leopoldo Gamberini,[19] the reviewer J. Murray Barbour remarks:

Gamberini wholeheartedly adopts Idelsohn's contention that the recitation formulas of widely separated communities of Eastern Jews are sufficiently alike that from them we can reconstruct a very early stage of Hebrew music. Even so, it remains a reconstruction, lacking the validity of the precisely notated songs found in the Greek fragments... The musical settings of the Hebrews were largely syllabic, like those of the Greeks, but with melismatic cadential formulas, similar to those of other peoples of the Near East. Since Hebrew poetry was a sort of poetic prose, with accent rather that quantity, Hebrew music was developed freely, both in rhythm and in pitch. The reciting tone is prominent, and Gamberini assumes that any occurrence of a reciting tone in later music is Hebraic in origin... Wellesz denies any direct link between ancient Greek music and that of the Byzantine Church, holding rather that the latter fell heir to the liturgy of the synagogue. Gamberini inclines to the opinion of Leo Levi that the Byzantine Christians assimilated elements of the popular music of Greece, as well as that of Syria and Palestine... Just as the accentual Hebrew chants afforded an opportunity for vocalizing, just so in the medieval chants lengthy melismas were placed upon syllables bearing the tonic accent. Above all, the settings of that most musical of Hebrew words, *Alleluia*, are melodically rich.

Some studies have been fired up in scholarly disagreement. For example, Helmut Hucke, in his article "Toward a New Historical View of Gregorian Chant,"[20] writes: "Other scholars have tried to demonstrate that specific Gregorian chants were derived directly from Jewish tradition, by comparing Gregorian melodies with Jewish songs collected in recent times in isolated Jewish communities. This kind of research was introduced especially by Abraham Zewi [*sic*] Idelsohn. It has been carried on by Eric Werner." In a footnote to that statement, Hucke takes specific issue with a study by Werner of the Jewish liturgical chant of *aleynu*, which appears to be similar to a Gregorian *sanctus*, citing as sources for his disagreement Idelsohn's published versions of *aleynu*. Here, Hucke shows his lack of understanding regarding the transmission of *mi-sinai* (from Mount Sinai) holy melodicals, the Jewish prayer tunes preserved over the centuries. Consequently, Hucke's citation of different versions from a 1763 cantorial notation, and alternatives given by Idelsohn and Werner, belie his refutations, for these versions are consistent with the time-honored orally transmitted flow of Jewish liturgical chant; that is, there are vocalized variants, but the significant melodic essence has been maintained by the singers in pious respect.

A colleague of Hucke, Leo Treitler, has also refuted the hypotheses advanced by Eric Werner. In his article "The Early History of Music Writing in the West,"[21] Treitler writes: "The principal recent proponent of a derivation of Latin neumatic writing from ecphonetic notation is Eric Werner. Werner's reasoning on this subject is a mix of appropriate observations and questions, baseless conjecture, and argument from premises that take their conclusions for granted... Werner claims that ecphonesis passed from the Hebrew, to the Byzantine, and thence to Western tradition." Treitler appears to ignore the random though potent influences of orally transmitted music as practiced among singers in emerging liturgical traditions during the early centuries of the Christian Era.

History belongs to those who leave behind a clear record, and therefore it is the responsibility of historians—in this case music historians—to search out, identify, document, and clarify those records. However, historicity can invite modifications to suit a current need or contemporary fancy, benevolent or otherwise. Therefore the scholarly duties are to collect, preserve, and interpret in such manner as to provide a representation of authenticity, tempered with a measure of creative thought and logical assumption.

NOTES

1. Abraham Z. Idelsohn, "The Value of Jewish Music in the Present Day Jewish Renascence," in *Avukah Annual*, ed. Leo W. Schwarz (New York: American Student Zionist Federation, 1930), pp. 79–83. Note: his name was incorrectly given in the publication as "I. Z. Idelsohn."

2. Menashe Ravina, *Abraham Zvi Idelsohn—Avraham Zvi Ben Yehudah*, issued as a pamphlet edition of *Renanim* (Songs of jubilation), eds. Emanuel Kipor and David Geshuri, (Tel Aviv: Music Education Publications, 1938/39), Hebrew text only.

3. Israel Adler, Bathja Bayer, and Eliyahu Schleifer, eds., and assisted by Lea Shalem, *The Abraham Zvi Idelsohn Memorial Volume*, Yuval Studies of the Jewish Music Research Centre, Volume V (Jerusalem: Magnes Press and Jewish National and University Library at Hebrew University, 1986), text and music; Eng. section—426 pages, Heb. section—242 pages. In addition to articles by the three editors, other contributors are (in the order of their contributions to the publication): A. Irma Cohon, Edith Gerson-Kiwi, Hanoch Avenary, Philip V. Bohlman, Dom Jean Claire, Dalia Cohen, Reinhard Flender, David Halperin, Ruth Katz, Kay Kaufman Shelemay, Eric Werner, Shlomo Hofman, Avner Bahat, Shelomo Morag, Yehuda Ratzaby, and Uri Sharvit.

4. Eric Werner, "Numerical Representation of Variants of orally Transmitted Tunes," in ibid., pp. 405–19. Here, Werner has used mathematical concepts to consider different oral versions of folk melodicals.

5. Eric Werner, *The Sacred Bridge: The Interdependence of Liturgy and Music in Synagogue and Church during the first Millennium* (New York: Columbia University Press, 1959; reprint ed., New York: Da Capo Press, 1979).

6. Between September 1940 and January 1956, ten editions of the *Jewish Music Forum Bulletin* were printed and distributed. In its first issue, the forum subtitled as "The Society for the Advancement of Jewish Music Culture," presented its organizational aims, serving all types of interests and activities in Jewish music. The issues of the *Bulletin* were given over to details of the usually monthly programs, along with abstracts of lectures and rosters of the participants, officers, and members.

Contents of the earliest meetings indicate that papers were given by the following: composer Mario Castelnuovo-Tedesco (1895–1968), journalist Artur Holde (1885–1962), and musicologists Paul Nettl (1889–1972), Curt Sachs, and Eric Werner. Among the first officers were: Abraham W. Binder (1895–1966), as chairman, with a governing board that included cantors Jacob Beimel (1880–1944) and Gershon Ephros (1890–1978), composer Paul Dessau (1895–1979), organist-educator Isadore Freed (1900–1960), and musicologist Joseph Yasser. The final issue of the *Bulletin* (concised as vol. 9, 1949–1955), reported on presentations by music educators Shalom Altman (1911–1986), Harry Coopersmith (1902–1975), and Rabbi Israel Goldfarb (1879–1967); composers Leonard Bernstein (1918–1990), Ernest Bloch (1880–1959), Lukas Foss, Darius Milhaud (1892–1974), and Robert Starer; synagogue choral directors Eric Mandell (1902–1984) and Lazare Saminsky (1882–1959); music publisher Henry Lefkowitch (1892–1959); scholars Solomon Rosowsky (1878–1962), Aron Marko Rothmueller, and Alfred Sendrey (1884–1976); choral conductor-arrangers Leo Low (1878–1960) and Lazar Weiner (1897–1982); opera tenor Jan Peerce (1904–1984); Yiddish folklorist Ruth Rubin; and Yiddish theatrical composer Sholom Secunda (1894–1974). In addition there was a formidable array of vocal and instrumental performers, and a membership roster of over three hundred.

7. For the preparation of my own bibliographic work, *The Resource Book of Jewish Music* (Westport, Conn.: Greenwood Press, 1985), I chose to define a more limited area, that of English language text, thereby setting the range and scope of materials covered. My compilation, however, affords full publication details, along with annotative explanations, for each of the entries. Sendrey was always in my mind as I worked on that project. I did have contact with him once, and felt deeply inspired by the dedicated respect that he maintained for the subject of Jewish music. It was a zeal and enthusiasm that belied his very advanced age at the time we met.

8. Alfred Sendrey, *Bibliography of Jewish Music* (New York: Columbia University Press, 1951; reprint ed., Millwood, N.Y.: Kraus Reprint, 1969).

9. Three works by Alfred Sendrey are:

Music in Ancient Israel (New York: The Philosophical Library, 1969).

The Music of the Jews In the Diaspora (Up to 1800): A Contribution to the Social and Cultural History of the Jews (Cranbury, N.J.: Thomas Yoseloff and A.S. Barnes, 1970).

Music In the Social and Religious Life of Antiquity (Rutherford, N.J.: Fairleigh Dickinson University Press, 1974).

10. Material in this section is based upon the recorded report of the April 12, 1943 meeting, as published in *Jewish Music Forum Bulletin*, vol. 4, no. 1 (1943).

11. Two articles by Joseph Yasser are:

"References to Hebrew Music in Russian Mediaeval Ballads," *Jewish Social Studies*, vol. 2, no. 1 (1949), pp. 21–48.

"The Magrepha of the Herodian Temple: A Five-Fold Hypothesis," *Journal of the American Musicological Society*, vol. 13, nos. 1/3 (1960), pp. 14–42.

12. Curt Sachs, *The Wellsprings of Music* (posthumously issued, prepared for publication by Jaap Kunst; The Hague: Martinus Nijoff, 1962).

13. Gustave Reese and Rose Brandel, eds., *The Commonwealth of Music*, (New York: Free Press-Collier/Macmillan, 1965).

14. In 1968, a bibliographic listing of one hundred of Eric Werner's works was compiled by Judith Cohen, and issued by the Tel Aviv University. Over the next twenty years until his death, Werner continued to write and publish prodigiously. In 1983, he gave me an augmented bibliographic roster, from which I selected only materials in English language text (not German, Latin, or Greek) for inclusion in my *Resource Book of Jewish Music*. I also omitted his many, often highly critical but always valid, book reviews.

15. Abraham Z. Idelsohn, *"Di Maqamen der arabischen Muzik,"* *Sammelbaende der internationalen Muzikgesellschafter*, vol. 15 (1913/14), pp. 1–63.

16. Milos Velimirovic wrote this as a memorial tribute to his teacher and mentor, Egon Wellesz. It appeared in *Musical Quarterly*, vol. 62, no. 2 (1976), pp. 265–77.

17. My copy of a bibliographic listing of the works of Henry George Farmer, along with other photocopy materials, was obtained from the Humanities Division of Glasgow University Library, Scotland, where the H. G. Farmer collection of books, music, and manuscripts is presently housed.

18. That roster includes: Israel Adler, Hanoch Avenary, Bathja Bayer, Dalia Cohen, Judith Cohen, Edith Gerson-Kiwi, Peter Gradenwitz, Don Harran, Jehoash Hershberg, Ruth Katz, Elihayu Schleifer, Lea Shalem, Uri Sharvit, Amnon Shiloah, Herzl Shmueli, and Michal Smoira-Cohen.

19. Leopoldo Gamberini, *La Parola e la Musica Nell' Antichita: Historiae Musicae Cultores, Biblioteca*, vol. 15 (Firenze: Leo S. Olschki, 1962). That book treats the relationships between Greek chant and its Greek, Hebrew, Gnostic, Syrian, Byzantine, and Ambrosian counterparts and antecedents. The book review by J. Murray Barbour appeared in *Journal of the American Musicological Society,* vol. 18, no.1 (1965), pp. 81–83.

20. Helmut Hucke, "Toward a New Historical View of Gregorian Chant," *Journal of the American Musicological Society*, vol. 33, no. 3 (1980), pp. 437–66.

21. Leo Treitler, "The Early History of Music Writing in the West," *Journal of the American Musicological Society*, vol. 35, no. 2 (1982), pp. 237–79.

Part II

Bible, Liturgy, and Cantorial Art

4

Jewish Music and Biblical Heritage

According to the Zohar, there is a Temple in Heaven that is opened only through song. Indeed, the Talmud scorns those who read the Holy Scriptures without melody and study its words without singing. A significant characteristic of Jewish religious service always has been its musical expression, based upon the chanting of Bible passages, and the intoning of prayer texts intoned by the leader together with the congregation. The founding shapers of Christian liturgy adapted earlier Hebraic customs and especially the post-Temple Era synagogue formulas with which many had been intimately familiar.

While chanting of biblical lessons and Psalms, along with essential avowals of faith remained for both religions the bedrock of the services during the early centuries of the Common Christian Era, structured organization for those rituals did not generally appear until about the fifth century, and then developed over considerable time. The codification and notation of the elaborate system of Hebrew biblical chant was the monumental contribution of the Masoretes, the Hebrew grammarian-scholars of the eighth and ninth centuries. Before then, exclusive reliance on special oral traditions had guided the continuity of these fundamental liturgio-melodic elements. Basically the Masorete versions of the biblical texts have been preserved zealously throughout the world by all Jewish traditions, complete with the neume signs, a musical notation code attached to every word in the Bible, above or below the letters.

Essentially, biblical cantillation was melodically shaped speech intonation, intended to focus attention upon the substance of the text. However, along historical byways, melodical qualities adhered to the essence of cantillation, and thereby generated discrepancies among many dispersed communities who otherwise maintained the same motival signs for that biblical text. The neumes (akin to the Hebrew word *n'ima*, meaning sweetness or melody) originated out of the hand signs and finger motions which were a Near Eastern singing custom, and which still accompany the religious singing of many Yemenite Jews. From antiquity onward, the custom of such chanting assured pleasantness of vocal rendition, served as a memory aid to readers, implied congregational respect for the text, and required devoted concentration. Since each of the neumes indicated a specific melodic pattern, a well-tutored reader could weave a line of melody that would be repeated in the same manner whenever the particular passage was chanted.

Originally, there were three systems of biblical neumes, or tropes: the Tiberian, which by the twelfth century pervaded all European Judaism and singularly has survived into present times; the old Babylonian; and the Proto-Palestinian. The basis of the Tiberian system consists of twenty-eight distinctive tropal signs, each designated by an Aramaic name. The neumes in themselves form a hierarchy of importance, with strict rules of relationships to one another and to the body of the biblical texts. While the same Tiberian configurations are now universally to be found, the motival elements that each of them represent differ quite markedly in the Ashkenazic and Sephardic performance traditions, and, indeed, even among the subdivisions of those branches of Judaism. Then, too, within the frame of each of these traditions are different melodic systems for the chanting of the Pentateuch (*Torah*, or Five Books of Moses), the Prophets (*Haftarah*, or prophetics), and for each of the other sacred Scrolls (K'*tuvim*, or holy writings): Song of Songs, Ruth, Esther, Lamentations, and Ecclesiastes.[1]

The abundant variety of different melodic systems in active practice among the many Jewish traditions represents an enormous reservoir of musical creativity, encompassing centuries of Diaspora life in many areas of the world. For this reason, collection and study of the diverse elements of the Jewish cantillations has attracted the interest of many musicologists and historians, Christian as well as Jewish. Moreover, from the late nineteenth century onward, composers began to turn to those neumes in a search for "authentic" Jewish musical expression. Significantly, with the rise of formalized cantorial education in America during the second half of the twentieth century, there have been efforts to establish more consistent and unified cantillation structures.

One of the leading scholars in that effort was Solomon Rosowsky (1878–1962), an internationally recognized authority on biblical chant who for a number of years, until his death, was on the faculty at the Cantors Institute of the Jewish Theological Seminary in New York City. His book *The Cantillation of the Bible* was the culmination of intensive scholarly research that he had begun in 1925 in Palestine, and constitutes a masterful treatise on the Sabbath chant of the Pentateuch in the Lithuanian-Ashkenazic tradition.[2] It remains an admirable resource for comparative investigations into the vast field of religious cantillation.

The son of a notable cantor, Boruch Leib Rosowsky (1841–1919), Solomon Rosowsky was born in Riga, Latvia. He studied music at the St. Petersburg Conservatory, where he took courses with Rimsky-Korsakov and helped to establish the pioneer St. Petersburg Society for Jewish Folk Music in 1908. A teacher and music critic, Rosowsky also composed for concert and theatrical presentations in

Europe and Palestine, and then, from 1950 onward, in the United States, where he was an active member of the Jewish Music Forum. As a highly specialized treatise on Jewish cantillation, the importance of Rosowsky's magnum opus lies in its significance for further scholarly research into comparative liturgical chant. Its broader importance relates to the manner in which Rosowsky points out the inherent musicality and ageless vitality of this liturgical heritage, and in his eloquent plea for wider appreciation of that art through more disciplined fidelity in its performance.

For the final edition of the *Jewish Music Forum Bulletin*, vol. 9 (1955), an issue that reported upon the forum meetings held from 1949 to 1955, Solomon Rosowsky contributed a summary of a lecture he had presented in February 1954 in connection with work on his book. He noted (p. 37):

When I began to interest myself in the biblical melodies some thirty years ago, I used to notate them in the accepted fashion prevalent at the time. In other words, I would notate the melodies, without any questioning, as sung for me by different cantillators. The results, however, did not satisfy me, for I felt that there was much more music in the tropes than the cantillators were able to bring out. It is certainly no secret that most cantillators do not possess the necessary musical background for bringing out the hidden beauty of the tropes. We must however treat these *Torah* readers with fairness and consideration, for even if they were to possess the necessary musical qualifications, they could not properly bring out the tropal melodies under the conditions which prevail in the synagogues during the *Torah* readings. These conditions are certainly not conducive to proper cantillation, since the time allotted for it is extremely limited. The reader has to chant a whole *sidra* (portion) and must therefore of necessity rush through the cantillation.

Joseph Yasser, in his reviews of Rosowsky's book,[3] pointed out certain affinities between those Jewish liturgical materials and elements of Gregorian chant. For centuries, scholars of music and philology have studied Hebrew biblical cantillation in search of reminiscences of biblical and Holy Temple music and roots of Christian plainchant. Among them were the German humanist Johann Reuchlin (1455–1522), who endeavored to notate the Hebrew tropes musically. His efforts were published in 1518 with the assistance of a Catholic priest and Hebraic scholar Johann Boeschenstein (fl. 15th–16th cent.). In his historical survey of Jewish music,[4] Abraham Z. Idelsohn cites that work, as well as those of other scholars who flourished in sixteenth- and seventeenth-century Europe.

Ironically, it was a Christian fascination for details of the biblical legacy that underscored for Jews a valid sense of their historical and cultural continuity. As though a blueprint for the ideal in literature and music had been established millennia ago in Jerusalem, Christian academics and theologians scrutinized details of the Temple Era, pouring over the *Talmud* and other Jewish sources for details. Scholarly interest in antiquity's creativity was further strengthened by the rise of nineteenth-century romanticism, displacing classicism's emphasis upon the Greek and Roman origins of Western civilization. Attention was directed toward the Holyland, and Christians scanned Jewish life in the European ghettos for vestiges of that biblical past. A newly developed discipline in the universities concentrating on the "scientific" study of music history began to attract European scholars.

An outstanding musicological treatise of that period was by Carl Engel (1818–1882).[5] Originally published in London in 1864, the book included an extensive section devoted to "Hebrew Music of the Present Day" presented as corollary to materials on the biblical era. Engel referred to then-contemporary musical services of Salomon Sulzer (1804–1890), Ashkenazic cantor in Vienna, and to David A. De Sola (1796–1860), Sephardic rabbi and liturgist of Amsterdam and London. Cited by Carl Engel also were the musical achievements of Mendelssohn, Meyerbeer, Halévy, and other musicians of Jewish lineage. He felt compelled to write (p. 348): "It is remarkable that the great susceptibility and fondness for music which the ancient Hebrew evidently possessed have been preserved by their race until the present day."

It was in the context of this intellectual environment that the German scholar Carl Heinrich Cornill (1854–1920) instructed students in Lutheran theology and published studies on Moses, the Prophets, the Psalms, and the people and culture of ancient Israel. His volume, *Music in the Old Testament*,[6] was originally prepared by Cornill for presentation in German lecture halls. The English translation was made for an American periodical, *The Monist*, a quarterly on philosophical topics issued at irregular intervals from 1890 to 1936 in Chicago. At the time of its publication, Cornill was professor of Old Testament theology at the University of Breslau. Another extended lecture by Cornill, *The Culture of Ancient Israel*, was also translated into English and published as a pamphlet in Chicago in 1914.

In his overview of music in the biblical era, Cornill noted the musical vitality of the people of Ancient Israel in their public and private lives, and especially the significance of music in their worship. The importance of Cornill's work rests in his sociological approach. However, while Carl Engel had perceived a viable Jewish musical continuity into modern times, particularly among Near Eastern Jews, and thus anticipated the research of Abraham Z. Idelsohn, Cornill concluded his own investigative studies with the concept of the Psalms alone as the residual treasury.

The work-legacy of Engel and Cornill was carried forward by Henry George Farmer (1882–1965) and Carl H. Kraeling (1897–1966), who in their studies of ancient and Biblical music began to trace common sources and intimate early relationships of Jewish and Christian religious music.[7] It was Eric Werner, in particular among the Jewish scholars, whose efforts were directed toward fathoming the early common roots of Judaic and Christian liturgical chant.

In considering the significance of the Dead Sea Scrolls,[8] Werner focused upon what they might reveal about the music of various Judaic sects during the Hellenist Era. For the history of musical notation, he observed that elaborate marginal signs in the manuscripts of "Isaiah" and "Habakkuk Commentary" bear more than casual resemblances to the musical shorthand for the early medieval Byzantine *Kontakia* (hymnals). Werner noted that this might alter theories as to origins of Church neumes and Hebrew tropal cantillation signs. Questioning whether to take literally the use of instruments repeatedly mentioned in the scrolls of "War of the Children of Light against the Children of Darkness," and in "Manual of Discipline," he emphasized the fact that singing with understanding was more important to the sects of that period than instrumentation, which had been primarily associated with the rituals of the Temple. Werner's magnum opus, *The Sacred Bridge*, originally published in 1959,[9] was the product of extensive and intensive study of comparative early church and synagogue liturgy, probing what he believed were common characteristics at the essential core of their musical substances.

Werner returned again and again over the following years to that thesis, and in 1984 under the rubric of "Volume 2" issued a collection of eight of those articles.[10] Here, his study "Liturgical Music in Hellenistic Palestine" examines the development of rabbinic-shaped Judaic rites following the destruction of the Temple and abandonment of instrumentation with a reformulation of vocally oriented devotions, noting the parallels between early synagogue and rising church. In another study, he proposes that St. Paul, who had been a pupil of Pharisee scholar Gamaliel the Elder, transmitted certain rabbinic attitudes toward music (opposition to instruments, emphasis upon vocal chant, silencing of women's voices) into formative Christian practices. In contrast to the Sadducees, who were the hereditary hierarchy vested in Temple ritual, the Pharisees had gradually assumed leadership among the general populace, forming communal devotional groups and study houses well before destruction of the Temple. Over all, Werner reiterates his firm belief in the roles of the bearers of liturgical musical elements between Judaism and Christianity. He maintains that plainsong in itself reflects Jewish roots, cantillation and melismatic chant patterns being germane to the liturgies of both. Moreover, psalmody remains the oldest common ground between the two faiths, springing from the critical significance of the 150 Psalms and their intonation in the litanies of ancient synagogue and early church worship services.

Of the twenty-four books of the Bible generally known as the Old Testament,[11] the Book of Psalms had constituted the bedrock of Judeo-Christian hymnology. Ascribed to King David, that most musical of all Biblical figures, its poetry has transcended time and place. The 150 Psalms have served devotional emotional needs of countless individuals and groups, ever since their introduction as texts for the music of the Levite choirs in the Jerusalem Temple. No other poetry has been set to music more often in Western civilization. The contents of those texts reflect an ancient age-old dedication to musical expression in instrumentation along with song, as climaxed with the panoply of musicians in concluding Psalm 150: "Let All Praise the Lord, Hallelujah." Over the centuries, scholars have sorted over that listing of musical instruments to recreate the original spectacle of Temple ritual and celebration, with its great choir of Levites accompanied by varied instruments of antiquity—strings, winds, and percussion. Of composite authorship during the hegemony of descendant monarchs of Ancient Israel, the Psalms constitute a literature of study in terms of historic analogies and liturgical interpretations. For the Jewish faith, there are specific Psalms intoned for weekdays and Sabbath, holidays and festivals, life-cycle events, and for personalized devotions. Above all, those texts constitute timeless inspirational expressions. For example, the very essence of centuries of Jewish Diaspora life is eloquently expressed by the text of Psalm 137, ascribed to a time following destruction of the First Holy Temple, early in the Babylonian exile: "By the Waters of Babylon, we sat down and wept when we remembered Zion... How shall we sing the Lord's song in a strange land?"[12]

Centuries of scholars and religious leaders have viewed the Psalms as a musical legacy, guiding liturgical practices. Intimations of their early performances have been perceived. Psalm 46 appears to indicate natural psalmody, or straight prayer intoned as solo or in unison chorus; Psalm 67 is clearly in responsive style, for two choral groups or a solo with chorus; Psalm 80 is a litany with a refrain; antiphony is indicated for parts of Psalm 103. Some Psalm headings may indicate melodic usages, and there certainly seems to be a relationship between text matter and style of musical presentation. Ensembles of such instruments as reed pipes and trumpets, lyres and harps, cymbals and drums, point to the conclusion that highly skilled musicians filled the ranks of the Temple performers.

Several obscure musical terms found in the Psalms have been of particular interest to scholars. The cantorial musician Jacob Beimel (1880–1944) was particularly intrigued by the word *selah*, and lectured on that subject at the March 1943 meeting of the Jewish Music Forum. He subsequently wrote a summary of that lecture, and it is here quoted in its entirety:[13]

The word *selah* occurs in the Book of Psalms seventy-one times. It is not to be found in any other book of the Bible except in the book of the prophet Habakkuk, where it appears in the middle of a verse. The word *selah* appears usually at the end of a Psalm or in the middle of it, at the end of a stanza. As to the meaning of *selah*, the opinions of the commentators of the Bible differ from each other. Aquilas [*sic*] in his Aramaic version of the Bible translates *selah* with the word *l'olam* or *almin*, meaning forever. This meaning of *selah* was adopted for many a Hebrew prayer of old. However, many commentators of the Bible, old and modern, Jewish and Christian, maintain that the term *selah* refers to music. It is a musical term. The reasons for these explanations are: 1. *Selah* appears in thirty-one Psalms which begin with the word *lam'natseyakh*, for the leader. It is therefore obvious that these Psalms were rendered under the direction of a leader. 2. The word *selah* appears in those Psalms (excepting Psalms 66 and 67) where their authors such as David, B'ney Korah, Asaph, and Ethan are mentioned. All these persons were musicians and conductors.

Accepting *selah* as a musical term, some commentators derive this word from the Hebrew verb *solal*, to raise or to cast a highway. Thus it may have meant *crescendo*. In the Septuagint, the early Greek Bible, *selah* is translated with the word *diapsalma*. Also about the meaning of the word *diapsalma* and what it stands for, there are different opinions, such as: 1. music between the songs (orchestral intermezzo or interlude); 2. pause; and, 3. change of the choir. There was also expressed the opinion that *selah* derives from the Syriac word *saloh*, supplication or prayer. Thus the word *selah* means prayer. Some commentators suggest that the three letters *s-l-h* with which the word *selah* is spelled in Hebrew, represent three words, namely: *sov l'ma-aloh ha-shar*—turn to the above of song, or *Da capo*.

The Hebrew lexicographer J. Steinberg, in his *Mishpat ha-Urim* maintains that *selah* refers to a musical instrument which had the shape of a basket, *sal* in Hebrew. Considering the fact that there were and still are drums which have had or have the shape of pots (India), barrels (China), and kettles (in the modern orchestra), it may be assumed that in the services at the Temple in Jerusalem there was used a drum which had the shape of a basket. This drum was possibly used for signals only. These signals may have been intended for the priests to continue or resume the sacrificial service, or for the congregation indicating that the services were finished.

In all probability, however, the signals were designated for the musicians who accompanied the singers on musical instruments. Like the accompanying musicians of our time, who in most cases do not know the texts of the songs which they accompany, so the Levitic players also may not have known the words of the Psalms which the Levitic singers sang. Thus a beat on the basket-drum may have indicated to them the change of the melody or the end of the Psalm. The verb *sollu* in Psalm 68:5 refers obviously to the *sal*, basket drum. It seems that no special musician was assigned to the task of beating out the signals. The conductor simply ordered a musician, placed nearest to the *sal*, to play the basket-drum by saying to him—to the *sal*, in Hebrew *la-sal* or *selah*. The *h* at the end of the word instead of the *l* at its beginning is a rule of Hebrew grammar.

NOTES

1. A good basic text for study-performance of the Ashkenazic cantillation formulas generally favored among American congregations is Abraham W. Binder, *Biblical Chant* (New York: Philosophical Library, 1959). Binder originally intended this book for the education of cantorial and rabbinical students at the Hebrew Union College-Jewish Institute of Religion.

2. Solomon Rosowsky, *The Cantillation of the Bible: The Five Books of Moses* (New York: Reconstructionist Press, 1957).

Unfortunately, the title of the book is somewhat misleading since it implies that all facets of the subject are discussed. The author, in fact, clearly states in his preface that he has treated only one specific aspect of biblical cantillation, that of the Sabbath chant for the Pentateuch in the Lithuanian branch of the Ashkenazic liturgical tradition. He explains that in order to present a thorough analysis of one form of cantillation, he chose the style with which he was personally most conversant and the one that has been most commonly adhered to by Ashkenazic traditions in America and Israel.

3. The two reviews by Joseph Yasser of Solomon Rosowsky's *Cantillation* can be found in *Musical Quarterly*, vol. 44, no. 3 (1958), pp. 393–401, and *YIVO Annual of Jewish Social Science*, vol. 12 (1958/59), pp. 157–75.

4. Abraham Z. Idelsohn, *Jewish Music in Its Historical Development* (New York: Henry Holt, 1929; reprint ed., Westport, Conn.: Greenwood Press, 1981), p. 346.

5. Carl Engel, *The Music of the Most Ancient Nations: Particularly of the Assyrians, Egyptians and Hebrews, With Special References to Recent Discoveries in Western Asia and in Egypt* (London: J. Murray, 1864; reprint ed., Freeport, N.Y.: Books for Libraries Press, 1970), pp. 277–365.

6. Carl Heinrich Cornill, *Music in the Old Testament*, trans. from German by Lydia G. Robinson (Chicago: Open Court Publishers, 1909).

7. Egon Wellesz, ed., *Ancient and Oriental Music* New Oxford History of Music Series, Vol. 1 (London: Oxford University Press, 1957). See the following: Chapters 5 and 6 by Henry George Farmer, "The Music of Ancient Mesopotamia," pp. 228–65, and "The Music of Ancient Egypt," pp. 255–82; Chapter 7 by Carl H. Kraeling and Lucetta Mowry, "Music in the Bible," pp. 283–312; and Chapter 8 by Eric Werner, "Post-Biblical Judaism," pp. 313–35.

8. Eric Werner, "Musical Aspects of the Dead Sea Scrolls," *Musical Quarterly*, vol. 43, no. 1 (1957), pp. 21–37.

9. Eric Werner, *The Sacred Bridge: The Interdependence of Liturgy and Music in Synagogue and Church During the First Millennium* (New York: Columbia University Press, 1959; reprint ed., New York: Da Capo Press, 1979).

10. Eric Werner, *The Sacred Bridge*, Vol. 1 (New York: Schocken Books, 1970), and *The Sacred Bridge*, Vol. 2 (New York: Ktav, 1984).

11. The Jewish Bible consists of the following twenty-four books: Pentateuch (*Torah*) or Five Books of Moses—Genesis, Exodus, Leviticus, Numbers, and Deuteronomy; Prophets (*Haftarah*)—Joshua, Judges, Samuel, Kings, Isaiah, Jeremiah, Ezekiel, Hosea, Joel, Amos, Obadiah, Jonah, Micah, Nahum, Habakkuk, Zephaniah, Haggai and Zechariah, and Malachi; Scriptures and Scrolls (K'*tuvim*)—Psalms, Proverbs, Job, Songs of Songs, Ruth, Lamentations, Ecclesiastes, Esther, Daniel, Ezra and Nehemiah, and Chronicles. The final two books treat the rebuilding of the Second Temple in Jerusalem and review Jewish history from Adam to the return to Judea in the Second Commonwealth Era. The apocryphal work, "Ben Sira/The Wisdom of Jesus the Son of Sirach" (or Ecclesiasticus) dates from a later period (ca.190 B.C.E.).

The *Septuagint* (Greek version) of the Jewish Bible, generally believed to have been translated by Aquila (ca.130 C.E.), was intended for the many Jews then living in

Greek-speaking areas. A Syriac-Eastern Aramaic version of the Old Testament was known as the *Peshitta*, and the *Targum* constituted a definitive translation for Aramaic-speaking Jews of the Near East. The *Vulgate*, or Latin language version of the Old Testament, has been attributed to St. Jerome (ca.400 C.E.).

12. For a masterful presentation on the Psalms, see Bathja Bayer, "The Titles of the Psalms—A Renewed Investigation of an Old Problem" in *Yuval: Studies of the Jewish Music Research Centre*, Vol. 4 (Jerusalem: Magnes Press and Hebrew University, 1982), pp. 29–123.

Bayer's highly analytical study of the ascriptions (in terms of origins, components, and interpretations) covers the range of Psalm headings. On page 91, She offers a particularly illuminating comment in her discussion of Psalm 137, "By the waters of Babylon": "There is ample documentation for the habit of the later Assyrian kings and their Babylonian successors to have original exotic music at their courts. The foreign musicians were obtained from client kings as part of their tribute, or taken as a special kind of living booty when a kingdom was conquered." Bayer's thesis might explain the chanting of Psalm 137 as a lamentation for those Temple musicians taken into captivity as slaves and compelled to entertain their captors.

13. Jacob Beimel, "Some Interpretations of the Meaning of *Selah*," *Jewish Music Forum Bulletin*, Vol. 4, no. 1 (1943), pp. 6–7. In her discussion, Bathja Bayer (ibid.) mentions the word *selah* several times, including its place within the text of Psalm 4, but does not discuss its meaning or possible musical function.

5

A Historical and Bibliographical Perspective on Jewish Liturgical Music in Eastern Europe to 1900

During earlier centuries when most musical talents were channeled into religious expression, there was an aesthetic conflict. In the Middle Ages, Erasmus feared that elaborate art would impinge upon piety and so he set extreme restrictions upon all music as detrimental to worship. In later times Martin Luther taught his followers that any music that emanated from the heart was fit to accompany the words of God. Yet liturgical music being first of all *music*, a product of man's creative urge, could never clearly be parceled into sharp categories of sacred-spiritual and secular-mundane. With the power of natural expression, the folk songs of the people themselves blended differing sounds, all but obliterating melodic boundaries. Music, as the most readily communicative of arts, was never an isolated form of expression; it was always influenced by time and place, and shaped by kindred as well as alien tonal ideas.

That musical conflict with its eventual compromises also raged within European Jewish communities, but essentially was tempered by the predominance of indigenous traditions. Historically, Jewish music evolved as a mirror of Jewish life, whether at religious observances or along the wayside of everyday individual and societal experiences. Moreover, its melodic elements were not confined by ghetto walls, and whether knowingly or not, Jew and non-Jew exchanged musical ideas. Indeed, the folk influence of Jewish music, particularly the motifs of synagogue cantillation and chant, remain yet to be traced and studied within the general sweep of musical history.

It is the purpose of this chapter to provide background information and to identify some important bibliographic references and collected source materials on Jewish liturgical music, as presently available to contemporary scholars for historical studies of ritual music in eastern Europe.

Civilization's reservoir of written music has been filled with those vital oral traditions that depended upon many informed and dedicated practitioners. This fact has been especially true for Jewish musico-cultural continuity, so profoundly based upon active individual association in creativity, performance, and transmission. For synagogue music, the religious functionaries were the bearers and preservers of a treasury of song. Before the Common (Christian) Era, the *mithpallel* (enabler to pray) was someone who seemed especially gifted with the power of musical prayer. Over the next centuries, this layman-precentor evolved into the *shaliakh tsibbur* (messenger of the people), an office of honor, for which assistance was often rendered by *soferim* (scholar-scribes) and *ba'aley korey* (master readers). By the fifth century, there were *tomeykhim* (supporters) or *mesayim* (task-doers), whose duties were to remember liturgical texts, melodic motifs, and the orders of various services. Toward the end of the following century, the office of professional precentor, called *paytan hazzan* (poet-beadle), arose to assume responsibility for liturgical duties. Increasingly, maintenance of precious synagogue traditions was entrusted to specially trained individuals as an ethical duty. In the ninth century, the rabbinical scholar Amram Gaon of Sura advised that boys of thirteen be properly qualified to officiate at services; such religious process was to be called *bar mitzvah* (son of holy deed) and to be considered as a sacred obligation among adult males in the Jewish community.

By the Middle Age, there were two types of precentors: *ba'al tefiloh* (master of prayer) as an honorary office, and the professional role of *hazzan* (beadle), often a gifted poet-musician or liturgical bard who created hymn texts and melodies. The secular counterpart in Jewish music was the *badkhen* (troubadour), who graced rabbinical gatherings, weddings, and communal celebrations, performing didactic ballads for the edification as well as entertainment of the people.

From the twelfth to the sixteenth centuries, the *rabbi* (teacher-spiritual leader) served also as *hazzan* (leader of services) in many European Jewish communities. Especially in eastern Europe, precentors with fine singing voices flourished, usually accompanied by *meshorerim* (choristers) who substituted for the banned musical instruments. An *ars nova* movement in synagogue music arose early in the eighteenth century with the notation, collection, study, and publication of this music.

Jews settled near Cracow in the twelfth century, though some had been in Poland since earlier times. Casimir the Great (ca.1333–1370) encouraged their migration to his territories. In 1364, the first Polish university was established in Cracow, with the aid of Jews appointed by the king to raise funds for teachers and students. Until 1764, Polish Jewry was organized by the government into the Council of Four Lands—Great Poland, Little Poland, Red Russia (East Galicia and Podolia), and Volhynia. Lithuania was a separate division. *Shtatlonim* (representatives) were permitted to attend sessions of the Polish Diet in Warsaw. Jews generally did not reside within the large cities until the nineteenth century. Living in small villages and rural areas among the other Polish peasantry, they were farmers, dairymen, millers, and artisan workers in the building and clothing trades. Formal public education was denied to most Jews, and so intellectual focus was Judaic. Hebrew was the sacred tongue, but the daily languages were Polish and Russian as well as Yiddish. That Jewish vernacular, composed of Hebrew, Aramaic, French, German, and Slavic elements, had developed from the twelfth century on. Jewish minstrels have been documented as entertaining in Poland as early as 1382, and Jews were permitted to perform as general musicians in Cracow by 1556. Among the seventeenth-century laws regarding Jewish musicians, there was a statute forbidding them to go through the streets at night singing and playing on their musical instruments.

Over the many centuries, three distinctive traditions of Jewish liturgical music had evolved: Sephardic/Judeo-Spaniolic (*Sefardim*)—derived from Iberia; Oriental—North Africa, Mediterranean area, and Near East-Asia; and Ashkenazic (*Ashkenazim*)—general Europe, derived from the early Jewish settlers in the Rhine Valley during the Roman Empire and documented as highly active communities by the time of Charlemagne. For all *minhagim* (traditions), there arose cantillation formulas for each of the three divisions of biblical readings: *Torah* (Pentateuch), *Nevi'im* (Prophets),; and *K'tuvim* (Holy Scrolls). The religious chants, or *nusakh ha-t'filah* (melodies of prayer) for the services—*shakharit* (morning), *musaf* (additional section for the Sabbath and holidays), *minkha* (afternoon), and *ma-ariv/arvit* (evening)—were shaped with the following characteristic constituents: specially improvisational elaborations of fixed musical motifs and modal patterns, particular well-revered chant melodies, and composed hymnology. Style of performance was that of precentor-soloist, with congregational participation in long or short forms of response. Different melodic elements also helped to define the calendar year: weekdays, Sabbaths, the great festivals (*Sukkoth*—Booths, *Pesakh*—Passover, and *Shevuoth*—Weeks), High Holy Days (*Rosh Hashanah*—New Year, and *Yom Kippur*—Day of Atonement), as well as such observances as *Rosh Khodesh* (New Moon), *Hanukkah* (Feast of Lights), *Purim* (Feast of Lots), and other minor fast and feast days. To some extent, music was an integral part of the significant life cycle events of birth, marriage, and death. In addition, much of centuries-old Jewish vernacular folk song related to the religious celebrations in the home, thereby constituting a unique musical and poetic blend of sacred with secular.

Eastern European Jewish liturgical music was Ashkenazic, and over the centuries in the Greater Polish area had evolved into a special variant, *minhag Polen* (Polish tradition), practiced with minor differences in Bessarabia, Hungary, Lithuania, Romania, Ukraine, and Volhynia as well as Poland. In other areas of Europe, such as Germany and the Lowlands, France, and Italy, Ashkenazic traditions evolved in other ways. Nevertheless, throughout Europe, Ashkenazic practices remained strongly akin notably to certain liturgico-musical formulas for the cantillations, the chants, revered (*mi-Sinai*—from Mount Sinai) melodic elements, and favored hymn tunes. Inevitably, however, certain qualities pervaded both the Slavic and Judaic liturgies of the eastern European region. The concept of minor as expressing sadness and of major as reflecting joy appears to have been western European, and not at all shared by Slavic area peoples. Analogous melodic elements and qualities may be found among Russian, Ukrainian, Polish, and Jewish tunes.[1]

A predilection for certain modal forms is apparent among all eastern Europeans, especially similar to two of the liturgical chant patterns of *minhag Polen*: *ahavoh rabboh* (with great love) mode, as a modified Gregorian Phrygian, and the so-called Ukrainian Dorian scalar pattern, as a form of ancient Dorian. Both have been favored by Jewish poet-singers, often using the Slavic-Oriental augmented second interval as a pivotal melodic figure. The linguistics of Jewish life in the region doubtless reinforced such melodic linkages. Some Jewish songs, including holiday tunes, were sung not only in Hebrew and Yiddish, but in combinations of Yiddish and Russian or Yiddish and Polish.[2]

For generations, collections of notated liturgical music were to be found among the private library holdings of many European rabbinical scholars. By the late eighteenth century, leading *hazzanim* (cantors) also collected the music manuscripts of their professional predecessors, adding their own particular works and then passing these materials along to their students and heirs as a precious legacy. The printing and publication of much of this music during the nineteenth and twentieth centuries has been a fortuitous consequence of those generations of dedicated oral and written preservation. As a result, there are several significant and comprehensive compilations of particular eastern European origin that should be examined by scholars interested in ritual music and text.

Abraham Baer (1834–1894) was chief cantor of a large congregation in Gothenberg from 1857 until his death. In 1871 in Leipzig, he published the first edition of his liturgical collection, *Ba'al Tefiloh, oder der Praktische Vorbeter* (Master of prayer, or the practical precentor). Six years later, he expanded that work, and it was reissued in Gothenberg in 1883. Posthumous reprint editions appeared in Frankfurt in 1901, Nuernberg in 1930, and then in New York City in 1953.[3] Baer's book provided a unique anthological source of Jewish liturgical music, consisting of 1,500 melody lines (with text) covering the entire calendar year of devotions for the Ashkenazic ritual in its variant traditions (*minhagim*)— German/western Europe, Polish/eastern Europe, and other Europeans. Also included were some liturgical chants from the Sephardic traditions. For his great collection, Baer had gathered a great number of eighteenth- and nineteenth-century liturgical manuscripts. He organized those materials according to functional ritual usage and added an introductory essay providing information as to their origins and styles of cantorial performance. The liturgical music book became a widely used reference work for European cantors, and after World War II an important text-source for traditional cantorial education in America and Israel.

A Russian cantor, Abraham Dunajewsky (1843–1911) published his collection, *Israelische Tempel Compositionen fuer den Sabbath* (Israelite temple compositions for the Sabbath) in Moscow in 1893 and then in 1898 in Odessa.[4] Though more modest in scope than Baer's work, the melodic components show stronger Slavic influences. A compilation by another Russian cantor, Eliezer Gerovitsch (1844–1913), *Synagogen Gesaenge: Shirey Zimroh, Shirey Tefiloh* (Synagogue songs: music of celebration, music of prayer) was musically skillful in presentation, and reflected creditably upon the formal training that Gerovitsch had received at the St. Petersburg Conservatory. Issued in two volumes in 1897, in both Rostov and Moscow, the collection covered the year-round liturgical services in the Russo-Polish tradition.

Throughout Europe during the nineteenth century, there were a number of important publications of cantorial collections treating the Ashkenazic ceremonial liturgy. In particular, three outstanding central European synagogue musicians flourished, each providing innovative ideas for ritual musical practice and leaving in legacy significant liturgical publications reflecting those musical ideas. Salomon Sulzer (1804–1890) was a notable cantor at Vienna's largest synagogue, Seitenstettengasse Shul, where he initiated ideas for more formal (though strictly observant) cantorial and choral practices, and thereby came to be considered the innovative father of the modern cantorial art. His published work, *Schir Zion—Gottesdienstliche Gesaenge* (Songs of Zion—songs in the service of God), was issued in three successive sections in Vienna in 1839, 1865, and 1889. In 1905, it was posthumously edited by his son Joseph Sulzer (1859–1926), and published there as one complete volume.

In Berlin, Louis Lewandowski (1821–1894) was a leading liturgical music director and composer-arranger; he introduced structured performances by well-trained choirs and cantorial soloists and became a historic role model for modern synagogue musicians. Two collections of his cantorial solos and choir responses (with optional organ accompaniments) for the full liturgical year, *Todah V'zimrah* (Thanksgiving and melody), were issued in Berlin, in 1876 and 1882. As a liturgical scholar as well as the cantor who served at the largest synagogue in Paris, Samuel Naumbourg (1815–1880) was an early advocate of the study of Jewish music history. With composer Vincent D'Indy (1851–1932), he edited and published liturgical compositions by Salomone Rossi, known in his time as Ebreo of Mantua, (ca.1565–ca.1628).[5] Naumbourg's own liturgical works in the French-South German Ashkenazic tradition were published in Paris, in 1847 and 1857, as *Chants Liturgiques des Israelites: Zemirot Yisroel* (Liturgical chants: songs of Israel), and in 1864 and 1874, as *Chants Religieux des Israelites: Agudat Shirim* (Religious chants of the Israelites: collected songs).

Those three gifted liturgists—Sulzer as uniquely innovative cantor and composer, Lewandowski as shaper of the role of professional choir leader, and Naumbourg as scholarly cantor—all strengthened and enriched the cantorial art throughout nineteenth-century European Jewish communities, east and west. They have had a lasting impact upon twentieth-century Jewish ritual musicians.

The traditional prayer melodies in the repertoires of two cantors from Odessa, Nissan Blumenthal (1805–1902) and David Nowakowsky (1846–1921), were collected in *Gebete und Gesaenge zum des Sabbath* (Prayers and songs for the Sabbath). Nowakowsky had succeeded his mentor Blumenthal at a prominent synagogue, Odesser Broder Shul, and in 1900 in Odessa, published this combined collection of their melodic chants. The music is somewhat modernized in style, yet adheres to the established Russian-Polish tradition. Another collector, Hirsch Alter Weintraub (1811–1882), had been trained for the cantorate by his father, Salomon Kashtan Weintraub (1781–1829), a widely respected musician who served a congregation in Alt-Konstantin. The younger Weintraub held cantorial posts in Dubnow and then in Koenigsberg, where he groomed as his successor the prodigious scholar and musician Eduard Birnbaum (1855–1920). In Koenigsberg, in 1859, Weintraub published a collection of his and his father's liturgical selections, *Schire Beth Adonai, Tempelgesaenge in der Gottesdienst der Israeliten* (Songs of the house of God, temple songs in the Israelite religious service). Birnbaum edited a posthumously expanded edition of that collection, published in Leipzig in 1901.

Eduard Birnbaum was a major East European liturgical leader with great general knowledge and an exceptional range of musical interest. Born in Cracow, he studied for the cantorate with Salomon Sulzer in Vienna, and then with Moritz Deutsch (1818–1892) of Breslau. Two collections of liturgical melodies by Deutsch, *Breslauer Synagogen Gesaenge* (Breslau synagogue hymns) and *Deutsche Synagogen un Shul Lieder* (German synagogue and school songs) were published in 1867 and 1871. Though ostensibly noted as German, that music appears firmly based on East European patterns, as stylized by Deutsch in a "Vienna-Berlin" manner.

By the time Birnbaum had arrived in Koenigsberg to apprentice with Hirsch Alter Weintraub, he already was a diligent copier-collector of liturgical music scores. Despite modest financial circumstances, to the end of his life Birnbaum accumulated and documented an enormous personal library of synagogue music. He maintained correspondence with leading musicians and historians. Much respected by his colleagues, he was teacher-mentor to many younger Jewish musicians. Some, like Vilna-born Arno Nadel (1878–1943), began their own extensive collections of music materials under Birnbaum's active guidance. In an article entitled *Polen und der Polnische Ritus* (Poland and the Polish rite), published in 1909 in an issue of *Oesterreichisch-Ungarische Kantorenzeitung* (Austro-Hungarian cantorial times), which he also edited, Birnbaum proposed a common Byzantine origin for the Polish-southern Russian traditions, and considered various means of melodic confluence between Slavic and Jewish ritual music.[6] Perhaps his greatest significance was that he showed how to combine scholarly musicality with a sense of the sweep of general history, and how to view Jewish music within that broader context.

In 1923, the complete holdings of the Birnbaum collection were purchased from his heirs and incorporated into the library of the Hebrew Union College at Cincinnati. The following year, Abraham Zvi Idelsohn (1882–1938) was engaged as archivist-cataloguer for those materials. Born in Filsberg, Latvia, Idelsohn trained as a cantor. He soon expanded his activities to ethnological investigation of music, an endeavor he actively pursued among the Yemenite, Near Eastern-Asian, and Sephardic-Mediterranean Jews whom he encountered in Jerusalem, where he lived from 1906 to 1922. By the time he arrived at Hebrew Union College, he had already completed work on five volumes of a major anthological resource based upon his research, *Hebraeish-Orientalischer Melodienschatz* (Thesaurus of Hebrew-Oriental melodies).[7] Idelsohn's appointment to oversee the Birnbaum collection proved enormously fruitful to his own anthological work. Following upon his examination of Birnbaum's rich treasury of eastern European liturgical music, Idelsohn developed five additional volumes for his *Thesaurus*, presenting the liturgical and secular folk music of the European Jews. He utilized materials from those holdings as the basis for Volumes 6, 7, and 8, and then fleshed out the final two volumes with over a thousand melodies of Hebrew and Yiddish folk songs, supplemented from other repositories and sources. The totality of the ten volumes constitutes a masterful achievement. Beyond incorporating the Birnbaum materials, Idelsohn sorted and organized them; he then placed all the constituent contents—collections and research—into a unified anthropological shape, substantively linking Ashkenazic, Sephardic, and Oriental traditions together in a common sociohistoric perspective.

Perusal of the ninth and tenth volumes of Idelsohn's *Thesaurus* yield salient examples of the dynamic relationship between eastern European Jewish melodies and Slavic songs. Indeed, Jewish musicologist Joseph Yasser (1893–1981) investigated musical parallels between the Russian art of *demestvo* (epic balladry) and the Polish-Russian *hazzanyah* (cantorial art) pointing out possible influences of Jewish Khazars from the eighth century into the Middle Ages.[8] While economics and politics has divided nations over the centuries, culture has made for integrity and unity among those peoples. Of the many instances of historic mutual musical enrichment between Slavs and Jews, there are two intriguing examples from more recent times, one theatrical and the other liturgical.

In 1896, at the old Windsor Theater on the Lower East Side of New York City, a Yiddish musical titled "Brokhoh, or the Jewish King of Poland for a Night" was created and performed. Its libretto was by Moses/Moshe Horowitz, also the impresario for that production. His scenario blended two different Jewish stories: the rabbinical legend of a heroic Jew, named Brokhoh, who fought alongside King Casimir on behalf of Polish freedom; and another relating to an actual event in Polish history. A Jew, Saul Wahl, was designated as king of Poland for one night until agreement could be reached between conflicting royal Polish factions on the choice of a proper monarch. Though history books have little if anything at all to say about that ephemeral reign, Jewish historical literature does. For that Yiddish American operetta, a special selection was composed by the chorus leader, Peretz Sandler, to be sung by the heroine while in great peril. The song was *Eili, Eili, Lomo Asavtoni* (My God, my God, why hast Thou forsaken me). With melodic elements of Slavic chant and Jewish liturgy and a poetic adaptation of Psalm 22, this song rapidly moved into the American and then international entertainment milieu. Transmuted over the decades from popular stage tune to religious folk hymn, the song has become widely recognized as a quintessential Judaic lament.

In the final years of the nineteenth century, Russian nationalist musicians, such as Stasov, Taneyev, Rimsky-Korsakov, and Mussorgsky, were charismatic figures who influenced the Jewish musicians at that time. Crimean-born Juli Dimitrovich (later name, Joel) Engel (1868–1927) was a favorite pupil of Sergei Taneyev at the Moscow Imperial Conservatory of Music, and when he graduated in 1895, became a highly respected music critic for the Moscow newspaper *Russkiya Vedomosty*. In 1898, on the eve of Russian Easter, Engel and his friend the Jewish sculptor Marek Antokolsky went to a Moscow hotel to see Vladimir Stasov, then visiting from St. Petersburg.[9] Over refreshments, they discussed Stasov's favorite topic, nationalism in the arts, and especially the matter of Slavic nationalism and Slavic art. Stasov was a great reader of the Old Testament, and felt a strong connection between the Bible and Western civilization. Suddenly, Stasov confronted Engel: "Where is your national pride in being a Jew?" Stasov was a tall man with a gray beard and looked like a fiery biblical prophet. He stormed through the room citing the glories of Jewish music—Temple Levites, synagogue liturgy, cantorial voices in melismatic chants, and the folk ballads of Yiddish-speaking Jews in eastern Europe. Within weeks, Engel resigned his newspaper post and went into the Russian Pale of Jewish Settlement to collect folk songs. When he published his first song collection in 1900, Engel sent it on to Stasov, inscribed with gratitude and respect. In 1908, Engel, among a number of other Jewish musicians, helped form the St. Petersburg Society for Jewish Folk Music, with a branch group in Moscow. Years later in New York City, one of that society's founders, Solomon Rosowsky (1878–1962), addressed a distinguished gathering of liturgists, scholars, and general musicians, all actively involved in the collection, study, arrangement, performance, and publication of Jewish music. He said to them: "We are all indebted to the Russians."[10]

NOTES

Much of this chapter originally appeared as an article on pages 441–47 of *Acta Musicologica: Musica Antiqua 8*, issued in Bydgoszcz, Poland, 1988. That publication was composed of papers delivered at the International Musicological Congress, *Musica Antiqua Europae Orientalis*, held September 5–10, 1988, under joint auspices of the International Musicological Society with the Polish Ministry of Art and Culture. For this present treatment, new text materials and footnotes have been added. That original version was developed as an historical survey of Jewish liturgical music, specifically for presentation at a conference composed almost entirely of non-Jewish Polish, Russian, and German scholars. Consequently, its contents focused upon the special interests of that constituent audience, and in particular, upon examples of Slavic connection with Jewish music in eastern Europe.

1. For example, the motival configuration of the Jewish anthem *Hatikvah* (The hope), which appears in Sephardic hymnology as well as Ashkenazic eastern European liturgy, may also be noted among Ukrainian, Polish, and Bohemian songs.

2. This custom was clearly underscored by evidence that well into the 1920s some of the favorite songs of the still Yiddish-speaking American immigrants were Slavic (Romanian, Russian, Ukrainian, and Polish). In the early decades of the twentieth century, American Jewish publishers issued sheet music editions with Cyrillic characters and Slavic poetic lyrics alongside Yiddish texts.

Not a little of that melodic influence penetrated into Yiddish American theatrical tunes, and eventually came into general knowledge, as for example the adaptation of Ivanovici's "Waves of the Danube" into a popular ballad, "The Anniversary Waltz." Well into the 1930s, American Jewish folk-style bands (*klezmorim*) introduced many Slavic dance tunes into the broader entertainment world by way of stage, radio, and recordings. In this manner, a form of Judeo-Slavic musical blend was often perceived in America as inherent in Yiddish musical performance. It was simply a case of melodies not only leaping back and forth over ghetto walls in eastern Europe, but traveling across the Atlantic Ocean to be adapted into a modern performance genre.

3. Abraham Baer, comp. and ed., *Ba'al Tefiloh, oder der Praktische Vorbeter* (reprint ed., New York: HUC-JIR Sacred Music Press, 1953). This extensive collection for the practice of traditional prayer leadership has been used as a training text at all the American schools of cantorial music—Orthodox, Conservative, and Reform.

4. During the 1950s, all of the liturgical publications listed and discussed in this chapter were reprinted in New York City by the Sacred Music Press of Hebrew Union College-Jewish Institute of Religion (HUC-JIR). Consequently, those works are available at most American public libraries and university collections, as well at each campus library of the three main American institutions of Jewish religious study: Hebrew Union College-Jewish Institute of Religion (HUC-JIR), Jewish Theological Seminary of America (JTSA), and Yeshiva University (YU). Copies are also likely to be found at libraries in the State of Israel and among the Judaica holdings of European institutions.

5. Samuel Naumbourg and Vincent D'Indy, comps. and eds., *Hashirim Asher Li'Shlomo* (The songs of Salomone Rossi) (Paris, 1877; reprint ed.,—New York: Sacred Music Press, 1954). Contents of this music collection (cantorial solos and choir responses, a cappella) were based upon the original edition which was published by Rossi himself in Venice, ca.1623.

6. For a bibliography of works by/about Eduard Birnbaum, see Edwin Seroussi, "Eduard Birnbaum—A Bibliography," in *Yuval Volume 4: Studies of the Jewish Music Research Centre* (Jerusalem: Magnes Press and Hebrew University, 1982), pp. 170–78.

7. Abraham Z. Idelsohn, comp. and ed., *Hebraeish-Orientalischer Melodienschatz—Thesaurus of Oriental Hebrew Melodies*, 10 vols. (Berlin, Leipzig, Vienna,

Jerusalem: Breitkopf u. Haertel and Benjamin Harz, 1922–1933; reprint ed., in four concise volumes, New York: Ktav, 1973).

8. Joseph Yasser, "References to the Hebrew Music in Russian Medieval Ballads," *Jewish Social Studies*, vol. 11, no. 1 (1949), pp. 21–48.

9. This material is based upon personal reminiscences told to me by both Solomon Rosowsky and Joseph Yasser.

10. Joseph Yasser recalled that Rosowsky made those remarks in his presentation at a meeting of the Jewish Music Forum. *Forum Bulletin*, vol. 9 (1948) gives the date as January 26, 1948. On that occasion a program celebrating the 40th anniversary of the founding of the St. Petersburg Society for Jewish Folk Music was held under the auspices of Temple Emanu-El as a tribute to its music director, Lazare Saminsky, an original member of that Russian society. Actually, Rosowsky appears to have echoed similar remarks made earlier by Joel Engel to Jacob Weinberg during their visit together in Tel Aviv in 1927, according to *Forum Bulletin, vols.* 7/8 (1946/1947), pp. 33–38. A fuller discussion of the St. Petersburg group is presented in Chapter 18 (Russian Nationalism and Jewish Music).

6

The Golden Age of the Cantorial Art

Why can some people in each generation sing so beautifully? On what basis is such a sublime gift placed in any particular human body? Does the use that is made of this special endowment justify its possession and ennoble its possessor? Cantorial tradition has always noted the manner in which the leader of prayer has lived his life and observed his duties to family, mankind, and God. Yet, a *hazzan* who also had an exceptional voice was considered as anointed. His renditions served a sacred mission in liturgy as the very essence of prayer becoming transparent through music, or what *Hasidim* (pietist Jews) deemed to be *hishtapkhut ha-nefesh* (outpouring of the soul). That type of musical expression would go beyond frail mortality and mundane matters, beyond human limitations or temporal locations. It was a form of complete mystery, reflective of the spirit as well as aesthetics. To be thus anointed could be a rapturous privilege that even the singer might not himself comprehend—a voice in dialogue with eternity.

Hazzanuth (cantorial art) abides as a composite of history and traditions, of holy music and sacred duties. In some form, music has always been an essential aspect in the ritual of all world religions, indicating that melodic expression ideally prepares an individual for a spiritual experience. Particularly in Western civilization, this music of the spirit has produced a profoundly inspiring and creative cultural history, and has vitally influenced the entire scope of musical artistry. Over the centuries, gifted musicians have fashioned religious works, their talents given over to the services of synagogue and church. As a result, the issues of form and style, of artistic leadership and congregational role, of instruments and vocalization always deeply occupied ecclesiastical considerations. Conflicts in shaping liturgical music raged throughout Europe within Jewish as well as Christian communities during those earlier times. In all locations of Diaspora life, the question so eloquently stated in Psalm 137 was asked of each generation of Jews: "How shall we sing the Lord's song in another land?"

As a result, Jewish music became a mirror of Jewish life, whether in the synagogue, the home, the community, or along the wayside of general experiences. Regardless of geographical locations, its hallmarks were a continuity of faith and peoplehood, reflected by dedicated observance of the time calendar and the life cycle. It was a Judaic musical heritage composed of sacred-liturgical and folk-secular materials, between which there could be no clear boundary. Devotional melodies and poetics moved freely and fluently between those areas.

Over the ages, the three distinctive branches of Diaspora Judaism—Sephardic (Judeo-Spanish), Oriental (Mediterranean-Near East-Asiatic), and Ashkenazic (mainland European)—each developed a distinctive style of liturgical interpretation (cantillation of biblical texts, prayer chants that evolved with modal motifs and vocal styles, and a special body of hymnology), as well as a vernacular folk culture. Ashkenazic Jews created a particularly multifaceted musical expression, composed of *nusakh ha-tefiloh* (melody of prayer), and certain fixed liturgical tunes, as well as a body of religious carols for Sabbath, holiday meals, and other festive celebrations. Secular songs, intoned apart from the rituals or ceremonials, took up folk texts in a daily language that for most *Ashkenazim* (Ashkenazic Jews) became known as *Juedisch* (Jewish), or Yiddish. There evolved a dynamic mixture of linguistics and melodies, an art nourished since Talmudic times by the *badkhen/badkh'n* (minstrel-bard), and often accompanied by the *klezmer/klezm'r* (instrumentalist). At the center of all this wealth of music was the sacred singer, a special minstrel of holy mission, the *hazzan/khaz'n* (precentor).[1]

The history of synagogue music cannot be understood apart from a consideration of its functionaries. As creators, performers, and preservers of this heritage, they served both art and religion. In the earliest devotional assemblies, the name *mithpallel* referred to someone who seemed especially able to lead others in prayer. During the first centuries of the Common Christian Era, that layman-precentor became the *shaliakh tsibbur* (messenger of the people), an office of honor in which he was often assisted by a *sofer/sofeyr* (scribe) and a *ba'al korey/k'rioh* (Bible master reader). Soon there were *tomekhim-mesayim* (prompters-aides) to oversee preservation of proper order in the rituals. Then there arose the liturgical bards, or *paytanim* (poet-singers), who wrote many lyrical prayers and composed melodies to be sung by the leaders with their congregations. Many of those *piyutim* (sacred poems) continue to enrich Jewish prayer books, as well as Judaic literature, into contemporary times. Some poet-singers also were rabbinical scholars, such as Meir of Rothenberg, respectfully known by a Hebraic acronym "Maharam," (1215–1293), and Jacob of Molin, similarly known by an acronym "Maharil," (ca.1356–1427), both of whom traveled throughout the Rhineland-Ashkenazic communities, strengthening the unique qualities of liturgical services. In those Germanic areas, the *hazzan* (cantor) also assumed the title of *vorbeyter* or *vorsaenger* (precentor).

Especially in mainland Europe, the professional office of Jewish precentor emerged by the eighth century, when the beadle-caretaker (originally known as *hazzan*) of a religious assembly assumed increased responsibility for ritual observances. Proper maintenance of liturgy was then entrusted to two types of specially dedicated leaders of prayer: an honorary layman called *ba'al tefiloh* (master of prayer), and the delegated *hazzan*. Beginning in the nineteenth century with such noted cantorial leaders as Salomon Sulzer, the *hazzan* began to assume another title as "cantor" and often in large communities was called *oberkantor* (chief cantor). Although the sounds of Jewish music commingled with non-Jewish melodies wherever Jews settled, there were some unique qualities that shaped and distinctively defined the Jewish liturgical genre: lyric facility, improvisational flow, modal patterns and motival phrases, fixed cantillation signs and specific chant elements, textual focus and clarity of emphasis, congregational interaction, and the strong influence of historic tradition.

For that Ashkenazic tradition, three Judaicized liturgical modes evolved as *shteyger* (leitmotif structures) for chanting of the sacred texts. With increasing Jewish migrations eastward to Slavic areas, those modal forms became the constituent basis for a widely acclaimed eastern European style of *hazzanuth* (cantorial art). Each so-called mode (*gust*) was popularly known by the name of the opening text of a particular prayer:

1. *Mogeyn Ovos* (Shield of the biblical patriarchs), an Aeolian minor (d-e-f-g-a-bflat-c-d) melodically utilized for biblical cantillation, (*Haftarah*), service chants of Sabbath and *Sholosh R'golim* (Three Festivals: *Sukkoth* or Booths/Tabernacles, *Pesakh* or Passover, and *Shevuoth* or Festival of Weeks), as well as some High Holy Days prayers. Its salient characteristics are a fluctuation to its relative minor, and frequent conclusions on the fifth step. Elements were further adapted as an intonation for religious studies. That mode has been associated with sentiments of peace, hope, and thanksgiving. It resembles the Near East *maqam nahawand*, and historically has been the most widely used of the Jewish modal patterns.

2. *Adonoy/Hashem Molokh* (God reigns), a modified Myxolydian with an ambiguity of major-minor and a wide range ([a-b]-c-d-e-f-g-a-bflat-c-[d-eflat]) used for biblical cantillation (*Torah*), and chants for the services of Sabbath and High Holy Days—*Rosh Hashanah* (New Year) and *Yom Kippur* (Day of Atonement), as well as some prayers for Three Festivals. It also appears in special prayers of petition (*tefiloh*) signifying spiritual meditation, and resembles the Near East *maqam rast*. Its plagal variant features major-minor excursions for the recitation of penitential prayers (*selikha/s'likho*) by which Hebrew name that plagal variant has generally been known.

3. *Ahavoh Rabboh* (Boundless love), an altered Phrygian ([csharp-d]-e-f-gsharp-a-b-c-d-[or dsharp]-e) for weekdays and Sabbath services, particular High Holy Day chants, as well as special blessings, and is reflective of deeply emotional expressions of supplication. It resembles the *maqam kar/hijaz*, and has been found in a Byzantine Greek Orthodox liturgical chant known as *ekhos*. Not widely utilized in the western

and central European Ashkenazic *minhagim* (customs), that modal form has most effectively permeated the Yiddish folk songs of eastern European Jewry.

4. Additionally, there is a variant Jewish mode known as *Mi Sheberakh* (He who blesses), a so-called Ukrainian or Hungarian Dorian (g-a-b-csharp-d-eflat-fsharp-g), employed for lamentations and penitential prayers, where it is treated as another formula for the *selikha/s'likho* mode. It also has appeared often in Hasidic *nigunim* (tunes), and was generally favored for Yiddish folk dances. Although the musical interval of the augmented second had long been a distinctive quality among Slavic melodies, by the nineteenth century it had become a readily identified characteristic of Jewish band entertainment music (*klezmer*) in Europe and then in America.

Until the sixteenth century, most of this music had not been notated or transcribed. It was an oral legacy passed on vocally between the generations, a truly remarkable phenomenon in cultural history. Scholars generally recognize that the written traditions of world music have been sustained for the most part by their oral traditions. The success of such supportive oral music has always depended upon the devotion of loyal and informed practitioners. Even after Jewish liturgical music began to be written down and then published, a particular pattern of oral musical transmission remained in fixed custom well into the twentieth century. It continues to constitute a significant method in the process of cantorial training, in essence a personal handing over of sacred melodic treasury from master to apprentice. After World War II, cantorial schools were established in America, offering formalized and structured courses of study for professional certification by each of the branches (Orthodox, Conservative, and Reform) of Jewish ritual observance.[2] However, in addition to textbooks and curricula, there still has remained the personal act of musical passage from teacher to student. Moreover, this is a definitive highlight in the cantorial training, a historic linkage of hazzanic continuity sealing a spiritual contract for holy duty. In precious circumstances, both mentor and recipient have been mindful of that sacred process.

The nineteenth century brought dynamic challenges as well as broadened opportunities to traditional Jewish life in terms of political, economic, social, and cultural issues. There were strong currents on behalf of "modernism" on both sides of the Atlantic Ocean, ideas of emancipation and adaptation as well as assimilation. There were ardent advocates for enlightenment (*haskalah*) and secularized education, as well as modifications in religious observances and customs. Reformist ideas pervaded in Europe, especially Germany, and culminated in the development of Liberal or Reform Judaism, as shaped by rabbinical and lay leaders in the communities of Seesen, Berlin, and Hamburg. When Rabbi Isaac Mayer Wise (1819–1900) came to the United States in 1846, he brought ideas of liturgical modification and structured hymnody, which were to take root and develop into the particular genre of Reform Temple musical services. Though most synagogues continued to follow the traditionally based liturgy, all cantors were influenced to some extent by those evolving trends, especially in terms of their congregational duties. This was true particularly for the rabbi, who assumed a more active role in the religious services as a minister-preacher.

Of far more direct impact upon Jewish liturgical music were those innovative "modernisms" that had been shaped by several leading cantorial figures of the nineteenth century. Of all, Salomon Sulzer (1804–1890) was the quintessential *hazzan*-cantor whose services in Vienna were widely celebrated for the musical fluency of precentor and choir and the arranged melodies for congregational response. In Berlin, Louis Lewandowski (1821–1894) raised the musical standards and advanced the role of the synagogue choirmaster as a professional music director. He also created courses of cantorial study and liturgical music at that city's Jewish Teachers Seminary. Samuel Naumbourg (1815–1880) of Paris was a fifth- generation practicing cantor and a scholar deeply interested in Jewish music history. He prepared a new edition of the liturgical works of Renaissance musician Salomone Rossi of Mantua (ca.1565–ca.1628), for which Naumbourg wrote the introductory biographical essay. Sulzer, Lewandowski, and Naumbourg also published notable collections of liturgical music and inspired a legion of musicians.

A number of traditional eastern European *hazzanim* (cantors) were also affected by those newer concepts in terms of vocal styles and music arrangements, applied, however, with abiding fidelity to the age-old chant formulas and modal patterns. Their honorary roster included: Bezalel Schulsinger, known as "Odesser" (1790–1860); Nissi Spivak, known as "Belzer" (1824–1906); Eliezer Gerovitsch (1844–1913); David Nowakowsky (1848–1921); and Boruch Schorr (1823–1904). Those liturgists gave substance to a truly distinctive form of cantorial artistry in performance, which reached even greater heights in American life during the early decades of the twentieth century. They had elaborated upon indigenous Jewish cultural custom, and thereupon introduced a style of cantorial performance as tour de force artistry.

For well over two hundred years, the phenomenon in Eastern Europe of itinerant cantors traveling a circuit of pulpits had gained wide popularity and significance. With their often acclaimed liturgical performances, they brought to city, town (*shtetl*), and village communities a combination of spiritual inspiration and aesthetic diversion. Rabbis assailed those touring *hazzanim* as mere minstrels and entertainers, and viewed their often flamboyant styles as excessive and unsuitable for serious devotions. Yet those liturgical performers brought a valuable form of music to congregants who were simple farmers, tradesmen, and artisans. The experience of hearing a guest *hazzan* at the local synagogue on a Sabbath or a holiday nourished their cultural needs. Those services were gala events, which focused upon faith, but also afforded the memorable excitement of a good (sometimes splendid) voice singing special Jewish melodies. The congregations were composed of people whose lives were harshly difficult and limited in scope. They were Jews unable by economic or social means to partake in the sophisticated cultural arts enjoyed by those who were more affluent and more broadly educated.

Indeed, the hazzanic entertainers understood their listeners and their needs, and highlighted the inspiring motifs of the traditional chants, blending familiar folk song elements (and in the late nineteenth century, even operatic snatches) into cantorial renditions. Many were famous for flexible vocalisms, skillful interpretations, sweet falsettos, and elaborate flights of melodic coloratura. Others were noted for their fine musicianship, shaping arrangements and free compositions for particular prayer settings. Excitement was generated by someone whose gifted on-the-spot improvisations could spin out in seemingly endless melodic invention. Led by such cantorial artistes, the services would last for hours, with time suspended for such a liturgical music feast. During the first decades of the twentieth century, many of those cantorial stylists emigrated to America, where for a time they and their art flourished. During earlier years, they entertained, comforted, and inspired struggling immigrant factory sweatshop workers, pushcart tradesmen, and grocery storekeepers; their liturgical artistry bridged the Old World *shtetl* (town) life with the New World city tenements.

As a rule, European *hazzanim* preferred to remain at a particular pulpit over an extended period of time, where as *shtot-hazzanim* (city-cantors) they might rise to prominence for their voices, musical scholarship, or liturgical compositions. Many took on a roster of apprentices, who then went forth to other congregations bearing the distinctive liturgical styles of their teacher-mentors. Among the traditional Ashkenazic cantors of eastern Europe, there emerged three different types of devotional intonation: *tefiloh/t'filah* (simple prayer chant); *k'riah* (motival readings); and *rinah* (singing) for which especially admired vocal qualities were improvisation, falsetto, and coloratura. For the *rinah*, brilliantly conceived and artfully executed melodic fantasies (which cantors called "recitatives") would be woven about the basic motifs and modal constructs. At its best, this was a virtuoso craft that required good technique in tonal production, vocal flexibility, and wide range to the upper register of the voice. The singer needed a secure musical ear and sensitive musicianship. That form of improvisation became a hallmark of the cantorial art in its "golden age."

For almost everyone, the main source of ear training and music education was the *shul khor/kor* (synagogue choir), a group that functioned, in the absence of instrumentation, as melodic support and accompaniment for the traditional cantor. By strict tradition, the Jewish liturgical choir was male only, and, in its historical development, varied as to substance and function according to circumstances. It usually consisted of young boys (treble-altos and sopranos) along with adult men (tenors and basses). Their vocal duties related to the year-round services and festive occasions. Compensation was often only room and board, and generally included the musical coaching and rehearsals necessary in preparation for proper liturgical renditions. Having choirboys as guests in their midst gave luster to hospitable households, and there also was some measure of *nakhes* (pleasure) for the parents of such young singers. The *meshorerim* (choristers) functioned as musical balance, echoing and harmonizing cantorial lines, and supplying melodic interludes. The choir also guided congregational responsive chanting, and served to underscore significant motival components of the melodies of prayer.

For centuries, that liturgical choir was a significant form of musical initiation. Its performances were daily and constant, attending upon a wide variety of religious occasions, in a broad range of communal presentations. When their voices changed at puberty, many boys matured into hazzanic apprentices. They would stay on as adult choir singers, assisting in other congregational duties in order to complete an adequate amount of cantorial training. Often their own pulpit appointments were secured through their cantor-teachers, or else because of the reputation of choirs in which they had sung. By the eighteenth century, many synagogue musicians could read and write music notation, and as a result the collection, preservation, and publication of Jewish liturgical manuscripts commenced in earnest. Increasingly, there were notated arrangements of solo and choir parts, and soon a functionary known as *meshorer ha-godol* (choir director) came upon the scene. He usually was an educated musician, often of limited voice but liturgically knowledgeable, and able to shepherd the group in its more elaborate performances.

During the latter decades of the nineteenth century, when Abraham Goldfaden (1840–1908) sought out musicians for the operettas of his fledgling Yiddish theater company, he found an abundance of talent in the synagogue choirs of the Ukraine and Bessarabia. Among those former choral singers were such gifted theatrical personalities as (Selig) Sigmund Mogulesco (?1856/8–1914) and (Borukh) Boris Thomashefsky (?1864/8–1939). Others who had benefited from such youthful musical duties in an eastern European *shul* were: the *badkh'n* (Yiddish bard) Eliakum Zunser (1840–1913); Yiddish American songwriters Solomon Smulewitz (Small) (1868–1943), Louis Friedsell (1850–1923), Joseph Rumshinsky (Rumshisky) (?1879/81–1956), and Sholom Secunda (1894–1974); as well as a legion of talented performers on the Yiddish stage in America.

In the large receiving hall for immigrants at Ellis Island, there was a Jewish prayer section, with an *Aron Kodesh* (Holy Ark) and a *Neyr Tomid* (Eternal Light). That initial experience of freedom for public prayer in an official environment remained a significant aspect of the Jewish immigrant mind-set. With the great movement of eastern European Jews to America from 1880 onward, an influx of exceptional liturgists also arrived, establishing a unique milieu for cantorial expression. Those decades of immigrant acculturation were a time of adaptation and evolvement, of survival and adjustment. That time also constituted a glory era for two distinctive cultural achievements, an invigoration of two basic age-old Judaic traditions implanted upon American shores: Yiddish theater, that unique composite of folklore, *purimshpil* (*Purim* holiday play) and *badkhonus* (minstrelsy); and *hazzanuth* (cantorial art) as a sacred religious artistry.

In twentieth-century America, prolific talents flourished on the stage and in the synagogue, supported by eager audiences in a free society. Stars of the theatricals were adored by Jewish audiences, and the vaudeville houses presented their favorite cantors. At concerts and charity benefits, popular performers included ballads from Yiddish shows, and arrangements of liturgical selections. Often a theater or meeting hall would be engaged to serve as temporary synagogue, with services advertised as featuring a renowned cantor, and that place would be filled with eager listeners. Moreover, their golden voices soon came to people through phonograph recordings, radio programs, and even films. However, by the 1930s, social and economic changes and the approach of World War II shifted public interests. Yiddish theatricals waned in popularity with a decline in Yiddish-speaking audiences. Synagogues adapted to more structured services in the Reform, Conservative, and Orthodox congregations. However, those two distinctive Jewish musical artistries—theatrical and cantorial—did succeed in blending into the creative mainstream of American life, with lasting influence upon performing arts and religious expression.

Yet recollections of that golden time linger on. Jewish immigrants had brought with them and then cultivated an abiding dedication to Yiddish song and liturgical melody. By 1870, notices were already being placed in eastern European journals seeking cantors to fill positions in America, and in the following decades congregations competed for the arrival of well-known *hazzanim*. Yearning to replicate the traditional life (or at least idealized versions) of their Old World origins, people from various eastern European geographical locations would gather together into benevolent societies and organize special *shuls* (synagogues) named for their old *shtetl* (town). At those services, they would willingly set aside the time to listen to long, elaborate cantorial renditions, savoring the pouring forth of familiar liturgical motifs. Social and educational groups organized gala liturgical concerts as fund-raisers. Tickets would be sold for sacred services, which were often prominently advertised in the Jewish newspapers.

In 1891, the first faltering efforts were made to organize an association of traditional cantors. Not until 1905 was that group firmly established as the Jewish Ministers Cantors Association, a group that has remained functional into present times.[3] Early on, there was hope that minimal standards could be set to regulate the conditions of cantorial employment and to ensure proper professional standards. Nevertheless, late in the twentieth century, many cantors (often still trained by personal apprenticeship to another cantor) continued to audition and negotiate privately for positions, usually appointments based upon inclinations of lay leaders in congregations. Nevertheless, viewed in professional perspective, the cantorate in America has reached a good level of intellectual quality, capable musicianship, and religious dedication.

In the early decades of the twentieth century, an honor roll of notable cantors settled in America. Many had fine voices and were charismatic musicians. Some also composed liturgical selections and set high standards for liturgical style. A number of their renditions were preserved on commercial recordings made during the heyday of the 1920s and 1930s. As a matter of fact, the recordings of cantors as well as Yiddish performers brought phonograph machines into many homes, all but displacing the ubiquitous parlor pianos. Moreover, those stars of pulpit and stage provided a wealth of Jewish talents for a rapidly growing radio industry, encouraging proliferation of local ethnic and religious programs in major cities throughout the country.

At one time, cantorials far outstripped other Jewish selections in record sales. Many of those old hard vinyl singles have become collectors' items, saved and played for nostalgia and religious reflection, and for the sheer magnificence of the vocal artistry.[4] Despite the limitations of early sound recording technology, the voices are surprisingly clear, powerful, and moving, retaining much of their musical artistry and charismatic appeal. The recordings, along with some music manuscript legacies from those cantors, preserve the essence of a long-gone heroic musical style. Given forth with panache and dramatic presence, it constituted a genre of operatic like grand performance in liturgy, a vocal and spiritual wonder gone forever.

There once was a time when a unique form of musical expression flourished among cantorial voices, when fans flocked to liturgical concerts, when families gathered around radios and phonographs listening to the singing of prayers. There once was a time when there were vigorous debates about the different merits of particular cantors. In America, the names were familiar: Berele Chagy (1892–1954), a lyric tenor with impressive coloratura; Leib Glantz (1898–1964), a flexible tenor whose fine musicianship made him a role model; Mordecai Hershman (1888–1940), a sweet tenor, equally impressive in folk songs and liturgy; Benzion Kapov-Kagan (1899–1953), a high tenor favorite of liturgical concerts; Alter Yechiel Karniol (1855–1928), a bass with wide range and the leading exponent of improvisation; Adolph Katchko (1886–1958), a flexible baritone who belied the idea that only tenors could execute the florid passages of coloratura; Moshe Koussevitzky (1899–1966) and his brother David Koussevitzky (1891–1985), both robust tenors who brought to America the great sounds of eastern European Jewry just when that cultural epoch was ending; Moyshe Oysher (1907–1958), a robust tenor who bridged liturgy to mainstream theater, performing on Broadway in *The Jazz Singer*; Pierre Pinchik (1900–1971), an expressive high tenor who incorporated Hasidic melodies into his chants; David Roitman (1884–1943), a lyric tenor whose keen appreciation for the authentic chants and motifs, along with his compositional talents, made him a "cantor among cantors"; and Leibele Waldman (1907–1969), a tenor with an exceptional falsetto technique. In eastern Europe, the last great cantorial generation included Gershon Sirota (1874–1943), a dramatic tenor of unusual strength and clarity whose perfect control and wide vocal register enabled him to perform coloratura feats and whose musicianship lent itself to masterful improvisations; he and his family perished in the Warsaw Ghetto on the last day of the Passover holiday.

An ornament to his profession as the "Jewish Enrico Caruso," it was (Josef) Yossele Rosenblatt (1882–1933) who epitomized the "golden" cantorial art.[5] Born in southern Russia into a family of nine daughters, he seemed especially cast for greatness. By the age of four he was singing with his father, an itinerant cantor. Maturing with a fine voice, he studied music industriously and showed particular talent in composition. After holding positions in Hungary, Russia, and Germany, he emigrated in 1912 to serve a congregation in New York City. Rosenblatt achieved great success in America. In the course of his numerous public appearances, he managed to adapt to the most bizarre of personal circumstances, and yet never compromised with his religious scruples. A good family man, well respected, and charitable to a fault, he was plagued by imprudent financial matters; those economic struggles likely shortened his life.

As a Jewish musician, Cantor Rosenblatt continues to occupy a historic position. He was something of a venturesome pioneer in his public performances. Always religiously garbed, he maintained his ritual observances wherever he went, and was not reluctant to sing his liturgical selections to mixed audiences everywhere. In this respect, he advanced the cause of Jewish musical artistry. Among the audiences were people who had never heard such music before, nor perhaps had ever seen a bearded observant Jew, certainly not on the concert stage or in the vaudeville halls, or even at Carnegie Hall. A creative and highly adaptable performer, he made many recordings that are still treasured and played, including some selections for the early talking picture *The Jazz Singer*. Though his fame grew because of the publicity, it took admirable strength of conviction to decline an invitation to sing with the Chicago Opera Company. His response was that the operatic stage conflicted with the dignity of his religious office. He passed away suddenly while on a musical tour in Jerusalem. Rosenblatt brought the sounds of traditional Jewish liturgical music to the general American public.

In 1927, a popular Yiddish American song, *Hayntigeh Hazzanim* (Cantors of today), was widely performed and recorded by Cantor Mordecai Hershman.[6] With ironic humor, its lyrics considered the comfortable lives and newer musical styles of cantors, with their homes, cars, and bank accounts, and all just for singing for a few hours. "Those cantors are no fools!" By that decade, many American Jews were attending Reform and Conservative congregations as alternatives to strictly traditional Orthodox observances. Not only were cantorial duties changing, but American rabbis were fast assuming the leadership roles at synagogue and temple services. Nonetheless, devotional music maintained its pivotal function, even for the most reformed groups in the Reform branch of Judaism. Affected by public acclaim for cantorial artists, congregants sustained their emotional linkage to qualities of the traditional music, and certain liturgical melodies continued to evoke spiritual responses. Especially after World War II, with the horror of the Holocaust destruction, there was a strong impetus for restoration (notably in Reform temples) to Judaic melodic resonance – biblical cantillation, cantorial chant, and congregational hymns. Many of the remaining star cantors continued to influence a younger generation of professional colleagues. Old recordings preserved that unique musical expression, and a movement to revitalize the cantorial art was spurred by scholars and musicians. The "golden age" had spun itself out. However, its essence could remain, infused into a contemporary mode of presentation of melody wedded to faith.

Jacob Beimel (1880–1944) was a unique figure among American Jewish musicians of his time. A dedicated liturgist and composer of prayer settings, he trained an array of younger cantors and wrote articles on liturgical music in Yiddish, Hebrew, and English for periodicals in Europe as well as America. He also briefly edited and published a journal on Jewish liturgical music.[7] To inaugurate that short-lived publication, Beimel wrote a moving tribute to liturgical song, from which the following paragraphs have been excerpted:

The human soul, which expresses itself in religious beliefs and customs, finds a medium for the utterances of its varied expressions in music. Moreover, that soul receives its very nourishment from these two attributes, religion and music. There has existed, from time immemorial, a strong and inseparable bond between divinity and the art of music. In the pagan world of polytheistic beliefs, the religious services were accompanied by music. Among the peoples confessing a monotheistic religion, music, of whatever variety and custom it may consist (vocal, instrumental, or both), has constituted an integral part of their divine services.

This has been especially so for Judaism and Christianity, where there can be no approach to the Almighty without song. In Judaism, morning prayers are begun by verses which refer to song as proper praise to the Almighty. The inseparable bond between God and the art of music is expressed time and again in the vast literature of the Jews. Rabbis wrote that the gates of song preceded the gates of repentance, and that the source of song is the nearest to the source of Holiness. According to the *Kabbalah*, there are gates in heaven which can be opened only by song.[8]

One salient quality that had infused the "golden age" cantorial performers was that of melody illuminating words, indeed transcending them as prayer made transparent through music. In those performances, there was vocal stamina and control, flexibility of intonation, and concentration upon textual content. It was the cantor's responsibility to interpret and inspire piety, and the cantorial art was a means to those ends. The sweet singer of prayers provided poetic mystical presence, a beauty of sound given over to the very heart of the matter. Creative improvisation was considered a religious duty, bonding infinite spirit to unlimited music.

Throughout Jewish history, there were certain qualifications that rabbinical sages consistently considered necessary for a truly fine leader of prayer: good personal character and devout belief, proper knowledge of the liturgy and its melodic components, and an acceptable voice. Singing was viewed as the most spiritual of the artistic gifts, but as invalid without proper devotion to the sanctity of life. One might possess a magnificent voice, but it would falter because the character of the singer was blemished and unfit. On the other hand, a simple voice might reach great vocal heights through holy faith, and with such accomplishments as the singer could neither expect nor even understand. Thus the true *hazzan* could give forth with heart and soul at the moment of intonation, in absolute trust that the more one created music for prayer, the more creativity one could summon forth from within. The vessel would simply never be emptied by its use.

NOTES

Portions of this chapter appeared in the introduction to a music collection: Velvel Pasternak, Noah Schall, and Irene Heskes, comps. and eds., *The Golden Age of Cantors: Musical Masterpieces of the Synagogue* (Cedarhurst, N.Y.: Tara Publications, 1991), pp. 5–11. That book presents liturgical selections from the repertoires of twenty-seven notable cantors, along with brief biographies, photographs, and other illustrations. New material has been added to this chapter, as well as an appended section of reference notes.

1. Detailed explanations of the background and musical functions of all these types of Jewish musicians may be found among the topical materials in the following encyclopedic works:

Cecil Roth and Geoffrey Wigoder, eds., *Encyclopaedia Judaica*, 16 vols. (Jerusalem and New York: Keter and Macmillan, 1971–1972).

Jacob Singer, ed., *Jewish Encyclopedia*, 12 vols. (New York: Funk and Wagnalls, 1901–1906; reprint ed., New York: Ktav, 1964).

Louis Finkelstein, ed., *Jews: Their History, Culture and Religion*, 3 vols. (Philadelphia: Jewish Publication Society of America, 1960).

2. Three cantorial schools were established: Reform, School of Sacred Music at the Hebrew Union College-Jewish Institute of Religion, in 1948; Conservative, Cantors Institute and Seminary College of Jewish Music at the Jewish Theological Seminary of America, in 1952; and Orthodox, Cantorial Training Institute at Yeshiva University, in 1964.

3. In America, professional cantorial organizations have been established for each of the three American branches of Jewish observance: Orthodox, Cantorial Council of America; Conservative, Cantors Assembly of America; and Reform, American Conference of Cantors.

4. A number of archives have collections of old cantorial recordings, particularly the Library of Congress, Music Division, and YIVO/Yiddish Scientific Institute in New York City. Jewish publishers and distributors, such as Tara Music Publications (Cedarhurst, N.Y.), have reissued that music on cassettes.

5. See Samuel Rosenblatt, *Yossele Rosenblatt: The Story of His Life as Told by His Son* (New York: Farrar, Straus and Young, 1954).

A collection of liturgical selections by Cantor Rosenblatt has been issued by Samuel Rosenblatt and Velvel Pasternak, comps. and arrs., *The Music of Yossele Rosenblatt* (Cedarhurst, N.Y.: Tara Publications, 1989). There also are many current cassette reissues of Rosenblatt's early cantorial renditions.

6. Lipa Feingold, words and music, *Hayntigeh Hazzanim: Humoresk* (Cantors of today: comic), song sheet, Yiddish text only (New York: Feingold, 1927).

7. Jacob Beimel, ed., *Jewish Music Journal,* published in New York by Beimel, 1934/35. There were five issues: vol. 1, no. 1, July 1934; vol. 2, no. 1, Mar./Apr. 1935; vol. 2, no. 2, May/June 1935; vol. 2, nos. 3/4, Nov./Dec. 1935. Among the contributors were Abraham W. Binder, Abraham Zvi Idelsohn, Adolph Katchko, and Bronislaw Huberman. In addition to the various articles and musical transcriptions, Beimel reported in the journal on the activities of the *Mailamm* Jewish Music Society. Beimel titled his prefatory tribute to Jewish liturgical music "Divinity and Music: A Jewish Conception." (vol. 1, no. 1; 1934; pp. 114–15)

8. The Hebrew word *Kabbalah* refers to a religious movement as well as the writings of certain Jewish religious mystics who flourished from the twelfth to the sixteenth century. Among them were liturgists who created poetics and melodies especially for celebration of the Sabbath.

7

Melodies of Prayer: The Jewish Liturgical Calendar

In addition to the holidays of the Jewish calendar year, the daily and weekly liturgies also contain numerous references to the historically significant past, thereby reminding the practicing Jew of the major formative events of his or her religion. It is explicitly remembered heritage underscored by religious observance, a process of continually reliving history through prayer and ritual duty. Therein lies the masterful challenge to a congregational leader who, by means of traditional melodies of prayer, bears a sacred mission affecting Jewish identity, continuity, and religious inspiration. Thus, the cantor assumes the role of the people's historian, presenting the liturgy in music as a mirror of Jewish life and Judaic history.

Jewish liturgical music for communal services developed following upon the great dispersion after the destruction of the Holy Temple, 586 B.C.E. Localized prayer-gathering and study groups had already been active in the areas outside of Jerusalem, led by laymen called *anshey ma-amad* (leaders). Those groups began to flourish especially in the growing diasporic communities of Babylon and Alexandrian Egypt, under the guidance of emerging rabbinical figures. Focused upon the Sabbath day of rest, as the particular Jewish religious custom, early rabbis concentrated upon Scriptures, Psalms, and supplicatory texts, with the active participation of congregants. Individuals of family descent from the Temple Priests (*kohanim*) and Levites were honored members, though not necessarily called upon to lead the assemblage. Mindful of the significantly growing role of these "houses of prayer and study," the Second Commonwealth Temple had a fixed location for this function, called *Beth ha-Knesseth* (House of Assembly). Especially after the second destruction in 70 C.E. by the Romans, the Jewish assembly for worship was no longer defined by a particular structure but by its liturgical functions. With the end to Holy Temple rituals accompanied by choral and instrumental performances, vocal chanting constituted the only musical resource for prayer devotions.

In the fifth century, "houses of Sabbath" for study and prayer were to be found throughout all the Roman Empire settlements, areas of the Mediterranean, Asia Minor, and well into northern Europe and the Rhineland Valley. Liturgical principles and year-round observances consisted of the following basic components, shaped to the particular day and holy occasion: cantillation for a prescribed cycle of portions from Pentateuch (*Torah*), Prophets (*Haftarah*), and Scrolls (*K'tuvim*); intonations of Psalms; chants of basic prayer texts— *Kedusha/Amidah* (order of benedictions), *Sh'ma* (Hear oh Israel, the affirmation of faith), *Kaddish* (sanctification); hymnology for specific observances; followed by festive blessings over wine. Prayer services were conducted three times each day: morning (*shaharit*), afternoon (*minkha*), and evening (*ma'ariv* or *arvit*). Since early times, ritual observances commenced on the eve of the day, at the *ma-ariv* (evening) services, in accordance with the biblical text of the creation, Genesis 1:5: "Evening came and morning came, making one day." Especially among European communities, rabbis and poetic liturgists soon began to develop and enlarge upon those basic prayer formulas in a dynamic manner, and then to expand the range of sacred domestic celebrations for Sabbaths, holidays, festivals, and the life-cycle events.[1]

By the time of Charlemagne in the ninth century, the traditions of the Iberian Sephardic (Judeo-Spanish) Jewry and the Ashkenazic Jews of mainland Europe had commenced to fashion a body of hymnology. Though essentially following along the same principles of calendar and liturgical observance, the traditions diverged in various prayers and customs. Ashkenazic traditions were guided by Babylonian Talmudic academies, while Sephardic and Oriental traditions were linked to Palestinian rabbinic sources. By the fourteenth century, the daily prayer book (*sidur*), and notably the full (*kol bo*) holiday cycle prayer book (*mahzor*) incorporated a highly diverse and intricate calendar of liturgical poetics. Particularly for the rapidly expanding Ashkenazic tradition, there emerged a growing body of *nus'kha-ot ha-tefilah* (melodies of prayer) for the services. Preeminent among those melodic elements were *mi-sinai* (from Mount Sinai) tunes, considered as holy melodies, and also called *scarbove* (sacred) songs. The liturgical developments were encouraged by Talmudists, who urged that prayer could be safeguarded against casual lip-service rendition through melodic renewal. There were gifted and dedicated poet-liturgists and rabbi-*hazzanim* (precentors) who created prayer poetics as well as melodies, and disseminated this devotional treasury throughout Europe. Notable among them were Rabbi Meir of Rothenberg, the "Maharam" (ca.1215–1293), and Rabbi Jacob Levi of Molin , the "Maharil" (1356–1427). They traveled to communities in the Rhineland areas, teaching the sacred poetry and prayer melodies and urging preservation of liturgical traditions.[2]

Over those centuries, a number of special liturgical melodies came to be shaped, chanted, and cherished by European Jews, notably the *mi-Sinai* tunes, which were a significant folk song accomplishment. Their melodic origins harkened back to traveling melodies of minnesingers and troubadours, the wandering minstrels (Jewish as well as Christian) of thirteenth- and fourteenth-century Burgundian-Rhineland. Among all Europeans, migrating tunes then were freely borrowed back and forth in a variety of changed versions. Entering church as well as synagogue, the tunes were a cultural interchange of medieval life. It was a matter of profane song being taken up and transformed into sacred hymn, *m'khadesh ha-nigun* (renewal of the tune). In their adaptation and Jewish liturgical performance, the holy tunes took on certain qualities: fixed melodic openings and endings, distinctive motifs applied in a particular order, fluent rendition by an interpretive singer, interrelationship between the various tunes, bonding to particular liturgical texts, and a sacred aura of *minhag* (custom) concerning their use in service chant.

Closely allied to those special tunes was the highly developed tradition of modes as a basis for elaborated cantorial music.[3] It is likely that those modal formulations evolved earlier than the fixed tune elements. By the sixteenth century, both bodies of musical resources constituted the fountainhead of Jewish liturgical music among the Ashkenazic groups of European Jewry. Soon, with the great migration of Jews eastward to Slavic areas, those traditions began to be further elaborated into a highly creative cantorial art of improvisational vocalism. Especially among eastern European Jews, by the nineteenth century there was a structured body of calendar melody for liturgical music, transcending differences of generation and geography. The simple idea was that a congregant might fall asleep in synagogue for some undetermined length of time, and upon awakening, by hearing the chanting of prayers, could straight away know the following: day of the week; time of day; month of the year; current or approaching holiday, festival, fast or feast day; and any local personal events—births, marriages, deaths. All this information would be conveyed through various liturgical melodies enlarging upon liturgical texts. In a timeless manner, devotional music chronicled Jewish continuity and communal life. Of course, it was axiomatic that all congregants fully recognized the melodies and poetics that constituted those sources of information. Largely because of dynamic changes and tragic events, especially in the twentieth century, such ritual awareness, along with its significant purposes, no longer constituted the norm for individuals in most Jewish communities. Nevertheless, that age-old melodic calendar abides, held fast by strictly observant ritualists; and it also remains as a fascinating topical study for ethnologists and music historians.

High Holy Days

Although in matter of fact they are the first days of the seventh month (*Tishri*) in the Jewish calendar, the High Holy Days usher in the Jewish New Year observance.[4] The ten days from *Rosh Hashanah* (New Year) through *Yom Kippur* (Day of Atonement) constitute the Jewish season of repentance and renewal, whose special prayer book (*mahzor*) is filled with poetics of historic as well as religious significance. Despite the solemnity of that annual observance, the *Talmud* notes that these are days when the devout should delight in song.[5] The New Year is known by other names: *Yom ha-Zikoron* (Day of Remembrance), *Yom ha-Din* (Day of Judgment), and most often as *Yom ha-Teruah* (Day of the Blowing of the *Shofar*). The *shofar* (ram's horn) is the ultimate musico-liturgical symbol, and throughout Jewish history it has held singular significance as musical and devotional centerpiece, likely beyond any other ethnic instrument in human civilization. Blown during the *Rosh Hashanah* services, it dramatically concludes the daylong fast of *Yom Kippur*. It is also sounded by the very devout at weekday morning services throughout the penitential (*s'lichoth*) period during the preceding sixth month (*Elul*).

The ram's horn is an ancient wind instrument known from biblical times, when it was an instrument used for sounding alarm and rallying for battle. It was said to have been the horn that Joshua used at the Battle of Jericho. There was a religious custom of sounding it on solemn occasions and at the beginning of each month, especially at *Tishri*, by the time of the Second Commonwealth Temple Era. As a recognizable symbol of the Jews, it was depicted in carvings on the Roman Arch of Titus. Early on, the tones of the *shofar* appeared to transcend words and to bear mystic significance. It came to signify a heralding of a Day of Judgment, of the Resurrection, and of the coming of the Messiah. The oldest written account of its special soundings dates from the tenth century, with the writings of the Babylonian Exilarch and scholar Sa'adyah Gaon (Sa'adyah ben Yosif ha-Pitomi, ca.892–942) who codified the formula of its sounds, as heard into present times.[6] For this holy ritual use, the *shofar* has continued to maintain its early primitive appearance. The hollowed-out horns of all clean animals may be valid in addition to the ram, except for the horns of the bull because of its linkage to the worship of the golden calf. The particular use of the ram underscores an important biblical passage read during this holiday, that of the *Akedah* (sacrifice), wherein the patriarch Abraham substitutes a ram for his son Isaac, as proper sacrifice to God.

The size of the *shofar* obviously determines the pitch of its calls; the smaller the horn, the higher the pitch. There is no mouthpiece. In order to sound the calls, the *ba'al t'kiyah* (master of sounding) blows across the hole at the narrow end of the instrument, tightening the lips to form an embouchure and shaping the overtones, which seem eerie and inexact. In recent times, some Reform Temples have substituted the musical performance of a trumpet or cornet. Practice is necessary for the privileged *mitzvah* (holy duty) of blowing the *shofar*, inasmuch as lip muscle and breath control determine the qualities and durations of the tones. The instrument itself must be kept clean and smooth. No dust may settle inside the narrow tube at any time, and there must not be any holes in the body of the horn permitting an escape of air. A special caller assists by announcing the names for each of the motifs, which are then blown in specified order.

There are three distinctive patterns of sounding: *tekiah*—long steady blast, *she-varim*—wavering sounds, and *teruah*—series of short staccatos. A full performance of calls concludes with *tekiah g'dolah* (great blast). In unique timbre, its intonations are an open fifth and octave. Following the patterns of soundings, the congregation responds with prayer chants.[7]

The liturgical music of the High Holy Days dramatically highlights the significance of the prayer texts. Musical leadership to inspire the prayerful participation of the congregation has three distinctive categories: (1) the *ba'al tefiloh* (master of prayer), usually a layman volunteer, who intones unelaborated pure chant for the *shaharit* (morning) services, but utilizes many of basic motifs of the day (that leader also conducts the *minkha* [afternoon] service of the day); (2) the *hazzan* (cantor), the professional leader whose musically adorned interpretations of the particular traditional motifs and prayer tunes round out the balance of the service, notably the *musaf* (additional) portion, and then the important *ma'ariv/arvit* (evening) service; (3) the *ba'al korey* (master reader) who intones the particular biblical portions of those services. For the High Holy Days, a special cantillation different from the rest of the year is used, based upon motifs attributed to the Book of Job. The Talmudic rabbis urged that this specific formula be used in order to remind congregants of the message of Job, that whoever cannot cry for another's sorrows does not merit salvation for himself.

Much of the musical substance sung by leaders and congregants varies by custom among communities adhering to three basic Judaic Diaspora traditions: Ashkenazic European, Sephardic Judeo-Spanish, and Oriental Near Eastern. The prayer texts are substantially similar for all. Particularly for the Ashkenazic traditions, however, the liturgical melody is elaborate and integral to the prayer text, elevating music to a sacred function. Particularly significant are the *mi-sinai* tunes. In the morning service, those tunes highlight three basic prayer concepts of the holiday: *malkhuyot* (kingdom of God), *zikhronot* (remembrance of the covenant), and *shofarot* (soundings of the *shofar*). In the additional service, historic tune motifs define in dramatic fashion the pivotal prayers: *ashamnu* (great confession), with its recitation of sins; *aleynu* (adoration of God), recalling text from third-century Babylonian exile, as poetically reshaped and chanted by subsequent martyrs for the faith; *yigdal* (religious attributes), dating from late Roman era and codified by Maimonides (Moses ben Maimon, 1135–1204); *bor'khu* (benediction), with a text composed by Eliezer ben Meshullam (fl. 11th cent., Mayence); *ovos* (the biblical patriarchs), the great benedictions shaped by the early rabbinical leaders.[8]

Of all, the most universally known Jewish musical theme is the chant of *kol nidrey* (all vows), which dramatically opens the *Yom Kippur* eve service, prior to sundown, for all Jews. Although Sephardic and Oriental congregations open their services chanting it in a simple penitential-style chant, both traditions have never quite elevated that Aramaic prayer text to the particular status that it holds in Ashkenazic tradition. Especially for these Jews, *kol nidrey* has been sung at least as far back as the eleventh century, and always to a fixed tune. Old French Jewry of the twelfth century began the custom of reciting it three times. The first printed version of the melody as known in present times was published in 1785 by a Berlin *hazzan* (precentor), Ahron Beer (1765–1821). In his study of that *mi-Sinai* holy tune, Abraham Zvi Idelsohn wrote: "While the text, a mere renouncement of vows, is devoid of religious emotions, its musical setting is generally accepted as an expression of the deep religious feelings which move the Jewish heart on the eve of the Day of Atonement."[9] The melody itself apparently is centuries old, and appears to combine elements of medieval German minnesong with motifs from the biblical cantillation of the *Haftarah* (Prophets).

The *shulkhan arukh* (standard code of Jewish law) considers the text of *kol nidrey* to be a precarious paradoxical statement, for which the author and circumstances of origin remain unknown. The scholarly Talmudic rabbis did not approve of vow making and regarded impulsive oaths as foolish, if not immoral. By the ninth century, however, recitation of the *kol nidrey* formula had become a general practice before *Rosh Hashanah*. It was not considered relevant to legal matters or religious affairs, but rather was applied to rashness of verbal expression. Indeed, the annulment of curses and oaths appeared to rabbinical thinkers as reflective of old pagan rituals. Nevertheless by about 1100, the custom had gained acceptance among all Jewish groups, and was soon attached to the commencement of *Yom Kippur* as part of atonement duties. The matter of text reference to either "past year" or "next year" (or often to both past and future) historically has been troublesome, and thus Jewish interpretation is that those time-frames are vague because the issue rests between man and God, not between man and man.[10]

In 1844, leaders of the emergent Reform movement in Germany sought to expunge *kol nidrey* from their prayer books, substituting Psalm 130 ("Out of the depths have I called to Thee, oh Lord") as the more appropriate supplication of a sinner seeking God's forgiveness for transgressions. European Jewish folk tradition prevailed, however, and *kol nidrey* was soon restored to the *Yom Kippur* service, where it has remained steadfastly in the prayers for all the branches of Judaic observance. With the passage of centuries, what was once a statement regarding impulsive oaths evolved into an intense expression of contrition, whose very recitation took on a mystic aura with linkage to martyrdom. Moreover, its distinctive melodic components achieved general recognition and was even widely performed in concert arrangements, most notably in a string solo version by the non-Jew, Max Bruch (1838–1916). More recently, a musical recasting of *kol nidrey*, composed in 1938 by Arnold Schoenberg (1874–1951), challenged the conception of its old text and familiar melody and, recast with the composer's extended tonality, highlighted a message of ultimate human renewal through faith.

As with the *Rosh Hashanah* services, devotions for *Yom Kippur* include traditional melodic chant formulas, along with some of significance to the Day of

Atonement. At essence again is the mighty confessional (*viddui*) with its stirring chant for *ashamnu* (we have sinned). *Yizkor* (remembrance), constitutes the great memorial to those who have passed away, family as well historic martyrs. The prayer *unesaneh tokef* (with utmost respect), whose majestic exposition dates from the ninth century declares: "God reviews the deeds and determines the destiny of every living soul." As the classic opportunity for hazzanic interpretation, cantorial settings of this text have been made by leading synagogue musicians and performed with heightened rendition on *Yom Kippur*. The ancient services of the priests in the Jerusalem Holy Temple is dramatically recreated within the *avodah* (service) text, and climaxed with the section *v'ha-Kohanim* (and the priests), detailing in thirteenth-century poetics how the High Priest would enter the innermost sanctuary, and then emerge to utter God's name before the prostrate congregation. Ernest Bloch (1880–1959) endeavored to interpret that prayer in 1929 with his composition "Abodah" for violin and piano. At sundown, at *ne'ilah*, (the concluding section of the daylong service), there is a great affirmation of faith, *Sh'ma Yisroel* (Hear, oh Israel), followed by a final blast of the *shofar* ending the penitential fast day. "Dost Thou not continually renew Thy creation, oh my Father? Take me, Thy child, and make me over. Breathe Thy spirit into me that I may live, that I may start life afresh with childhood's unbounded promise."[11]

Three Great Festivals

Following closely upon the High Holy Days in the month of *Tishri* is the first of the three ancient Temple pilgrimage festivals, *Sukkoth* (Booths or Tabernacles). In fact, upon the conclusion of *Yom Kippur*, traditionally Jews begin to assemble a temporary *sukkah* (booth). While much of the liturgical music (cantillation, chant motifs, *mi-sinai* tunes, special hymns) is similar for *Sukkoth*, *Pesakh*, and *Shevuoth*, each of those festivals also has some distinctive melodic elements. Originally a holiday of thanksgiving for the harvest, *Sukkoth* historically has become a great celebration of the annual cycle of biblical readings. However, in recollection of that earlier era, during the *hallel* (praise) portion of prayers, branches of four plants are festively blessed: *lulav* (palm), *ethrog* (citron), *hadasa* (myrtle), and *arava* (willow). A particular chant of *hoshana* (prayer for salvation) characterizes these services. The holiday lasts eight days, during which a Sabbath occurs and the biblical Book of Ecclesiastes is recited. On the seventh day of *Sukkoth* (called *Shemini Atsereth*), there is a memorial (*yizkor*) service. Then, in recollection of ancient agricultural life in the Holyland, a special motival chant also is intoned as a prayer for *geshem* (rain). Over many centuries of Diaspora settlement in places where rain was an all-too- common occurrence, that prayer for the divine bounty of rain has resonated in Holyland geographical remembrance among all Jewish traditions. The final festival day is called *Simhat Torah* (celebration of the Bible), and the synagogue is given over to joyful singing, dancing, and parading with the biblical scrolls. Vernacular Jewish folk songs enter into the celebration at this time.[12]

The second of the three pilgrimage festivals is *Pesakh* (Passover), known as the holiday of liberty, of freedom from slavery. It begins on the eve of the fourteenth day of the Jewish month of *Nisan*. As with *Sukkoth*, the festival lasts eight days. For Reform congregations, Passover lasts only seven days. There is a *yizkor* (memorial) service on the last day, and on the Sabbath during that holiday, the biblical *Shir ha-Shirim* (Song of Songs) is chanted. At the services, there is a special motival chanting of the prayer for *tal* (dew), which in ancient times provided the necessary moisture for young plants during the spring planting season.[13]

The truly distinctive musical experience of Passover belongs to the home festive meal called *seder* (order of service), which is conducted on the first two evenings of the festival. It is a sacred bridging celebration, in that Jewish ritual unites with custom, domestic life dominates a liturgical event, and synagogue chant bonds to folk song. The special text for the *seder* is called the *haggadah* (homiletic guide), composed of various ceremonials and benedictions along with a narrative discussion of the holiday itself. That text began to be shaped in the Second Temple Commonwealth Era. Its importance grew with the dominance of the Roman Empire, evolving into a celebration of freedom from bondage. The paschal lamb harkened to ancient priestly sacrifices, while wine and unleavened wafer (*matzoh*) became dominant symbols of the ritual meal. As the unseen honored guest at the *seder*, Elijah the Prophet was considered to be the herald of a messianic era to come, the time of perfect universal freedom.

By the thirteenth century, the *seder* text was part of the prayer book, especially in the Sephardic tradition. Among the Ashkenazic Jews, the custom arose of a separate *haggadah*. Its essential ritual elements, based upon events in Exodus 12 with rabbinical commentaries, were set during the earliest period of the Common Christian Era. Over the subsequent centuries, poetic materials were added. haggadic tradition soon became fixed, and into modern times has abided in the following manner: text recited by table leader with participation of gathered group; traditional asking of four specified questions by the youngest in attendance, intoned in the formula of traditional study chant; and, after the festive meal, the grace, chanted in liturgical style. Beyond this order of service, a custom arose among fourteenth-century Rhineland Jews to sing the special poetry of the *haggadah*, and the practice grew rapidly throughout Europe. While particular *seder* melodies have varied greatly from place to place and from generation to generation, the singing of poetic texts has remained a consistent part of the festivities.[14]

Earliest to be sung were the *hallel* (praises: Psalms 113–118). Since its inclusion in the sixth century, the liturgical poem *adir hu* (Glory to His name) has had many melodies associated with it. The one that is currently most familiar first appeared in a German *haggadah* in 1644, and more recently has been printed in English hymnals as "God of Might." Another poem *v'haya biktsos ha-layla* (And it came to pass at midnight) written by Yannai (fl. 6th cent.), has been favored musically by Sephardic and Oriental as well as Ashkenazic traditions. Most widely recognized are some tunes of Ashkenazic origin. One for *adir bimlukha* (Praise Him in the highest), a poem by Eliezer Kallir (fl. 8th cent.), comes from seventeenth-century Bavaria. The riddle poem *echod mi yodeya* (Who knows one) originated in medieval European minstrelsy. In 1838, its already popular melody was musically notated as *alte weise* (old tune) by Isaac Judah Eberst (1779–1850), the father of Jacques (Jacob Levy von) Offenbach. Ernest Bloch used it as a melodic motif in the final movement of his "Israel Symphony." The cumulative Aramaic rhyme *khad gadyo* (An only kid/goat), with its intriguing allegorical interpretations, first appeared in a Prague *haggadah* in 1590, and to this day is widely sung to an adaptation of the old German folk song *Raetsel*. Of more recent Jewish folk source is the lively tune sung for the venerable poetic *dayenu* (It is enough). In twentieth-century America and Israel, a number of newer melodic settings for the poetics have been introduced into the *seder* celebration.

Shevuoth is the third of the *sholosh r'golim* (three pilgrimages), recalling the ancient wheat harvest and seasonal observances in the Holy Temple. Known as the Feast of Weeks, it is the celebration of revelation on Mount Sinai, of the giving of *Torah* (Holy Writ), and occurs fifty days after Passover, on the sixth day of the Jewish month *Sivan*.[15] It lasts two days, and the services, like the other two festivals, include the chanting of *yizkor* (memorial) and *dukhan* (priestly blessing). A salient musical feature of the *Shevuoth* liturgy is the Aramaic prayer *akdamuth* (Prelude). That text has been attributed to Meir ben Yitzhok of Worms (fl. 11th cent.), and the distinctive chant motifs are interspersed with the other liturgical melodies. On this festival, the biblical *Megillat Ruth* (Book or Scroll of Ruth) is chanted.[16]

Hanukkah and Purim

Over the centuries, two Jewish holidays have acquired a particular secular folk culture of literature and music: *Hanukkah* (Feast of Lights) at dark of winter, and *Purim* (Feast of Lots) in early spring. *Hanukkah* is an eight-day observance commencing on the twenty-fourth day of *Kislev*. Candles (or bright lights) are lit in a *menorah* (candelabrum) one by one on succeeding nights, until all eight plus a *shamesh* (guardian candle) are burning. They are kindled and blessed in celebration of the victory of Judas Maccabeus against the Syrians, and the rededication of the Holy Temple in Jerusalem in 165 B.C.E.[17] The holiday is a composite of historic facts, traditional customs, and cultural inspiration.[18]

While there are special prayers in the services for *Hanukkah*, its focus is upon domestic celebration. Two prayers, *ha-nerot ha-lolu* (These candles we kindle) and *al ha-nissim* (For the miracles), chanted in synagogue and at home, are based upon texts that originated in the fourth century among the Babylonian Jews. The leading hymn of the holiday is *ma-oz tsur* (Rock of ages). Its text is attributed to an Italian Jew, Mordecai ben Yitzhok (fl. 13th cent.). Entering early on into the services, it was sung to various tunes as early as the fifteenth century. Its Sephardic version was used by Benedetto Marcello (1686–1739) for his setting of Psalm 15 ("Lord, who shall sojourn in Thy tabernacle"), in a collection of music arranged for the Venetian Jewish Community and published there in about 1724. That particular melody had also been used by Sephardic Jews for singing Psalm 137 ("By the Waters of Babylon"). It is still popularly sung as a *Hanukkah* hymn, especially in the State of Israel. A more widely recognized melodic version is of Ashkenazic origin; based upon two (possibly three) elements of medieval German folk tunes, it became popular among Jews throughout Europe by the eighteenth century. Its tune even appears in 1815 in London for a setting of Lord Byron's poem "On Jordan's Banks," and this *ma-oz tsur* remains the most widely sung of the *Hanukkah* melodies. Max Bruch (1838–1916) incorporated it into his *Hebraeische Gesaenge* (Hebrew melodies) for chorus and orchestra.

A number of *Hanukkah* songs were created by folk minstrels among eastern European Yiddish-speaking Jews in the eighteenth and nineteenth centuries.[19] The theme of this holiday has inspired several composers, most notably George Frideric Handel (1685–1759), who composed the oratorio *Judas Maccabaeus* in 1746. The work was premiered at London's Theatre Royale of Covent Garden, and proved highly successful subsequently, with fifty-five performances, which helped improve the composer's failing finances and public reputation before his death. As to the real Judas Maccabeus and his followers in ancient times, there was a distressing sequel to that heroic victory of the Maccabees. In 132 B.C.E., battles again raged in defense of the Holy Temple, this time against powerful Roman legions. Defeated and martyred were the Hebrew leaders Simon Bar Kokhba and Rabbi Akiva. Jerusalem was conquered and became a Roman citadel, thus shaping the following centuries of Judaic and Christian history. Nevertheless, *Hanukkah* remains an integral part of Jewish annual observances. The lighting of holiday candles on the darkest winter days honors the universal virtues of steadfast courage and spiritual resilience.[20]

Purim is celebrated on the fourteenth day in the Jewish month of *Adar*, joyously heralding the approach of Passover in four weeks and the promise of spring. During Talmudic times, it already was a popular holiday, in which the biblical Scroll (*megillah*) of Esther was chanted in synagogue, retelling the story of King Ahasuerus of ancient Persia, his Queen Esther, her uncle Mordechai, and wicked Haman, who tried to destroy all the Jews. Early on, domestic celebrations began to include a festive meal (*seudah*) with music and pageantry as well as the giving of gifts. Over the centuries, Jewish minstrelsy elaborated upon those *Purim* entertainments, attracting general interest for them among Christians as well as Jews throughout Europe. Public *Purim* festivities were known to have been held in northern Italy in 1531, 1558, and 1592, particularly in such locations as Mantua, Venice, Florence, Genoa, and Ferrara.[21] By the seventeenth century, the biblical story had become a topic for musical presentations. George Frideric Handel was inspired to write an early opera, *Haman and Mordecai*, and then in 1732 his oratorio *Esther*, as a result of attending *Purim* celebrations in the Venetian ghetto while he was in Italy from 1704 to 1710. In Frankfurt, in 1708, an *Ahasuerus Spiel* (Ahasuerus play) was published with a text and some tunes. Already notable in Prague by 1720 was the annual *Acta Esther*, performed by *Yeshiva* (seminary) students singing and playing musical instruments. A Yiddish play with music, *Esther und Mordechai*, was published in 1780 in Amsterdam, and a German text version appeared in Fuerth in 1828. Particularly in eastern European communities, the *Purimshpil* (*Purim* play) assumed heightened cultural significance with the creativity of Yiddish folk performers: *klezmer* (instrumentalist), *leytz* (jester), and *badkhon* (minstrel/bard, or singing poet). Late in the nineteenth century, those flourishing popular artistries inspired the development of the modern Yiddish theater in Europe and then in America.[22]

Generally, the music associated with this festival has blended liturgy and chant with folklore and song. Sections of the prayers, especially for the afternoon service, are parodied with pseudorabbis and pseudocantors, usually play acted by youngsters. In synagogue, by long observed custom, whenever the name of Haman is mentioned, congregants respond by sounding noisemakers. In earlier times (and currently among some Near East Oriental Jews), people would stamp their feet or bang on drums. During the thirteenth century, among Jews in the Rhine Valley area, the now-prevailing custom first arose of whirling *groggers*, which are types of scrapers or rattles made of wood or metal. The sacred services conclude with a holy poem (*piyut*) known as *Shoshanath Ya-akov* (The lily-rose of Jacob), which is sung to various folk melodies. The text of this hymn is in the form of an acrostic eulogizing Esther and Mordechai, and is intoned by all traditions of Judaism. The communal festivities feature all sorts of vernacular songs and popular dances. In more recent times, costume parades highlight celebrations in America and Israel.[23]

Sabbath

The Sabbath affords a dynamic combination of synagogue liturgy and home ritual. Over centuries of Jewish history, a body of significant literature, folklore, and music has been created in dedication to that weekly day of rest. Of particular interest are special table songs, carols for the Sabbath meals that provide an atmosphere of both sanctity and culture. The religious poetry of those songs dates from early medieval times, and their musical settings consist of age-old melodies as well as more recent tunes. Along with that range of special domestic music, various liturgical prayers for evening, morning, afternoon, and concluding services are chanted with particular melodic motifs. Music is integral to the entire Sabbath observance.[24]

On Friday evening at sundown, the Sabbath is inaugurated at home by a woman who kindles the Sabbath candles and intones the blessing. As part of the opening synagogue devotions, the hymn *Kabbalat Shabbat* (Welcome to the Sabbath) is sung. Its poetic text was written by Solomon (Shlomo ben Moses) Halevi Alkabez (ca.1505–ca.1580) at the request of the Palestinian mystic and liturgist Isaac Luria (1534–1572), and is chanted by all Jewish traditions.[25] Home from Sabbath eve services, the head of the house blesses his family and then joins them in a religious hymn, *Shalom Aleykhem* (Peace be with you), whose poetry dates from the sixteenth century. Blessings are then intoned over bread and wine to commence the festive meal. Before the concluding grace, the table songs (*z'miroth*) are sung by all assembled. This custom arose during the era of the Second Temple Commonwealth and was encouraged by the Talmudic rabbis. Its popularity spread to all Jewish communities, and by medieval times had become the creative focus for much devotional poetry, which was chanted in musical inspiration by groups around a festive domestic table.[26]

Though other songs may also be sung, there are several customary holy poems (*piyutim*) for the Friday evening repast: *Kol mekadesh shevi-i* (Whoever sanctifies the seventh day), and *Menukhah v'simkha* (Rest and joy), both acrostics attributed to Moses ben Kalonymos (fl. 10th cent., Provence); *Mah yedidus* (How lovely Thy peace), by Menahem ben Makhir (fl. 11th cent., Ratisbon); *Mah yofis* (How sweet the day), by Mordecai ben Isaac (fl. 14th cent., Carpentras); *Yom Shabat kodesh* (Sabbath day is holy) attributed to a liturgical troubadour known as Jonathan ha-Meshorer (the poet-singer) (fl. 14th cent., southern France); *Yom zeh l'Yisrael* (This day is for Israel), by Isaac Luria (1535–1573, Jerusalem/Safed); and *Yoh ribon olam* (God of the world) by Israel Najara (1550–1620, Safed/Gaza). A concluding carol, *Tsur mishelo* (From God's bounty), based upon the three blessings of grace, is of anonymous origin and dates from the earliest centuries in the Common Christian Era. The chanting of grace includes Psalm 126, *Shir ha-ma'aloth* (Song of ascents).

At the second festive meal of the Sabbath, after morning services, table songs are again sung before grace. Traditionally, the singing includes the following: *Dror Yikrah* (He will proclaim) by Dunash ibn Labrat (fl. 10th cent., Fez/Morocco); *Barukh Adonoy* (Bless the Lord), by Simon bar Isaac (fl. 11th cent., Mayence); *Barukh Eyl elyon* (Blessed be God on highest), by Barukh ben Samuel (d. 1221, Mayence); *Yom zeh mekhubad* (This day is special) attributed to a liturgical troubadour known as Israel/Judah ha-Meshorer (fl. 13th cent., Provence); *Ki eshmera Shabbat* (I will observe the Sabbath), by Abraham ibn Ezra (1093–1168, southern Iberia). In more recent times, many newer carols are also sung to currently popular Jewish tunes, but their texts remain suitable to celebration of the Sabbath day.

The third of the special Sabbath meals (*shalosh seudoth*) occurs between the afternoon and evening services, and serves to precede the ceremonial *Havdalah* (Separation), prayers that usher out the Sabbath day. Two poetics: *B'ney heykhala* (Children of Thy Holy Temple) and *Asadeyr l'seudoso* (I shall keep the meals), both by Isaac Luria and in Aramaic, favor language of medieval Jewish mystic poets. A grace is chanted, and here hasidic pietistic groups have further elaborated upon the festivities in song and dance, creating a particularly rich musical experience.[27] Blessings over wine, spices, and a braided candle-taper are recited, along with chanting of the *Havdalah* (He who makes distinction between holy and profane). That poetic prayer text is chanted in all Jewish communities, and has been attributed to Isaac ibn Ghayat (fl. 11th cent., southern France). Most significant among other sacred poems chanted at this concluding ritual are some in tribute to *Eliyahu ha-Navi* (Elijah the Prophet). From the eleventh century onward, the belief has grown among devout Jews that Elijah himself will herald the Messiah, appearing just as the Sabbath is about to be concluded and thereby prolonging that "day of man's rest and delight" into unending eternity.

Especially among eastern European Jews, there evolved the custom of a woman's prayer at the conclusion of the Sabbath. Parallel to her kindling of the Sabbath eve candles, she would snuff out the braided *Havdalah* taper and chant in Yiddish *Gott fun Avrohom* (God of Abraham), praying for the health and safety of her family over the days ahead into the next Sabbath of joy.

The *z'miroth* of Sabbath are religious folk songs of good cheer and thankfulness to God, celebrating the ideals of life. They arose during a period in history when Christians, as well as Jews, were creating literary tributes to the duties of their respective religions. The monk Albinus Flaceus Alcuin (d. 804) wrote special poetics to be sung with the grace at meals, as did an Iberian troubadour named Aurelius Clemens Prudentius (d. 1348). Over the centuries, however, Christians devoted their sacred liturgics to church rituals, and the sacred meal became not a domestic observance but rather an essential part of the Holy Mass itself. A tradition of folk caroling in celebration of Christmas did evolve, and has been sustained as a valued communal and family custom.

Other Observances

Over the centuries of Diaspora life, *Tisha b'Av* (ninth day in the Jewish month of *Av*) has been considered second to *Yom Kippur* as an important fast day. It commemorates the destruction of the first and second Holy Temples, the fall of Jerusalem, and the great dispersals. At services, poetic elegies or lamentations (*kinoth*) are chanted, in an order of ritual dating from Gaonic-Talmudic times. The biblical Book of Lamentations is cantillated, and the special melodic motifs interspersed throughout the services reflect upon the chant for the biblical passages of *Ekho*, opening with: "How solitary is the city, bereft of its glory." Verses are also intoned from the Book of Jeremiah, as well as appropriate Psalm texts, as for example, Psalm 137: "By the Waters of Babylon." A special hymn for the day is *Eyli Tsiyon* (God of Zion). It is generally sung to a favored old folk melody, that likely originated as a wandering troubadour tune of the Rhine Valley during medieval times.

Scattered throughout the year are other special days of religious significance, each with some liturgical additions. Of particular note is the celebration of *Rosh Khodesh* (the beginning of each Jewish month), prompting special liturgical prayers and communal observance. Of the usual daily services, the morning prayers for each Monday and Thursday also include cantillation of selected biblical passages. Customarily at those readings, prayers may be intoned for those who are ill or troubled, and blessings may be chanted announcing newborns and betrothals. As all of the ritual services conclude, a mourner's *kaddish* (benediction) is chanted for the recently deceased. Through time-honored liturgical customs, congregants are informed about life-cycle events in their community.

Hymns

Of the well-known hymns sung by Jewish congregants at services, three are of special interest. Based upon an anonymously written theological poetic of twelfth century Iberia (though often attributed to Solomon ibn Gabirol), *Adon Olam* (Lord of the world) entered into the service prayer books of all Jewish traditions by the fifteenth century. The text is either chanted simply or sung to a folk tune or composed melody, at daily morning services, and as a closing hymn at the evening services for Sabbaths and holidays. By tradition, it is also the prayer recited before retiring to sleep and at the deathbed: "And if my life-strength departs, God is with me and I shall have no fear." Among some Oriental and Sephardic Jews, it is also intoned at wedding ceremonials. Over the centuries, this *piyut* (sacred poem) has been a favorite for choral compositions as well as congregational hymn settings. Its most widely recognized tune in current times has been ascribed to Eliezer Mordecai Gerovitsch (1844–1914), who likely adapted its metered melody from an older folk song. Gerovitsch was both a rabbinical scholar and a thoroughly schooled cantor who had studied music at the St. Petersburg Conservatory. He served a congregation in Rostov for almost three decades and published collections of his liturgical music.[28]

Eyn Keloheynu (There is none like our Lord) is a liturgical poem of unknown but venerable origin, likely from the late Middle Ages, and is in the prayer books of Ashkenazic traditions. As a hymn, it is sung at the conclusion of the morning additional (*musaf*) services for Sabbaths and festivals, and it has been set to numerous melodies. By far its most popularly sung tune was shaped from elements of an old German folk song and march melody by a leader of the rising Jewish reformist movement in Germany, Julius Freudenthal (1805–1874).

The text of *Yigdal* (Praise to the living God) has been ascribed to Daniel ben Judah (fl. 14th cent., Rome), and poetically lists the thirteen principles of Jewish faith as delineated by Maimonides. Though Sephardic tradition also has this prayer, Ashkenazic congregations customarily conclude the Sabbath evening with this hymn. Its most generally sung tune has been attributed to Meyer Leoni (ca.1740–1800), who likely adapted its melodic elements from earlier folk songs of Jewish and Slavic origins. Soon widely recognized as the "Leoni Yigdal" tune, it was taken over in the late eighteenth century by Wesleyan English congregations as their hymn "God of Abraham, Praise," and may be found in a number of Christian hymnals.

Life Cycle Chants

Musical elements of liturgical chant are integral to the rituals associated with the three great life-cycle events—birth, marriage, and death. For funerals and burials, Psalms and the prayer *Eyl moley rakhamim* (God of abundant mercy) are chanted. Regarding wedding ceremonials, only if they are held in a synagogue before or after a particular service of the day are any of the ritual prayers chanted. Otherwise, an officiating minister (rabbi or cantor) intones the traditional marriage benedictions. Additional selections appropriate to the occasion may be sung and instrumentally performed. Upon the occasion of the naming of a child in synagogue, the blessings are chanted by a cantorial leader and congregation.

The melodies of Jewish liturgical tradition and theological custom constitute a body of artistry developed over centuries, creatively shaped, spiritually integrated, and respectfully preserved. Sustained over so many centuries, the music of prayer was the spiritual sustenance and devotional expression of generations in all parts of the world. The great upheavals in the earlier twentieth century, with their human tolls and dynamic changes, have not yet settled into historic perspectives. Meanwhile, culturally as well as spiritually, the viable centers of Judaism have shifted to America and Israel. Yet throughout the world, Jewish religious traditions continue to be observed, along with the heritage of music—secular and sacred. There still are Jews who delineate time and place by means of liturgical poetics and melody. Historians recognize that the continuity of civilization depends upon a dedicated few, who in every time and each place, honor and safeguard their cultural and intellectual treasures and endeavor to ensure that whatever is of spiritual value will remain and be sustained. For the survival of Jewish liturgical music, there is also abiding and hopeful prayer.

NOTES

1. The following publications treat in detail the range of liturgical music developments in the synagogue:

Abraham Z. Idelsohn, *Jewish Music in Its Historical Development* (New York: Henry Holt, 1929; reprint ed., Westport, Conn.: Greenwood Press, 1981).

Alfred Sendrey, *The Music of the Jews in the Diaspora (up to 1800)* (Cranberry, N.J.: Thomas Yoseloff/A. S. Barnes, 1970).

Eric Werner, *A Voice Still Heard: The Sacred Songs of the Ashkenazic Jews* (University Park: Pennsylvania State University Press, 1976).

2. In addition to the references in note 1, topical listings treat aspects of liturgy, liturgical music and musicians, and the Jewish holidays in the following publications:

Jacob Singer, ed., *The Jewish Encyclopedia*, 12 vols. (New York: Funk and Wagnalls, 1964; reprint ed., New York: Ktav, 1964).

Cecil Roth and Geoffrey Wigoder, eds., *The Encyclopaedia Judaica*, 16 vols. (Jerusalem: Keter, 1971; New York: Macmillan, 1972).

Macy Nulman, comp., *Concise Encyclopedia of Jewish Music,* single vol. (New York: McGraw-Hill, 1975).

3. For detailed descriptions of various cantorial vocal styles and the Ashkenazic liturgical modes, see Chapter 6 (The Golden Age of the Cantorial Art).

4. The twelve months of the Jewish calendar year are: *Nisan, Iyar, Sivan, Tammuz, Av, Elul, Tishri, Cheshvan, Kislev, Tevet, Shevat, Adar* 1, and *Adar* 2—a leap month.

5. The *Talmud* is the *corpus juris* of Judaism.

6. See Henry George Farmer, *Sa'adyah Gaon on the Influence of Music* (London: A. Probsthain, 1943).

7. See Cyrus Adler, *The Shofar: Its Use and Origin* (Washington, D.C.: Smithsonian Institution, U.S. Government Printing Office, pamphlet no. 936, 1894).

8. For particular musical examples, consult the following liturgical collections:

Abraham Baer, comp. and ed., *Ba'al Tefiloh, oder Der Praktische Vorbeter* (The master of prayer, or the practical precentor) (Leipzig/Gothenberg: Baer, 1883; reprint ed., New York: Sacred Music Press, 1953).

Gershon Ephros, comp. and ed., *The Cantorial Anthology: Traditional and Modern Synagogue Music,* 6 vols. (New York: Bloch Publishing, 1929–1975).

9. See Abraham Zevi Idelsohn, "The Kol Nidre Tune," *Hebrew Union College Annual,* vols. 8 and 9 (1931 and 1932), pp. 493–509. Idelsohn places the oldest text reference as early as the ninth century, and indicates that the presently known tune had been sung in Prague by 1600. He notes that a melodic blend of it was performed by Ashkenazic Italian Jews of sixteenth-century northern Italy, notably in Venice.

10. For an interesting study of that text, see Herman Kieval, "The Curious Case of *Kol Nidre,*" *Commentary,* vol. 46, no. 4 (1968), pp. 53–58.

11. Excerpted from a poem, "That We Be Reborn," by Hillel Zeitlin (1871–1942), trans. from the Hebrew by Eugene Kohn; included in many modern prayer books.

12. Most general collections of Jewish folk songs include a wide array of the various holiday tunes. A good summary of the festival music is Paul Kavon, "Music for *Sukkoth* and *Simhat Torah*," in *The Sukkoth and Simhat Torah Anthology*, ed. Philip Goodman (Philadelphia: Jewish Publication Society of America, 1973), pp. 434–42.

13. See Judith Kaplan Eisenstein, "The Music of Passover," in *The Passover Anthology*, ed. Philip Goodman (Philadelphia: Jewish Publication Society of America, 1961), pp. 272–94.

14. Many *haggadah* booklets also include some melody lines of the *seder* folk songs. For additional information on this music, see Eric Werner, "The Tunes of the *Haggadah*," in *Studies in Bibliography and Booklore*, vol. 7 (Cincinnati: Hebrew Union College Press, 1965), pp. 57–83. For a collection of those songs, see Richard Neumann and Velvel Pasternak, comps. and eds., *Seder Melodies* (Cedarhurst, N.Y.: Tara Publications, 1977).

15. General information concerning *Shevuoth*, as well as the other Jewish calendar holidays may be found in Hayyim Schauss, *The Jewish Festivals: From Their Beginnings to Our Own Day* (Cincinnati: Union of American Hebrew Congregations, 1938).

16. See Paul Kavon, "Music for *Shevuoth*," in *Shevuoth Anthology*, ed. Philip Goodman (Philadelphia: Jewish Publication Society of America, 1974), pp. 323–37.

17. By the second century B.C.E., Jewish communities were already scattered from Babylonia to Italy and Asia Minor, with a heavy concentration in Egypt, particularly at Alexandria. David Flusser, a leading authority on the theology of the Second Temple period, in an article for *The Jerusalem Post* (International Edition, May 2, 1992, p. 9), notes that Judas Maccabeus had written a letter to the Jewish community in Egypt just after Jerusalem had been recaptured and the Holy Temple was to be cleansed and restored, expressing the hope that God would now gather Jews "from everywhere under heaven." Flusser further notes that he found the very same theme of Jewish ingathering upon his examination of texts in fragments of the Dead Sea Scrolls, indicating that even then the motherland was deemed to be Jerusalem, though actual physical residence might be elsewhere in the world.

18. For additional information on the background of the *Hanukkah* holiday, see

Emily Solis-Cohen, ed., *Hanukkah, the Feast of Lights* (Philadelphia: Jewish Publication Society of America, 1937).

Philip Goodman, ed., *The Hanukkah Anthology* (Philadelphia: Jewish Publication Society of America, 1976).

19. For a collection of *Hanukkah* music, see Richard Neumann and Velvel Pasternak, comps. and eds., *Hanukkah Melodies* (Cedarhurst, N.Y.: Tara Publications, 1977). It is important to know that most general collections of Jewish songs include a suitable array of tunes for all of the year-round holidays.

20. In the early 1930s, with the rise of Nazi terror in Europe, the Hebrew Publishing Company issued a pamphlet: Rabbi A. Hyman, comp., *Megillas Hanukkah* (Scroll of *Hanukkah*). The booklet was distributed to religious schools and synagogues as an educational aid. The contents commenced with an inspirational narration of the heroic struggles against the tyranny of Antiochus Epiphanes by Mattathias of Modin and his

sons, Simon and Judas, the Maccabees. Included was the order of religious service for that holiday, along with a collection of appropriate poems and songs.

21. See Cecil Roth, *The Jews in the Renaissance* (Philadelphia: Jewish Publication Society of America, 1959).

22. For further discussion in this book concerning the custom of *Purimshpil*, as well as its influential role on the development of the modern Yiddish theater, see Chapter 17 (Yiddish Musical Theater: Its Origins in Europe).

23. Additional information on the *Purim* holiday and examples of its music may be found in:

Philip Goodman, ed., *The Purim Anthology*, (Philadelphia: Jewish Publication Society of America, 1949).

Richard Neumann and Velvel Pasternak, comps., and eds., *Purim Melodies* (Cedarhurst, N.Y.: Tara Publications, 1978).

24. Although an overview of Sabbath music is presented here, for further background information and musical selections, see

Abraham E. Millgram, ed., *Sabbath: The Day of Delight* (Philadelphia: Jewish Publication Society of America, 1944).

Jacob Beimel, Harry Coopersmith, and Gershon Ephros, comps. and arrs., *Sabbath Services in Song* (New York: Behrman House, 1947).

Neil Levin and Velvel Pasternak, comps. and arrs., *Z'miroth Anthology: Traditional Sabbath Songs for the Home* (Cedarhurst, N.Y.: Tara Publications, 1981).

Sabbath selections are included in most of the general collections of Jewish songs.

25. Much of the poetic liturgy for the Sabbath was created by religious mystics of the ninth to sixteenth centuries. Their formative interpretation, which has continued into present times and to current observances among observers of traditional Judaism, was to view the Sabbath as a bride-queen who, as celebrated with poetics and songs, arrives (*bo-i kallah*, greeting the bride) on Friday eve, and then departs (*melaveh malkeh*, escorting the queen) on Saturday at nightfall.

26. An interesting source about the *z'miroth*, with a collection of the songs, is Herbert Loewe and Rose Henriques, comps. and eds., *Medieval Hebrew Minstrelsy* (London: J. Clark, 1926).

27. Fuller discussion on the topic is presented in this book as Part IV (Music of Mysticism and Piety).

28. Eliezer Gerovitsch, *Shire Simrah—Synagogen Gesaenge*, and *Shire Tefiloh—Synagogen Gesaenge* (two collections) (Rostov/Moscow: Gerovitsch, 1897 and 1904; reprint eds., New York: Sacred Music Press, 1953).

Part III

The Musical Heritage of Sephardic and Oriental Jewry

8

Judeo-Spanish Moroccan Songs

On March 31, 1492, an edict of expulsion was issued for all Jews in the Spanish domain. In August of that same year, Christopher Columbus sailed from the Spanish port of Palos, and on October 12 disembarked in the New World upon an island he called San Salvador, more recently known as Watling Island, in the Bahamas. Earlier, in 1469, Spanish-Jewish balladeers, minstrels, and dancers had participated in the wedding celebrations uniting Ferdinand of Aragon with Isabella of Castile. Unfortunately, raging pogroms had already started in 1391 with the destruction of the Jewish community in Seville, spreading over the next decades into Cordova, Toledo, Barcelona, Catalonia, and Valencia. Soon there were *conversos* (converts) or *marranos*,[1] a term of reference for Jews who felt compelled to convert publicly to Christianity. Many still privately observed Judaic rituals. By 1483, the religious inquisitions in Spain promulgated by the Dominican Tomas de Torquemada, confessor to Queen Isabella, had begun in earnest.

Despite the vicissitudes of life in those times, Jews flourished in Spain in what they considered to be a "golden age" of cultural enrichment and intellectual achievement, a great era of Sephardic (Judeo-Spanish) civilization. Consequently, when they were officially expelled in 1492, they considered themselves to be in a second exile. It was another dispersion, which over the following centuries was to scatter Sephardic Jews throughout the Mediterranean areas of North Africa, southern Europe, and the Near East to the mainland European countries, and then to the New World of the Americas. They brought along into that worldwide dispersal the manifold cultural ingredients of a special Hispanic-Jewish heritage that has been cherished and preserved over five centuries into present times.

Jews having sojourned in the Iberian peninsula since Roman times, Jewish liturgical chants and folk melodies had successfully blended with Visigothic, Moorish, and Hispanic musical elements. Small wonder that such notable twentieth-century scholars as Higinio Angles and Medina Anzara have stressed the influence of Judaic elements upon old Spanish secular and religious folk songs. In addition to their continuity of liturgical Hebrew, the Jews in Spain had spoken Old Latin under the Romans and Visigoths, Arabic under Moorish Islam, and then, in Christian Spain, a Romanic Old Spanish combined with Hebraic vocabulary, which they called Ladino. Over the later centuries, it was to take on linguistic elements from other countries. That special Jewish vernacular of Ladino is still spoken by contemporary Sephardic Jews, and remains essentially a Hispanic tongue.

The preserved culture of Ladino is composed of poetry and literary works, theological writings, and liturgical music as well as folklore and folk songs. The religious hymns and mundane songs especially reflect upon Old Spain, with visions of Iberian *cantigas, coplas, romanceros,* and *endechas,* and even of *chansons,* recollecting one-time relationships between the courts of Spain and those of the French in Flanders and Burgundy. The father of modern Jewish musicology, Abraham Z. Idelsohn (1882–1938), devoted the fourth volume of his monumental *Thesaurus of Oriental Hebrew Melodies* to the songs of the Oriental Sephardim.[2] For that volume, he compiled and annotated a collection of liturgical chants, religious hymns, and Ladino folk songs, many of which he had heard sung by Sephardic Jews in Jerusalem early in the twentieth century. In the fifth volume of his *Thesaurus,* treating the songs of the Moroccan Jews, Idelsohn included liturgical music and religious folk music that he had gathered from the Oriental-Moorish Sephardic traditions practiced in Jerusalem.

A more recent collection, issued in 1989 by Susana Weich-Shahak, is a compilation of some Judeo-Spanish Moroccan music source materials as prepared in collaboration with the National Sound Archives of the Jewish National and Hebrew University Library in Jerusalem. It consists of melodic transcripts, as notated from the oral amateur performances, and their original poetic texts, along with synoptic translations in both English and Hebrew. Presented with a trilingual (English, Ladino, and Hebrew) introduction are fifty selections, some as variants of thirty-two different folk song elements. They were collected among an older generation of Israeli settlers from the Moroccan communities of Tetuan, Tangier, Larache, Arcila, and Alcazarquivir. In addition to the music and poetry, the compilation includes a listing of reference works and a comparative table of sources. There is also a companion cassette affording the opportunity to hear thirty-six of the original ethnic recordings gathered in the research project. The folk songs are highly topical and relate to the life cycle, treating circumcision celebrations and lullabies, children's tunes and *bar mitzvah* festivities, courtship songs and wedding odes, funeral dirges and mourning ballads.

Following their expulsion from Spain in 1492, many Jews fled south of the Iberian peninsula across the Mediterranean to communities in North Africa, where they resumed their lives under a Moorish hegemony. Settled there, they developed a variant of their Ladino vernacular that they called Hatakia, a combination of the Old Castilian Spanish and Hebrew, with an added dialectal form of

Arabic. In the mid-1950s, there was a great emigration to Israel of Jews from North Africa, spurred by the French government withdrawal and growing political and social unrest in the area. The folk songs in Weich-Shahak's anthology are generally in Hatakia, and were collected during the years 1976–87 from Moroccan immigrants who had settled in the Israeli communities of Ashkelon and Ashdod. The selections are given without detailed musical analysis or ethnological discussion. While issues of musical interchange and adaptation surface, those matters are not explored. The music is presented in an unaccompanied melody line for solo voice, but several of the songs on the cassette are intoned by a small group, and some selections are accompanied by a simple percussion ensemble that includes castanets and darbuqqa, underscoring a distinctive rhythmic pulse for folk dance. In several examples, the women singers ululate in a Near Eastern manner. The lyrics are mixed in form, sometimes strophic or metered, at other times narrative and balladic. The source performers for the most part have clear diction, and their singing is well intonated, demonstrating a secure knowledge of the materials.

Obviously, these songs of the life cycle are part of the women's cultural legacy, and most likely are still sung among them on special occasions. While there seems to be a male voice in the folk group chants on the cassette, it is likely incidental to the original ethnic gathering and recording, rather than representing an authentic practice. Men and women generally were separated at the festivities for those life-cycle observances. The selections gathered in Weich-Shahak's book constitute a sampling of the genre rather than a comprehensive treatment. Although limited in number, the unique qualities of the materials are musically intriguing. One senses the poetic and melodic influences of old Spanish culture, yet the impact of Arabic North Africa is pervasive. For example, *Eres Chiquita*, a *coplas de matesa* from Tetuan, is a courtship song whose lovely melody and narrative couplets are reminiscent of Spain, though its language is Hatakia. In particular, the fragments of wedding folk ballads demonstrate how richly varied was the old Moroccan Jewish folk music allied to traditional ceremonies of uniting bride and groom. In the alternate versions provided for several songs, the reader may perceive similarities that illustrate common root origins with much older Iberian melodies. The mourning dirges are especially touching ballads portraying the sadness of life itself along with the fact of death. In *Muerte que a todos convidas*, the singer chants: "One cannot bargain with the Angel of Death; even a king must die." That text remains as a literary legacy from Sephardic Spain.

To round out her song collection, Weich-Shahak added a brief citation of resource publications.[3] Most studies of this subject area focus upon comparative literary and musicological issues rather than on the actual musical substance of the Spanish-Jewish heritage. The 1992 observance of the Columbian 500th anniversary has provided opportunity to reexamine a significant folk song legacy that abides to this day as the melodic documentation of events in Spanish history.[4]

Among their number, the Sephardic Jews, while flourishing in Iberia, included a host of notable historic and creative figures. One of them, the Castilian Spanish-Hebrew philosopher from Toledo known as Yehudah Halevi (1085–1145), wrote in his monumental literary work *Kuzari*: "And if thy joy lead thee so far as to sing and dance, it becomes worship and a bond of union between thee and the Divine influence."

NOTES

Most of this chapter originally appeared as a book review in *Notes*, the quarterly journal of the Music Library Association, vol. 48, no.3, pp. 1086–89. The book reviewed was Susana Weich-Shahak, comp. and ed., *Judeo-Spanish Moroccan Songs for the Life Cycle/Cantares Judeo Espanoles de Marruecos para el ciclo de la vida*, Yuval Music Series, 1 (Jerusalem: Jewish Music Research Centre and Hebrew University, 1989). Reference notes in this chapter have been appended.

1. During the inquisition, the Spanish word *marrano* meaning "pig," became a pejorative epithet for any Jews converted to Christianity. The general belief at the time was that those *conversos* (converts) still secretly observed Judaism, including the Jewish dietary laws abstaining from eating pork meats.

2. Abraham Z. Idelsohn, comp. and ed., *Hebraeish-Orientalisher Melodienschatz/Thesaurus of Oriental-Hebrew Melodies*, 10 vols. (Berlin, Leipzig, Vienna, Jerusalem: Breitkopf u. Haertel and Benjamin Harz, 1922–1933; reprint ed., New York: Ktav, 1973). See Vol. 4, *Gesaenge der Orientalischen Sefardim* (The songs of the Oriental Sephardim), and Vol. 5, *Gesaenge der Morakkanischen Jueden* (The songs of the Moroccan Jews).

3. That author's listing was quite limited in scope. The following sources are recommended:

Manuel Lopez Alvar, comp. and ed., *Cantes de Boda Judaeo-Espagnoles* (Madrid: Instituto Arias Montano, 1971).

R. D. Barnett, ed., *The Sephardic Heritage: Essays on the History and Cultural Contributions of the Jews of Spain and Portugal* (New York: Ktav, 1971).

Meir Jose Benardete and Marc D. Angel, *Hispanic Culture and Character of the Sephardic Jews* (New York: Sepher Hermon Press, 1982).

Izaak Langnas and Barton Sholod, eds., *Studies in Honor of M. J. Benardete: Essays in Hispanic and Sephardic Culture* (New York: Las Americas, 1965).

Moshe Lazar, *The Sephardic Tradition: Ladino and Spanish-Jewish Literature*, trans. David Herman (New York: Norton, 1972).

Manuel Ortega, *Los Hebreos en Marruecos* (Madrid: Ediciones Nuestra Raza, 1934).

Arcadio de Larrea Palacin, comp. and ed., *Cancionero Judio del Norte de Marruecos*, 3 vols. (Madrid: Instituto de Estudios Africanos, 1952–54).

Raphael Patai, Abraham Lopes-Cardozo, and David de Sola Pool, eds., *The World of the Sephardim* (New York: Herzl Press, 1960).

4. Suggested anthological sources of traditional liturgical music of Sephardic Jews and their special Ladino folk songs are:

Eliezer Abinum, Ovadiah Camhy, Joseph Papo, and Franz Reisenstein, comps. and eds., *Liturgie Sephardie* (London: World Sephardi Federation, 1959).

Emanuel Aguilar and David Aaron de Sola, comps. and eds., *The Ancient Melodies of the Liturgy of the Spanish and Portuguese Jews*, 2 vols. (London: Wertheimer, 1857).

Leon Algazi, comp. and ed., *Chants Sephardis* (London: World Sephardi Federation, 1958).

Maurice J. Benharoche-Baralia and Moise Alvarez-Pereyre, comps. and eds., *Chants Hebraigues Traditionnels en Usage Dans la Communaute Sephardie de Bayonne* (Biarritz: Zadoc Kahn, 1961).

Abraham Lopes-Cardozo, comp. and ed., *Sephardie Songs of Praise.* (Cedarhurst, N.Y.: Tara Publications, 1989).

Federico Consolo, comp. and ed., *Libro dei Canti d'Israele: Antichi Canti Liturgici del Rito degli Ebrei Spagnoli* (Florence: Bratti, 1892).

Alberto Hemsi, comp. and ed., *Coplas Sefardies* (Alexandria, Egypt: Edition Orientale de Musique, 1938).

Elias R. Jessurun, Emanuel A. Aguilar, and David A. de Sola, comps. and eds., *Sephardi Melodies* (London: Oxford University Press, 1931).

Emile Elihu Jonas, comp. and ed., *Recueil des Chants au Temple du Rite Portugals de Paris* (Paris: A. Durlacher, 1854 and 1886).

Isaac Levy, comp. and ed., *Antologia de Liturgia Judeo-Espagnola* (Jerusalem: Ministry of Education and Culture, 1974).

Isaac Levy, comp. and ed., *Chants Judeo-Espagnols* (London: World Sephardi Federation, 1960).

Richard Neumann, comp. and ed., *The Nico Castel Ladino Song Book* (Cedarhurst, N.Y.: Tara Publications, 1981).

9

Three Important Collections of Sephardic Music

Three particular publications present collections of many Sephardic religious and secular melodies of rare beauty, constituting a special musical treasury from a significant Judaic heritage.[1]

After the expulsion of 1492, the Jewish community of Spain scattered to many different geographical locations. They retained their medieval Castilian speech, called *Judezmo* or Ladino, maintaining it as a distinctive language wherever they settled. Enlarged with Hebrew and Aramaic vocabulary, Ladino became for the *Sephardim* (Sephardic Jews) what Yiddish became for the *Ashkenazim* (Ashkenazic Jews) of East Europe—a unifying vernacular tongue. The *Sephardim* also took with them from Spain their special synagogue traditions of worship, along with their distinctive literature and folklore, a folk art and music. Some even retained in their families for generations the very keys to their former homes in Spain.

It must be noted in this discussion that not all of the Jewish groups who follow the Sephardic musical traditions have had direct historical connection with Spain. Some Oriental-Near East Jewish communities in Egypt, Syria, Iran, and Iraq subsequently took on many of those folk traditions and liturgical practices from the Spaniolic Jews.

Sephardic religious melodies were transmitted orally from generation to generation by the *hazzan* (precentor), whose office often was filled by a *haham* (sage) or rabbi. His role in the services was that of reader and leader for the congregational chanting. The musical style was more austere and less elaborate than that which evolved for the cantorial expositions among mainland European *Ashkenazim*. In sharp contrast to the especially ornate melodies of prayer improvised and spun out by the *hazzanim* (cantors) in eastern Europe, Sephardic liturgical performance continued to follow a principle of strict adherence to the purity and simplicity of religious chant.

Particularly the women of Sephardic tradition maintained their Spanish-Jewish culture and Ladino language. Over generations, they preserved and transmitted cherished *romanceros*, the medieval romantic ballads from Old Spain. Generally, it was the men who, in their day-to-day contacts with outsiders, took up other languages and secular customs. Although Ladino poetics were chanted in the synagogue during Sabbath, festivals, and other holiday celebrations, the vast body of Sephardic liturgy was in Hebrew, and therefore was the domain of the men. For the women, on the other hand, Ladino became an important tongue of spiritual comfort as well as daily life over the generations, precisely as Yiddish served those functions for Jewish women in eastern Europe. It appears that among themselves, women strengthened the Judaic qualities of their respective vernacular tongues and enlarged upon native folklore with the poetics and music that enhanced the important events of their lives—births and lullabies, love and marriages, domestic celebrations for Sabbath and festivals. Transmitted more casually than the traditions of synagogue liturgical chant, there was no strict adherence to purity of musical style nor to melodic origins. Cultural expression was often a matter of subjective choice and popular sentiment.

Issued between 1958 and 1960, three volumes of Sephardic secular and religious music constitute important additions to that body of Jewish ethnomusical literature. Though comprehensive compilations, they by no means cover the entire scope of that treasury. Clearly, further collection projects and scholarly studies of Sephardic music are warranted. Time is running out for those materials, because it appears that only older generations wish to remember what the young people are not interested in learning. This is also the case with eastern European Yiddish folklore and folk song.

As to the publications themselves, the collection by noted liturgical musician Leon Algazi (1890–1971) consists of eighty-one liturgical melodies and folk tunes in Hebrew, Aramaic, and Ladino. For a number of years, Isaac Levy had been in charge of all Sephardic radio programming at *Kol Yisrael,* the broadcasting station in Jerusalem, and his compilation presents ninety-seven Ladino folk ballads. Ovadiah Camhy (1890–1971) served as director of educational activities for the World Sephardi Federation and supervised publication of all three of these volumes. The book that he coedited with Eliezer Abinum, Joseph Papo, and Franz Reisenstein contains one hundred liturgical chants, including characteristic chants for the entire religious calendar.

Among the wealth of synagogue music in that latter volume is the ancient melody that Sephardic congregants vigorously intone together every Sabbath morning as the triumphant *Shir Moshe* (Song of Moses). In all branches of Judaic liturgy, special attention is paid to the chanting of this biblical passage annually on *Shabbat Shirah* (Sabbath of Song). Another Sephardic liturgical melody of special interest included by Camhy and his colleagues is the traditional chant for *tal* (dew), intoned at the Passover services. It is an old liturgical melody of early medieval origin whose melodic elements have been favored among Christians as well as Jews over the centuries. Wandering minstrels, traveling and performing throughout Europe during the Middle Ages, brought many melodies to diverse communities. This particular melody for dew has attracted the interest of many folklorists and musicians. The *Sephardim* have cherished and sung it over the centuries, and in more recent times, elements of its melodic motifs were re-shaped for *Hatikvah*, the Jewish anthem.[2]

NOTES

This material has been adapted from a review of three books that originally appeared in *The Jewish Frontier* vol. 28, no. 2 (1961), p. 29, published in New York. Excerpts from that review were subsequently published in *Le Judaisme Sephardi* no. 22 (1971), p. 973, published in London by the World Sephardi Federation. Footnotes have been added for this chapter.

1. The three books discussed are:

Leon Algazi, comp. and ed., *Chants Sephardis* (London: World Sephardi Federation, 1958).

Ovadia Camhy, Eliezer Abinum, Joseph Papo, and Franz Reisenstein, comps. and eds., *Liturgie Sephardie* (London: World Sephardi Federation, 1959).

Isaac Levy, comp. and ed., *Chants Judeo-Espagnols* (London: World Sephardi Federation, 1960).

2. For a more extended discussion of *Hatikvah* and its poet-author Naphtali Herz Imber, see Chapter 21 (Hope and the Man: *Hatikvah* and Naphtali Herz Imber).

10

Sephardic Music Conference in Jerusalem

The musical traditions—liturgical and secular—of the Sephardic Jews and the Oriental Jews were significantly highlighted during an important international musicological conference held in Jerusalem August 5–12, 1963. The "East-West in Music" conference was organized by the Israel National Council of Culture and Art, in cooperation with the International Music Council of UNESCO and the International Folk Music Council, and with the assistance of Kol Israel Broadcasting Services and Hebrew University. At this conference were gathered 127 representatives from thirty-five countries, as well as 130 registered Israeli scholars and musicians. In addition, students in the music departments of Bar Ilan University and Tel Aviv University as well as Hebrew University attended and assisted in various duties. Delegates came from the Far East, from many of the African countries, and from every European country except the former Soviet Union. This was a great musical encounter of many ideas and traditions, a world meeting of outstanding Jewish and non-Jewish composers, educators, and music scholars from five continents.

Fifty excellent papers on folk music studies and musical techniques of collection and composition were presented during regular sessions held in the Kaplan Building on the Hebrew University campus. Among the subjects were many of specific interest to Sephardic communities, such as Oriental elements in Israeli song, polyphony in Jewish music of the Near East, aspects of the liturgical music of Sephardic Jews in Bulgaria, and analogies between Spanish folk song of early times and the formation of Gregorian chant.

In connection with this international conference, the Israel Music Institute published nine important pamphlets by leading Israeli music scholars, covering such areas as Persian-Jewish folk song, Israeli folk song analyzed in terms of influences of Sephardic and Oriental Jewish music, and the cantillation traditions of Tunis.[1] Courtesy of the Israel Institute for Sacred Music and the government's Ministry of Religious Affairs, ten booklets of recently published liturgical music, collectively titled *Renanot* (Songs of exultation), were distributed to all delegates. Those materials consisted of twenty-nine selections arranged for synagogue rendition during Sabbath and holidays according to the traditions of Jews from Tunisia, Iraq, Yemen, Morocco, and Algeria as well as mainstream Israeli Ashkenazic and Sephardic liturgy.[2]

Among the many excellent concerts especially prepared and presented for the distinguished guests at the conference were two presentations of particular Sephardic relevance. One, held at Hebrew University, was the premiere of a choral work by Mordecai Seter, an arrangement of salient elements of traditional Sephardic liturgical melodies as performed by an SATB (soprano, alto, tenor, bass) choir ensemble. Copies of the musical score of this work by Seter were distributed to all attendees. At the other, also held on the university campus, a program was presented which could not have been heard anywhere else in the world. The Bible cantillation-reading for the previous Sabbath's portion of the week was chanted in succession by *hazzanim* (precentors) representing the great spectrum of Jewish groups ingathered to Israel. In addition to varied presentations by Ashkenazic and European Sephardic Jews, there were chants from the following traditions now resident in Jerusalem: Aleppo, Babylonian-Bagdad, Bukhara, Djerba, Iraq, Morocco, Persia-Iran, Turkey, and Yemen. In addition, comparable biblical intonations were provided by several different Christian sects and from Islamic readers of the Koran.

The International Folk Music Council is an organization composed of a worldwide membership devoted to the collection, preservation, study, and performance of the folk music heritages of mankind. Its president at the time of the conference (1963) was Hungarian folk composer Zoltán Kodály (1882–1967), who actively participated in all of the conference sessions and concerts. The stated objective of the Music Council of UNESCO is to foster international cultural understanding through musical studies among all nations of the world. This branch of UNESCO seeks to apply the universal language of music toward a goal of better human relations between all peoples.

The conference in Israel was an academic and musical success. Its papers were of high caliber, and the concerts provided valuable intellectual as well as aesthetic musical experiences. The delegates appeared to mingle well and to enjoy their stay in Israel, some remaining after the conference itself in order to tour the country. Many delegates paid warm public tributes to Israel as well as to Israeli music. Iranian professors of music listened seriously to performances of Persian-Jewish folk songs, folk dances, and folk instruments. African musicians, generally clad in native costumes, observed intently as Yemenite Jews chanted special hymns. Valuable contacts were made between Israelis and their musical counterparts from other parts of the world.[3]

It was obvious at the conclusion of the conference that the sacred and secular musical creations of all the traditions of Judaism—Sephardic, Oriental-Near East, and Ashkenazic—constitute a viable historic heritage of world-wide cultural significance.

NOTES

This chapter was originally published in *Kol Sepharad,* vol. 7, no. 43 (1964), pp. 7–8, in London by the World Sephardi Federation. It is given here with minor editorial changes and added reference notes.

1. Among the pamphlet publications issued at that time (1963) by the Israel Music Institute (Tel Aviv) were:

Hanoch Avenary, *Studies in the Hebrew, Syrian, and Greek Liturgical Recitative.*

Bathja Bayer, *The Material Relics of Music in Ancient Palestine and its Environment: An Archeological Inventory.*

Edith Gerson-Kiwi, *The Legacy of Jewish Music through the Ages.*

Avigdor Herzog, *The Intonation of the Pentateuch in the Heder of Tunis.*

Menashe Ravina, *Organum and the Samaritans.*

Michal Smoira-Roll, *Folk Song in Israel: An Analysis Attempted.*

2. Avigdor Herzog, comp. and ed., *Renanot/Songster of Sacred Music* (Jerusalem: Institute for Sacred Music [ISM], 1962–63. Also issued and distributed at that time was another collection prepared by Avigdor Herzog: *Rinatyah/Canticles and Songs* (Jerusalem: ISM, 1963); with an additional fourteen liturgical selections.

3. For a more detailed treatment of music in Israel, see the material in Part VIII (The Music of Zion and Israel).

11

Sephardic Traditions and Mediterranean Styles

By the time that Charlemagne (C.E. 768–814), king of the Franks, assumed control of western Europe, Moors had established strongholds in the Iberian area and were spreading their hegemony throughout the Mediterranean rim in southern Europe and northern Africa. Jews had resided in Iberia (which they called in Hebrew *Sefarad*) since Roman times. During the subsequent Visigothic occupation, they established many viable communities that continued to flourish under the later Moorish rulers. As Christianity grew stronger in Europe, there were forced conversions of Jews, as well as other political subjects (considered pagans) in the areas. The Hebrew word for those "forced ones" was *anusim*, and many of them secretly still observed Judaism over the succeeding generations. Rabbi Gershom of Mayence (fl. 1000 C.E.) counseled many of those crypto-Jews. The notable rabbinical scholar Solomon ben Isaac of Troyes, known by the acronym of his title and name as "Rashi," (1040–1105), aided the return of converts and preached kindness toward their families. The Middle Ages were centuries of Jewish martyrdoms and forced baptisms. Small wonder that for a long time afterward the general belief was sustained that in Europe, especially among the duchies of France and Italy, Jewish blood flowed in the veins of royalty. However, over those centuries there were Iberian Moorish rulers and Christian Spanish kings who permitted, even encouraged, Jewish communal life, and thereby enabled development of a "golden age" for Hispanic-Jewish cultural creativity and spiritual enrichment.[1]

Early in the fourteenth century, withdrawal of the Moors left Iberia-Spain to the Christian kings. With the rise of anti-Semitic public riots, many Jews began to migrate, mostly by sea route, to the areas around the Mediterranean that offered more hospitable surroundings.[2] On Ash Wednesday, March 15, 1391, the flourishing Jewish community of Seville was sacked and destroyed, commencing an era of overt and intense hostility to Iberian Jewry. In quick succession, the thriving Jewish communities in Cordova, Toledo, and Barcelona were decimated. Pillage and destruction, murder and forced conversion (pogroms) raged unchecked throughout the kingdoms of Aragon, Castile, Catalonia, and Valencia. The devastation took its desperate toll in such once thriving Jewish communities as Arevalo, Avila, Burgos, Segovia, Soria, and Tolevera. By this time, converts known as *nuevos cristianos* (new Christians), or *conversos* (converts) and contemptuously called *marranos* (an old Spanish word for "swine") were entering into general Spanish society, some rising to high royal positions and even to significant religious offices. In 1478, an inquisitional edict was initiated by a group of bishops who resented those successful *conversos*, and in 1483, the confessor to Queen Isabella, Tomas de Torquemada, became head of the Supreme Inquisition of Spain.

The official excuse for the decree of Jewish Expulsion in 1492 was that Spanish Jews were forcing converts back to Judaism. In 1496, the edicts issued in the Portuguese territory of Iberia ordered the mass eviction of Jews, but for economic reasons compelled thousands of them to convert and to remain there. By the end of the sixteenth century, the "golden age" of Jewish life in Sefarad-Iberia had ended with the emigration of many *conversos* along with the last of the Spanish Jews. Likely, Jewish blood lines did remain behind among Spaniards. Although inquisitional decrees followed all Spanish settlements, even across to the Americas, crypto-Jews abided for generations in new territories, and very likely exist into present times.

The cultural legacy of old Judeo-Spanish folk song has best preserved the history of Iberian-Judaism. That music was created and appreciated during the old "golden" times, and then was brought over to areas of Sephardic resettlement in other areas of the world, where it has been preserved and cherished. Those distinctive melodies and Ladino poetics echo with old Castilian, Aragonese, Catalonian, and Andalusian tunes and folklore. Scholars of Spanish history study them for information about the culture of Old Spain.[3]

Between the seventh and fifteenth centuries, there had been great cultural and scholarly achievements among the Jews residing in realms stretching from Baghdad (seat of the Babylonian Gaonate or Jewish Exilarchate) across to numerous Jewish communities in southern France and the Iberian peninsula. Music, along with literature, always constituted a special interest. Leo Hebraeus Gersonides (Levi ben Gershom, d.1344) wrote a significant Latin treatise on music at the invitation of Philippe de Vitry, bishop of Meaux in Provence (1291–1361), and thus helped the rise of the *ars nova* (new art) movement that was to flourish during the Renaissance. Rabbi Moses Batarel (fl. late 14th cent., southern France) analyzed, in Hebrew and Old French, a system of ascending and descending tones to prove that melody is a science. An Andalusian Jewish scholar of that same century, Shemtob ibn Falaquera, created an Arabic classification of musical theory.

During that time, Jewish performers were popular at Christian festivities, creating dramatic pageants and musical entertainments. Jewish troubadours and minstrels shaped ballads and romances on heroic subjects. Instrumental ensembles that included Jews played at the courts of the Moorish sultans and Christian nobles throughout the Mediterranean area. Old records of Navarre and Pamplona show that there were popular Jewish mimes and dancers as well as musicians. In 1469 in Palermo, official public celebration of the wedding of Ferdinand of Aragon and Isabella of Castille included Jewish entertainers—dancers, singers, and instrumentalists. A first illuminated edition of the biblical *Song of Songs*, with poetic annotations and musical indications, was issued in mid-fifteenth-century northern Spain. In the face of growing hostility, however, many noted Spanish Jewish musicians fled well before 1492, some leaving to serve at other royal courts in Europe, and even for the popes of Rome. Ramon de Pareja of Baeza (fl. late 15th cent.) left in 1491 to perform at several northern Italian ducal courts, where he developed a system of equal temperament of twelve semitones for tuning of the lute and guitar. Sadly, already by the late fourteenth century, there were popular Spanish ditties deriding the Jews, in poetic broadsides and in parodies of known Judaic melodies.

Their great dispersal drove the Sephardic Jews far from Iberia and exposed them to other cultures, which varied widely according to geographical area. In northern Africa, Arabic influences emerged, while in Greece, Turkey, and the Balkans, other particular qualities were incorporated. It is important to recognize that the most strictly defined and maintained musical tradition was for their liturgical services. This was a male domain wherein the basic language remained Hebrew, with some Aramaic and a few poetic Ladino insertions. Care was taken to preserve biblical cantillation patterns and to formalize the special motival chants for the prayers, all according to the Jewish calendar year of observances. Hymnology for the rituals was somewhat more variable, yet also was monitored zealously by religious leaders. Transmitted orally between the male officiants from generation to generation, Sephardic devotional melody was first formally collected, notated, and printed in the early sixteenth century, as supplement to the venerated contents of the traditionally established prayer book. It was for a body of sacred folk songs that some additions and changes gradually came about with the passage of time. Ladino remained as the vernacular tongue of certain religious celebrations, especially for the life cycle rituals, and domestic observances of Sabbath and the festivals. Performed by women as well as men, that music constituted a cultural bridge between holy and mundane and took on the folkloric qualities of improvisational embellishment and emotional intensity.

In an article treating "Some Sefardi Melodies and Customs," Rabbi D. A. Jessurun Cardozo noted:

An interesting custom prevailed among the Sephardim, to gather on the eve of important private celebrations in the home of the celebrant for what was called a reading. Appropriate passages were chanted from *Torah* and *Haftarah*, followed by the singing of the *hallel* (liturgy of praises), other Psalms, and *zemiroth* (table carols). Such readings could be arranged for important occasions, such as the eves of a wedding, a *bar mitzvah,* special anniversaries, and important birthdays. For *Purim,* there were of course many special songs, some very ingeniously using Hebrew words that have the same sounds as well known Spanish words, and also singing Hebrew text interspersed with Spanish expressions.[4]

The departing Sephardic Jews took with them a great many secular songs and other forms of general music and poetry, all reflective of earlier cultural life in Iberia. Though cherished and performed elsewhere, this was not "frozen" music, but rather, as an expression of everyday life, it readily incorporated melodic elements and qualities from newer places. Those Spaniolic Jews also retained an Iberian mind-set that viewed music as a science worthy of intellectual significance. In Amsterdam, Samuel Usque (fl. early 17th cent.) instituted courses of musical study (including lessons in harp, vihuela de arco, and harpsichord) into the curriculum of a school that he established for the education of young Sephardic Jewry. Among the students there were Isaac Aboab de Fonseca (1605–1693), the first rabbi in America, and also the philosopher Baruch Spinoza (1632–1677).

However, it was especially in the areas around the Mediterranean and in the hegemony of the Turkish Empire that a strong musicality ensured cultural continuity among many reestablished Jewish communities. In particular, cultural interaction with Arabic society proved especially congenial for retention of the Ladino heritage and its later melodic elaboration and augmentation. Enhanced were the older preferences for the voices of flexible lyric tenors and darkly dramatic sopranos. Cast into newer environments were liturgical hymns—*t'filoth* (prayers), *bakashot* (petitions), *z'miroth* (carols), *pizmonim* (sacred poetics)—sung with texts created by gifted poets of faith. Melodies ranged from fixed patterns of motival chant and simple lines of limited tessitura, to musical fantasies abounding with melodies, melismatic passages, and vocal embellishments. In particular, secular Ladino songs preserved the cultural styles, folk music, and literary legacies of Iberian bards, troubadours, and storytellers (*balladas, canciones, cantigas, coplas, rascas, romanceros,* and *villancicos*), as well as earlier Moorish influences of *conte hondo* and *al andalus flamenco.*[5]

In the course of its geographical transplantation, the Jewish vernacular language of Ladino (*Judezmo*) retained both its Hebrew and Old Castillian-Catalonian roots, appending more of the later local vocabularies along the way. Its linguistics parallel that of another Jewish vernacular tongue, Yiddish, which arose centuries ago as a dynamic combination of Hebrew with Old Rhenish German, and then over time acquired Slavicisms as Jews settled in eastern Europe. Ladino palpably differs from the modern Spanish language as to style of pronunciation and particularly in terms of its verbal endings, certain vowels sounds, and some grammatical usages.[6]

NOTES

1. For detailed historical background on this topical area, see these publications:

Israel Abrahams, *Jewish Life in the Middle Ages* (Cambridge, England: Goldston, 1896; reprint ed., Philadelphia: Jewish Publication Society of America, 1958).

Jacob Rader Marcus, *The Jew in the Medieval World* (Philadelphia: Union of American Hebrew Congregations [UAHC] and Jewish Publication Society of America [JPSA], 1938; reprint ed., New York: Harper & Row, 1965).

Cecil Roth, *A History of the Marranos* (Philadelphia: Jewish Publication Society of America, 1932; reprint ed., New York; Meridian Books, 1959).

2. Ancient patterns of communal activities by the early Phoenician settlers in Iberia were substantially enhanced during the Roman and then Visigothic eras. The people of that peninsula, especially along coastal areas, were merchant-traders, seamen, and shipbuilders. To a great extent, they were involved in sea and land commerce with other communities in the Mediterranean area. Especially in the port towns, many Jews were prominently involved in those enterprises.

3. Among the modern Spanish scholars who have studied the folklore and folk songs of the Sephardic heritage, and in particular the Ladino materials, are two of notable significance: Felipe Pedrell (1841–1922) produced many collections of old Spanish folksongs, among them, *Cancionero Musical Popular Espagnol*, 4 vols (Valla, Catalonia: E. Castella, 1919–1920). Don Ramon Menendez-Pidal (1869–1968) was a preeminent cultural historian whose range of considerations included Judeo-Spanish folk elements and linguistics. He published annotated compilations of old Iberian romances and ballads (Madrid: Pidal, 1928), in which he underscored the historic importance of Judeo-Iberian poetry and melodies

4. D. A. Jessurun Cardozo, "Some Sefardi Melodies and Customs," *Jewish Music Forum Bulletin*, vol. 10 (1956), p. 22.

5. Two important scholarly studies treating aspects of this musical legacy are:

Edith Gerson-Kiwi, "The Musical Sources of Judeo-Hispanic Romance," *The Musical Quarterly*, vol. 50, no. 1 (1964), pp. 31–43.

Hanoch Avenary, "Persistence and Transformation of a Sephardic Penitential Hymn under Changing Environmental Conditions," *The Abraham Zvi Idelsohn Memorial Volume* (Jerusalem: Magnes Press and Hebrew University, 1986), pp. 181–237.

6. Additional sources on Sephardic culture are:

David M. Bunis, *Sephardic Studies: A Research Bibliography Incorporating Judezmo Language, Literature and Folklore, and Historical Background* (New York: Garland, 1981).

Moshe Lazar, *The Sephardic Tradition: Ladino and Spanish–Jewish Literature*, trans. David Herman (New York: Norton, 1972).

12

The Music of Oriental Jewry

In traditional terminology, diasporic Jewry may be divided into three definitive groupings. (1) *Ashkenazim,* mainland Europeans, or the major portion of continental Jewry and the Yiddish–speaking Jews of Eastern Europe; (2) *Sephardim,* originally settlers in the Iberian peninsula whose dispersion from Spain soon divided them into two distinctive categories, (a) Spanish-Portuguese, or European Sephardics who went to Holland and Germanic areas, southern France, northern Italy, and by the early seventeenth century also began colonizing in the Americas, and (b) Oriental Sephardics, or those who resettled in the Balkans, the old Turkish Empire, Greece and the Aegean area, and northern African regions of Morocco, Algeria, Tunisia, and Egypt. (3) *Ur-Orientalim,* a category of Jewish groups who had always resided in the Near Eastern-African-Asiatic areas, composed of those in Yemen (southern Arabia), Iraq and Syria (Babylonian-Baghdad), Persia (Bukhara, Afghanistan, Daghestan, and Georgia), and Cochin (southern India on the Malabar Coast). In addition, there also arose over the centuries dissident sects relating to Judaism, such as Bene Israel in the Bombay area of India and Falasha-Amharics of Ethiopia, and such dissident groups as Samaritans in Judea, Karaites in Iraq and Kurdistan, and Sabbatheans or Subotnikis in the Caucasus and Siberia.

As a natural course of development among Jews residing in the same geographical regions, secular and sacred cultural intermingling came about between Oriental Sephardics and Ur-Orientals. In sharp contrast to any of the *Sephardim,* whose religious customs and communal folklore had been shaped during several centuries of residence among the Moors and Christians, the Afro-Asiatic Judaic culture was deeply influenced by a thousand more years of Islamic dominance and the Arabic language. The clearest of those latter Judaic folk patterns may be noted among the Yemenite and Babylonian-Baghdadi Jews.

With the exception of dissidently related sects, all traditions of Judaism have the same fixed Jewish calendar year of religious observances, with an essential consistency in the prayers and prayer rituals. There is further significant constancy in that Hebrew is the holy tongue, and the services are a male domain. Moreover, in every case, there are special domestic sacred duties and festivities shared by the entire family, for which song and poetry are integral. In addition, each traditional grouping has its own secularized vernacular communal culture of customs, folklore, and music, in which women as well as men participate.[1]

According to legend, the Jews had resided in coastal northern Africa since the era of the first Holy Temple in Jerusalem, likely as early as the reign of King Solomon. In antiquity, there were settlements during the time of the Phoenician sea traders. in southern Arabia (Yemen), Jews have been documented as flourishing for centuries until the last of the Himgaric-Jewish kings, Joseph du Nuwas (d. 525 C.E.). Subsequently, Yemen was taken over by Islamic conquest. Under that Arabic domination, Jews spoke a vernacular dialect of Arabic with some Hebraicisms, and reserved pure Hebrew for holy expression. At their services, tenor-voice precentors led the congregations in modal chanting of the prayers. For religious doctrinal matters, Yemenite communities maintained contacts with the Gaonate rabbinical academy and the Talmudic leaders in Baghdad, until the death there of the last Gaonic Exilarch (1038 C.E.). Afterwards, Yemenite rabbis sought out the writings of Maimonides and other religious thinkers, especially in the Moorish hegemony. Then, spurred by the movement of Jewish mysticism and Cabalists in Safed during the sixteenth century, the Yemenite Jews added poetic songs (*zemiroth*) to religious celebrations. Their most noted liturgical bard, Mori Salim (Shalom) Shabazi (fl. 17th cent.), collected a great number of those Yemenite sacred poetics.

Into modern times, along with their great devotion to singing, the Yemenites have customarily favored dances, and for secular music use various types of percussion instruments in rhythmic patterns of accompaniment. The women, in particular, have taken on the arts of singing, dancing, and instrumentation. Much of that musical expression over the centuries has been linked to the romantic life-cycle event of the wedding. Folk customs adorn that life-cycle ceremony with mystic and religious significances beyond the union of a man and woman, to signify the relationship of God and Israel. Special songs and dances were performed for prenuptial preparations of bride and groom as well as for festivities after the rite itself. In the late nineteenth century, because of increasing difficulties with the rulers of Yemen, a Jewish movement of return to Jerusalem began. Then, after establishment of the State of Israel, Operation Magic Carpet enabled air transport and resettlement of most Yemenite Jews in 1949 and 1950.[2]

The Iraqi-Baghdadi Jews are believed to have settled in that area during the first dispersion in 586 B.C.E., following the Babylonian captivity and destruction of the Holy Temple in Jerusalem. They retained their Aramaic (*targum*) vernacular language, but gradually adapted a form of Arabic for general daily life. For over a thousand years, the Babylonian area was the location of the great rabbinical academies headed by *Gaonim*, or Jewish Exilarchs, whose influences through their rabbinical teachings and Talmudic writings constituted the fountainhead of Judaic religious development during that period of history.

Considered to be of even older origins are Jewish settlements in Bukhara, Afghanistan, and Daghestan (old Persia), descendants of the Hebrew tribes in the North Kingdom of Israel, who left there 135 years before the Great Babylonian exile. The biblical Book of Esther is likely to have originated there. Many of the Caspian Sea region Jews, *Girgasim*, or Georgians, and the "mountain Jews" of Transcaucasia hold that they arose from the Jews carried into captivity by the Assyrian kings (8th cent. B.C.E.) and even Nebuchadnezzar (11th cent. B.C.E.). Their essential patterns of sacred and secular musical expression are akin to those of the Yemenites. However, the music sounds different because of an assimilation of Persian and other local melodies into the folk songs, and even into modal qualities of the liturgical chants. Abraham Z. Idelsohn in his *Thesaurus* cited the Babylonian and Persian musical traditions, especially their biblical cantillations and Psalm chants, as the most ancient of Judaic melodic expressions.[3]

Considering the far-flung geographical dispersion of all the various Judaic groups as well as their different historic experiences in so many areas of the world, it seems quite remarkable that there has evolved such a spiritual kinship and a unifying quality of expression in their Jewish traditions: year-round and daily sacred rituals and prayers, communal and domestic religious and secular observances, ways in which different Judaic vernaculars have been incorporated into mundane Judaism, and well-defined societal roles of men and women in religious and secular matters. All those abiding similarities serve to highlight a determined maintenance of lineage and of communication between all the traditions, spanning centuries of the Common Christian Era (C.E.). Despite hardships encountered in Diaspora life and the vicissitudes of history, those Jewish traditions survived, and at certain periods in history managed to flourish. Though this may seem to be a guarded reflection, it is meant as a celebration of faith, culture, and continuity.[4]

NOTES

1. Extensive liturgical and folk music materials for each of these groups may be found in: Abraham Z. Idelsohn, comp. and ed., *Hebraeish-Orientalischer Melodienschatz, Thesaurus of Hebrew-Oriental Melodies*, 10 Vols. (reprint ed., New York: Ktav, 1973). Of particular interest for this discussion are: Vol. 1, *Songs of the Yemenite Jews*; Vol. 2, *Songs of the Babylonian Jews*; Vol. 3, *Songs of the Jews of Persia, Bukhara and Daghestan*; Vol. 4, *Songs of the Oriental Sephardim;* and Vol. 5, *Songs of the Moroccan Jews*. Idelsohn has provided illuminating annotative information in each of those volumes.

2. A helpful bibliographic listing on Yemenite history and music is Paul Marks, comp., *Bibliography of Literature Concerning Yemenite-Jewish Music* (Detroit: Information Coordinators, 1973).

3. A comparative survey of the music of Asiatic Jewish communities is provided in Edith Gerson-Kiwi. "The Legacy of Jewish Music through the Ages." *In the Dispersion*, Vol. 3 (Jerusalem: World Zionist Organization, 1963–1964), pp. 149–72.

4. An important collection of the folk songs of Ur-Oriental Jews was gathered in modern Israel from among the resettlers by the foremost exponent of Yemenite folk song: Bracha Zefira, comp. and ed., *Kolot Rabim (Many Voices): Anthology of Oriental Jewish Hymns and Songs* (Ramat Gan, Israel: Masada Press, 1978).

Part IV

Music of Mysticism and Piety

13

The Mystics: Poet-Bards of the Liturgy

By the seventeenth century, the Ashkenazic traditions had become the predominant influence among European Jewry. Nevertheless, many aspects of Sephardic Judaism and its culture had entered into the liturgical poetry of the prayer book and notably the celebration of the Sabbath. By this time, all Jewish traditions, including the Ur-Oriental, adhered in religious commitment to the basic rabbinical writings of the *Talmud* (*Bavli*-Babylonian and *Yerushalmi*-Palestinian versions), as well as the *Mishnah Torah* and other writings of Maimonides.[1] In addition, all held in high esteem the *Zohar* (Splendor or brightness), a collection of religious writings, and venerated its putative author, the martyred Rabbi Simeon bar Yohai (Johai) (fl. 2nd cent.), who had been a disciple of the historic figure Rabbi Akiba ben Joseph (ca.40–135 C.E.), also killed by the Romans. Written in Aramaic, it was in the form of a commentary upon the Pentateuch (Five Books of Moses), introducing the essence of Jewish mysticism, the *Kabbalah* (Reception or tradition). Subsequently, the *Zohar* was reshaped as a composite of those oral sources and written materials by the Sephardic philosopher-scholar Moses ben Shem Tov de Leon (1250–1305), who, in the growing trend of Judaism of his time, wove concepts of mysticism, messianism, and spiritual folklore into interpretations of the Bible. Though those writings were widely circulated among Jews as well as Christians and Moslems, a printed edition of the *Zohar* was first published in Mantua, Italy, in 1558–1560.

For musico-poetic expression, the *Zohar* provided a formative guide, especially as elements of pious mysticism entered Jewish liturgical practices and folk customs. The idea of celestial holy melody also was attributed to Simeon bar Yohai, who is reputed to have taught his pupils: "Hearken well to the music of the spheres. There are choirs of angels intoning the music and harmony of the spheres. The prophets, the singers, the seers, and the mystics, when they feel themselves possessed of the Divine Spirit, and their spiritual eyes see naught but the whiteness of a mirror, are able to disengage themselves from this material world and to vision themselves climbing to the heights to music of this Divine melody."[2] Throughout, the *Zohar* iterates such sentiments as "In the highest heavens there are gates which open only through the power of song," and "All creation sings glorious songs of praise to the Creator." Likely, the author was reflecting upon similar concepts in the biblical Book of Job 38:7: "Who laid the cornerstone, when the morning stars were singing, and all the angels chanted in their joy."[3] The English poet and artist William Blake (1757–1827) admirably portrayed this same sentiment in the fourteenth of his twenty-one illustrations for "A Vision of the Book of Job," which he titled: "When the morning stars sang together, and all the sons of God shouted for joy."[4]

Early on, such sanctification of melody found its way into Ashkenazic and Sephardic prayer books, notably in the *Birkoth ha-Shakhar* (Morning benedictions): "Blessed be the Lord's glory throughout all space. Thus they chant in melodious psalmody to the blessed God. They raise their songs of lauding and praise to their King, the eternal God of life."[5] A great rabbinical leader of Ashkenazic Jewry in the Rhineland Valley, Jacob Levi of Molin "Maharil" (1356–1427) officiated as the *hazzan* (precentor) at services and traveled to many communities, instructing those congregations to hold fast to liturgical poetry and *mi-Sinai* (from Mount Sinai) tunes. His ideas spread widely throughout Central Europe, promoting the enrichment and preservation of holy rituals and folk customs, prayer texts, and special chants. Thus, the distinctive Jewish observances in synagogue devotions and studies and in communal and domestic life prevailed there during the fifteenth and sixteenth centuries, and then traveled along with a great eastward movement of many Jews to settlements in the Slavic countries.

What constituted that sacred treasury of literature and song? In addition to the basic prayer formulations for each of the daily and holiday services, there were the religious poems, variously called *kerovoth, ofanim, pizmonim*. Many were anonymous creations, but the earliest of known liturgical bards was Eliezer Kallir (fl. late 8th cent.), who is believed to have resided in Palestine and Syria. His metrical works were related to the services of the holy festivals, particularly of Passover. Between the tenth and fifteenth centuries, most of the religious poet-singers were of Sephardic origin, and were greatly influenced by the Moorish-Arabic meter and style of literary expression. Their works were characterized by an exalted spirituality, with purity of expression and intense devotion to the Almighty and His works. Those *paytanim* (liturgical poets) were imbued with a pious mysticism that focused upon messianic hope, and a glorification of the Sabbath as a celestial bride-queen. The Sabbath day itself became particularly significant as an earthly sample of the ideal world to come. As a result, its liturgical services and domestic rituals were elaborated and celebrated with special songs, poetics, and folklore. To a lesser extent, the same mind-set was applied to the Passover *seder* (ritual meal) with its *haggadah* (ritual narrative).

A movement of Jewish mysticism first arose during the tenth century among Iberian Sephardic Jewry. By the twelfth century, it had spread to the Rhineland European Ashkenazic Jews, as a pietistic reaction to hard times of crusaders, plagues, and Christian church edicts. Many significant prayer texts were written during that period, for example, the great statement of belief, *aleynu*: "We bow in homage only to Thee, Almighty God." It was first intoned by Jewish martyrs for the faith in France and soon entered into the daily services, and in fourteenth-century Rhineland attained particular significance with a specific motival chant intoned in the High Holy Days doxology. Its verses were set into their present form by Herz Treves of Frankfurt (1470–1550). Also at that time, the poetics and chant of *kol nidrey* (all vows) became the opening passages of the *Yom Kippur* (Day of Atonement) eve service. Freely chanted at first, its present distinctive melodic contours arose among Ashkenazic Jews late in the fourteenth century. Other important prayer texts and their motival tunes were created during that period, including devotional sections for various High Holy Days prayer texts. Also arising during this period were such poetics as the thirteenth-century *Ma-oz tsur* (Rock of ages) for *Hanukkah* (Feast of Lights), whose most well-known melody evolved from a late fifteenth-century military march refrain. For the Sabbath, an acrostic poem by Isaac ha-Koton (fl. 13th cent.), *Hamavdil* (the separation), became a defined part of the liturgical ritual concluding the Sabbath.

Following the death of the last of the great leaders of the Talmudic Gaonate in Babylonia, Rabbi Solomon ben Isaac of Troyes , known as "Rashi" (northern France, 1040–1105), took up and carried forward the range of Judaic studies, spreading principles of rabbinic Judaism throughout Europe. In addition to expounding upon the Talmud, he wrote extensive commentaries on the Pentateuch (Five Books of Moses) and established a rabbinical academy at Mayence. It is intriguing to know that he had three daughters, all of whom were taught the Scriptures and even the Talmud.[6] However, it was the strong influence of the Sephardic rabbis and liturgical bards that permeated religious expression of medieval European Jewry. Among them were such outstanding doctrinists as Moses Nachmanides (1194–1270) and especially Moses (ben Maimon) Maimonides (1135–1204), of Cordoba, Iberia, and then Fez, Morocco. The philosophical ideas and writings of Maimonides in his monumental *Mishnah Torah* became essential to the theological concepts of Judaism, and even influenced the thinking of theological leaders of Christianity as well as Islam.[7]

Yet it was the poetic works of the Iberian *paytanim* that all Judaic traditions found deeply expressive and inspirational, a celebration of the mystery of religious faith. Beginning with Hasdai ibn Shaprut (915–970 C.E.), Samuel ibn Nagrela (993–1056 C.E.), and Dunash ibn Labrat (fl. 10th cent.), all of whom were deeply influenced by Moorish literary forms, Hebrew and Aramaic poetic creativity flowered in celebration of the Jewish calendar and life-cycle observances. Between the tenth and sixteenth centuries, numerous devotional poems were written, many of which were sung to special tunes. Although most of the manuscripts of that great period of creativity were lost, collections of *pizmonim* (sacred poems) were gathered by Israel Najara in 1592–1599, Joseph Gonsho in 1600, and Menahem Lonzano in 1618. Published in northern Italy, those compilations were circulated among all Jews in Italy, France, the Rhineland, and soon in other areas of Europe. Ashkenazic Jews added those literary works, including a *piyut* (liturgical poem) of twelfth-century anonymous origin, *Adon Olam* (Lord of the World), to their own tradition of religious poetry, and particularly began to favor the poetics of *zemiroth* (carols) for the Sabbath.[8]

Most of the poetry was of anonymous sources, but among the known authors were several Iberian poet-bards: Moses ibn Ezra (ca.1070–1138), Abraham ibn Ezra (ca.1092–1167), Menahem ben Makhir (fl. 11th cent.), Mordecai ben Isaac (fl. 11th cent.), Solomon ibn Gabirol (1021–ca.1058), Yehudah Halevi, Judah ben Samuel ha-Levi (ca.1085–1145), Judah al-Harizi (d.1235), and Abraham Abulafia (1240–ca.1291). Yehudah Halevi, of Cordova and then Grenada, was a notable teacher-philosopher as well as literary figure. He wrote the *Kitab al Kuzari* (Writings to the Kuzari), a classical exposition on the essence of Judaism, originally written in Arabic for the King of the Khazars in Central Asia. Late in his life, Halevi embarked upon a pilgrimage to Jerusalem, dying on the way there in the Egyptian desert.[9]

By the sixteenth century, expulsion from the Iberian peninsula had shifted that flowering of religious mysticism and poetic spirituality to Safed in Palestine. Gathered there were Sephardic *hasidim* (pietists) inspired by the *Zohar* and *Kabbalah*, who highlighted and embellished upon celebration of the Jewish holidays, and especially upon the holiness of the Sabbath day as a foretaste of the messianic era.[10] Joseph Judah ben Ephraim Karo (1488–1575) was the leading intellectual figure among the pietists in Safed. His rabbinical writings included a masterful exposition on Judaic laws, *Shulkhan Arukh* (known as the table of custom). First issued in Safed in 1515, it attracted wide interest across Europe, and was published in Lublin in 1551. Karo was a charismatic *maggid* (preacher) who had many disciples in Safed, many of them *paytanim* (liturgical bards). It was Isaac Luria also known as "ha-Ari" (1534–1572) who introduced the concept of three special Sabbath repasts (*s'udoth*), at which festive poetry and song would enhance the pleasure (*oneg*) of the holy day. He first introduced the concept of the *dibbuk* (enjoining spirit), as well as the mystic essence of melody in prayer, in his treatise *Etz Khayim* (Tree of life). Luria's writings influenced the subsequent rise of Ashkenazic Hasidism (pietism) in eastern Europe. Solomon Halevi Alkabez (1505–1580), with his poem *L'kho dodi* (Come, my beloved), created the traditional serenade of welcome to the Sabbath as a bride-queen. That lovely concept was taken up, cultivated, and highlighted by the later Hasidic movement as a focal religious custom, in which the Sabbath day was concluded ceremonially with the *melaveh malkeh* (escorting away the bride-queen). Israel Najara (d. 1587) was not only a prodigious collector of the sacred poetry but also wrote a writer of some, including an Aramaic ode sung at the poetry but also wrote a writer of some, including an Aramaic ode sung at the Sabbath evening repast, *Yah ribon olam* (God, ruler of the world).

Early on, it became customary to create melodies as well as adapt known tunes for the singing of the poems, the texts of which often were bilingual, using Hebrew and some vernacular words. That music was pleasurably elaborated at Sabbath meals, but was entirely vocal. While there are no specific references to women's musical role, it may be assumed that women also participated domestically in this music and poetry of mystic piety. There was, however, a basic difference between pietistic musical expression in Safed and the later Hasidic movement in eastern Europe. For the bard-singers of Safed, the words of the text were of utmost significance in reaching out toward mystic devotional rapture. For the European Hasidic Jews, on the other hand, melody itself prevailed, and wordless singing brought one closest to the religious communion. The fact that hasidism could at times dispense entirely with text on behalf of spiritual expression, could detach prayer essence from language itself, remains a unique phenomenon in Judaism, which otherwise has been a religion historically bonded to the word.

NOTES

1. However, the dissident Judaic groups (Samaritans, Karaites, and Sabbateans) did not accept the principles of rabbinic Judaism, the Talmud, or the theological writings of Maimonides.

2. Ariel Bension, *The Zohar in Moslem and Christian Spain*, intro. by Denison Ross (New York: Hermon Press, 1974), p. 162. In addition, although some of its documentation is weak, the following publication offers an interesting treatment of the subject: Yehuday Ashlag, *An Entrance to the Zohar: The Key to the Portals of Jewish Mysticism*, ed. Philip A. Berg (New York: Research Centre of Kabbalah, 1974/1975).

3. James Moffatt, trans., *The Holy Bible* (New York: Harper, 1922), p. 600.

4. William Blake, *The Portable Blake*, ed. Alfred Kazin (New York: Viking Press, 1946), p. 644.

5. This translation is from David de Sola Pool, ed. and trans., *The Book of Prayer: According to the Custom of the Spanish and Portuguese Jews* (New York: Union of Sephardic Congregations, 1974), p. 54. A similar morning liturgical passage may be found in Ashkenazic prayer books as, for example, A. Theodore Philips, ed. and trans., *Daily Prayers* (New York: Hebrew Publishing, 1920), p. 79.

6. For further information on this period, see Max I. Margolis and Alexander Marx, *A History of the Jewish People* (Philadelphia: Jewish Publication Society of America, 1941).

7. In addition to the Holy Scriptures, the great classic works of rabbinical Judaism are:

Mishnah—a second century compilation and editing of Jewish Oral Law that has been attributed to a rabbinical leader of that era, Yehudah Hanasi.

Talmud—compiled between 200–500 C.E. by rabbis of the Babylonian Gaonate, in order to provide guidelines and values for Judaism. It consists of expositions upon the earlier *Mishnah* as well as *Gemarah* (commentary), which is further divided into *Halakhah* (doctrine), *Agadah* (narrative), and *midrashah* (homiletics).

Mishnah Torah—written by Moses Maimonides in the twelfth century. It is a significant compendium of interpretations of the Jewish laws and a guide to the living of a proper Jewish life.

8. There are many currently available collections of the poetic *zemiroth* (carols). The following offer especially fine samplings as well as informative annotations:

Herbert M. J. Loewe and Rose L. Henriques, comps. and arrs., *Mediaeval Hebrew Minstrelsy—Songs for the Bride Queen's Feast* (London: J. Clark, 1926).

Herman Mayerowitsch, comp. and arr., *Oneg Shabbat: Ancient Hebrew Table Songs, or Zemiroth* (London: E. Goldston, 1951).

Neil Levin and Velvel Pasternak, comps. and arrs., *Zemiroth Anthology: Traditional Sabbath Songs for the Home* (Cedarhurst, N.Y.: Tara Publications, 1981).

9. Yehudah Halevi's poem "Longing for Jerusalem" may be found in a translation from the Hebrew by the Sephardic-American poetess Emma Lazarus (1849–1887) in Leo W. Schwarz, comp. and ed., *A Golden Treasury of Jewish Literature* (New York: Rinehart, 1937), pp. 579–80.

10. Two good sources of further information on this topic are:

Perle S. Epstein, *Kabbalah: The Way of the Jewish Mystic* (Garden City, N.Y.: Doubleday, 1978).

Sheila A. Spector, *Jewish Mysticism: An Annotated Bibliography on the Kabbalah in English* (New York: Garland, 1984).

14

The Music of Hasidism: Melodies of Spiritual Ecstasy

The leading Jewish philosopher of modern times, Martin Buber (1878–1965), a profoundly religious man, wrote concerning the unique Hasidic musical experience: "The soul lays hold of the voice of a man and makes it sing what the soul has experienced in the heights, and the voice does not know what it does. Thus, one *tsaddik* (saintly man) stood in prayer during the High Holy Days and sang new melodies, wonder of wonders, that he had never heard and that no human ear had ever heard, and he did not know at all what he sang and in what ways he sang, for he was bound to the upper world, to the *Shekhina* (Divine Presence)."[1]

Mysticism and messianism pervaded Judaism during the sixteenth and seventeenth centuries, culminating in such self-proclaimed "messiahs" as Sabbatai Zevi of Smyrna (1626–1676) and Jacob Leibovicz Frank of Lemberg (d. 1791). Despite the social unrest and spiritual disillusion generated by such false pretenders, Jews throughout Europe clung to those hopes. As a result, rabbis feared for their congregants, not only in terms of religious faith but also for their safety in the face of hostile reactions by rulers of lands where they lived. At a rabbinical conference held in Brody in 1756, the rabbis from areas of greater Poland and Russia agreed that none of their students under the age of thirty should study the *Zohar* and *Kabbalah*, and then only after having mastered the Talmud.

In the midst of this spiritual turmoil, the movement of Hasidism arose, and by the end of the eighteenth century had spread among groups of pious Jews throughout eastern Europe. Its acknowledged founder who had studied the *Zohar*, was Rabbi Israel ben Eliezer Ba'al Shem Tov (1700–1760) of Podolia and Galicia. Known as Ba'al Shem Tov (the acronym B'ShT), Hebrew for "Master of Good Name," he preached a simple but ardent faith, emphasizing the attainment of spiritual ecstasy in joyful devotions, wherein music was an important form of religious expression. With melodies of *hasiduth* (piety), time would shrink, eternity disappear, and only the moment come alive for the Hasidim (pietists), in their oneness with *Shekhina* (Divine Presence). It was a prayerful search for the unfathomable God (*deus absconditus*) and the mystery of His Spirit. As this form of Jewish observance subsequently evolved, Hasidic *rebbes* (rabbinical leaders) encouraged their followers to join together in song and even in dance, so that music might blend with holy thoughts and enhance concentration upon communion with God. Moreover, worship in melody might likely achieve what worship in tears could not, and so the worshipper would not cry but rather sing his prayers with such intensity as though his soul might be prepared to expire.

For Hasidim, body motions became intrinsic to total concentration upon study as well as prayer. In an article on Hasidic religious customs, Louis Jacobs notes that: "Both the *Zohar* and Yehudah/Judah Halevi's *Kuzari* refer to the Jewish practice of swaying the body while studying the *Torah*, and it would appear the practice was also widespread in the Middle Ages of swaying during prayer."[2] Such bodily movement was spontaneous and unselfconscious, and *simkha* (exaltation) was expressed with *rikud* (dance). As a result, male dancing, or at least body motion, among *hasidim* was elevated to an expression of religious fervor, in reflection of biblical King David, who danced before the Holy Ark.

An important early Hasidic leader was Rabbi Nachman of Bratzlav (1772–1811), who advocated freely improvising liturgical chant and spinning holy *nigunim* (tunes). He took particular pleasure in creating new tunes, and urged that ordinary melodies be sought out and "rescued," or revised for sacred purposes. It was a form of musical adaptation that he termed *m'khadesh ha-nigun* (renewal of the tune). Other *rebbes*, such as Dov Baer of Mezeritsch, known as *ha-maggid* (the preacher), (1710–1772) and Levi Yitzkhok of Berditschev (1740–1810), created and sang special prayers and petitional dialogues with the Almighty. Schneor Zalman of Liadi (1747–1813), who founded the Lubavitcher sect of Hasidism, preached that musical talent is one of the greatest of God's gifts. Eventually, Hasidic wordless song—melody intoned without text—was felt to attain for the singer what might not be reached by words, a vocal meditation in partnership with mystical thought.

By the early nineteenth century, rabbinical courts of ardent followers had developed for particular *rebbes* and their versions of Hasidism. There were court *shuls* (synagogues), *yeshivas* (study academies), and favorite singers—*hazanim* (cantors) and *badkhonim* (poet-bards). Special new *nigunim* (tunes) in particular styles for various courts were learned, sung, and then disseminated by attendees at rabbinical *farbrengen* (gatherings). There were different "mood" melodies as spiritual preparation for prayer, study, and the contemplation of religious discourses. At the *se'udot* (meal gatherings) and festive celebrations for the Sabbath and holidays, congregations of devout adherents would join together in song.

What sort of music was this? Essentially, it was derived from prayer chant modes, cantillation motifs, and hymn themes, all of which were elaborated and embellished. Particular Psalm passages and religious texts were excerpted for the worded songs. In addition, folk songs of Jewish, and especially Slavic, origins were adapted and incorporated into that body of Hasidic melodies. For the dances, vigorous rhythms were added. This was a process of conscious addition, wherein peasant tunes, dances, and marches became Judaized. Music making was viewed as a universal quality of Hasidic life. *Klezmorim* (instrumentalists) often participated, though never at liturgical services. It was a male domain, and the women made their music entirely separately, even at weddings and other communal festivities.

In its full flowering at the turn of the nineteenth century, the Hasidic movement had over four million adherents in eastern Europe, among various sects located in Poland, Lithuania, Galicia-Austria, Hungary, Romania, Russia, and the Ukraine, and following a number of rabbinical family dynasties. There were two leading branches of Hasidism. One was Besht (*B'Sht*) whose various local dynasties claimed direct lineage from the Ba'al Shem Tov *rebbe* himself, and emphasized the mystic power of spontaneous creative improvisation for melodies of prayer and dance. The soul could not soar without melody. The other was Chabad (*khabad*), a Hebrew acronym meaning *khokhma* (wisdom), *bina* (insight), and *da-as* (knowledge). It was founded by Schneur Zalman of Liadi, whose dynastic sects evolved and practiced a series of six spiritual levels for their devotional song and dance: *hishtapkhut ha-nefesh* (outpouring of the soul), *hitorerut* (spiritual awakening), *hitpa-alut* (contemplation, insight), *d'veykut* (communion with the Almighty), *hitlahavut* (religious ecstasy), and *hitpashtut ha-gashmiyut* (soul as disembodied spirit). Mystic ascent could be achieved through stages of melody. Moreover, melodic configurations were set aside for each of the four realms of the universe, as noted in the *Zohar*: *bri-ah* (inanimate matter); *yetsirah* (living things); *asiyah* (mankind); and, *atsilut* (heavenly spheres).[3]

It was inevitable that the Hasidic concept of sanctification of melody would affect general Ashkenazic liturgical services in eastern Europe. Among influential changes were a freeing up of cantorial styles, with the rise of "artiste" cantors who could create melodies and improvise elaborations upon traditional chants. Congregants began to take part more actively in hymnology at services. Jewish folk songs also drew inspiration from the Hasidic *nigunim*. Religious tunes of the domestic celebrations for Sabbath and festivals were enhanced by wider melodic scope. Despite determined efforts of *mithnagdim* (opponents) led by strict rabbinical theologians, Hasidism's ideas, with its emphasis upon music and joy in religious experience, entered the mainstream of eastern European Jewish life, and pervaded the folklore and culture with essences of messianic fervor and spiritual renewal. Two important developments arising in the late nineteenth century took their impetus from that Hasidic emotional fervor: *haskalah* (enlightenment), which sought the modernization intellectually and culturally of the Jewish people, and *va-ad Zion* (Zionism), which sought reestablishment of *Erets Yisrael* (Land of Israel), the ancient Jewish homeland. Both movements utilized songs to imbue people with hope and faith. The idea of Jewish music making as *mitzvah* (holy duty), became fixed in the customs of all eastern European Jewry.

Among the newer Jewish folk songs, a genre arose as an expression of protest to Hasidism. The opponents were lead by intellectuals and doctrinal rabbis who perceived extremist elements of pantheism and mysticism in Hasidic practices, notably in the "miracles" of *rebbes* and their devoted emphasis upon particular "regal" rabbinical lineages. Originally created and sung by those *mithnagdim*, the songs parodied the Hasidic *nigunim*, imitating the musical styles and adding satiric texts. Many of those parodies were widely sung, and became popular for their own vitality and happy tunes. By the twentieth century, people often could not distinguish between the two types of songs, those for and those against Hasidism, and sang them all without taking sides, or even caring either way.

The Holocaust destroyed Hasidic dynasties and their courts, and the movement itself was essentially gone from the European areas where it once had flourished. Surviving leaders and followers resettled for the most part in North America, and to a lesser degree in the State of Israel.[4] However, the qualities of Hasidic song remain in Zionist and Yiddish folk songs, and also in resonances from the heyday of Yiddish American theater music. One of the most widely recognized of Hebrew folk songs, *Hava Nagilah* (Let us be merry) was originally a favored tune at the Hasidic court of the *rebbe* in Sadigora.

Abraham Zvi Idelsohn, father of modern Jewish musicology, considered Hasidic music as a wellspring of Judaic spiritual expression. The nigunim (tunes) blended into the folksongs of European Jewry for over two hundred years, and well into the twentieth century supplied rich melodic source materials for the people. At its best, it was a folk musical expression on an exalted level. Although much of that heritage, along with other cultural aspects of European Jewry, may no longer be viable, research and collection have enabled publication of many fine examples of this music now available for study and performance.[5] For example, followers of the Chabad Hasidic sect residing in the United States have begun to compile and annotate collections of their own special *nigunim*. Hasidic spiritual tunes remain as unique examples of folk creativity preserved and transmitted orally, an artistry inspired by religious fervor and performed in order to reach out to the infinite Almighty.

NOTES

1. Martin Buber, *Hasidism and Modern Man*, trans. Maurice Friedman (New York: Harper & Row, 1958), p. 79.

2. Louis Jacobs, "Chap. 10: Hasidic Prayer," in *Essential Papers on Hasidism: Origins to Present*, ed. Gershon David Hundert (New York: New York University

Press, 1991), p. 346. There are fourteen articles in this collection of scholarly studies treating Hasidism. Among the array of other authors are Martin Buber, Simon Dubnow, Solomon Maimon, and Gershom Scholem.

3. For a technical discussion of this music, see Ellen Gilbert Koskoff, "The Concept of Nigun Among Lubavitcher Hasidim in the United States," (unpublished thesis, University of Pittsburgh, 1976, available on microfiche [University Microfilms international]).

4. Additional information on the sects of Hasidism and their groups in more recent times may be found in Harry M. Rabinowicz, *Hasidism: The Movement and Its Masters* (Northvale, N.J.: J. Aronson, 1988). This book has an extensive bibliography on the subject.

5. See the following collections:

Abraham Z. Idelsohn, comp. and ed., *Thesaurus of Oriental Hebrew Melodies*, Vol. 10, *Songs of the Hasidim* (reprint. ed., New York: Ktav, 1973).

Joachim Stutschewsky, comp. and ed., *Chassidic Melodies* (Tel Aviv: Israel Culture and Education Department, 1950).

15

Collections of Hasidic Music

The Anthology of Jewish Music, compiled and edited by composer and conductor Chemjo Vinaver (1900–1973), was a notable achievement.[1] For many years, Vinaver's choral groups had afforded concert audiences in American cities a unique Jewish musical experience. The programs were not only of impressive quality but were inspirational and, to many Jewish musicians, quite challenging. With great skill and sincere dedication, he presented choral arrangements of liturgical and Hasidic selections, many for the first time on any public stage.

In culmination of that long and busy career, Vinaver prepared a book reflecting in print his lifelong zeal for Jewish music, and notably highlighting melodies of Hasidism. Fortunately, he was both a scholar and musician, with a respectful understanding of Judaic folk and cultural traditions. As a result, by notating and documenting oral sources and gathering and editing manuscripts, Vinaver managed to assemble a body of previously unpublished and unrecorded choral and solo works. He then endeavored to present that music in its own authentic style, as the best examples of what he considered to be an abiding and still viable legacy from the Old World of eastern Europe.

Chemjo Vinaver was born in Warsaw to a devoutly Hasidic family that traced its lineage to the Lithuanian-Polish *Vorke rebbe* and a branch of the *Chabad* sect. By the time that he emigrated to America in 1938, Vinaver had achieved early professional success in Europe as a choral conductor and composer-arranger, and was active in sacred as well as secular musical performances. His main liturgical connections had been with several Hasidic courts in eastern Europe. In America, Vinaver was associated with synagogue choirs and several cantorial artists, and in 1969 he settled in Israel, where he died. The great storehouse of his musical gatherings are presently housed as the Chemjo Vinaver Archives at the Jewish National and University Library of Hebrew University in Jerusalem. A posthumously prepared collection of materials from that collection was issued in 1983.[2]

Vinaver's own *Anthology*, issued in 1955, includes his commentaries and annotations for the selections, along with English translations of the Hebrew texts. His informative introductory essay (presented in Hebrew as well as English) cogently describes the scope of contents and objectives of the collection. His intent was to present the music as a living, rather than resurrected, art form; many of those selections merit general concert performances. The book consists of two main sections. The first covers sacred liturgy, encompassing scriptural cantillations in Hasidic style, prayer chants in choral (all-male) arrangements, and musical settings of Psalms. Included are Vinaver's arrangements of cantorial solos with chorus, in a style reminiscent of the old Hasidic *shul* (synagogue) services. There are rediscovered examples of nineteenth-century eastern European *shtetl* (town) liturgy. Among the selections are works for the High Holy Days by Moses Milner (1886–1953) and Pinchos Minkowsky (1859–1924), both celebrated liturgist-composers.

It is important to remember that true four-part choral singing was not traditional for the liturgy of eastern Europe. The cantor and chorus were male only, and instrumentation was forbidden. Where the voices assumed distinctive, though limited, harmonious parts, the bass was carried by an adult chorister echoing the tenor cantor. Passages for soprano and alto were intoned by young choirboys, whose immature voices often had phenomenally high ranges. At a Hasidic court *shul*, the congregants generally participated along with the choir. Although Vinaver's arrangements creatively reflect all those customary strictures, the musical writing is so secure that those works may be effectively performed by mixed singing groups and still retain their original traditional qualities.

Interestingly, Vinaver included an all-male quartet by the American composer Frederick Jacobi (1891–1952). Written in 1942, it is an excerpt from the hymn *Teyfen l'hakshiv* (Turn to heed). The setting is modern and the strict prayer chant (*nusakh*) has been forsaken. Yet the work is entirely devotional in character, reaching a compelling musical climax and admirably fitting a liturgical text that is more than a thousand years old. This musical section is rounded out with some lovely settings for Psalm 24 ("Unto Thee, O Lord, do I lift up my soul"), Psalm 126 ("When the Lord brought back those that returned to Zion"), and Psalm 130 ("Out of the depths, I have called to Thee, O Lord"). Psalm 130 is presented in two sharply contrasting settings: first, as Vinaver's notation of a Hasidic melody, and second, as a composition for chorus by Arnold Schoenberg (1874–1951). The composer wrote it in 1951, in response to a request by Vinaver, who had sent Schoenberg a copy of the Hasidic version to serve as a musical basis. The work is intriguing, as the voices alternately sing and declaim. It is a remarkable musical exercise by a great modern composer, crafted in reference to a Jewish spiritual theme, a *nigun*.

The second section of Vinaver's book presents various examples of Jewish table-carols or spirituals (*zemiroth*) and Hasidic melodies (*nigunim*), which he collected and notated in simple vocal lines. The Jewish folk songs of religious character had their origins during the Middle Ages, similar to Christmas carols. At that time, both forms of carols were extraliturgical songs linked to festive celebrations. Those melodies had been popularized by the traveling minstrels, who brought that music to many geographical areas. Soon, however, their respective literary references and musical styles took on widely different patterns as a result of the increasing divergence of cultural outlook and theological expression between Jews and Christians. The *zemiroth*, based upon medieval poetry of great piety, became closely tied to the Sabbath and to domestic observances of Jewish religious traditions. The formative leaders of the Hasidic movement assigned special significance to songs at the Sabbath meals, and shaped the poetry and melodies to reflect their philosophy. Particular Hasidic table carols were sung and cherished over generations in numerous places. Vinaver chose a good sampling from that legacy.

To complete the second section of his book, Vinaver edited a group of textless, or wordless, Hasidic melodies and some dance tunes. Some have been attributed to the Ba'al Shem Tov and other revered Hasidic leaders, and others are tunes from Vinaver's own Vorke-Chabad sect rounded out with a madrigal arrangement based upon some of the Vorke melodic fragments. The music collection concludes with a musical tribute to lost European Jewry. It is a choral selection by Warsaw ghetto martyr David Eisenstadt (d. 1943), who had thematically elaborated a popular Hasidic melody known as *ha-Rav's nigun* (The rabbi's tune). for this publication, Vinaver rearranged Eisenstadt's work for mixed voices (SATB), rather than the original all-male version, likely intending it for subsequent performances at concert halls in America, Israel, and even Europe. Indeed, this is an apt final selection, because adherents of Hasidism believe that from every ending, there arises a new beginning.

Almost twenty years after Chemjo Vinaver's publication first appeared, another dedicated collector and arranger of Hasidic music, Velvel Pasternak, began to publish melodies gathered from different viably active sects resident in the United States and Canada. Musically knowledgeable and keenly aware of the customs and practices of the American *Hasidim*, Pasternak has endeavored to make a great many of these otherwise orally transmitted tunes available to the general public. As notator-editor as well as publisher, he has shaped his music collections into practical performance resources.[3] For the six collections issued, the vocal lines have been clearly defined; there are chord indications, transliterated song texts, and some brief informative annotations. Clearly, the books primarily function as songsters.

Although Pasternak's Hasidic collections are not scholarly works, they constitute comprehensive sources for this musical genre. The contents overlap from book to book, and the quality of the materials varies widely. Included are wordless as well as textual tunes, and in many cases there are connections to the various Hasidic dances. In his annotational remarks, Pasternak has endeavored to place into proper perspective the musical differences between authentic Hasidic melodies and those tune parodies which in many cases have passed into general recognition as "Hasidic" folk songs.

Granted that much of this area of Jewish folk song may be naïvely constructed and melodically derivative, it nevertheless remains a singular folk art delineated by a philosophic purpose. This music was created to serve a religious revival, to inspirit an impoverished portion of society during a century when European political and social humanitarianism did not extend to consideration of the Jews. Hasidism, with its music, went straight to the heart of the matter. And the honest fervor of that melodic expression has vitally influenced creative Jewish musical expression, secular and sacred, folk and art, into the concluding years of the twentieth century, and likely will influence it well beyond, into the future.

NOTES

1. Chemjo Vinaver, comp. and ed., *Anthology of Jewish Music: Sacred Chant and Religious Folksong of the East European Jews* (New York: Edward B. Marks Music, 1955).

2. Elihu Schleifer, comp. and ed., *Anthology of Hasidic Music: Chemjo Vinaver* (Jerusalem: Magnes Press and Hebrew University, 1983).

3. Velvel Pasternak, comp. and ed. (Cedarhurst, N.Y.: Tara Publications):

Songs of the Hasidim: An Anthology, vols. 1 and 2 (1968 and 1971).

Hasidic Favorites (1972).

Rejoice: Songs in Modern Hasidic Style (1973).

Hasidic-Style Songs of the 1970s (1975).

Hasidic Hits (1977).

Part V

The Yiddish Musical World of Eastern Europe

16

Music and Yiddish

The art of music has been celebrated as a language, a vehicle of human communication par excellence, transmitting ideas as well as cultures and reflecting periods in history. Scholars concerned with music as an intellectual as well as artistic discipline have verified the dynamic role of music-language as historical documentation, the trackings of civilization. The study of music may properly provide a significant view of the history of mankind. In nineteenth- century Europe, along with rising concepts of political, economic, and social nationalism, there was a movement for musical nationalism and an intensification of interest among musicians for the folk songs and indigenous cultures of their native countries.

Particularly for Jewish history, cultural expression over centuries of Diaspora life had created the very folk essence that territorial nationalism had held for other peoples. Jewish music, in particular, became a mirror of Jewish life everywhere in the world and also a significant factor in Jewish identity and continuity. There once was a time when the Yiddish language and culture, notably its folklore and folk songs, were vital to European Jewry. Like *Judezmo*, or Ladino, for Sephardic Jews, *Juedisch,* or Yiddish, had evolved over a thousand years into an endeared vernacular language for Ashkenazic Jews. It became especially important to Jews who, by the early fourteenth century, had begun to settle in the Slavic areas of eastern Europe. There, as the secular voice of Judaism, Yiddish developed distinctive customs, folklore, literature, and music. In 1908, an international conference on the Yiddish language was held in the city of Czernowitz, then part of the Austro-Hungarian Empire. Recognition was sought for Yiddish as a modern literary and national language, beyond merely a folk tongue of Judaism. Conferees claimed that Yiddish had the right to a legitimate place among the languages of the world, and that it constituted a vital means of ethnic linkage for Jews everywhere.

In his book on the various linguistic branchings of the German language, William B. Lockwood has ably summarized the distinctive odyssey of the Yiddish language in Europe.

It is estimated that in 1939 between ten and twelve million people spoke Yiddish, of whom more than two-thirds lived in Eastern Europe. But after the catastrophe that overwhelmed Eastern Jewry in World War II. these figures and the outlook for Yiddish have been radically changed. Of some six million done to death. a good majority were Yiddish speakers, and the survivors have mostly left Eastern Europe. Brought almost to the verge of extinction in the areas that nurtured it as a primary medium, Yiddish now faces rapid decline. for linguistic assimilation is today nearly everywhere the rule. The largest Jewish populations are now in the Soviet Union and the United States. The Russian Jews seem to have largely abandoned Yiddish, while in America the younger generation has gone over to English either exclusively or as the main medium. In Israel, only Hebrew is recognized as the official language, so that Yiddish seems destined to disappear there as well in a couple of generations or so.[1]

At the approach of the twenty-first century, only two general groups remain actively interested in Yiddish: those who for various reasons never severed their connection with the language, among them notably members of Hasidic sects resident in the United States and Israel, and a small but active group of newcomers to Yiddish, who are either in personal quest for an earlier European heritage or, more likely, are scholars investigating this important ethnosociological portion of Jewish history. In addition, there still is a sustained general interest in Yiddish folk songs, and therefore a number of studies, collections, and books have been published in America and abroad.[2]

The topical range of Yiddish folk songs covered all aspects of human life as it was lived from birth through death, encompassing childhood, courtship, family, livelihood, and religious observances. Though usually brief in poetic text, the songs were always of deeply emotional nature with an underlying Judaic component. Melodies were rooted in the age-old mystique of Jewish musical expression, and resonated with sacred chant and secular tunes. Their lyrics bespoke both eternity and immediacy, and reflected the communal as well as personal concerns of survival, encompassing economic, social, and political woes. When new ideas and movements began to transform Jewish life in nineteenth-century eastern Europe, there was a ready voice in Yiddish songs about mounting tsarist oppression, migrations westward and to America, the emergent Zionist movement, secularism in conflict with strict rabbinical tradition, and the desperate yearning for cultural enrichment and intellectual fulfillment without the restrictions of prejudice. Created by gifted popular entertainers, though more often of anonymous origin, those songs and poetics were forthright, and reached out more widely than did most published journals and public figures. The medium of music became a messenger of change.

Any consideration of the Yiddish musical heritage, of course, is overshadowed by the Holocaust. In an important sense, the destruction spread beyond Europe, depriving Yiddish culture everywhere else of its historic continuity and artistic nourishment. Elements of an earlier "golden age" of flourishing American Yiddish theatrical artistry have all but been absorbed in the mainstream American entertainment scene. Nevertheless, important creative ingredients of that eastern European melodic treasury have survived, and not only in song compilations or because of dedicated efforts by the new Yiddishists. What remains to inspire Jewish musical expression into the twenty-first century is best explained by Hasidism, which teaches that life is impoverished without music. The poet-singer is the voice of the people, and with songs the soul reaches out to the Almighty. And, of course, Jewish music is the voice of Jewish history.

NOTES

1. William Burley Lockwood, *An Informal History of the German Language: With Chapters on Dutch, Afrikaans, Frisian, and Yiddish* (London: Andre Deutsch, 1965), p. 237.

2. Most general collections of Jewish songs include Yiddish materials. The following are comprehensive resource compilations:

Sussman Kisselgof, Alexander Zhitomirski, and Pesach Lvov, comps. and eds., *Lider Sammelbuch* (Song collection) (Berlin: Juwal, 1923).

Sarah P. Schack and Ethel S. Cohen, comps. and eds., *Yiddish Folksongs,* New York: Bloch Publishing, 1924.

Moisei Beregovskii and Itzik Feffer, comps. and eds., *Yiddisher Folkslider* (Yiddish folk songs) (Moscow/Kiev: Meluche Ukrainishe Natsion, 1938).

Yehudah Leyb Cahan, comp. and ed., *Yiddishe Folkslider Mit Melodien* (Yiddish folk songs with melodies) (New York: YIVO, 1957).

Ruth Rubin, comp. and ed., *Voices of a People: The Story of Yiddish Folksong* (New York: McGraw-Hill, 1973).

Eleanor G. Mlotek, comp. and ed., *Mir Trogn a Gezang* (We carry a tune) (New York: Workmen's Circle, 1977).

17

Yiddish Musical Theater: Its Origins in Europe

The phenomenon known as Yiddish musical theater was crafted out of Jewish traditions that date back to the Talmudic era: *badkhonus*, or Jewish folk minstrelsy, and *purimshpil* (*Purim* play), or holiday celebration with songs, stories, and pageantry. Cast in the varied vernaculars of the various Diaspora communities, those forms of entertainment took on many qualities from their local environments. Over the centuries, many poetic and musical ideas were exchanged between Jewish and non-Jewish entertainers. Especially during the Renaissance, *Purim* presentations among Ashkenazic Jews began to be shaped as *commedia dell'arte*, a form of structured story line with improvised dialogue and music. The artistries of *badkh'n* (minstrel) and *purimshpiler* (*Purim* player) flourished particularly well in eastern Europe, and during the nineteenth century those types of Jewish performers achieved great popularity among the people in small towns and rural hamlets.

Avrum Goldinfodim (Abraham Goldfaden) was born in 1840, in the city of Altkonstantin, Volhynia, Imperial Russia.[1] His father, Khayim Lipeh, was a watchmaker, and he called his son *Avrumeleh badkh'n* because the little boy liked to sing and recite poems. He sent him to a tsarist public school so that he would not be taken away by the Russian army. It was a general practice for the authorities to gather up Jewish male children, often taking them far from their families to be kept in service for decades. In 1857, Goldfaden went to study at a government-endorsed rabbinical seminary in Zhitomir, Ukraine. By that time, he already had performed at local weddings and knew songs and poems by such well-known eastern European folk entertainers as Mark Warshawsky (1845–1907), Velveleh Zbarzher (1826–1883), and Berl Broder (1817–1880). As a student in Zhitomir, he was exposed to Hebrew and Yiddish literature along with liturgical chants and religious folk songs. He learned to write poetry, stories, and songs reflecting that treasury of Jewish culture. Under the direction of Hayim Selig Slonimsky (fl. 19th cent.), that rabbinical academy was a rather worldly institution. Among the teachers were Abraham Ber Gottlober (1810–1899) and Menashe Margolis (fl. 19th cent.), all advocates of *haskalah* (enlightenment), the nineteenth-century Jewish modernist movement. The school was a nest of writers and would-be writers, perilously labeled as *apikorism* (lapsed ones), renegades from strict religious observances. Zhitomir city itself was cosmopolitan, with theaters for Russian-Ukrainian as well as French and Italian drama, music, and dance. Goldfaden, with a new friend, fellow student Yitskhok Joel Linetzky (1839–1916), began to thrive in this environment.

Goldfaden had no formal musical training but possessed a good ear and reliable memory, and early on he learned how to avail himself of the skills of those who could notate his tunes. In 1862, Slonimsky married a highly educated Jewish woman from Warsaw, and she brought to the academy a manuscript copy of the play *Serkele* by Solomon Ettinger (1803–1856). Goldfaden worked with her to arrange a public performance, assisting in the staging and direction and himself playing the female role of Serkele. It was a formative experience that shaped the rest of his life.

At that time, Goldfaden also began to write for Hebrew and Yiddish journals. In 1865, he published a collection of his Hebrew poems, *Tsitsim U'ferakhim* (Blossoms and flowers), dedicated to his father. The following year, he issued his Yiddish poetic materials in a volume entitled *Dos Yideleh* (The little Jew), with this dedication to his father and mother: "Dear parents, you have done so much for me. With what can I repay you? Poor as I am, the pen is my wealth. Weak as I am, my poems are strong. From my whole heart, I give you this gift of my ideas. Your son, Avrum." That collection included a didactic piece, *Dos pinteleh Yid* (The essence of being a Jew). Excerpts from that poem were set by Goldfaden to an old Yiddish folk melody, and later in America it was the very song featured in Jacob Gordin's (1853–1909) powerful drama, *Gott, mensh un toyfel* (God, man and devil), or the Jewish Faust. Also included in Goldfaden's early collection was a satirical Sabbath song that he had composed at the Zhitomir academy. It soon became popular among students at other *yeshivoth* (seminaries), who added other verses, some in parody of Hasidic ideas. Goldfaden's poem paraphrased the *havdalah* (prayer concluding the Sabbath day): "Light the *havdalah* braided candle, hold the incense box aloft, say the prayers, and sip the ceremonial wine. Then, begin a week-long struggle to fill your pockets. Alas, if you cannot earn a livelihood, you cannot live. I know this for a fact." To sing it, Goldfaden adapted traditional *havdalah* chant motifs. Subsequently, it was published in Europe and America as an anonymous folk song.

Upon graduation from the academy in 1866, Goldfaden was sent to teach in Simferopol. However, he soon left for Odessa at the invitation of an uncle, Yidel Keselman, whose prosperous household had a piano. Goldfaden took advantage of the opportunities to have his cousins play and write down his growing repertoire of songs and poems. While there, he tutored students, performed as a *badkh'n*, and attended general theatricals and concerts. He also was involved in private performances of Yiddish works, including Israel Aksenfeld's (1787–1866) play *Di Rekruten* (The recruits). In 1869, Goldfaden published a companion volume to his earlier Yiddish collection, this time entitled *Dos Yideneh* (The little Jewess). In addition to songs, it had texts for two of his playlets: *Tsvey Sh'khinos* (Two female neighbors), and *Di Mumeh Susyeh* (The aunt Susyeh [Susie]). That year, he met and married Paulina (Pereleh) Werbel, daughter of the noted Hebraist Eliyahu Mordechai Werbel (1806–1880). Through his early publications, Goldfaden began to achieve recognition, and his works were taken up and performed by other entertainers. With his friend Linetzky, he wrote for Jewish papers under the pseudonym of "Yisrolik," and in 1871 they tried to publish a Yiddish literary magazine, but were unsuccessful.

In 1875, Goldfaden traveled to Lemberg, Galicia, with the purpose of studying medicine. However, he soon abandoned that idea in favor of performing and writing, along with efforts at establishing a newspaper called *Yisrolikel* (Little Israel). The next year, he went on to Tschernowitz in Bukovina, where another of his publishing enterprises, *Israelitishe Folks Blatt* (Israelite folk folio) failed. By 1876, he had made his way to Iasi, Romania, then the commercial crossroads between three European empires—Russia, Austria-Hungary, and Turkey. Sometime before his death, Goldfaden wrote some memoirs in which he reflected upon that turning point in his life:

The Jewish public used to be entertained by certain types of singer-jesters who performed their songs in wine cellars and coffee houses. They also used my songs, which became very popular. One time, while I was listening to these singers, the idea came into my mind that I should combine those songs of mine with spoken words and thereby make a theatrical piece. I immediately set to work, and in this manner during *Sukkoth* (Feast of Tabernacles) holiday, I laid the cornerstone of the Jewish theater. My heart was filled with pain to see my people in a low state of spiritual development. I realized that they were utterly ignorant of the holy spark of their peoplehood. So far, I had tried to infuse it into their hearts by means of my songs. The people needed a school. They needed to understand their own life and that of our people. They needed a means by which to truly understand their traditions. Historic pieces should be given before their eyes, so that they can learn their background, and find out who they really were.

I came to Iasi in Romania from the big world, very well acquainted with the classics of literature, drama, and opera. I already had known of Shakespeare, Ibsen, Molière, Goethe, and Lessing. I already had heard the operas of Meyerbeer, Halévy, and Verdi. I already had listened to the greatest singers and actors perform. Jewish history and literature were also well in my mind, and opened a new way before me. My head was filled with subjects like Joseph and his brothers, King David and King Solomon, the heroic Maccabees and Bar Kokhba, the wise Rabbi Akiva, the poet Yehudah Halevi, and so many others. However, to reach the people I first had to descend from my high thoughts, by necessity using themes like *Ni-ben-ni-meh* [Tra-la-la], the comic fool

Shmendrig, and other such. I had to ignore my antagonists, who pointed to those works as proof that I lacked the knowledge of better subjects.[2]

In this respect, Goldfaden adopted the concept of the theater as a school whose presentations afforded educational opportunities for the audiences by means of humanized role models and ethical lessons. The ancient Greeks had viewed drama as true education and not as mere entertainment. Early on, rabbinical sages had abjured idle leisure pastimes in favor of the didactic and enriching experiences that could provide a learning process throughout life. With Goldfaden as its ideological father, the unique modern Yiddish theater was born during *Sukkoth-Simkhas Torah* (Festival of Tabernacles-Celebration of the Bible) in September 1876, with a presentation at Shimon Marek's (fl. 19th cent.) *Pomel Verda* (Green Tree) wine garden in Iasi.

When Goldfaden came to Iasi in 1876, he met a Yiddish entertainer named Yisroel Grodner (1841–1887), who happened to be using his songs and poetics, along with works by Eliakum Zunser (1840–1913) and other Yiddish minstrels, for his own presentations. Grodner was particularly skillful at utilizing costumes and props. His performances always included songs and ended with a little dance, even if the material was sad or dramatic. Goldfaden put aside efforts at starting yet another newspaper and began to collaborate with Grodner. Their first formal production at the wine garden received a warm response, thereby launching the theatricals. Goldfaden soon added more music and a violin, as well as a stronger story line with dialogue. For a time, his friend Linetzky was also in Iasi, and he encouraged Goldfaden to pursue this new venture.

Grodner's specialty was a parody character that he called *freylikher husid'l* (merry little *hasid* or pietist), for which Goldfaden wrote variants of his earlier poems and songs. The pair soon took on a young man, Sacher Goldstein (1860–1911?)) who played the female roles. Goldfaden realized that he needed a larger cast in order to perform his playlets, especially a new set piece, *Di kats un dem brunem* (The cat and the well), based upon a story by his father-in-law, Werbel. That dramatic idea later became the basis for Goldfaden's famous operetta *Shulamith*. Unfortunately, bad winter weather halted those early performances, which were held outdoors or in cold indoor rooms. Then the fledgling troupe traveled to Galatz, another Romanian town, where Goldfaden was able to improvise a tiny theater in the coffee room of a hotel, complete with a little stage and some scenery. He developed a form of vaudeville presentation that he called *Dos bintel holts* (The bundle of wood). One evening, a girl of sixteen approached Goldfaden and asked to join the troupe. Because her mother was concerned about her virtue, Goldfaden arranged to have her marry their male juvenile, Sacher Goldstein. Thus, Sureh Segal became an actress named Sarah Goldstein, and later was known as the famous soubrette Sophie Karp (1861–1906), who in 1896 introduced the dramatic ballad *Eili, Eili* (My God, my God) on a Bowery stage in New York City.[3] Starting her career with Goldfaden,

Karp's first role was as a wordless heroine in his playlet *Di shtumeh kalleh* (The silent, or mute, bride).

While in Galatz, the struggling Yiddish theater was favorably reviewed in a Romanian newspaper. After Passover 1877, the troupe all traveled on to Bucharest. War had broken out between Russia and Turkey. Romania became an important source of provisions for the Russian army, with Bucharest as a military supply center, and soon its people prospered. As a result, Goldfaden's troupe began to thrive, and even acquired its own little theater hall. In that city, there was a large synagogue with a full male choir assisting the cantor, following the elaborate liturgical style of Vienna's Cantor Salomon Sulzer (1804–1890). At that time, music reading and notation skill was not a general accomplishment among traditional cantors. As a result, choristers were expected not only to have good voices, but also be able to memorize the special compositions of their cantors. Goldfaden realized that he would need such musical talents for his theatrical works. He attended that synagogue's services and induced three of the choristers to sing at his performances. Among them was Zelig Mogilevsky, soon known as Sigmund Mogulesco (?1856/8–1914), who had also managed to sing in the chorus of the local opera house. Initially, Mogulesco played secondary support and female parts. For his first star role, Goldfaden adapted a then-popular Romanian folk sketch, *Vladuku mamu* (Mama's little Vlad) into a Yiddish production, *Shmendrig* (the name of the comic hero), which was an immediate success. He followed this with an early version of *Di tsvey Kuni-Lemel* (The two [boys] named Kuni-Lemel), another good vehicle for the rapidly developing stage presence of Mogulesco. Yisroel Grodner left Goldfaden and formed his own acting company, and not too long afterwards managed to lure Mogulesco away. By that time, Grodner had also enlisted his own writers, Joseph Lateiner (1853–1935) and Moshe Horowitz (ca.1850–1910), both of whom subsequently emigrated to America; from 1886 onward they were actively creating Yiddish theatricals in New York City. Meanwhile, Grodner had resettled in London, where he died.

Sigmund Mogulesco rapidly became a great favorite, versatile as a singer, actor, mime, dancer, and also as a prolific creator of his own materials. He traveled first to London and then, in 1886, to New York, where he achieved great success and was lauded as the Yiddish Offenbach. Mogulesco's numerous stage works, shaped in association with various scenario writers, included *Dovid's fideleh* (David's fiddle), *Homon der tsvayter* (The second Haman), *Di sheyne Miriam* (The lovely Miriam), *Di akeyda* (The binding), *Degel makhaneh Yehudah* (Banner of the Judah encampment), and *Blihmeleh* (Little blossom), in which his famous wedding ode, *Khoson kalleh mazel tov* (Bridegroom and bride, good luck) was introduced.[4] Throughout his career, Sigmund Mogulesco continued to play characters that were versions of his original roles in the early Goldfaden productions.

The idea of Yiddish theater, by this time, had spread widely and was imitated by many other itinerant eastern European Jewish entertainers. Goldfaden took his troupe back to Galatz, where they flourished for a time, until the Russo-Turkish War ended. Then, at Passover 1879, he returned to Odessa with a theatrical troupe enlarged with a retinue of actors, musicians, choristers, and their families. That season, they performed augmented versions of his "operas" *Shmendrig* and *Kuni-Lemel*, in which he already showed a distinctive creative style of blending different musical ingredients—liturgical chants, adapted Jewish and Slavic folk melodies, Hasidic tunes, and borrowed themes—to highlight his poetic lyrics and dramatic story ideas. The next year, Goldfaden successfully introduced a new work, *Di kishifmakherin* (The sorceress), about a Yiddish Cinderella.[5] With this work, Goldfaden's concept of Yiddish musical theater had truly come into its own: a regular theater stage with scenery and costumes; a scenario with fixed dialogue; solos, choruses, dances, and musical interludes; and versatile and trained male as well as female performers. His fame spread throughout eastern Europe, and articles were written about him and his theatrical ideas in the Russian as well as Yiddish journals. However, Goldfaden realized that a growing number of other entertainers and writers were imitating, indeed copying, his works. Even his brother Naftuli had tried to start his own acting troupe!

Goldfaden felt justified in calling his musical theatricals "operas" or "operettas." Before the performances of his works, he began to present introductory lectures before the performances of his works, in which he told the audiences that songs constituted a dominating element in these dramatic works and that without songs, it simply was not Jewish theater. Consequently, all of his actors had to sing, and to sing well! It was those musical qualities that early on bridged the linguistic gap and attracted non-Jewish audiences. His works, as each in turn were introduced to the public, reflected in their narratives much about the people in that area of Europe, their historical traditions and cultural customs, their struggles and aspirations. Often the issues were universal, general, rather than only Jewish, offering theater as the societal documentation of a particular time and place. In every sense, he spoke to the situation of Ashkenazic Jews living in eastern Europe during the final decades of the nineteenth century.

The lifetime creativity of Abraham Goldfaden may be placed into three categories: (1) the early materials before he returned with his troupe to Odessa; (2) the fruits of his great era of success, from 1879 to 1883; and (3) the works he shaped during the aftermath years of bitter personal and artistic struggle. During the first period of Goldfaden's theatricals, he experimented by developing materials he had originally collected and published between 1866 and 1869. With extended dialogue and songs, he shaped skits and little scenes first into set pieces and then into such playlets as: *Di tsvey sh'khinos* (The two female neighbors), *Di mumeh Susyeh* (The aunt Susyeh), *Ni beh ni meh, oder Kamf tsvishen bildung un fantasie* (Tra-la-la, or conflict between idea and fantasy), *Der bintel holts, oder a Glas vaser* (The bundle of wood, or a glass of water), *Di shtumeh kalleh* (The silent, or mute bride), *Di rekruten* (The recruits), *Di tsvey toybeh* (The two deaf ones), *Di bobeh mit'n eynikel* (The grandmother with the grandchild), and *Der leybedigeh toyter* (The lively corpse). Then, in more structured form, came *Shmendrig* (the hero's name), the story of a pampered ninny whose marriage was being arranged by his mother; *Di beydeh Kuni-Lemel* (The two Kuni-Lemel), a satire on the self-importance of *yikhus* (family lineage), concluding with the triumph of true love; and *Brayndeleh khozak* (Brayndeleh, the strong), adapting some popular Ukrainian folk themes.

Goldfaden's most significant works were created during the singular period of his life, 1879–1883, in which he enjoyed personal success and led a thriving theatrical troupe. Those were the years, in Odessa and on tour in areas of Russia and the Ukraine, when he wrote and presented to the public such works as: *Di kishifmakherin, oder Di tsoyberin* (The witch, or the sorceress), the story of a Jewish Cinderella; *Shulamith, oder bas Yerusholayim* (Shulamith, or daughter of Jerusalem), a romance set in Jerusalem during the era of the Second Jewish Commonwealth; *Dr. Almasada, oder di Yiden in Palerma* (Dr. Almasada, or the Jews in Palermo), based on historical events during the fourteenth century; *Bar Kokhba, oder suhn fun dem shtern* (Bar Kokhba, or son of the star), depicting events of 132–135 C.E. during the revolt in Judea against the rule of the Roman Empire; *Keynig Akhashverush, oder Keynigen Esther* (King Ahasverus, or Queen Esther), a fully developed *purimshpil*, adapted from the biblical narrative; *Akeydas Yitskhok* (Binding of Isaac), including other stories from the Bible; *Dos Tseynteh Gebot, oder lo takhmod* (The Tenth Commandment, or do not covet), a version of Goethe's *Faust*; *Di tsigayne baron* (The gypsy baron), adapted from a popular general operetta of the time; and *Todros Bloz, oder der ligner* (Todroz Bloz, or the liar), a morality piece.

From an established theatrical base in Odessa, Goldfaden toured widely during his prosperous years. In 1881, the tsar was assassinated and a much more reactionary era began throughout the Russian Empire under his successor, Tsar Alexander III. That April, during Passover and the concurrent Easter season, pogroms broke out in southern Russia and the Ukraine, and more restrictive laws were instituted oppressing Jews in those areas. That summer, Goldfaden took his troupe to St. Petersburg, where he encountered a different public. There, while his innovative theatrical ideas were appreciated, his comic satires on Jewish life were attacked as subjecting up Jews to ridicule at a time of great peril in eastern Europe. Moreover, the Russian newspapers made fun of what they called silly Jewish jargon plays. Goldfaden brought his troupe back to Odessa in February 1882, and immediately embarked on writing serious works treating Jewish history and traditions. By 1883, his *Bar Kokhba* was being hailed by the Yiddish press as a great Jewish theatrical achievement. In his memoirs, Goldfaden acknowledged that he had then found his true artistic vocation, that of educating and inspiring the people by means of musical dramas. He had just about reached his true theatrical stride.

Then, unfortunately, catastrophe struck in February 1883, with a complete government ban upon all Yiddish theater throughout tsarist Russia. Perhaps the great general popularity of a Jewish drama about Bar Kokhba's historic rebellion against the oppressive Romans was considered too dangerous politically by the Russian officials. At any rate, by that summer all Yiddish stage presentations ceased, whether those of Goldfaden or any of his numerous imitators. The entertainers and fledgling troupes started to emigrate westward to various other European countries, and many then followed the rapidly rising flow of immigrants to America. It was at this time that the era of lonely struggle and diminished fulfillment began for Goldfaden, an era that was to be the sad final period of his life.

Returning to Odessa, he published a collection of poetics and songs, *Dos fideleh* (The fiddle), and he began to read his plays at public lectures. He also issued a folio of his theatrical works. However, interest in his materials declined, and so he traveled to Warsaw in 1885, and there tried to resume his work, calling it *Yiddish Daytsh Teater*, (Jewish German Theater). There, his *Shulamith* again was a resounding success, and for a while he had a regular theater, with an acting troupe and a small instrumental ensemble. From 1885 to 1887, he toured Lodz and other Polish cities. Yet the tsarist ban had dimmed his creative energies and had discouraged him spiritually, because he believed his mission was particularly to Russian Jews. He had always written fresh materials in each community as he toured, but he wrote nothing new for performances in Poland. By this time, Yiddish theater had begun to take root on the Lower East Side of New York City. It had rapidly grown in the five years since the Thomashefsky troupe had arrived in 1882 and had presented Goldfaden's *Di kishifmakherin* to an American public. And so in 1887, Goldfaden went to America. It was to be a bitter disappointment for him.

The popular Yiddish American actor David Kessler (1860–1920), who had started out in Europe with a Goldfaden troupe, recalled that there was no great reception in America for the father of Yiddish theater, yet Goldfaden had expected and probably deserved a warm welcome.[6] Goldfaden's relationships in Europe with most of the performers had been stormy, likely due to his often autocratic behavior and haphazard economic planning. Moreover, many of the performers were still using his materials, or else creating close adaptations, and thus feared a rumored (but unfounded!) form of Russian copyright which Goldfaden actually never possessed. Goldfaden dearly wished to establish his own theater in America and to present his authentic works. At the time, the two leading impresarios in New York City were Lateiner and Horowitz, who banded together to keep Goldfaden away from the actors and the stage in the city.

In 1888, Goldfaden started a theater club in New York, *Dos Lyra* (The Lyre), where he gave lessons in acting and singing and lectured on Jewish music and the stage. Thoroughly discouraged, in 1889 he returned to Europe by way of London, where he tried unsuccessfully to start a theatrical troupe with his protégé Jacob P. Adler (1855–1926). Soon, Adler also left for New York City, where he was to rise to eminence on the Yiddish stage, and Goldfaden went to Paris. There, he wrote to his friend the Yiddish writer Sholom Aleichem (1859–1916): "I stand again at the brink of life, waiting for something good. Whatever has happened to me in America, I shall soon write down fully. For me, life is a fight for existence, but I have not lost hope. Now, I am in Paris to start a Yiddish theater and perhaps remain here."[7] He was not successful in Paris either, and lived there in abject poverty, writing to friends: "The theater is my life, and it has taken my blood and breath away."[8]

By late 1890, Goldfaden had managed to return to Lemberg, where he resumed his activities—writing, lecturing, revising and publishing his earlier materials. He also created a final group of dramatic works: *Moshiakhs tsayten, oder bilder der Russishen Yiden* (Messianic times, or pictures of Russian Jewry), a didactic script including ideas based upon his trip to America; *Meylits yoshor* (Righteous advocate), a serious morality tale; *Kabts'nzon un Hungerman* (Beggarson and Hungryman), adapted from a Moliere play about the tragedy of great pride; *Rabbi Yoselman, oder di gezeyrus fun Elzas* (Rabbi Yoselman, or the edict of Alsace), a historical narrative; *Rothschilds geshikhte* (Rothschild's story), a drama about that Jewish banking family; *Uriel Acosta* (the hero's name), a literary piece; *Yehudah ha-Maccabee* (Judah, the Maccabee), a dramatic account of Jewish heroism and the origins of the Hanukkah holiday; *Yehudis un Holofern* (Judith and Holofernes), based on biblical passages; *Der eviger Yid* (The eternal Jew), an allegorical panorama of Jewish history; and *Ben Ami, oder zuhn fun mayn folk* (Ben Ami, or son of my people), based on George Eliot's novel *Daniel Deronda*.

Goldfaden's travels to New York, London, and Paris had proved to him that he no longer was the leading figure in the growing modern Yiddish theater of Europe and America. He had conceived and shaped a special theatrical art out of historic Jewish traditions and the customs of Diaspora life in the towns and villages of eastern Europe. He had initiated careers and shaped talents of artists whose proliferating stage productions now far surpassed his own pioneer efforts. Still endeavoring to train young actors, he urged them in his lectures to understand the meaning of each story and the parts that they played, to try to live the characters as they played them.

In 1896, in Europe and America there were celebrations honoring the twentieth anniversary of the founding of the Yiddish theater. In New York, there was a full production of Goldfaden's *Shulamith* featuring his protégés Sigmund Mogulesco, David Kessler, and Bertha Kalish (1872–1939). At that time, Goldfaden traveled to Galicia, Romania, and Bukovina, where he was honored at numerous performances of that work, already deemed a Yiddish theater classic. He issued another collection of his later dramas, for which a literateur named Abraham

Broides (fl. late 19th cent.) wrote this foreword: "The theater which you founded never made you rich. Yet, your works are played everywhere, and your songs are sung by everyone. Comfort yourself, for yours is the fate of a great Yiddish folk poet."[9]

There was some recognition of Goldfaden's sixtieth birthday in the Yiddish press of Europe and America in 1900. His letters of acknowledgment to those journals were bitter and full of sad lament, echoing a familiar Yiddish lament of old parents: *Varf mir nisht avek oyf der elter.*(Do not cast me aside in my old age). Goldfaden was now an outsider to the very artistry that he had sired and nurtured. He no longer was involved in the creativity and excitement of the busy theatrical troupes; he was now estranged from a stage culture that was truly coming into its own. He had been cast aside!

Goldfaden returned briefly to Paris in 1902, and then continued on to New York City, where he remained until his death in 1908. He was not economically self-sufficient in America, and he was supported to the end of his life by funds collected from loyal theater patrons and from some of the performers who owed their early start to him and still performed his works. Goldfaden would often be seen walking on the busy thoroughfares of the Lower East Side of New York City. Many there felt a special need to tender him food and other comforts, without taking money, or at least with as little payment as possible. A proud man, he bore himself with worn gentility and regal bearing, with his white neatly brushed hair, pince-nez glasses, black frock coat and formal trousers, white cravat, top hat, and walking cane with a silver gilt handle.

During those last years, Goldfaden revised his final work, *Ben Ami*, and sought desperately to have it performed. Conceived as a drama with incidental music, as a Yiddish *Daniel Deronda*, it was the story of a disaffected and worldly aristocrat who rediscovers his own Jewish heritage and ends his days as a simple farmer in Jerusalem. Boris Thomashefsky (?1864/8–1939) decided to present it, in collaboration with Sigmund Mogulesco. For that production, as a concession to more popular audience appeal, Goldfaden was induced to add couplet verses for some light tunes created by Mogulesco and music director Louis Friedsell (1850–1923). The work reached the stage in December 1907, and Goldfaden attended every performance, until he became ill and died on January 9, 1908. After his death, *Ben Ami* played to packed houses for six months, a remarkably long run for any Yiddish stage vehicle, then or ever!

A large funeral procession escorted Abraham Goldfaden to his burial place at the Washington Cemetery in Brooklyn. There on his tombstone was inscribed: *Fater fun der Yiddishe teater* (Father of the Yiddish theater). In July 1908, at the nineteenth annual meeting of the Central Conference of American Rabbis (CCAR), held in Frankfort, Michigan, the following motion was presented by its Committee on Contemporaneous Jewish History and published in its annual report (Cincinnati, 1909):

Your committee further suggests that this convention record its deep sorrow at the
death of Abraham Goldfaden, the popular playwright and composer, in New York in
January 1908. The Yiddish stage, while of recent date, is no longer an anomaly, but has
produced and popularized works of art, elevated the standards of taste, been a teacher
of social problems, raised the self-respect of the Jews and the standing of the Jew in
the literary world. Be it therefore resolved, that this conference express its admiration
of the work done by the late Abraham Goldfaden, and extend to his widow the most
heartfelt sympathy of its members.

Over his lifetime, Goldfaden wrote twenty-six opera-operettas, as well as
many shorter dramatic pieces for which he shaped plots, dialogues, and songs.
His works featured historic themes and didactic topics of ethics and morality.
They reflected Judaic traditions as well as universal ideals and values; they highlighted religious observances, historical events, the human life cycle, and the
communal society; they brought into the theater an intensity of emotional involvement that could captivate as well as educate an eager public. Goldfaden
introduced upon the stage many memorable character roles, delineated not only
with identifiable human aspects but also with special set turns, or star *shtik*
(pieces). Solos, duets, choruses, and dances, were interspersed with the action,
and were augmented or deleted according to the abilities of particular performers. All of those qualities were to distinguish the American Yiddish theatricals
and vaudeville shows during their heyday, and were then brought along by many
talented Jewish artists as they mainstreamed into the realm of general American
entertainment.

Goldfaden's musical elements were derived from a broad range of nineteenth-century eastern European sources: synagogue cantillation, prayer chant,
and hymnology; Yiddish folk songs; Hasidic tunes; Russian, Ukrainian, and
other Slavic melodies; and arias from French and Italian operas. According to
Jewish musicologist Abraham Z. Idelsohn, a particular source of Goldfaden's
liturgical motifs was Cantor Wolf Velvele Schestopol (1832–1872) of Odessa.[10]
Schestopol, who had studied in Vienna with Cantor Salomon Sulzer (1804–
1890), was a prolific composer of hymn melodies, often based upon folk themes
or reminiscent of popular Italian operatic arias. Schestopol's music was widely
known, though never published, and it is likely that Goldfaden became familiar
with those materials when he resided in Odessa. It was just that sort of melodic
variety that Goldfaden was able to shape and adapt to enhance his poetic texts.
Perhaps this unique mixture provided the qualities of accessibility and universality that enabled a number of his songs to survive well beyond their original
settings and to become ageless "classics" treated as folk songs. Indeed, his particular attraction to Hasidic tunes and dances and to Judeo-Slavic melodic
formulas likely had a dynamic influence upon the styles of performance of
twentieth-century American Jewish entertainers.

Some of the characters in Goldfaden's dramatic works have passed into Yiddish and even general English usage, as for example, the antihero Shmendrig, or Shmendrik, as any gullible fool, or the witch in *Di kishifmakherin*, Bobeh Yakhne, the ultimate busybody gossip. Not only did he provide the initial opportunities for women to perform on the Yiddish stage, but he also crafted female roles that honored women and highlighted their important roles in biblical lore and Judaic history. One may consider whether Goldfaden's plays have retained an independent literary significance. Could they be performed without their songs? Before her death, Goldfaden's widow sent the texts of his last works, those strongly nationalistic ones including *Ben Ami*, back to relatives in eastern Europe, and some of those materials were published in Vilna in 1930. At that time, excerpts from his poetry and song lyrics were printed on Jewish calendars in Poland.

Goldfaden had been an early advocate of Zionism as a solution to the mounting Jewish problems in eastern Europe late in the nineteenth century, and he applied those ideas especially in his last dramas and songs. In 1905, at a public meeting held in New York at Cooper Union Hall to memorialize the father of modern Zionism, Theodor Herzl (1860–1904), Goldfaden joined a crowded speakers platform along with another eulogist, Eliakum Zunser, once a highly celebrated *badkh'n* (folk minstrel) in eastern Europe. In 1889, Zunser had emigrated to New York, where he operated a small printing shop and languished in obscurity, unnoticed by the artists on the Yiddish stage. At that Herzl memorial gathering, Zunser chanted a special elegy for which he had written an extended literary text. In turn, Goldfaden read his own tribute to Herzl, and then as he began to sing one of his own songs, *Di Yiddishe hofnung* (The Jewish hope), the entire assemblage joined him in the singing.

Early in the twentieth century, Abraham Goldfaden's works had already entered into Jewish folk culture in Europe and in America. He had created a distinctive art form, and thereby set in motion artistic ideas that were to flourish over the rest of the century. He had helped transport centuries-old eastern European Yiddish musical culture to American shores.

NOTES

This chapter is an adapted version of the author's introductory essay in Irene Heskes, comp. and ed., *The Music of Abraham Goldfaden: Father of the Yiddish Theater* (Cedarhurst, N.Y.: Tara Publications, 1990). With an introductory essay, this is a collection of fifty songs reprinted as originally published in early commercial sheet music and in the arrangements performed at that time. Background information is also given for each of the selections, along with synoptic translations and transliteration of the Yiddish lyric texts. Included are many well-known selections from the leading

Goldfaden theatricals. Some new information has been added to this chapter, as well as reference notes.

1.. For extensive background on the life of Abraham Goldfaden, I am indebted to an excellent Yiddish pamphlet from which I have derived valuable information: Nakhman Meisel, *Abraham Goldfaden* (New York: Yiddish Cooperative Book League of the International Workers Order, 1938). I gratefully acknowledge the opportunity to quote, in my own English translations, from this fine biographical source that also includes excerpts from Goldfaden's own writings.

2. Ibid., Meisel, unpaginated text.

3. For information about that premiere performance, as well as fuller details concerning the song *Eili, Eili,* see Irene Heskes, *Yiddish-American Popular Songs, 1895 to 1950* (Washington, D.C.: The Library of Congress, 1992), intro. pp. XXXV–XXXVII, and also the appropriate copyright song entries in the volume.

4. Although this song was published in New York in 1909 by the Hebrew Publishing Company, it was never copyrighted by Sigmund Mogulesco. He had adapted the melody of a hasidic *nigun* (tune) with his own lyrics, and then throughout his career performed it as an encore solo. Since its original introduction by Mogulesco in his operetta *Blihmeleh,* it probably has been performed more widely at Jewish weddings than any other song, and is generally treated as a folk song of anonymous origin. During the heyday of the Yiddish *klezmer* (folk instrumental) bands in the 1920s, the tune was widely recorded, and thus entered into the mainstream of American and European dance music.

5. Variously titled as *Di kishifmakherin,* or *Di tsoyberin* (The witch, or The sorceress), this work was the first formal Yiddish production to be introduced in America, premiering in 1882 at Turn Hall, New York City, in performances by the then recently arrived Thomashefsky family, with the young Boris Thomashefsky as star. A complete edition of songs from this opera-operetta was published in 1900 in New York City, by Katzenelenbogen and Rabinowitz Company, and was subsequently reissued by the Hebrew Publishing Company. Many of the songs in Goldfaden's theatrical works became perennial favorites. Over the decades of the twentieth century, they were performed and issued in many arrangements in America and abroad. Unfortunately, Goldfaden never copyrighted any of those materials, neither the music, the lyrics, nor the scenarios.

6. Meisel, excerpts from unpaginated text materials.

7. Ibid.

8. Ibid.

9. Ibid.

10. Abraham Z. Idelsohn, *Jewish Music in Its Historical Development* (New York: Henry Holt, 1929; reprint ed., Westport, Conn.: Greenwood Press, 1981); pp. 308–9.

18

Russian Nationalism and Jewish Music

By the end of the nineteenth century, Jewish music had entered into its modern era. Often termed a musical renaissance, it was more truly a newly emerging dynamic force in both liturgical and secular forms reflective of changing Jewish life in Europe and America. Looking back over the earliest years of those developments, one senses mounting appreciation of historic cultural continuity, along with a growing impetus toward further creative achievement. For a time in that process, early in the twentieth century, the Russian folk nationalism movement was a significant influence upon Jewish cultural self-awareness in eastern Europe.

All Europeans had awakened to their various national identities during the nineteenth century, in the wake of the post-Napoleonic era. In a historical sense, it had been Napoleon Bonaparte (1769–1821) who set a course for Jewish nationalism and gave impetus to a consequent rise of the *haskalah* (enlightenment) movement for intellectual and cultural auto-emancipation. In 1799, as first Consul of the French Republic, Napoleon identified the Jews as Frenchmen among other French, granting them full citizenship entitled to liberty, equality, and fraternity. Extending tolerance toward all religions, including Judaism, he organized an assembly of Jewish rabbis and notable laymen, which in 1807 met in Paris as a Grand Sanhedrin, a form of consistorial organization. Ironically, it was the rising tide of European nationalism initially advanced by Napoleon in his conquests that ultimately defeated his ambitions to rule the entire continent. The concept of nationhood and of national mission energized Jews and Jewish life itself, reaching over into the ghettos of eastern Europe. Before its final defeat, Napoleon's army had been on Russian soil and had left behind there those political ideas of folk self-awareness.

The movement for Jewish nationalism began primarily as a Diaspora-centered phenomenon. The word *haskalah* was derived from the Hebrew and Yiddish word *seykhel* (wisdom, good sense), and its followers were called *maskilim* (intellectuals, enlightened ones). For Judaism, it meant expansion of opportunities for broader education and wider range of life-styles, along with the confrontation of political, social, and economic realities within the context of Christian civilization. In Europe, over the centuries, there had been Jews functioning in the general scholarly and artistic world. By the late nineteenth century, many of those who prospered outside the ghetto confines were experiencing a pendulum swing in their perceptions, oscillating between a complete social and intellectual assimilation and the earnest search for self-realization in terms of traditional Jewish cultural and spiritual values. This ambivalence in personal quest particularly affected Jewish musicians, who, suppressing their personal background, had fitted themselves into a Procrustean bed of Christian culture. Thus, while the rest of Europe seethed with mounting nationalism, many Jews also felt impelled to justify their particular ethnic existence, at least among themselves.

Like all other national movements expressed through music, Jewish folk awareness began with the gathering of indigenous folk songs, mainly of Yiddish genre. In the beginning, those simple tunes were arranged to fit the formal musical ideas and principles of conservatory-educated Jews, who set them as pseudo-art songs or instrumental solo themes. In retrospect, it does not really matter how many melodies were actually collected, or even the altered manner in which they were initially presented to the general public. What does matter, however, was the acknowledgment of their intrinsic cultural value among those who collected, arranged, performed, and published them. The importance rests in the recognition of this Jewish musical folk legacy and its taking a rightful place among the other worldwide ethnic musical expressions.

The father of that emergent Jewish national music was Joel Engel (Yulius/Yuli Dimitrievich Engel, 1868–1927). Until his death in Tel Aviv in 1927, Engel was to insist to everyone that he owed everything he had tried to accomplished in Jewish music to the Russians. There had been a dramatic conversion in his musical and personal life for which he always credited the Russian nationalists.[1] Born in the Crimea, he attended Kharkov University to prepare for a career as a lawyer. A brief meeting early in his life with the composer Peter Tschaikovsky (1840–1893) led him to enter the Moscow Imperial Conservatory of Music in 1893, where he became a favored pupil of Sergei Taneyev (1856–1915). Upon completion of his formal music education in 1897, Engel joined the staff of the Moscow journal *Russkaya Vyedomosti* as an assistant editor in charge of music. His articles were acclaimed by the Russian music nationalists, notably Cesar Cui (1835–1918) and Nikolai Rimsky-Korsakov (1844–1908). It was a time when Slavic folk songs and liturgical chants were being collected and many of those melodies had begun to appear, arranged as serious musical works.

On the eve of Russian Easter 1897, Engel and his friend the Jewish sculptor Marek Antokolsky (d. 1917?) went to a Moscow hotel to see Vladimir Vasilevitch Stasov (1824–1906), then on a visit to the city from his home in St.

Petersburg. Stasov was Russia's most eminent music critic, and an ardent advocate of Russo-Slavic national art. He confronted Engel with the challenging question of Jewish national pride, and cited the glories of Jewish music that he himself had heard, the Hebrew liturgical chants and Yiddish folk ballads. That summer, Engel took leave of his newspaper post and headed into the Russian Jewish Pale of Settlement to collect Jewish folk songs among the people in the villages. When he returned to Moscow, he edited and arranged those materials and presented them in lectures at the Moscow Polytechnic Museum and the Imperial Ethnographical Society in St. Petersburg. In 1900, Engel prepared an edition of some of those songs, and a copy was sent to Stasov, inscribed with sentiments of gratitude and respect.

About this time, two Jewish historians, Pesach Marek (1862–1920) and Saul Ginsberg (1866–1940), had also embarked upon the extensive collection of folk songs among Russian Jews. They published those materials in St. Petersburg in 1901. The following year, Engel and Marek presented examples from their respective collections before the Moscow Society for Natural Science and Anthropology. By this time, a number of other Jewish musicians had begun to work with that folk resource. Several were then at the St. Petersburg Conservatory of Music, studying with the Russian music nationalists Nikolai Rimsky-Korsakov and Mily Balakirev (1837–1910). Among them were Ephraim Shklar (1871–1941?), Michael Gniessin (1883–1957), Solomon Rosowsky (1878–1962), and Lazare Saminsky (1882–1959), who gathered together in 1908 and formed the St. Petersburg Society for Jewish Folk Music, with the formal approval of the Russian District Commissioner.[2] The society functioned from 1908 to 1918 as a pioneer group in this endeavor. In 1913, a branch was established in Moscow; it was disbanded after the Russian Revolution.

In 1922, Joel Engel went to Berlin, where he established a Jewish music publishing company, *Juval Verlag*, and issued a number of his folk song arrangements. In 1924, he resettled in Tel Aviv. There, until his death three years later, he helped institute a communal folk cultural celebration of the Sabbath day, now widely observed as *Oneg Shabbat* (Sabbath pleasure). Some years later, an "Engel Room" of Jewish folklore was set aside at the Kiev Museum in the Ukraine, and an Engel Street was named in Tel Aviv. From 1914 to 1919, Lazare Saminsky, with a commission from the Baron Guinzbourg Ethnological Fund, traveled to various areas of the Russian Empire, as well as Turkey and Palestine, collecting Jewish folk materials. In 1920, he emigrated to America, and four years later became the music director at Temple Emanu-El in New York City, a position he held until his death.[3] Solomon Rosowsky went to Jerusalem, and then to New York City, where until his death in 1962 he was actively involved in the many activities of the Jewish Music Forum and in the formation of schools for cantorial study. The other members of the society remained in the Soviet Union.

An excellent overview of the St. Petersburg-Moscow Society and the consequent influence of those Russian Jews upon twentieth-century developments in
Jewish music has been provided by Albert Weisser in his book *The Modern
Renaissance of Jewish Music*. It is a narrative account of the emergence of Jewish self-consciousness on the part of that influential group of musicians.[4] In
particular, the author discusses the careers and contributions of such early activists as Joseph Achron (1886–1943), who settled in the United States in 1925, and
Alexander Krein (1883–1951) and Moses Milner (1886–1953, who, with Michael
Gniessin, remained in the Soviet Union. Weisser appears to highlight the leadership role of his own mentor-teacher Lazare Saminsky and to somewhat dim the
luster of Saminsky's philosophical rival Joel Engel. Nevertheless, Weisser's detailed treatment of their respective innovative musical ideas places both Engel
and Saminsky in significant ethno-historic context. Included in his book are listings of early publications by the Society for Jewish Folk Music and by Joel
Engel's *Yuval/Yibneh Verlag* as well as rosters of subsequent compositions by
the Russian Jewish musicians.[5] Rediscovery and performance of all these works
is long overdue. Although their musical qualities vary widely, and indeed often
appear to be experimental ventures in the integration of Judaic folk elements,
there are some fine instrumental and vocal compositions among them. Clearly,
the important contribution by the Russian musicians was the emergence of professional musical interest in the secular-folk and liturgical-sacred treasury of
Judaism.

During the Stalinist and later regimes of the Soviet Union, music was used as
a deliberate means of public control. Creativity in literature and the arts was particularly harnessed. Even in music, governmentally authorized works were
produced expressing the "correct" ideological concepts. Unacceptable art and
artists were banned and even penalized. For Soviet Jews, the matter was even
more crucial. Yet over the years, journalists often described scenes in which
groups of Jews thronged outside of old synagogues, singing Jewish songs.
Through that musical expression, volumes of unutterable words were spoken.
These people constituted a surviving branch of Jewish life in eastern Europe following the Holocaust; many of them had been cut off from the continuity of
their cultural as well as religious heritage. Jewish intellectual expression and artistic creativity had been silenced or was practiced in secrecy. It was a form of
cultural genocide, a systematic draining of a distinctive ethnicity as well as a religion. Hebrew was acceptable only in a prayer book, and even the Yiddish
language was discouraged. Secular Jewish education was discouraged. Moreover, to a great extent, old-style tsarist anti-Semitism abided, especially outside
the large cities.

During those years, there were numerous Soviet Jews who managed to have
musical careers, especially virtuoso performers whose public recognition belied
their Judaism. Of the earlier musical leaders who initiated the modern Jewish
music movement with the St. Petersburg Society, three of those who remained in

the Soviet Union—Gniessin, Krein and Milner—became decreasingly involved with Jewish music itself. By the end of their lives, those three gifted musicians had ceased to have any association with the musical ideas that they had enthusiastically espoused. They were, however, widely noted as Russian music educators and founders of music conservatories. Gniessin himself had two successful Jewish protégés: Isaac Dunayevsky (1910–1955), heir of a great hazzanic name, wrote the theme song for the official Moscow radio broadcasting station and was president of the Union of Soviet composers; he never was associated with the music of the synagogue. Samuel Feinberg (1890–1952?) won a Stalin prize in composition and was music critic for *Pravda*, the official newspaper.

In contrast to hundreds of Soviet publications on music, many treating the folk songs of various ethnic groups, scant materials referred to Jewish music. By the end of the Stalin era, scholarly musicological and ethnological studies omitted references to that musical genre. Two collections of Jewish folk music had been issued under governmental sponsorship, the Institute for Jewish People's Culture of the Ukrainian Education Academy. The volumes were compiled and edited by Moisei Beregovskii (1894–1941?), a Yiddish folklorist, in association with Yiddish journalist and poet Itzik Feffer (1900–1952) and with a musician named Meir Viner (fl. early 20th cent.).[6] Feffer, who had been considered at the time to be a major Russian writer, was murdered along with twenty-three other Jewish intellectuals, on direct orders of Stalin. It is unclear how and where Beregovskii died. Public performances of Jewish music were limited following the Stalinist purges of 1948–1952.

Some Soviet Jewish folk songs were written and sung over the decades, but in the Russian and Ukrainian languages rather than Yiddish; they were political statements or social commentaries that could be sung by anyone, Jews or others. Most of those songs originated in Birobidzhan, the location where Stalin had sought at one time to resettle Russian Jews. In Moscow, an officially approved Yiddish theater, which employed Jewish musicians Lev Pulver (b. 1883), Lev Knepper (b. 1898), and Zinovy Komponeets (b. 1902), was closed in 1949.

Ironically, over the decades Jewish musicians and musical performers have been highly active in Soviet popular entertainment—via radio, television, theater, and cinema—as performers, composers, and writers-lyricists. They have filled the rosters of orchestras, opera companies, and music conservatories, and at least a third of the listed members in the 1990 roster of the Soviet composers union were known to be of Jewish descent. Moreover, a number of Soviet so-called mass songs (military marches and patriotic tunes) were written by Jews, including the highly prolific Matvey Blanter (1903–1974). It is likely that Jewish melodies have become ingredients in general Soviet music. At the same time, some "underground" collections of Jewish songs were printed and distributed, including such protest songs as the Russian *Otpusti narod moy* (Let my people go) and the Yiddish *Antshuldikt mir* (Excuse me) and *Vayt, vayt* (Far, far away).

Several noted non-Jewish composers have risked their careers in order to support Jewish musical ideas. Sergei Prokofiev (1891–1953) composed an overture on Jewish themes (1919), which he himself performed in a piano arrangement at concerts. Dmitri Shostakovich (1906–1975) wrote a work "From Jewish Poetry" (1948), and dedicated his Symphony No. 13 (1962) to the memory of the Russian Jewish men, women, and children who were victims of the infamous slaughter at the Ukrainian Babi Yar ravine during World War II.

With the ascendancy to power of Mikhail Gorbachev and the ideas of *glasnost*, restrictions on religious observances, including Judaic ones, were eased, and terms of permission were granted for the emigration of Russian Jews to Israel, America, and other countries. Only with the breakup in 1991 of the Union of Soviet Socialist Republics, which politically separated Russia, Ukraine, and the other Soviet republics, has there been a rising sense of personal freedom among those people. With the dynamic political changes and an upheaval in search of a new economic system, it remains to be seen what the developments will mean for Jewish life there. Moreover, in those regions sectional nationalism may bring difficulties for Jews, as ethnic and religious outsiders. Will the rise of militant nationalism throughout Europe and Asia constitute a threat to viable Jewish existence on those continents? Meanwhile, it appears that the musical sounds of Slavic Judaism—religious and secular—have begun to be heard again.

NOTES

1. For further biographical information about Joel Engel, see:

Israel Rabinovich, *Of Jewish Music: Ancient and Modern* (Montreal: The Book Center, 1952), pp. 145–53.

Albert Weisser, *The Modern Renaissance of Jewish Music* (New York: Bloch Publishing, 1954), pp. 41, 71–80. In particular, Weisser's book provides an extensive discussion of Joel Engel and the other Russian Jewish musicians of that time and place. He includes important details about their activities on behalf of the emergent movement for Jewish folk music in Europe, America, and Palestine/Israel.

2. There is a personal reminiscence concerning the formation of the St. Petersburg Society for Jewish Folk Music, provided by Solomon Rosowsky, in *Jewish Music Forum Bulletin*, Vol. 9 (1948), pp. 9–10. Other extended discussions of the Petersburg Society and its members may be found in: Rabinovich, *Of Jewish Music*, and in Weisser, *The Modern Renaissance*.

3. Lazare Saminsky wrote two books on Jewish music:

Music of Our Days: Essentials and Prophecies (New York: Crowell, 1932). It includes critiques of the composers Schoenberg, Bloch, and Copland as well as of several Russian-Jewish musicians.

Music of the Ghetto and Bible (New York: Bloch Publishing, 1934). It includes Saminsky's personal recollections of some of "the Russian group," and an essay in strong response to the ideas of Joel Engel. Saminsky, in sharp contrast to Engel, believed that for modern Jewish music, the biblical Hebraic elements were more significant than the diasporic Yiddish melodic expression. Ironically, Engel resettled in Palestine and learned at the end of his life to speak Hebrew, and, on the other hand, Saminsky emigrated to America, where most of his fellow New York Jews came from a background of Yiddish language and many still spoke it.

4. Weisser, *The Modern Renaissance*.

5. Another source for suitable music lists is Irene Heskes and Arthur Wolfson, comps. and eds., *The Historic Contribution of Russian Jewry to Jewish Music* (New York: National Jewish Music Council, 1967).

6. Moisei Beregovskii and Meir Viner, comps. and eds., *Yidisher Musik-Folklor* (Yiddish folk music) (Moscow: Meluxiser Musik, 1934), and Beregovskii, and Itzik Feffer, *Yidisher Folkslider* (Yiddish folk songs) (Moscow and Kiev: Meluche/Ukrainishe Natsion, 1938).

Part VI

The Holocaust Era

19

The Musical Legacy of the Holocaust

Early on in the 1920s, the Nazis had clearly perceived music to be a formative social factor and political tool, useful for their own propaganda purposes and beyond mere cultural expression. Control of music was not a new concept. Plato, after all, had urged that the role of music in society be given serious consideration. The National Socialist idea of the politics of music, however, negated the right of musical expression to any autonomy. Moreover, there was a distinctive German "own people" (*Volk*) music, determined by facts of race, and inherent in the specific ideology and practice of the Nazi movement.[1]

As soon as Hitler came to power in 1933, a movement for the so-called purification of German music began with a day of boycott on April 1, 1933. Joseph Goebbels, as overseer of the government's Ministry of Propaganda, had formed the Chamber of Culture, with a special section for music called the Reich Chamber of Music (*Reichsmusikkammer*).[2] That department was to supervise all musical activities and musicians, and to monitor the music that would pervade the concert halls, radio programs, schools, factories, offices, homes, and soon also the army barracks and wartime battlefields. Hitler's ideas about music, as well as all the other arts, shaped the German cultural atmosphere from the very start of his regime. In 1934, a formal ban was instituted against Jewish music and musicians, and the next year Jews were no longer to be employed by musical groups nor to perform publicly for general audiences. Also strictly banned were compositions written by Jews or by those suspected of being pro-Jewish. With the Chamber of Music as its instrument of action, the Gestapo took control of this "cleansing" of German culture. Following publication of government listings of forbidden musicians and musical selections, the ban spread to all aspects of music and became a total fact.

There had been precedents in Germany for such listings and for an overt anti-Semitic movement in music. In 1869, Richard Wagner penned an infamous tract: *Das Judentum in der Musik* (The Judaism in music), a vicious and rambling diatribe attacking Jewish influences as impure and negative cultural forces and stressing that anything by Jews did not properly belong in the European Occident.[3] Subsequently, a son-in-law of Wagner, Houston Stewart Chamberlain, also railed in print against Jewish musicians and their works. During the 1920s and the rise of the Nazi movement, several publications underscored antipathy toward Jewish musicians and Jewish music. In 1926, a reworking of Wagner's infamous essay was prepared by Heinrich Berl and published under Wagner's same title in the cities of Stuttgart, Berlin, and Leipzig by the publishing house of Deutsche Verlags-Anstalt. Berl, an active member of the Nazi party in Stuttgart, went even further by denying any value at all to Jewish cultural and intellectual expression, emphasizing Wagner's argument that anything Jewish and consequently oriental does not belong in occidental Europe.[4] In Munich in 1932, another party member, Richard Eichenauer, at his own expense published his book *Musik und Rasse* (Music and race), which further advanced the Nazi theory that Jewish musical ideas polluted the purity of German musical expression and therefore had to be erased. In rapid succession after Hitler came to power, there were more such racist publications, not only from the offices of propagandist Joseph Goebbels and his associate Peter Raabe, but also written by a number of so-called music scholars: Michael Alt, Karl Blessinger, Joachim Du-Kart, Werner Egk, Carl Heinzen, Hans Hickmann, Hans Koeltzsch, H. W. Kulenkampff, Hans Joachim Moser, Helmuth Sommerfeld, and Guido Waldmann.[5]

The public removal of Jewish musicians began in 1933 with compulsory registration rules instituted by the Reich Chamber of Music. Soon the following were appointed: Paul Graener, head of the Reich Union of Composers; Karl Straube, head of the Reich Union of Church Musicians; Fritz Stege, head of the Reich Union of Music Critics; and a committee, led by Werner Lodwig, Max Trapp, and Hermann Matzke, to serve the Reich Union of Music Educators and Education. By 1935, Goebbels had formally begun to purge Jews from all German cultural life. A first listing for the banning was prepared in 1935–36 in Munich, *Judentum un Musik: Mit dem ABC juedischer und nichtarischer Musikbeflissener* (Jews in music: with the ABC study of Jewish and not proper music) compiled and edited (and self-published) by Christa Maria Wiesner-Rack and Hans Brueckner. An augmented version appeared two years later, with eight blank pages appended for additions to the 300 pages of listings. In 1940, the first official edition of *Lexikon des Judens in der Musik: Mit einem Titelverzeichnis juedischer Werke* (Lexicon of Jews in music: with a title index of Jewish works) was prepared for general distribution throughout Germany. It was issued in order to guarantee the exclusion of any Judaic elements in all public music anywhere—concert halls to restaurants, radio programs to cabaret shows. Published in Berlin and in Frankfurt am Main by B. Hahnefeld, it was reissued in augmented form in 1943. Again, blank pages were left in that *Lexikon* for the insertion of more names and compositions. Its prodigious compiler-editors,

Theophil Stengel and Herbert Gerigk, worked at the Berlin central office of the NSDAP, officially known as the Workshop for Research in the Matter of the Jewish Problem.

By 1935, Jews already were rapidly disappearing from the ranks and programs of orchestras and other instrumental groups, conservatories and university music departments, publishers and libraries, opera houses and concert halls, newspapers and periodicals, radio and recording studios. Music ascribed to Jews was rapidly being erased from all types of programs. Jazz music was regarded as non-Aryan Negroid and was also banned, along with most American popular music, whether by Jews or not.[6] Inasmuch as Richard Wagner's music was adored by Hitler, his operas were instituted as ritual events. The performances at Bayreuth assumed a particularly intense atmosphere. The music of Anton Bruckner, a disciple of Wagnerian ideas, was also frequently performed at Nazi functions.

German radio broadcasts were increasingly utilized for propaganda purposes, and music became a significantly serious aspect of those programs. Suitably nazified music was performed at mass rallies and public events. In 1938, Hitler proclaimed a national Day of Music for which Goebbels drafted a list of commandments to be observed by all German musicians, citing that music deeply affected the spirit of man.[7] Throughout Hitler's regime, many musicians were exempted from actual military combat service and instead were sent out to entertain field soldiers and factory workers. During the final critical months of the war, there were broadcasts of American popular music to the barracks and hospitals. However, those songs were heard only with German lyrics, and without any references to their original musical sources. In that way, the melodies by Irving Berlin, Duke Ellington, George Gershwin, Jerome Kern, and so forth were enjoyed by men fighting for Hitler.

To carry forward their objectives, the Nazis early on took on the practice of adapting music, giving their own new texts to favorite German songs and old folk ballads. Music was a strong part of the Nazi movement propaganda, and its special programmed purposes continued up to the very last days of the regime. The rationalization among many of the musicians who remained active on behalf of Hitler was that good German music would purify the spirit. The official National Socialist (NSDAP) song book, *Was der Deutscher Singt* (What the Germans sing), was compiled and edited by Reinhold Zimmerman and issued in Berlin in 1933 for general national distribution commencing in all schools.[8] The official songster featured the Nazi party anthem, *Horst Wessel Lied* (Song of Horst Wessel), which was also highlighted in a collection of band tunes, *Horst Wessel Marschalbum* (Horst Wessel march album). Its melody was that of an old beer hall ballad that had first been adapted with new lyrics and then retitled as *Die Fahne Hoch* (Lift up the banner) by a member of the SA Brown Shirts named Horst Wessel, who was injured in a street brawl and died of blood poisoning. Thereupon, Wessel was made a Nazi martyr, and a party musician,

Herman Blume, revised the song to honor *Kamerad Horst Wessel* (Comrade Horst Wessel). The house where Wessel had lived in Vienna was maintained as a public shrine from the 1938 Austrian Anschluss until the Nazi defeat in 1945. In 1923, the Hitler rally song, *Bundeslied, oder Lied den Sturmabteilungen* (Group song, or song of the storm troopers), was shaped by an early Nazi party member, Erich Tessemer. He adapted its melody from an earlier American soldier song, "Blue Eyes, We Must Part," ascribed in 1904 to Theodore Morse. Tessemer's first version was revised in 1933 and updated for publication in the NSDAP song-book. Several well-known Prussian army marches also were refashioned with special lyrics that lauded Hitler and Nazism and lashed out against Jews. With the actual outbreak of World War II, lyrics were added denouncing the English, French, Americans, and others.

Throughout the time of Hitler, parading Nazis sang out such lyrics as: *Wenn das Judenblut vom messer spritzt, dann gehts noch mal so gut* (When Jewish blood flows from the knife, then everything goes so well). Thus, ideology was defined through musical expression. Music could be used to create an atmosphere in which mass murder would be sung about as a justified patriotic duty, and the victims described as subhuman. Musical propaganda was everywhere, and as the concentration camps were established, music followed into those infamous places. At the arrival depots, at least during the first years, all prisoners were questioned about their musical abilities, and a special sorting out was done among them for notable musicians. In Terezin Camp, very many famous European artists performed for their captors before being sent away to be tortured, gassed, and incinerated. As early as 1938, a *Lagerskappelle* (prison band) was organized in Buchenwald Camp. An all-female orchestra was formed at Auschwitz Camp. The ranks of those performers were constantly filled with newer prisoners as the others died of disease or starvation or were slaughtered. A number of postwar publications describe those macabre musical activities.[9]

In the concentration camps, when musicians played and sang for their captors, it was not music by Jewish composers. Often, however, the prescribed repertoire included mocking parody performances of Jewish selections. At least at the outset, musicians were relieved from some of the work details, and often given different outfits to wear. In the early years of the camps, some funds were allocated for scores and instruments, but soon those music materials were only acquired as property confiscated from the inmates. Prisoner-ensembles played for the physical exercises and military drills of the guards as well as for their leisure entertainment. All too frequently, musical performances accompanied the marching off to death of fellow victims. Survivors recall hearing radio broadcasts over camp loudspeakers, even of the Berlin Philharmonic Orchestra, playing music as men, women, and children were being enslaved, abused, and then murdered.

During the first years of the Hitler regime, German Jews, in reaction to the bans and even encouraged for a while by the Nazis, organized their own

Kulturbund Deutscher Juden (Cultural organization of German Jews) with branches in many of the larger cities. Among their wide range of artistic and literary activities were music events held at private homes, meeting halls, and synagogues. As the oppressive measures grew worse and the societal isolation of Jews became almost complete, those Jewish groups were filled with famous people, and for a brief time there was much creative activity. Quite soon, however, the atmosphere of human jeopardy proved to be overwhelming, and there were desperate efforts to find ways to escape to another country. For notable figures in the arts, this may have been a feasible possibility, but only those who actually left the European continent ultimately managed not to be trapped and destroyed.[10]

Years later, Willy Brandt, then Chancellor of West Germany, addressed a gathering of scholars on September 25, 1973, at a meeting marking the fortieth anniversary of the New School for Social Research. Earlier known as the "University in Exile," the New School had been founded in 1933 as a haven for scholars fleeing Nazi persecution. According to a text published in the *New York Times* the following day, Chancellor Brandt said: "The great loss Germany suffered in the thirties by the exodus of so many of her most gifted and learned men and women is still being felt in the Germany of today. Our cultural scene, lively as it is, has never regained the diversity and creativity it had under the Weimar Republic. Frankly, the Jewish element in our society is sorely missing."

Those musicians who had devoted their talents to Jewish liturgical traditions were prime visible targets in every country that the Nazis occupied, and were least able to evade capture. Their lives had been bound up with the Jewish faith, in service to synagogue and temple congregants. Most *hazzanim* (precentor-cantors) went along with their local communities into the ghettos and concentration camps, where they perished. Thus ended an unbroken continuity of Judaic liturgical musical traditions that had flourished throughout Europe since the early era of the Roman Empire.

Inasmuch as Hitler's deliberate endeavor was to destroy Judaism along with the Jewish people, the Nazis worked ceaselessly to denigrate and distort Jewish religion and history. The objective was to erase any tangible evidence of that heritage as a viable living force, to write Jews entirely out of the chronicles of Western civilization. Small wonder that along with the six million Jewish human beings lost, little of substance remains from their lives, especially during the years 1933 to 1945. There was a further profound diminution as the consequence of the burning of books and the destruction of libraries and archival collections of Judaica. In terms of music and literature, any creative works during that period had to be secretly written down and then zealously saved from destruction or else had to be preserved by word of mouth and orally transmitted to the few who, it was hoped, might not perish. As a result, some personal accounts, touching poetry, and simple songs are the essence of the legacy.

Postwar collections of those materials, shaped amidst tragic circumstances, not only provide a priceless remembrance but also constitute for historians a significant form of documentary evidence describing the times and events. Some postwar collectors have managed to gather remnants of vocal and instrumental compositions, to be valued less as works of artistry than as a sustained tribute to the greater amount of what was irrevocably lost. Surviving elements of Jewish music, in particular, ought not to be judged by the usual rules of aesthetic evaluation. The songs of the period are like old faded and torn photographs, dimmed and damaged likenesses from the past. They must be viewed in the context of their creative origins and the circumstances of expression, as symbols of unfinished lives and shattered continuities. In a sense, they may also be viewed as a form of protest and an eloquent if muted echo of voices resistant to spiritual destruction.

Details of events during those dreadful years in Europe serve to underscore the impact upon Jewish musical expression at the time. By the so-called *Krystalnacht* (crystal night) in November 1938, with the shattering and looting of Jewish homes, commercial establishments, and houses of worship, Jews were in grave peril. Mass deportations to the detention camps had begun. Then, as the German army entered into each unlucky country, Jewish professionals and notable figures were the first targets. By late 1941, thousands of them were being rounded up and sent in particular to Theresienstadt (Terezin), located north of Prague in Czechoslovakia. This concentration camp had been set up in 1934 as a special holding place for those Jews (and "problem" non-Jews) prominent in politics and public life as well as in the various arts. Terezin was to become the final known place of residence for very many famous people. For a time at that camp, the inmates were allowed to organize their own special activities, especially music, and to develop various artistic projects. The Nazis used those activities as a deceitful instrument of propaganda, purporting to illustrate how the affluent Jews were resting and enjoying themselves, while the good Germans— or Austrians, Czechs, Poles, and so on—were laboring so hard during such difficult times.

As conditions degenerated at Terezin and became desperately impossible by late 1942, ensemble and solo instrumental concerts as well as operatic and oratorio performances continued on.[11] And so musicians rehearsed and performed, composers wrote and conducted, music teachers taught and lectured. That particular concentration camp became a grotesque microcosm of the former flourishing European musical society. Music sustained the spirit, numbed the anguish, entertained for brief fleeting hours, and strengthened personal resolve. Even more than that, musical expression became a defiant act of affirmation. Josef Bor, a Czechoslovakian Jew, was imprisoned with his entire family at Terezin, and alone of them all subsequently managed to survive. He wrote movingly of the inmates' grim rehearsals of Verdi's *Requiem* at that concentration camp for a command performance before Eichmann and a contingent of SS troops.[12] Why Verdi's *Requiem*? Busy grinding out the final destruction of European Jewry, Eichmann was amused by the very idea of Jews singing their own death knell. According to author Josef Bor, who participated in the chorus, Eichmann's victims appeared to transcend his warped humor. Exalted by the beauty of the music, they sought to triumph over provocation, exhaustion, and terror, and found a measure of liberation in the glorious power of the music. At that command performance, the ensemble gathered whatever strength they had within themselves, and sang across the dark abyss to their audience of murderers: *Libera me, Domine, de morte aeterna* (Free me, God, from eternal death).

Over the months, starvation, disease, and then the death transports decimated the ranks of musicians and other inmates at Terezin. Finally the music ended there, and that anteroom to hell became merely a gathering point stopover on the road to gas chambers at Auschwitz, Belsen, Buchenwald, and others. In recent years several music scholars have recovered and collected some written scores from Terezin—works by Holocaust victims Pavel Haar, Gideon Klein, Hans Krasa, and Viktor Ullman, each of whom had begun a notable musical career before the Nazis came into power. Ullman had been a pupil and protégé of Arnold Schoenberg.[13] In particular are two operas, *Brundibar*, a children's opera in two acts composed by Hans Krasa with a libretto by Adolf Hoffmeister, and *Der Kaiser von Atlantis, oder Tod dankt ab* (The emperor of Atlantis, or death abdicates), a chamber work in four scenes, with music by Viktor Ullman and libretto by Peter Kien. Krasa, Hoffmeister, Ullman, and Kien all perished at Auschwitz in 1944. Over recent years, both of those works have been performed in the United States, Israel, England, Holland, and Czechoslovakia. In addition, there are collections of instrumental and vocal selections culled from manuscripts found at the Terezin camp, many remaining anonymous creations. Of the literature and art, there also are remnants, most poignantly drawings and poems by the Terezin children.[14] A legacy of the songs and poems of the once-noted German folksinger and educator Ilse Weber (d. 1943), are among the collected literature and music that may be found in Israeli libraries and Holocaust memorials. While at Terezin she composed and sang her songs for the children, and she was transported with a group of them to Auschwitz to be gassed.[15] A survivor, Susan Cernyak-Spatz, speaking of her own incarceration at Terezin to an interviewer, said: "We lived as much as possible. Maybe we somehow supported the German efforts in sustaining this normalcy, but it had a much farther effect in that we kept our cultural and intellectual aspects very high and very intense on all levels."[16]

For eastern Europe, which for centuries had been the golden area of Yiddish culture, the artistic as well as human destruction proved catastrophic. Inspired by leaders of the nineteenth-century *haskalah* (enlightenment) movement in Judaism, which encouraged a broader range of educational and intellectual quest, Jewish life in that part of Europe had fast become remarkably productive in literature and the arts. Much of that creativity was expressed in a distinctive

Yiddish folk medium. During the first four decades of the twentieth century, there was a particular abundance of musical activities, both sacred and secular. It was as though, in final urgency, a burst of great expression erupted before the total extinction.

The Ashkenazic communities of Jewish Diaspora life in Europe over many centuries had elaborated, sanctified, and preserved the age-old religious musical traditions that illuminated their precious liturgy. For over four hundred years, the geographical area of eastern Europe was the most productive center for the training of *hazzanim* (precentors) and other musicians of the congregational rituals—bible chanters, choir singers, choral directors, liturgical composers, and music arrangers. Born, bred, and trained, they went forth to serve Jews throughout Europe and overseas in America. Synagogue music, based upon many centuries of unbroken lyric and poetic inspiration, was passed along the generations by means of personal instruction and apprenticeship. Handed on in that process of oral dissemination were unique cantorial styles, the techniques and nuances of devotional music making. By the eighteenth century, much of that great musical repertoire had begun to be committed to written scores and liturgical publications. As a result, by the early decades of the twentieth century, substantial libraries of liturgical music, either in the form of one-of-a-kind manuscripts or in books of liturgy, filled the sanctuaries and shelves of European synagogues, schools, and homes. Most of these were lost or went up in flames when those buildings were desecrated and destroyed. A torch was put to Judaica as the Nazis swept through all of the eastern European countries.

In secular music affairs, large choral groups and skillful composer-arrangers had emerged on the scene during the decade preceding World War I, including the famous *Hazamir* choirs of Vilna, Warsaw, and Lodz. Beyond the usual *klezmer* folk bands, there were musical ensembles that featured Jewish selections in concert halls and at communal events. Yiddish theater groups flourished, as for example the *Azazel* in Warsaw and the *Ararat* in Lodz, where general popular tunes were performed along with the Yiddish favorite songs before appreciative audiences of all types. Jews filled the vocal and instrumental performing ranks of eastern European orchestras and opera companies, appearing at light musicales and cabarets and on radio programs. They were music publishers, entrepreneurs of productions, creative figures, and reviewer-critics. They participated in the entire range of musical endeavors.

Bridging those active secular and sacred genres were the special folk songs and distinctive musical expressions of Jewish social and educational societies, labor groups, and organizations of secularists and of Zionists. There was the music of the ever-popular balladeers and instrumentalists at weddings, communal celebrations, and holiday festivities. Yiddish folk songs reflected all aspects of life, and most entertainers presented tunes with lyrics touching upon subjects of timely interest, of specific political, economic, and societal concerns. During the late 1920s and early 1930s, many balladeers warned in their songs about the dark menace emerging to the west in Germany.

After World War I, a new educational concept known as *tarbuth* (culture) had taken hold among eastern European Jews. Its purposes were the teaching of the Hebrew and Yiddish languages, along with Jewish history and customs, all by means of the arts, and particularly with music. As a result, a number of song-sters were published for that pedagogical outlook, whose ideas had also spread to American shores with the growth there of late-afternoon Hebrew academies and Jewish Sunday schools. For a while in the 1920s, American Jewry still looked to eastern Europe and the *tarbuth* concept for inspirational leadership in Jewish education. The development of children's schools and clubs afforded great impetus for the creation of new Jewish tunes and poetics. Here, as well as in the genre of popular Yiddish songs, the music favored by the Hasidic (pietist) sects throughout eastern Europe influenced the rhythms and melodies of the newer songs and dance tunes. In addition, there had always been a fluidity of musical movement, a symbiotic adaptability of melodic elements between Jews and Slavic Christians over the many centuries of Jewish settlement and accul-turation in the Slavic area of Europe. Moreover, during the first decades of the twentieth century, many of the ballads of Yiddish-American theatricals became popular in eastern Europe—in theaters, radio programs, recordings, and even sheet music. A number of the performing stars of those Jewish theatricals re-turned to European shores on tours of the large cities.

After 1939, musical expression persisted, as Jews were herded into the ghet-tos and then into the boxcars transporting them to the death camps. Their great resource of music served as a form of basic life force, likely affording a sem-blance of sanity in the face of the most insane of circumstances.[17] In the shrinking ghettos, adult choirs served as a last means of communication, and children's choruses became devices for the care of orphans. Finally, into the transports went the great body of Jewish melodic expression: liturgical musical traditions, holiday and Sabbath chants, favorite songs of family life and com-munity history, folk tunes from countless past generations, popular songs and art selections, street ditties and broadside ballads. Rapidly added to all that old fa-miliar music was a much newer expression—songs with special lyrics shaped to be sung in reaction to the most dreadful of human conditions. There can be no doubt that there was music making to the very end. It was a folk artistry wrought out of sheer necessity and age-old cultural habit, and in defiance of the Nazis and their malevolent helpers, in so many infamous places in Europe.

In some strange way, those freshly created songs traveled from ghetto to ghetto, and among the various concentration camps. One of those songs, known everywhere as the chant of the *frumer Yidn* (pious Jews), was *Ani Ma-amin* (I believe). It is an example of remarkable musical adaptation, the reshaping of mundane melodic elements into a chant song of profound spiritual significance. The brief Hebrew verse was chanted as an affirmation of a principle of Judaic faith at the very moment of death: "I believe, with true hope and trust, in the coming of the Messiah; and though that coming be delayed, I shall never stop believing." Its melody combines fragments of a well-known Jewish cabaret ballad of the 1920s with elements of the traditional *lernsteyg* (learning chant), a motival pattern traditionally intoned by the rabbinical students at their studies.[18]

Although the popular East European *badkh'n* (folk balladeer) Mordechai (Mordkhe) Gebirtig (1877–1943) had written *Es Brennt* (It is burning) in 1938 as an early warning song, it was sung with added lyrics over the following years as an ironic outcry to the outside world: "Our little town is on fire; it is burning and you helplessly stand by, watching as the flames grow wilder and higher. Who will quench the blaze, my brothers? All our world is on fire!"[19]

So many gifted musicians were lost! A few of their names now are known only through reports of some final musical activities. It is by means of those meager recollections that the enormous artistic loss is underscored. David Eisenstadt, noted scholar and musician, organized a symphonic ensemble and chorus in the Warsaw ghetto. His daughter, Maryasha Eisenstadt, was called "nightingale of the ghetto." Both were murdered in 1942 when they resisted capture for deportation. Israel Faiveshes, music educator and conservatory director, organized children's choruses in the ghettos of Warsaw, Lodz, and Vilna. Sent to the Piantova Concentration Camp, he continued to teach youngsters to sing, and perished there with them. Jacob Glatschtein had been a prolific writer of pedagogical songs and choral works for the Yiddish schools. Imprisoned at Treblinka, he gathered the children together and taught them songs before they were all gassed. In the Vilna ghetto, Abraham Slep, who had founded and directed a major music institute in Vilna, led a chorus performing elegies in open defiance of the Nazis following a particularly savage massacre in April 1943 at Ponar (much like what had taken place at Babi Yar in the Ukraine). Slep was thereupon transported to Esthonia, where he was shot as a dangerous political leader.

Jewish musicians were treated especially harshly in the camps because their music influenced the people, helped keep bonds of relationship, or at least afforded some essence of humanity and continuity. Jewish music was used to communicate between ghettos and camps, and to share information among resistance fighters. In the Vilna ghetto, a music contest was held. The winning song, *Shtiler, Shtiler* (Quiet, quiet), was submitted by an eleven-year-old child, Alex Volkovisky, who survived and later emigrated to Israel. The melody and words were elaborated upon by many others at the camps, singing to each other: "Quiet, silence! Make no noise; graves around us are growing. Roads lead to Ponar, to terrible places, but none lead back. Days are black with endless grief, and hearts are frozen numb. Our crime is to be hated, to be Jews. Who can understand that?" There were many more poetic lyrics that outlasted the melodies to which they had been sung in the camps. Some texts begged those who might survive never to forget what had happened to the others. There were songs and poems of the barely alive mourning those who had died, of those who did not know where loved ones had gone, of pleas to the outside world for rescue. It is likely that every possible emotion was expressed during that era. The traditional Jewish love of music and literature had blended with a desperate will to prevail, if only posthumously, through an artistry that might last beyond the awful times and tell the whole dreadful story to generations ahead. Fortunately, some of the songs and their poetics survived their creators, and have been published in collected arrangements.[20]

Most pathetic were the lullabies sung by strangers to orphans, by bereft mothers alone, and by children to each other. Among remnants of such songs is the eloquent *S'dremlen Feygel oyf di Tsvaygen* (Birds are sleeping on the branches): "Sleep poor baby, hungry baby. On the cold ground beside you, a stranger softly sings, a stranger softly weeps." Another one is an ironic refashioning of the original words and melody of a widely known and beloved lullaby composed by Abraham Goldfaden, *Rozhinkes mit Mandlen* (Raisins and almonds),[21] retitled and sung as *Nit Kayn Rozhinkes, Nit Kayn Mandlen* (Not any raisins, not any almonds): "Little ones, here you are all alone. Father will never bring you any sweets, and mother is also gone forever." The original *Rozhinkes mit Mandlen* was also altered textually, playing upon its lovely tune in a poignant way. Retaining the exact melody, the newer lyrics (attributed to an Orthodox Jew from Kovno named Axelrod) was sung as *Di Letsteh Videh* (The last testament or will): "To my fellow Jews, and all my brothers, I leave this final message. Tell your children of our grievous suffering and terrible destruction, Never forget us." Newer texts were constantly sung to old familiar melodies, and familiar melodies were altered to suit newer poetic purposes.

Survivors relate how the imprisoned in ghettos and concentration camps endeavored to maintain their cultural and intellectual expression with ever more intensity as they faced death. It was a reaffirmation of will. Promises were made that those who might survive would never forget, making certain that the world would know and also remember: "Live, so you can tell everyone what happened here!" The shriek of spiritual resistance was: "I have taken an oath to remember it all; to forget nothing, forgetting nothing of this until the tenth generation disappears. To the last, to its ending, till the punishing blows are ended for good, I swear this night of terror shall not have passed in vain. I swear this morning I will not live unchanged, as if I were no wiser even now" (by Abraham Shlonsky and Chaim Stern).[22]

Ethnic folklore arose out of such desperate need. Beyond comfort or communication, people wrote songs, poems, and messages to the future, transforming themselves into real individuals rather than faceless tattoo numbers. Realizing that this singing particularly afforded dignity and strength, the Nazis often shot singers on sight. Escaping from a roundup in the Vilna ghetto in 1941, a writer named Abraham Sutzkever hid in a closed box for hours. While there, he composed a poem: "So this is the rule. Here today, somewhere else tomorrow; and in this coffin now as in stiff wooden clothing, my speech still moves into song."[23] In this manner, simple poetry and melody transcended the label of mere folklore and, passing into the realm of art, became historic documentation.

Among the Jewish partisan fighters, whistles and tunes were used as signals, especially one particular song, *Zog Nit Keynmol as du Geyst dem Letsten Veg* (Do not say you are going on the final road): "Never say that this is the end of the way. Though all around is darkness and death, the time is coming soon when our footsteps will resound in triumph. Wherever our blood has red-stained the ground, from there will our courage and strength take root and blossom forth anew. The world will surely know that we are still here!" The author of that text was Hirsh Glik (1920–1944). Born and bred in Vilna, he organized the resistance groups there, and then in 1943 escaped the ghetto to join partisans outside of the city. Glik was captured and shipped to a camp in Esthonia, where he again escaped, but he soon died in the woods nearby battling against Nazi soldiers. He had wanted to be a journalist, and wrote this poem among other protest pieces. It was immediately sung to a well-known march melody of the time, and became such a widely popular song during the final months of the war that even many non-Jews fighting the Nazis sang it.[24]

Although Yiddish had rapidly become the predominant language in the ghettos and death camps, among the prisoners were many Jews of other vernacular backgrounds, including those of the Judeo-Spanish tradition known as *Sephardim*, who had lived in Holland, Belgium, France, Italy, the Balkans, Greece, and Turkey. Before they lost their lives, many maintained their particular cultural heritage and sang their own traditional *ladino* (Judeo-Español) ballads and liturgical chants. Dismayed that less is generally known concerning those Jewish victims of the Holocaust, scholars have endeavored to collect any remnants of literature, especially poetry, as a particular Sephardic legacy from the camps.[25]

The period from the surrender of the German army in May 1945 to the formal creation of the State of Israel in May 1948 was a twilight era in Jewish history. It was a time of full realization of the enormous crime done to six million men, women, and children, all punished simply for being Jewish. Almost immediately, efforts were begun to salvage what was left, in terms of any human survivors as well as the legacy of all who had been murdered. Gathered were a variety of materials—letters, documents, communal records, literary pieces, notes of communication, Nazi reports, and camp dossiers—that testified to what actually had happened. That process of collection grew rapidly as a mission of verification, along with the tallying of what had been destroyed. In terms of music and poetics, there emerged a modest body of precious works, consisting of timely and poignant lyrics, some sung to adapted familiar tunes and others to melodies composed on the spot. Some were merely fragments of ditties or snatches of chants. The songs had served the needs of their martyred singers.

Most of the texts were created in Yiddish, a language of intense resonance for the victims. Yet, the strength of that human expression readily has passed into English and other linguistic translations. Each item of poetics embodies a special message, reflecting emotional reactions and relating details of actual events. Most notable among the postwar collectors of these materials was a concentration camp survivor, Shmerke Kaczerginski (1908–1953), to whom lasting gratitude must be expressed for his undaunted dedication to gathering together a truly comprehensive volume of priceless cultural resource materials.[26]

In response to the full knowledge of what had happened and the consequent impact of that catastrophe upon general society, all types of creative artists, especially writers and musicians, have been inspired to express their reactions to the Holocaust in a wide spectrum of works and activities. Composers in particular have taken on the almost impossible burden of interpreting and memorializing by means of music. In this case, as with actual Holocaust songs, the usual yardsticks of aesthetic principles ought not be applied. Indeed, since all of this music is by no means pleasurable, performances are likely to be rare. However, memorial compositions continue to be written. Perhaps a future music genius will fashion a masterpiece worthy of this subject, successfully moving beyond the actual horror and anguish to a sublime level of artistry.[27]

In 1962, Dmitri Shostakovich wrote his thirteenth symphony, *Babi Yar*, memorializing the thousands of Ukrainian Jews murdered in 1941 at a location known as Babi Yar, or Old Wives Ravine, an area outside of Kiev. Arnold Schoenberg, who found refuge from the Nazis in America in 1934, composed "A Survivor from Warsaw" in 1947. Scored for speaker, male chorus, and chamber orchestra, it was commissioned by the Serge Koussevitzky Foundation. Schoenberg wrote an English text for it, and this brief musical work is starkly powerful, building up to a highly dramatic chanting of *Sh'ma Yisrael* (Hear, Israel), the age-old Jewish affirmation of faith.

Accounts of post World War II musical activities in Germany, Poland and other European countries reveal much in what they do not contain, in what is missing. For a good while after the end of the war, the special Jewish music ingredients—composers, vocal and instrumental performing artists, conductors, educators, scholars, entrepreneurs—were absent from the scene.[28] The elements of distinctively European Jewish music have been transplanted elsewhere, and the creative vitality indigenous to Yiddish eastern European life is gone forever. As the twentieth century draws to a close, Jewish musicians from America and Israel have become familiar participants in European musical activities of all types.[29]

The master scholar of Jewish history, Heinrich Hirsch Graetz (1817–1891) characterized Jewish history as *Leidens und Gelehrtensgeschichte* (martyrdom and scholarship). The Bible itself provides ample examples of Judaism's martyrology: the later Psalms, Scroll of Esther, and Book of Maccabees. Accounts of the torturous deaths of Rabbi Akiva and other Jewish sages at the hands of the

Romans are recalled not only in historical chronicles but in traditional memorial prayer texts, notably in the *makhzor* (sacred devotional text) of the High Holy Days. Inflictions and injustices as well as pogroms and banishments crowd the annals of centuries of Western civilization, culminating in the raging and ravaging wrought at the mid-twentieth century. During the hardships of the Middle Ages, an anonymous Jew wrote a bitter personal commentary for the local martyrologies that were listed in old communal prayer books: "Master of the Universe. I know You are doing everything to make me test my faith, to desert my people and my heritage. And yet, You know that I am a Jew, and I will remain a Jew. And through all the sufferings, through flame and flood, I shall never cease to be a Jew."

Social historians cannot afford to ignore the significance of the art of music, and most especially of those songs created by and for the people themselves. In partnership with poetic expression, such songs have served mankind as a valuable form of information concerning times, places, and events. They have been written and sung by so many individuals striving in the maelstrom of mortal existence and seeking verification of human continuity. Viewed in such perspectives, the music from the Holocaust era constitutes a particularly valuable documentary resource. Reflective of an abiding historical tragedy, those musical materials serve to underscore the critical role of poetics and melody as intrinsic to the totality of experience and expression. Arising out of the confines of ghettos and concentration camps, sung at the very edge of destruction, the songs constitute a unique cultural expression crafted under the worst of circumstances. In every sense, such ad hoc artistry amplifies the facts of recent history and the enormous loss suffered not only by Jewry but by all of humanity. We have been bequeathed this legacy, a melodic portrait set within a landscape of screams.

NOTES

This chapter was originally prepared as an essay "Music of the Holocaust" for the publication *Handbook of Holocaust Literature*, edited by Saul S. Friedman (Westport, Conn.: Greenwood Press, 1993). For this chapter, additional detailed information on this entire topic has been added, along with appended reference notes.

Additional comment: I purposefully have not provided biographical dates for any of the Nazis mentioned in this chapter. They are all gone at this writing, and the important matter is only to note their names and to document some part of the horror that they perpetrated, in specific relating to the field of music, during their lives.

1. An exceptionally valuable study of the Nazi political and social attitudes and policies concerning music has been presented in the doctoral thesis of Michael Meyer: "Assumptions and Implementation of Nazi Policy toward Music" (University of California at Los Angeles, 1970–1971; typescript, University Microfilms, Ann Arbor,

Mich.). With extensive documentary treatment, Meyer discusses the following significant topics: the background of German musical nationalism before 1933; ideological
cultural attitudes in Germany, including Richard Wagner and issues of "music and
race"; the emergence of National Socialism and the use of music in its rise to power;
the organizational control by Nazis of music; and an overview of Hitler's "new" German music and musicians. I am much indebted to this fine research work on the part
of Michael Meyer for some valuable information included in this chapter.

2. Joseph Goebbels had been associated with Hitler since 1926. An amateur pianist
and sometime painter and writer, he had been promised the post of jurisdiction over
German culture. His rival for that position had been Alfred Rosenberg, who in 1929
with Alfred Heuss had founded a "combat league" to fight for pure German culture.
Associated with Rosenberg at that time was Hans Pfistner, the music ideologue for the
National Socialists, who along with Siegmund von Hausegger, Hermann Abendroth,
and Hugo Rasch, wrote articles attacking Jewish and Negro music and musicians.
While Pfistner had fully expected to become the director of the Chamber of Music,
Goebbels appointed his own party allies, first Hans Hinkel, and then Peter Raabe.

3. "Whether the decadence of our culture can be prevented by forcible expulsion of
foreign elements of pernicious character I cannot say, as powers for this purpose are
requisite, of the existence of which I am not aware." Richard Wagner, *Das Judentum
in der Musik*, trans. Edwin Evans (London: Reeves, 1910), p. 93.

4. Another exposition advancing the anti-Semitic musical ideas of Richard Wagner
was issued by *Schriften des Reichsinstitut fuer Geschichte des neuen Deutschlands*
(Writings of the German Institute for History of the New Germany): Karl Richard Gan-
zer, *Richard Wagner und das Judentum* (Hamburg: Hanseatische Verlagsstelt, 1938–
1939).

5. Among those infamous pseudoscholarly works were:

Michael Alt, *Deutsches Art in Musik* (German art in music), issued as part of a series of writings, *Bildung und Natsion, Schriftenreihe zur national politischen
Erziehung* (Culture and nation, a series of writings on national political educational
matters) (Leipzig: Eichblatt-Verlag, 1936).

Joachim DuKart and Guido Waldmann, eds., *Rasse und Musik* (Race and music)
(Berlin: Lichterfelde and C. F. Vieweg, 1939).

Karl Blessinger, *Judentum un Musik: Der Jude als Kulturparasit, ein Beitrag zur
Kultur un Rassenpolitik* (Jews and music: the Jew as cultural parasite, a contribution to
[essay on] culture and racial politics) (Berlin: B. Hahnefeld, 1943–1944). Issued just at
the time of the worst massacres in the concentration camps, Blessinger's work described the music creativity of Jews—particularly of Mendelssohn, Meyerbeer, and
Mahler—in the most despicable of terms.

In addition, as late as 1944–45, Helmuth Sommerfeld penned a work, *Judesches
Weisen in musikalischen Darstellung* (Jewish ways in musical performance), issued in
Berlin by the German Office of Youth and Folk.

In 1937, Hans Joachim Moser had personally distributed his own book, *Di Musik
der Deutschen Stamme* (The music of the German tribe). Crafted to curry favor with

Nazi leaders of German academia, it was rampant with crude racism, factual distortions, and sloppy scholarship. After the end of World War II, Moser continued to be active in German music affairs. In 1957–1958, he compiled a roster of biographical briefs, *Musikgeschichte in hundert Lebensbildern* (Music history in one hundred life stories) (Wiesbaden: R. Lowit). Included were a number of Jewish composers. No mention was made by Moser, in any part of his book of over a thousand pages of biographical material, regarding Nazi bans of music, exiles of leading Jewish and non-Jewish musicians, numerous anti-Semitic officially published diatribes issued during the Nazi regime, nor the concentration camps where so many musicians perished. Moser had "erased" the entire Nazi era.

6. For an excellent study of this musical topic see Michael Kater, *Different Drummers: Jazz in the Culture of Nazi Germany* (New York: Oxford University Press, 1992). Kater treats popular music by Jews as well as by Afro-Americans. I am indebted to him for some interesting information, as, for instance, the fact that before Jesse Owens was insulted at the 1936 World Olympics in Berlin, the contralto Marian Anderson had been barred in 1935 from performing any concerts in Germany. Kater notes that swing music as well as jazz was officially forbidden, although there was much "underground" jazz even through the war years, when German bands played camouflaged arrangements of the American popular styles, adapting liberally from Duke Ellington, Benny Goodman, Artie Shaw, Chick Webb, and early Nat King Cole. Efforts at German *Volk* (people) jazz were generally ignored by the public. Toward the end of the war, their radios were tuning to foreign stations as much for the pop tunes and other forbidden music as for the outside news itself.

7. It was not until September 1938 that Goebbels himself issued a ban on all songs by Irving Berlin and George Gershwin (his two private favorites) as well as on the many recordings of such American favorites as the English version of Sholom Secunda's *Bei mir bistu sheyn*.

8. "The melodies of the NSDAP songster literature were to a large extent borrowed. Most of them were old German folk or soldier songs; others included an American soldier song, but also some of other nations." Meyer, "Nazi Policy toward Music," p. 508.

9. Among those publications are:

Josef Bor, *The Terezin Requiem*, trans. from the Czech by Edith Pargeter (New York: Knopf, 1963).

Fania Fenelon and Marcelle Rautier, *The Musicians of Auschwitz*, trans. from the French by J. Landry (London: Atheneum, 1977).

Emilio Jani, *My Voice saved Me—Auschwitz 180046*, trans. from the Italian by Timothy Paterson (Milan: Centauro Editrice, 1961).

Zdenek Lederer, *Ghetto Theresienstadt/Terezin* (London: E. Goldston, 1953).

10. For information about many of the European musicians who perished and those who were able to flee abroad, see Artur Holde, *Jews in Music: From the Age of Enlightenment to the Mid-Twentieth Century*, revised edition by Irene Heskes (New York: Bloch Publishing, 1974).

In Germany, Artur Holde (1885–1962) had been a composer, choral conductor, and music journalist. After 1933, he and his wife, the concert pianist Heida Hermanns, were active with the *Kulturbund*. They managed to escape to America in 1937 under a guise of concertizing abroad. Over a number of years, Holde served as a music director and organist for synagogues in New York City and was music editor of a German-American weekly, *Aufbau* (Rebuilding). He also wrote monographs on various musical figures and contributed to music journals.

11. A good source of detailed information about the camp and its musical activities is Joza Karas, *Music in Terezin 1941 to 1945* (New York: Beaufort Books, 1985).

12. Bor, *Terezin Requiem*.

13. See Max Bloch, "Viktor Ullman (1898–1943): A Brief Biography and Appreciation," *Journal of the Arnold Schoenberg Institute*, vol. 3, no.2 (1979), pp. 150–77.

14. A collection of those poems, posthumously titled *I Never Saw Another Butterfly* has inspired a number of musical settings, among them a cantata composed by Jewish liturgist Charles Davidson.

15. An edition of some of Weber's poetry was issued in Israel in 1964 and then published in its original German in 1991: Ilse Weber, *In deinen Mauern wohnt das Leid: Gedichte aus dem KZ Theresienstadt* (Within your walls dwells sorrow: poetry from Terezin Concentration Camp) (Gerlinger, Germany: Bleicher, 1991).

16. Esther Katz and Joan Miriam Ringelheim, eds., *Proceedings of the Conference on Women Surviving the Holocaust* (New York: Institute for Research in History, 1983), p. 30.

17. A number of studies concerning the therapeutic role of music among Nazi victims have been published over recent decades. Of special interest are two published studies by a Polish psychologist, A. Kulisiewitcz: "Psychopathology of Music and Songs in the Nazi Concentration Camps," *PRLKA—Przeglad Lekarski* (Warsaw, 1974), pp. 39–45, and "Music and Songs as a Factor of Self-Defense among Inmates of Nazi Concentration Camps," in *PRLKA-Przeglad Lekarski* (Warsaw: 1977), pp. 66–77. Both articles are available from the American Institute of Therapeutics Research in New York.

18. This song is highlighted in the following publications:

Emma Schaver and Lazar Weiner, comps. and arrs., *Songs of the Concentration Camps* (New York: Transcontinental Music/UAHC, 1960).

Ruth Rubin, ed., *The Warsaw Ghetto Memorial Program* (New York: Workmen's Circle Organization, 1967).

Among the very many published vocal solo and choral performance arrangements of *Ani Ma-amin* and other Holocaust songs are those by Abraham W. Binder, Julius Chajes, Charles Davidson, Abraham Ellstein, Michl Gelbart, Max Helfman, Henoch Kon, Velvel Pasternak, Maurice Rauch, Joseph Rumshinsky, Sholom Secunda, and Lazar Weiner.

19. For additional information about Gebirtig and some of his other songs, see Joseph Mlotek, *Mordechai/Mordkhe Gebirtig, Martyred Troubadour of Our People* (New York: Workmen's Circle Organization, 1970).

20. There are several well arranged collections of Holocaust songs and poetics:

Ernest Horvitz, comp. and arr., *Out of the Depths: From the Songs of the Ghettos* (Tel Aviv: Histadruth Organization, 1949).

Shoshana Kalisch and Barbara Meister, comps. and arrs., *Yes, We Sang! Songs of the Ghettos and Concentration Camps* (New York: Harper & Row, 1985).

Henoch Kon, comp. and arr., *Songs of the Ghetto*, Vols. 1 and 2 (New York: Congress for Jewish Culture/CYCO, 1960 and 1972).

Chana Mlotek and Malka Gottlieb, comps. and arrs., *Twenty-Five Ghetto Songs* (New York: Workmen's Circle Organization, 1968).

Chana Mlotek and Malka Gottlieb, comps. and arrs., *We Are Here! Songs of the Holocaust* (New York: Hippocrene Books, 1983).

21. For further information about the song *Rozhinkes mit Mandlen* and Abraham Goldfaden, refer to Chapter 17 (Yiddish Musical Theater: Its Origins in Europe).

22. This text may be found in the official Reform prayer book for the High Holy Days, *The Gates of Repentance* (p. 432), and has been set for mixed choir and organ by Michael Isaacson (New York: Transcontinental Press/UAHC).

23. Sutzkever survived and resettled in Israel. I am indebted for this excerpt of his poem to an article by Ruth S. Wisse, "The Ghetto Poems of Abraham Sutzkever," *The Jewish Book Annual*, Vol. 36 (New York, 1979), pp. 26–36; poem trans. by Seymour Mayne, p. 31.

24. Two studies treating the significant role of songs created and sung in the ghettos and concentration camps are:

Gila Flam, *Singing for Survival: Songs of the Lodz Ghetto*, 1940–1945 (Urbana.: University of Illinois Press, 1992).

Ruth Rubin, "Yiddish Songs of World War II," *Jewish Quarterly*, vol. 2, no.2 (World Jewish Congress) (1963), pp. 12–17.

25. For additional information, see Isaac Jack Levy, "Holocaust Poetry: The Forgotten Sephardim," *The Sephardic Scholar*, vol. 4, ed. Rachel Dalven (New York: Yeshiva University Press, 1979–82), pp. 111–24. Scholars associated with the American Society of Sephardic Studies, including David F. Altabe, Salomon Gaon, and Mitchell Serels, have collected poetics and other writings as well as communal records. All of those materials are available at the library of Yeshiva University in New York City.

26. Shmerke (Shmariah) Kaczerginski, comp. and ed., *Lider fun di Getos un Lagern—Songs and Poetry from the Ghettos and Concentration Camps*, with additional annotations by H. Leivick (Leivick Halper), and musical notations by Michl Gelbart (New York: CYCO/Congress for Jewish Culture, 1948).

27. Among the many composers who have taken on the subject of the Holocaust are Samuel Adler, Emanuel Amiran, David Amram, Abraham W. Binder, Uriah Boscovitch, John Cage, Mario Castelnuovo-Tedesco, Charles Davidson, Lukas Foss, Herbert Fromm, Arthur Gelbrun, Srul Irving Glick, Morton Gould, Max Helfman, Sergiu Natra, Oedoen Partos, Kryzysztof Penderecki, Shulamith Ran, Eda Rapaport, Heinrich Schalit, Arnold Schoenberg, Mordecai Seter, Dmitri Shostakovich, Robert Starer,

Mikia Theodorakis, Franz Waxman, Hugo Weisgall, Richard Wernick, and Yehudi Wyner.

28. A good description of that absence is Lidia Rappaport-Gelfand, *Musical Life in Poland: The Post-War Years 1945–1977*, trans. Irina Lasoff (New York: Gordon and Breach, 1991).

29. In 1969, I met with the Yiddish actress Ida Kaminska (d. 1980), then a recent arrival in New York City. She readily discussed her hopes for a renewal of Yiddish theater and Jewish music in Poland. For some years after World War II, Kaminska and her acting troupe had been performing in Warsaw and other Polish cities, where a renewal of general interest in the old Yiddish productions and their tunes had heartened her and others who had returned to eastern Europe. In Poland, the theaters were state run and the artists received their salaries from the government. Most of the people in her audiences were non-Jewish and highly appreciative. By the late 1960s, however, that sunny climate appeared to have changed for the worse. A remarkably resilient artist, Ida Kaminska commented to me upon the fact that, as in so many times in the past, she and her family of actors were making a new start in yet another country. She said then: "Everyone hopes for the beginning of a new life. Jews have to be optimistic; otherwise there is no chance for them."

Part VII

America

20

Three Hundred Years of Jewish Music in America

The music of American Jewry is a specific ethno-geographic matter as well as an intricate integration of worldwide Jewish musical elements created and acquired, developed and transmitted, over centuries of Western civilization. Composed of tradition and history, liturgy and folklore, custom and artistry, Jewish music delineates the calendar of the year and the human life cycle. It has qualities of timelessness, yet is deeply rooted in the here-and-now of existence. Although personally focused, it is communally oriented. Its melodic diversity is word centered. Above all, it is a lively complex of nonmusical as well as musical components.

Early in the twentieth century, the philosopher-educator Horace Kallen propounded the concept of cultural pluralism in America. Reflecting upon the viable differences among American people, he rejected the inevitability of a melting pot ideal. Kallen justified the continuity of different racial, religious, and ethnic expressions in the country as being compatible with an American way of life, and in fact as the wellspring of strength in a free society. Since 1654, Jewish settlers on American shores have discovered an extraordinary environment in which to seek fulfillment. The arts, and music in particular, have amply reflected that fruitfulness. Indeed, there has been a modern renascence, the rise of a distinctive American Jewish musical genre well beyond echoes of the past in other lands.

The Jewish people who emigrated to continental America from many areas of the world brought along a complex legacy of melodic influences, both religious and mundane. What happened to that music, as implanted in this new environment?

Early Arrivals

Following their expulsion from Spain in 1492, Sephardic Jews divided into two distinct groups: Spanish-Portuguese, settling at first in northern Europe, especially the Netherlands and France; and, Mediterraneans, migrating among the sea islands to southern Italy, and then populating areas of Greece, the Balkans, and the Turkish Empire. Many also joined with the "Oriental" Jews living in North Africa, Palestine, and other areas of the Near East. Generally, all retained the Ladino vernacular tongue and old Spaniolic customs and folklore, along with a significantly consistent order of liturgy and liturgical chant. Over the next centuries, each group of those *Sefardim* enhanced their reservoir of religious music and secular folk songs, influenced by newer geographical circumstances and ethnic influences. Many of them were seafarers, involved in shipbuilding and ocean commerce. A persistent story places a crypto-Jew (*marrano*) named Luis de Torres as one of the map makers on the historic voyage of Christopher Columbus. Torres is believed to have finally settled on the island of Cuba. By the early seventeenth century, Sephardic Jews were reported to have colonized in the West Indies, Cuba, Mexico, and various areas of Central and South America, including Curaçao, Surinam, and Paramaribo.

The first Jew on Manhattan Island was Jacob Barsimon, who arrived on a ship from the Netherlands in August 1654. The following month, twenty-three Sephardic Jews came to New Amsterdam as subjects from a former Dutch colony in Pernambuco, Brazil. Expelled and set adrift by the Portuguese, they were rescued from attacks of Spanish pirates by a French ship that brought them to New Netherlands. Upon orders of the Dutch West India Company, Governor Peter Stuyvesant admitted them, with the proviso that they be entirely responsible for their own welfare. Their leader was Asser Levy, and they called their religious congregation *Shearith Israel* (Remnant of Israel).[1] In 1658, a Sephardic group from Curaçao settled in Newport, Rhode Island, welcomed there by Roger Williams.[2] Then, in 1733, Jews from London came to Savannah, Georgia, and in 1741, some *Sefardim* helped establish the community of Charleston, South Carolina. Soon afterwards, other Jews settled in Philadelphia and Baltimore. By the outbreak of the Revolutionary War, there were an estimated 3,000 Jews in the Thirteen Colonies, most of whom were of Sephardic origins. While some Jews remained loyal to British rule, three hundred served in the Revolutionary Army under George Washington,[3] among them his staff officer Benjamin Nones. By that time, there were also Ashkenazic Jews in America, including Hayim Salomon from Poland. As ratified in 1790, the American Constitution provided there not be any religious test for public offices, and in 1791, the First Amendment guaranteed that there not be any established governmental religion and assured the right to free exercise of one's faith.[4]

Initially, Jewish religious services were held in private homes. Congregation Shearith Israel dedicated its first building in 1730 at Mills Street in Lower Manhattan. Soon afterwards, there were other houses of worship, appropriately named *Yeshuah Israel* (Salvation of Israel), later known as Truro synagogue in Newport, Rhode Island; *Beth Elohim* (House of God) in Charleston, South Carolina; and *Mikveh Israel* (Hope of Israel) in Philadelphia, Pennsylvania.

Although the Shearith Israel group had appointed someone named Saul Brown in 1682 to serve as its nominal minister, the first officially designated *hazzan* (cantor or precentor) in America was Isaac da Costa (1721–1796). He came from London in 1750 and began to serve the congregation in Charleston in 1756. However, Isaac Touro was the earliest fully professional *hazzan* to officiate in America. He had emigrated from Amsterdam in 1760 to lead the congregation at Newport in the very building (ca.1763) that stands to this day. The first American book of prayer for Jewish observances was printed in 1761, with English text in addition to an abridged Hebrew liturgy. It was for the ritual of the High Holy Days, and believed to be the work of someone named Isaac Pinto. In 1809, a separate Hebrew book of the Psalms was published.

The Pilgrims had brought to America their Psalm book (Ainsworth, 1612), a psalter with thirty-nine tunes. That book constituted an influential musical source because the Puritans preferred songs whose texts were based upon Scripture. Melodies familiar also to French Huguenots and Pietists in Holland were sung. For those early settlers, prayer with music was integral to daily life. When Sephardic seaman Isaac de Rasieres visited the Plymouth colony in 1627, he noted in his diary the importance of Psalm singing and the absence of instrumentation at the services. Musical instruments were permitted at home, where there were viols and harmoniums. The first book printed in the English-speaking American colonies was the *Bay Psalm Book*, published in 1640 in Cambridge, Massachusetts. It had only text, but it did include references to known melodies from the *Ravenscroft Psalter* (London, 1821). When in 1698 music was added to that early Cambridge Psalm book, it became the first music collection to be published in America. By the 1700s, there were many different types of immigrants arriving in America, bringing along their varied musical traditions and tastes. However, psalmody and hymnody had become the characteristic aspects of religious musical expression, and those liturgical qualities were recognized and appreciated by Jewish settlers. When Nathan Levy died in 1752 in Philadelphia, his legacy included numerous music books, including English psalters, and a viol. In 1753, a Jew named Joseph Ottolenghi was observed teaching Psalm singing to the Negroes on plantations in the Georgia area.[5]

In 1976, during the celebration of the American Bicentennial, Shearith Israel (now more familiarly known in New York City as the Spanish and Portuguese Synagogue) held a commemorative service. Exhibited was a Torah scroll mantle that still showed blood stains and bullet holes sustained during a conflict in 1776 between colonists and British soldiers. The celebrative 1976 service replicated the religious devotions of two hundred years earlier, and concluded with a Sephardic memorial prayer (*hashcabah*) intoned for their congregants and for all the other Jews who had served in the American War of Independence. In those earlier revolutionary times, the religious officiator (*haham*) had been Gershom Mendes Seixas (1745–1816), who served there (except for some war years) from 1768 to 1816. Born in America, he was a dedicated spiritual leader who brought to the religious office a strong tradition of Sephardic ritual and musical heritage, including the Ladino sacred and secular folk songs. As a precentor, he set standards for strict intonation of cantillations and for limited improvisation upon the modes and chant motifs of the prayers. He also structured the congregational responses and hymnology and trained volunteers for an all-male choir. During the nineteenth century, Shearith Israel followed its congregants, moving further uptown in Manhattan. In 1897, the synagogue was established at its permanent location on Central Park West, where the liturgical music standards set by Gershom Mendes Seixas continue to prevail as the twentieth century draws to a close.

After Independence

When he came to America, Gustavus Poznanski (1805–1879), though of Ashkenazic background, was an assistant officiant at Shearith Israel in New York. He soon went on to serve as precentor-minister at Congregation Beth Elohim in Charleston, South Carolina. By 1830, a number of dynamic changes had occurred among Jewish immigrants to America. Not only were the mid-European Germanic and Prussian-Polish Jews fast becoming the dominant groupings, but the new ideas of Jewish liturgical reform had arrived on American shores. In 1832, Poznanski compiled a first American Jewish hymnal, which was formulated like the American Protestant hymnals. Then, in 1838, he introduced an organ-harmonium into religious services, soon leading a breakaway group of congregants to establish the Reform Society of Israelites, an earliest formal implantation of that movement on American shores. Eventually Beth Elohim incorporated many of the Reform Society practices for a reunited congregation. In 1865, Poznanski returned to New York City to become a textile merchant. At that time, he applied for membership at Congregation Shearith Israel, where he worshipped at those traditional Sephardic services to the end of his life.

By 1840, there were over 15,000 American Jews settled in the South and Midwest, especially in Indiana, Illinois, Missouri, Ohio, Kentucky, Louisiana, Georgia, and the Carolinas, and a decade later, in the Far West: California, Oregon, and Utah. A naval hero of the War of 1812 had been Uriah P. Levy, of German birth. Out in the Texas territory, Adolphus Stern had established the town of Nacogdoches in 1824, and Moses Albert Levy served as surgeon to Sam Houston. A first *Yom Kippur* service was held in San Francisco in 1849, and the following year two congregations were established there, a reformed, or "German," and a traditional, or "Polish." By 1860, there were many Jewish congregations throughout the country, and some officially listed their leader as a minister, in the manner of the Protestant churches. Temple Emanu-El in New York City was established in 1845 with a rabbi, Leo Merzbacher (d. 1856), as well as a music leader, Gustave M. Cohen (fl. 19th cent.), who served until 1852. Cohen had come from Germany in 1844, and was considered the first professional precentor of Emanu-El. According to archival records, the rabbinical sermons were given in German and English, and the duties assigned to the cantorial officiant included leadership at services, training of a choir, teaching children, and, ministering at births, marriages and funerals. In 1853, there was a public concert with soloists, chorus, and orchestra in order to raise funds for the purchase and installation of an organ in the sanctuary. Temple Emanu-El moved to its current Manhattan site in 1930.[6]

The earliest published popular music selection of Judaic content in America was "The Sorrowing Jew," originally composed in London by George J. Webb (fl. 19th cent.) with lyrics by Matthew A. Berk (fl. 19th cent.). A sort of hymn tune, it was printed in Boston in three editions between 1841 and 1843. The music was issued in the form of a commercial song sheet with an elaborate lithographic cover design featuring an old Jew mourning for the destruction of the Holy Temple in Jerusalem, along with an undertext: "If I forget thee, O Jerusalem, may my right hand forget its cunning" (Psalm 127). At the same time, music for various Jewish hymns began to be included in the issues of a Philadelphia Jewish periodical called *The Occident*.[7] Meanwhile, in Philadelphia in 1838, Rebecca Gratz (1781–1869) had started the first American Sunday School for Jewish children, utilizing liturgical poetics and hymn tunes for the religious lessons.

A revised and enlarged version of Gustavus Poznanski's earlier hymnal was published in 1843 and issued again in 1856 by the reconstituted Temple Beth Elohim in Charleston. The 1856 publication of their hymnal, titled *Hymns Written for the Use of Hebrew Congregations*, indicates on the title page that it is the "third edition, revised and corrected." The hymns are all in English text and topically sorted, with an index listing of first lines. That hymnal included many of the German Reform materials, as compiled, translated, and edited by Sephardic poetess Penina Moise (1797–1880), with the addition of some of her own texts. Indeed, she may be considered the first American Jewish hymnodist of record. Her edition, consisting of fifty English hymns for Sabbath, High Holy Days, festivals, and confirmation, became very popular throughout the American South, and was reprinted for the dedication in 1873 of a new congregational building in Charleston. Its musical settings were highly derivative of Protestant anthems, along with adapted snatches of classical melodies. There was meager resonance with traditional Jewish music, but some elements were still retained from the Sephardic liturgical chant, such as Poznanski's metered version of the traditional *hallel* (Song of praise). Rendered with a newer English text ("For still in rev'rent tones is heard"), that particular hymn tune bears a striking similarity to the melody of the modern Jewish anthem *Hatikvah* (The hope).

Emergent Reform Judaism

The Reform movement in Judaism may have arisen in Europe, but when transplanted to American soil, it came into full flower, with highly significant

Jewish musical developments. The winds of political, social, and religious change had swept across western and central Europe early in the nineteenth century. European Jews trusted that this new age of humanism would be their era of *haskalah* (enlightenment and auto-emancipation), a time of greater opportunities for general education and for participation in the intellectual and cultural mainstream. Some sought to modernize Judaic customs and ceremonials and to bring those Jewish observances into greater consonance with the rest of society. The initial efforts in that direction were made by laymen. In Berlin, David Friedlaender (1750–1834) advocated the use of an organ at services. Israel Jacobson (1768–1828) established a first Reform Temple in 1810 in Seesen, Westphalia. Then, in rapid order, he abridged the order of liturgy, abandoned traditional cantillation and prayer chant, and eliminated the hazzanic precentor in favor of a rabbinic leader-preacher. For the music, he added an organ, and adapted Protestant-style chorales and hymns for a mixed choir and the congregation. In 1815, Jacobson settled in Berlin, and there, in association with Jacob Herz Beer (fl. 18th–19th cent.), father of Giacomo Meyerbeer (1791–1864), he formed another Reform Temple. Meyerbeer composed some hymns for those services, but the group soon was disbanded.

The Temple congregation (*Tempelverein*) in Seesen flourished, and in 1833 its congregants engaged an official precentor who retained the organ and newer hymnology but resumed some biblical intonation and prayer chants. The most dynamic change by the reformers concerned the role of the rabbi at services. Traditionally, rabbis prayed with their congregants but preached only at the religious convocations and educational gatherings. They were spiritual leaders, teachers, scholars, and ethical communal arbiters. They were guiding figures at the life-cycle events of birth, marriage, and death, and if priests by family descent (*kohanim*), they blessed the congregants in a formal order of prayer. Especially in Ashkenazic synagogues, it was the *hazzan* who officiated and led the prayers. The movement for reform permanently shifted that historic balance of religious duties. Early on, reformers instituted musical instrumentation, generally an organ, and a female and male choir of mixed voices (SATB), instead of any cantorial leader. However, wherever that religious officiant was subsequently reinstated, he served as a precentor of limited liturgical and musical prominence. Those changes profoundly influenced the subsequent developments in American synagogue music.

Until well into the nineteenth century, almost all American Jewish congregations had been led by cantorial officiants who conducted the liturgical rites. In addition, they had taken on other pastoral duties, such as counseling, performing marriages, and burying the dead. Many also circumcised male infants and supervised ritual food preparations. Without rabbinical training, they were nonetheless recognized publicly as ministers. That unique American view of cantorial duties as akin to ministerial ones, and beyond musical duties, has persisted well into the end of the twentieth century. When the first organization in

America of traditional precentors was formed in 1897, it took the title of Jewish Cantors Ministers Association.

In Europe, Hirsch Goldberg (1807–1893) had served as liturgical music leader for the Seesen Reform Temple until he was called to the German synagogue of Brunswick in 1842. There, together with the organist and court musician Julius Freudenthal (1807–1874), he arranged many liturgical melodies, and in 1844 published a collection of hymns for soloist, choir, and congregation. Included was Freudenthal's *Eyn Keloheynu* (There is none like our God) to be sung as a concluding hymn. Its melody had been derived from a German march tune and reshaped as a setting for a venerable liturgical poem (*piyut*) found in both Ashkenazic and Sephardic prayer books. Melodically newly hatched, it early on was brought over to America. Though once facetiously known as the "battle hymn" of American Reform Judaism, this anthem has since become one of the most frequently sung ones at traditional as well as Reform liturgical services.

Especially after 1848, with the years of political, social, and economic upheaval in the European German Confederation, large numbers of Jews from that area of Europe began to emigrate to America. Some were adherents of the new Reform movement, including several young rabbis dedicated to those ideas, and in particular to the innovations made by the Hamburg congregation organized in 1817. In America, those congregants rapidly instituted changes according to the Seesen model. However, they went much further, adopting the Sephardic pronunciation of Hebrew and using some prayer texts and chants from that branch of Judaism. The 1845 edition of the Hamburg hymnal became the preferred one brought over to America. The Seesen-Hamburg services had been conducted in German as well as Hebrew, and that linguistic custom was also transferred to American Reform congregations. The German-Jewish Reform Society of Baltimore was established in 1845, and well into the end of the nineteenth century used the original Hamburg prayer book and hymnal.

By the outbreak of the American Civil War, there were over 200,000 Jews in the country, mostly of mid-European Ashkenazic background. About 6,000 served in the Union Army, and another 1,200 joined up with the Confederate forces. Judah P. Benjamin (1811–1884) was Secretary of State under Confederacy President Jefferson Davis. During the war, Abraham Lincoln commissioned the first Jewish chaplain to the American military services. He was Jacob Frankel (1808–1887), cantor-minister to Rodeph Shalom Congregation in Philadelphia. Born into a cantorial family, Frankel had been trained as a *hazzan* in his native Bavaria, and served at a traditional synagogue in Mainz before emigrating to the United States in 1848 to assume the post in Philadelphia. He served there as the congregational minister as well as cantor until a year before his death. As a chaplain in service to the government military from 1862 until the end of the war, Frankel primarily visited hospitals, where he chanted the prayer services, celebrated Jewish holidays, and ministered to Jewish soldiers in the Union Army.[8]

Post Civil War Era and Jewish Hymnology

Over the decades following that war, a distinctive American Judaic hymnody began to be shaped, reflecting age-old sacred observances in dynamic collaboration with the forces of acculturation, accommodation, and integration. A growing number of religious leaders arrived, called to American congregations that were generally of liberalized or Reform outlook. Their efforts to strengthen the integrity of the rituals and liturgical texts, to educate as well as serve congregants, led to a rapid growth in Jewish hymnology and structured prayer singing. Regardless of the presence or absence of special musical leaders, most rabbis advocated the use of hymnals along with the prayer books.

At the same time, in nineteenth-century America, the heritage of old Jewish folk songs appeared to languish in the wake of the lure of popular American songs. Then, too, many immigrant Jews had brought along their predilection for the general musical culture of Europe. Much in the pattern of the Damrosch, Goldmark, and Mannes Jewish families of that era, their secular music activities blended increasingly into the mainstream of American cultural life. As a result, while the religious carols—Sabbath and holiday tunes—were still remembered and sung, secular Jewish ballads from mid-Europe were fading from memory. However, a new liturgical music creativity had begun to be endorsed and published, and it was finding its way into Jewish homes as well as the houses of worship.

A significant, indeed protean, figure in the American Reform movement was Isaac Mayer Wise (1819–1900). He had come from Europe in 1846 to serve as the rabbi for Temple Beth-El in Albany, New York, and then in 1854 went to Temple B'nai Jeshurun in Cincinnati, Ohio. There, he prepared a new prayer book that was rapidly taken up by other groups. Soon after, Rabbi Wise compiled a hymnal using forty English poetic texts that had been translated from the original Hamburg hymnal by members at Temple Emanu-El in New York City. In 1873, he helped to found an association of Reform temples, called the Union of American Hebrew Congregations (UAHC). Two years later, with Rabbi Wise as its first president, Hebrew Union College was established in Cincinnati for the training of Reform rabbis. In 1889, Wise also started the Central Conference of American Rabbis (CCAR), and that organization set up a music committee in order to commission and publish volumes of American hymnology and Jewish holiday songsters.

Editions of Jewish hymnals published during the nineteenth century reflected to a great extent the evolving musical tastes of American congregants. Some of the better-known European hymnals were reprinted in America. For example, a collection of Jewish religious songs, *Auswahl Israelitisch Religioser Lieder* (Selection of Israelite religious songs) with musical arrangements attributed to a musician named Wilhelm Filcher, a book originally published in Germany, was reissued in its original form in Philadelphia in 1863, but with an American copyright. Along with the text in Hebrew and German, its original elaborately detailed iconographic cover, as signed by lithographer L. N. Rosenthal, was also retained.[9]

The first edition of *The Sacred Harp of Judah: A Choice Collection of Music for the Use of Synagogues, Schools, and Home*, compiled by synagogue musician Gustave M. Cohen (fl. 19th cent.) was published in Cleveland in 1864 by S. Brainard Company. The texts were in English, Hebrew, and German, and the music cover noted that Cohen's work was "The Result of 25 Years Experience and Gleanings." Until 1856, he had been the music leader at Temple Emanu-El in New York City. In a brief preface for his collection, Cohen wrote:

To the congregation belongs properly the response, to the choir the singing. The minister reads the prayer and causes by the recitative either the congregation to join by responses, or the choir by singing. And this great objective can only be effected by a musical work, properly arranged for such a purpose. All musical works for the synagogue used at present are too complicated and designed only for well drilled choirs and competent solo singers. Furthermore, in the works that are now extant, we find them devoid of responses for the congregation. And not only is a musical work desired for public worship, but also for home devotion, and for schools. (unpaginated text)

True to his word, Cohen's arrangements for part singing were simple yet musically interesting; he included a nicely accessible version of Psalm 150. In 1878, S. Brainard Company published Cohen's collection *The Orpheus*. Substantially based upon his earlier songbook, it was comprised of fifty anthems, hymns, and psalms that were arranged with organ or piano accompaniment for four-part voice lines. Again, Cohen's preface to the music cites the value of both congregation and family singing, and in this work acknowledges having taken materials "from Dr. Wise's hymn book."

In 1873, Adolph Huebsch (1830–1894), of Temple Ahavas Chesed in New York City, compiled a hymnal with German poetry and adapted Protestant and general melodies, which for a time was widely circulated. Three years later in Chicago, Otto Loeb (fl. 19th cent.) circulated his own songster for Sabbath and festivals, with melodies adapted from various European composers. In Evansville, Indiana, in 1878, Simon Hecht (fl. 19th cent.) issued his collection, *Jewish Hymns for Sabbath, Schools, and Families*, whose fifty-two selections in English and German were set to music written by Mozart, Gluck, Mendelssohn, and the like. However, that particular hymnal was soon rejected for endorsement by the Union of American Hebrew Congregations on the grounds that its music materials did not use any traditional Jewish themes or motifs.

Alois Kaiser (1840–1908) in 1879 published his composition, "Requiem for the Day of Atonement," for mixed chorus (SATB) and organ, with English and German text, as commissioned by the Baltimore German Reform Society. The following year, a sheet music edition of the *Yom Kippur* liturgical prayer *kol nidrey* (All vows), arranged for piano solo without text by Joseph Seebaum (fl. 19th cent.), was published by the Chicago Music Company. The cover design featured elaborate lettering and noted that this version of the "celebrated Hebrew song" was both "original" and "simplified." Also in 1880, a temple organist and choral leader, Gustave S. Ensel (fl. 19th cent.) of Paducah, Kentucky, published an essay with musical examples titled: "Ancient Liturgical Music: A Study of Comparative Music in the Worship of Synagogue, Church, and Mosque." At New York City's Temple Emanu-El, cantorial leader Gustav Gottheil (1827–1903) and organist A. J. Davis (fl. 19th cent.) were commissioned by the congregation to revise and enlarge the 1875 edition of their widely used hymnal. As a result, a work was published in 1887 as *The Music to Hymns and Anthems for Worship*, with Hebrew and English (but no longer any German) texts and a roster of selections for the entire calendar year of Jewish observances. That new edition also included some devotional poetry contributed by Emma Lazarus (1849–1887).

Some Leading Figures

There were several seminal figures, late in the nineteenth century, whose musicianship and dedication to the Jewish liturgical genre produced valuable contributions to Jewish hymnology, indeed, to an emergent literature of American Jewish music. Some, like Alois Kaiser, served as cantorial leaders and choir directors. In Baltimore, Kaiser composed and arranged music for Congregation Ohev Sholom. When the Central Conference of American Rabbis organized its special music committee, Kaiser was selected as music editor for the preparation of a first officially endorsed hymnal. Originally, he had gathered a melodically diverse group of 117 selections, an amalgam of works from preceding hymnals, with some American patriotic songs and anthems for children. When Kaiser's subsequent edition of a Reform Union Hymnal, companion volume to the Reform Union Prayer book, was published in 1897, that compilation of 149 selections included forty of his own compositions, along with materials from the earlier volume. Alois Kaiser also collaborated with William Sparger (1860–1903), then cantor at Temple Emanu-El in New York City, on a brief history of synagogue music based upon articles that they had co-authored and contributed to several general American periodicals during the 1880s. Entitled *A Collection of the Principal Melodies of the Synagogue*, the monograph was published by T. Rubovitz Company in Chicago in 1893. That elaborately designed and illustrated booklet was distributed by the Jewish Women's Section of a Parliament of Religions, which was held in Chicago during the Colombian Exposition. For the historical essay, Kaiser and Sparger introduced two sections of musical examples: fifty "traditional" liturgical melodies for Sabbath and festivals, with English text and organ or piano accompaniment, and sixteen "modern" hymns for the Reform services. Examination of the first group of those selections indicates a growing influence in America of Ashkenazic liturgical customary usage (*minhag*), though in a more stylized manner.

William Sparger also composed anthems and compiled songbooks for the religious education of the children. Then, in 1901, in association with organist and choral director Max Spicker (1858–1912), he prepared a two-volume edition of selections for the Sabbath eve and morning services at Temple Emanu-El, scored for solo voice with mixed choir (SATB) and organ. It was designed for use with the official Reform Union Prayerbook. As published by G. Schirmer Company, the liturgical works no longer had any German text, only English and Hebrew, and the music incorporated elements of traditional liturgical melodies and chants.

At that time, two non-Jewish musicians, both German born and formally trained, played significant roles in these American Judaic musical developments: Sigmund Schlesinger (1835–1906), and Frederick Emil Kitziger (1844–1903). Schlesinger was the organist and choral director for Congregation Sha-arey Shomayim in Mobile, Alabama, from 1863 until 1903. Over that long tenure, he collected and arranged liturgical music, compiling several full liturgical services for Sabbath, festivals, and High Holy Days, and also wrote additional anthems. His music was utilized well into the twentieth century by professional musicians employed for the Reform services. It was skillfully prepared music, but of a Protestant quality, with operatic-classic elements, and it omitted almost all traditional synagogue chant motifs. Nevertheless, over the decades, Schlesinger's renditions remained in the standard Reform temple repertoire.

Frederick Emil Kitziger came to New Orleans in 1865, where he first performed as a brass player in marching bands and opera orchestras and then was a music teacher and organist. In 1881, he became the choral director and organist for that city's Judah Touro Synagogue, where he appears to have found his musical metier. By 1888, he had published the first volume of his arrangements and compositions for Sabbath eve and morning, *Songs of Judah/Shirey Yehudah*, set for solos, chorus, and organ. Successive augmented editions issued by Kitziger appeared in 1891, 1892, 1895, 1897, and 1899, adding music for the High Holy Days, festivals, and special religious occasions. Those collections were to be used in association with the Reform Union Prayerbook, and included texts in German as well as in Hebrew and English.

Kitziger very wisely copyrighted his volumes, for they became widely known and used throughout America, most especially in the South. In his preface to a second edition, Kitziger wrote: "May therefore also this Second Edition find favor in the eyes of American Israel, and, above all, stimulate others to enlist their heart and their talent for the purpose of enriching the sacred songs of the synagogues of our country." He also published a separate collection of twenty hymns for Jewish worship in English text. Many of his liturgical compositions were issued and sold in individual octavo form. Indeed, Kitziger's home became a publishing house dedicated to his own works. He labored in close association with the rabbis of his congregation as well as leaders of other Reform groups, notably Isaac Mayer Wise. Well along into the twentieth century, Kitziger's liturgical collections were in standard use in Canada as well as the United States. It was not until the 1930s that his particular styles of organ accompaniment and of trained choir part singing were supplanted by the return of the cantorial solo voice to a more active role in the Reform services. Frederick Emil Kitziger was a Christian musical voice in the synagogue who appeared to have found professional fulfillment there and to have served with great artistry and dedication.[10]

Particularly during the final years of his work, Kitziger developed increasing interest in using Jewish melodic elements and acknowledged his musical indebtedness to the leading figures of nineteenth-century European synagogue music. The 1893 Colombian Exposition publication on Jewish music prepared by Kaiser and Sparger had included materials from Ashkenazic liturgists who were then developing a different form of musical "reformation" by working within the age-old religious traditions. Their objectives were to preserve, enhance, and renew, not to supplant or replace, the age-old Judaic chants and melodies of prayer. Historic synagogue music was to be viewed as sacred and inherent to Jewish spiritual expression. During the nineteenth century, three significant European leaders in that traditionalist mode of reformation were Salomon Sulzer (1804–1890) of Vienna, Louis Lewandowski (1821–1894) of Berlin, and Samuel Naumbourg (1815–1880) of Paris. While they never left Europe, their musical ideas and creative achievements became dominant qualities in the establishment of a distinctive twentieth-century liturgical style at American synagogues. Indeed, one of the most influential leaders of Reform Judaism in America, Rabbi Isaac Mayer Wise, had been a boy chorister in the Vienna choir of Salomon Sulzer.[11]

Salomon Sulzer became the role model for the American cantorate in terms of musicianship and religious outlook. As a dedicated and highly skillful choirmaster and liturgical coach, Louis Lewandowski became the ideal prototype for American synagogue music directors. Samuel Naumbourg was a broadly educated musician of serious intellectual bent, qualities that became the hallmarks of cantorial education as it was later formalized at American Jewish theological institutions. Those three liturgists had inaugurated dynamic changes in Jewish sacred music, which proved appealing to observant Jewry, because their ideas of reformation did not entail displacement of traditional devotional melodies nor time-honored prayers. This was to be an evolutionary development whose objectives were liturgical continuity, preservation, and enrichment. Late in the nineteenth century, those ideas had begun to sweep across Europe and eastward to the Jewish communities in the Slavic areas, from where a great wave of immigrants had already started to come to America. The eastern European Jews would bring with them different sounds of music, secular as well as sacred. Meanwhile, however, the Jewish music of the German reformers still predominated on the American scene.

Toward the end of the nineteenth century, several American cantors contributed noteworthy musical resources to the services of increasing numbers of Reform congregations. Morris (Moritz) Goldstein (1840–1906) had sung as a chorister in Salomon Sulzer's choir, and then emigrated to serve a synagogue in New York City, before joining B'nai Israel Temple in Cincinnati in 1881. In that city, the Bloch Publishing Company, a newly founded publisher of Judaica, issued two hymnals by Goldstein: one in 1885, for the Sabbath, and one in 1895, for the High Holy Days. Both were for use with the official Union Prayerbook, and included materials for children's participation. Texts were in Hebrew and English, and this collection was endorsed by Rabbi Isaac Mayer Wise. In his own preface to the editions, Goldstein wrote: "While I retain almost all of the traditional melodies and chants, as well as many of the compositions of Sulzer, Lewandowski, and Lowenstam of Munich, I have also included a number of original compositions and harmonized others, clothing them in modern form and fitting them to the new texts... The place for the organ should be exclusively in the house of worship. I have therefore endeavored to treat the organ in that light, and not as a pianoforte, as is often the case in this country."[12]

Isaac Moses (1847–1926), who served at the (Reform) Ahavath Chesed Central Synagogue in New York City, had also trained as a cantor in Europe with an Orthodox strictly traditional congregation. In 1894, he published his *Sabbath-School Hymnal* for year-round use in school, synagogue, and home.[13] By 1920, that collection had been reissued by the Bloch Publishing Company in a fourteenth revised and expanded edition of 250 selections. It was one of the earliest hymnals to include the anthem *Adon Olam* (Lord of the world), which was originally written by a Ukrainian cantor and music scholar, Eliezer Gerovitsch (1844–1913). Since then, that hymn has become ubiquitous at all Jewish services throughout America. Isaac Moses also included the ever-popular hymn *Eyn Keloheynu* (None like our God), and the original Hebrew chant *Yigdal* (Praise), also known as the "Leoni Praise," which was adopted in England and America as the melody for a Wesleyan hymn, "Praise to the Living God." In the brief preface to a 1904 eleventh edition of his hymnal, Isaac Moses wrote: "The improvement of this book will be found not only in the larger number of hymns, but chiefly in the Jewishness. It is eminently proper that hymn books intended for Jewish worship should be Jewish in character, and that the hymns of prayer should be the products of Jewish authors... Trained choirs will always be necessary in our synagogues, for the highest class of music now forms an indispensable element of our services; but the choir should not usurp the function of the congregation." (unpaged) This widely used hymnal greatly influenced the revisions made for a 1914 edition of the official Reform Union Hymnal.

Edward Stark (1856–1918) was born in Hohenems, Austria, as the son of a cantor (Josef Stark, fl. 19th cent.) who had trained in Vienna with Sulzer. The father had officiated at several European congregations before emigrating with his family in 1871 to serve a traditional congregation in New York City. Edward

Stark was in his father's choir, and developed a strong baritone voice in early adulthood. He sang solos in the synagogue as well as at public performances of light operettas favored at the time, and also composed some sacred and secular songs. In 1885/86, a member of the community financed his trip to Vienna and Leipzig for cantorial and general musical studies. Stark's first appointment (ca.1891) was to Temple Beth Elohim in Brooklyn, where he followed William Sparger, who had gone on to the larger Temple Emanu-El in Manhattan. In 1893, Edward Stark was called to serve at San Francisco's Temple Emanu-El, and he remained there until 1913, when he resigned because of illness. He was then succeeded by Cantor Reuben Rinder (1887–1966), who in the course of his own fifty-year tenure commissioned Ernest Bloch and Darius Milhaud to compose Sabbath sacred services.

In San Francisco, Stark flourished as a fine musician and singer, and was afforded the advantages of a professional choir and organist, to which he often added stringed instruments. The congregation used the official Reform Union Prayerbook, for which Stark arranged and composed settings. His collection of sacred melodies for the entire year, *Sefer Anim Zemiroth* (Book of melodies), published by Bloch Publishing Company, was issued in four volumes between 1909 and 1913. Its contents reflected Stark's firm knowledge of traditional chant, notably with Sulzer and Lewandowski as models. In 1900, he privately published a volume of special religious music for children's services, which included his own musical playlets for *Hanukkah* and *Purim*. Over the years, Bloch Publishing Company and G. Schirmer Company published his compositions and arrangements of various liturgical selections, including adaptations of selections by Halévy and Meyerbeer. Stark formed the first Society of American Cantors, and was an active member of music committees for Reform organizations. He helped prepare the contents of the first officially endorsed Reform Union Hymnal (Cincinnati: Bloch Publishing, 1897). That collection of 129 anthems included materials from the early Seesen-Hamburg hymnal as well as from the American collections of Kaiser, Sparger, Spicker, and Stark. It also had chants from Sulzer and Lewandowski as well as some melodies by Mendelssohn, Gounod, Haydn, Hiller, Mozart, and Schubert.[14]

By the turn of the century, American synagogue music varied in quality and substance from bare minimum content to a great array of cantorial intonation and choral selections, congregational responses, hymnology and psalmody, and instrumental or organ accompaniments. Not all Reform congregations adopted the endorsed Reform Union Prayerbook and Hymnal, often preferring to shape their own versions. For example, in 1904, Temple Keneseth Israel in Philadelphia privately published a combined prayer book and hymnal, The Service-Hymnal, with the text compiled by Rabbi Joseph Krauskopf (fl. 19th–20th cent.) and the music notated by an organist, Russell King Miller (fl. 19th–20th cent.). In its brief preface, the compiler wrote: "Traditional melodies have been preserved wherever possible, and the musical settings of responses have been taken mainly from Jewish sources." (unpaginated text) With some revisions in a 1922 edition, that volume served its congregation for almost three decades.

Not too long after the appearance of the first official Reform Union Hymnal in 1897, plans were under way for a different edition. That second edition, expanded to 226 selections and issued in 1914, still utilized almost all of the materials from the 1897 hymnal. Though enhanced with devotional poetry by such literary figures as Emma Lazarus, Penina Moise, Isaac Mayer Wise, and Israel Zangwill (1861–1926), it did not find widespread acceptance. Within ten years, a music committee had been formed to review ideas for a completely different hymnal, one that would "ring true," particularly for the increasing numbers of Reform congregants coming from eastern European Yiddishist backgrounds.

Increasing Influences of Eastern Europeans

A first Polish-Russian congregation had been organized in 1852 in New York City, and by 1879 there were more than twenty-five Orthodox (traditionally strict) eastern European congregations in that area. The demographic growth was almost as rapid in many other American cities, producing two distinct branchings of Judaism—Reform and Orthodox. Then around the turn of the century, a uniquely American bridge between the two emerged as Conservative Judaism.

The new wave of Jewish immigrants from eastern Europe truly were birds of flight. Like other immigrants to America, they were fleeing from economic, political, and social distress. Significantly, Jews also were seeking haven from the anti-Semitic pogroms in Russia that had erupted in the 1870s and would not subside. They had lived in the Slavic areas of Europe for hundreds of years. There, Ashkenazic religious traditions had developed in particular ways, enhanced by special folklore and customs inherent to geography and ethnology, and the Jewish vernacular tongue was Yiddish.

The Yiddish language uses Hebrew characters in print and script, with modifications derived from German and Slavonic phonetics, and is read from right to left. Yiddish arose over a thousand years ago in the Rhineland Valley area of Europe, incorporating Old German as well as elements of Latin and Old French, combined with Hebrew and Aramaic. Following a particularly significant Jewish migration eastward to the Polish-Russian areas commencing early in the fifteenth century, Yiddish began to incorporate idioms from those languages. Over the next centuries, it developed three regional dialects: Northeastern, in Byelorussia, Estonia, Latvia, and Lithuania; Central, in Austria, Galicia, and Poland; and Southeastern, in Bessarabia, Hungary, Romania, Ukraine, and Volhynia. However, the Yiddish-Hebrew characters as printed and written, along with the entire range of vocabulary, remained essentially the same for all. In essence, eastern European Jewry was trilingual: Hebrew, Yiddish, and the particular resident tongue of a country.

Eastern European Jewish liturgical music was Ashkenazic, and had been further refined into a special usage as practiced with some variations in all Slavic areas. Inevitably, certain melodic qualities pervaded the region. The concepts of minor as expressive of sadness and major as reflective of joy appear to have been general European ideas not shared by the Slavonic and Jewish peoples. Certain analogous musical elements were readily found among Polish, Russian, Ukrainian, and Jewish tunes. There also was a kindred predilection for certain modes and motival forms. For example, melodic configurations of the Jewish anthem *Hatikvah* appear in Sephardic and Ashkenazic liturgy, but may also be found among Russian and Bohemian folk songs. Moreover, the musical interval of an augmented second has been a salient quality among many Slavic melodies, and this interval also came to be a readily identified characteristic of Jewish music in eastern Europe and then in America.[15]

The historic word-focused nature of Jewish music shaped the creation of a dynamic Yiddish folk song. eastern European Jews sang in Hebrew, Yiddish, and a variety of Slavic tongues. A custom prevailed of combining Yiddish with Russian, Ukrainian, and Polish in terms of texts as well as melodies. Jewish minstrelsy was especially popular in *shtetl* (town) and farming village communities, reaching a particular apex of creativity and popularity by the end of the nineteenth century. Generations of traveling *badkhonim* (folk troubadours) and *klezmorim* (folk instrumentalists) provided entertainment at weddings and other festivities, public wayside inns, and taverns. Their artistry became an integral cultural ingredient of Jewish Diaspora life, and their repertoire included historic ballads, contemporary broadsides, folk narratives with music, wedding odes, and holiday tunes. Materials, composed originally or borrowed and adapted from non-Judaic sources, were heavily based upon familiar liturgical chants as well as old sacred and secular Jewish folk songs.

The Yiddish-speaking immigrants brought all that musical heritage to America, along with two distinctive types of Jewish professional musicians—minstrel entertainers and cantorial artists. They all rapidly accommodated and acculturated creatively. By 1880, notices were being placed in journals throughout eastern Europe seeking qualified cantors for positions at American synagogues. Over the next decades, communities vied for well-known cantorial leaders and sought to replicate in America the traditional sounds of eastern European services. Early on there were cantorial concerts, and sacred services were advertised as featuring particular precentor "artistes."[16] Some famous European cantors, like the gifted Pinchos Minkowsky (1859–1924), did not do well in America, and left to serve at European congregations. Most did stay, however, often touring the country. For a period early in the twentieth century, there was a "golden age" of old-style cantorial artistry in America. The first faltering efforts to organize an association of traditional cantors were made in 1891, but not until 1905 was a group to be firmly established as the Jewish Ministers Cantors Association. Professional cantorial training remained a matter of personal apprenticeship and oral transmission, and not until mid-twentieth century in America were historic changes made in that process.

The restrictive Reed-Johnson Immigration Act became effective in 1924, a watershed date for immigrant and native-born Jews in America, and a substantial subsequent influence on their ethno-cultural activities.[17] For over three centuries, millions of people had emigrated to the United States in what may be considered one of the greatest population shifts in human history. Between 1880 and 1924 alone, over twenty-four million entered, of which about two and a half million were eastern European Jews. That time was a great era for certain forms of Jewish musical artistry in America: cantorial vocal stars, gifted Yiddish theatrical entertainers, lively tunes of Slavic-Jewish folk bands played on vinyl recordings, prolific creation of a unique genre of Yiddish American songs, publication of ethnic Slavic as well as Jewish music, and amateur singing societies and mandolin ensembles.

Cantorial Artistry

An honor roll of great liturgical precentors had settled in America. They possessed fine voices and were trained, dedicated synagogue musicians. Some of their charismatic renditions at the height of their powers were preserved on early recordings. The most notable and widely recognized was Cantor (Josef) Yossele Rosenblatt (1882–1933). In 1924, he was touring American vaudeville theaters singing cantorial works and Jewish folk songs as well as Irish, Italian, and general American ballads, and also featuring his own composition, "America." For the general American public, Rosenblatt became the epitome of a Jewish cantor. Born in the Ukraine into a cantorial family, by the age of eighteen he was serving a congregation in Hungary. In 1912, he was called to a synagogue in New York City, and he made his first public concert appearances in America during World War I on behalf of war bonds and charities. Though Rosenblatt declined to sing in opera, he did perform at Carnegie Hall in 1918, and began to make numerous recordings of liturgical music and Jewish songs. His voice was compared to that of Enrico Caruso, and his audiences at major American cities were filled with non-Jews, most of them hearing for the first time the special melodic qualities of Jewish sacred song. He composed and arranged selections, some of which were published. Yossele Rosenblatt died in Jerusalem, after completing a film there and a singing tour abroad.[18]

Cantorial artistes provided a cultural bridge between the synagogue and public entertainment, blending spiritual song with minstrel balladry, a phenomenon then unique to American society. It was not unusual for an urban meeting hall to be temporarily converted into a holiday *shul* (synagogue), with services publicly advertised as led by a prominent cantor. The eastern European Jews who were beginning to worship at Reform temples were familiar, indeed accustomed, to that type of liturgical music. This fact influenced the reformers, began to make their congregational hymnals more traditional in content. Moreover, the popularity of that devotional artistry affected all synagogue musicians in terms of their vocal styles, professional standards, and relationships to rabbinical and communal leaders. While the rabbi had become the minister-preacher, the American cantor still evoked the deepest spiritual response of congregants.

One abiding quality that infused cantorial performances was that melody transcended words. Music not only enhanced text, but went beyond to the heart of the matter. This was a direct influence of the intensely emotional tunes of the Hasidim (Jewish pietists), whose religious movement had been founded in eastern Europe by Rabbi Israel Ba'al Shem Tov (1700–1760).[19] During the nineteenth century, Hasidism flourished, with proliferating sects in areas of Russia and Poland, and developed its own special melodic expression. Hasidic *nigunim* (tunes) were integral to both prayer and study. Melody was the means for reaching God; song could open up the very gates of heaven. As a result, words were almost extraneous to that prayerful communion, and creative vocal improvisation was valued as a noble religious duty. The ecstasy of melody was wedded to a form of rhythmic *rikud* (dance) movements, for which Slavic tunes were often adapted. By the nineteenth century, Hasidic music permeated Jewish folk song. Either in imitation or in parody, those elements became an important part of the stock-in-trade of Jewish minstrels as they migrated across Europe and on to settle in America.

Yiddish American Minstrelsy

When Yiddish writer Sholom Aleichem (1859–1916) came to America toward the end of his life, he brought along the ballads of Mark Warshawsky (1845–1907) with whom he had toured in areas of the Ukraine. Among those songs were: *Oyf'n Pripetshok* (By the fireside), a loving tribute to the Hebrew alphabet, and *Di Mezinkeh Oysgegeyben* (Giving the youngest child in marriage), whose melody was subsequently quoted by Ernest Bloch (1880–1959) in his instrumental work "Ba'al Shem Suite." By the early twentieth century, eastern European Jewish minstrelsy had become increasingly polemical, with broadsides and commentaries, information and advice, treatments of current events and timely issues. There always had been songs of childhood, courtship and family, of travels, towns and communities, of tradesmen, artisans and farmers, of religion, history, and culture. Then came songs of poverty, pogroms and communal displacements, of the homeless, ill and orphaned, and soon, songs of migration, resettlement and adjustment.

By 1900, *America di goldeneh medineh* (America the golden land) was a favorite lyric topic on both sides of the Atlantic Ocean. Back in the Old Country, the popular poet-singers continually reflected upon that theme: "Play *klezmer* (musician), your fiddle in hand; play the song of the golden land. Long ago by my cradle, my mother sang it to me. It was her dream and she gave it to me. Play *klezmer*, sing that sweet melody" (from a lyric of Mordechai Gebirtig, 1877–1942). For settlers in the New World, the Yiddish songs continued to be deeply subjective in nature. Although some older balladeers like Eliakum Zunser (1840–1913) had come over, a younger generation of immigrants soon became the prolific creators of a newer song genre, a minstrelsy intrinsic to the special flowering of Yiddish theater in America.[20]

Yiddish theater was crafted as a modern composite of historic Jewish entertainers: *Purim* holiday player (*purimshpiler*), minstrel-bard (*badkh'n*), comic-jester (*leyts*), dance master (*tantsfirer*), band musician (*klezmer*), narrator (*marshalik*), and the cantorial artistry (*hazzaniyah*). It arose as a distinctive artistry in the wayside inns of eastern European villages, but reached its fruition in the theater houses of New York and other American cities. Late in the nineteenth century, Abraham Goldfaden (1840–1908) had put all those cultural ingredients together into productions for which he fashioned more than twenty-six Jewish operettas.[21] Those works were light dramas, generally of biblical, historical, or didactic nature, highlighted by solos, choruses, and instrumental tunes with dances. For the music, Goldfaden adapted or arranged synagogue chants, religious hymns, holiday songs, Hasidic tunes, and Yiddish folk songs as well as Slavic melodies and European grand opera arias. The theatrical characters he created and the songs he wrote, rapidly became folk favorites. His casts were recruited from minstrel troupes and synagogue choirs. A legion of performers began their careers with him, including Jacob P. Adler (1855–1926), Bertha Kalish (1872–1939), Sophie Karp (1861–1906), David Kessler (1860–1920), Sigmund Mogulesco (?1856/8–1914), Regina Prager (1874–1949)), and Boris Thomashefsky (?1864/8–1939). Regardless of how elaborately embellished the Yiddish theater in America would become, Goldfaden had set the tone and delineated the métier. Without music, it was not a Jewish theatrical production; songs were the dominating elements in drama as well as comedy, and everyone on stage sang.

Boris Thomashefsky brought the first Yiddish acting troupe to America, arriving in New York City in 1882, and opening to the public that year with Goldfaden's operetta *Di kishifmakherin* (The sorceress). Soon afterwards, a retinue of other immigrant performers came, and settled into theaters around the Bowery area of Lower Manhattan. The Bowery had been a lively entertainment area specializing in variety programs, melodramas, and comedies. By the 1870s, the more stylish patronage moved uptown to Fourteenth Street and beyond, leaving behind many amusement halls, beer gardens, and vaudeville houses. Then Yiddish theatricals and revues gradually took over those places, located well within the Jewish immigrant tenement section. The old theaters were occupied and renamed as the Roumanian, Oriental, Thalia, and Windsor, or were known by the names of a succession of popular Jewish performers. By 1910, weekly audience attendees had swelled to the thousands, borne forward with the tide of immigration. On the eve of World War I, what had once been only a cottage industry had developed into big business. There now were a great variety of actors, musicians, playwrights, composers, costumers, set makers, impresarios, and a host of other types of theatrical employees, along with program printers and sheet music publishing houses. This was the era of a unique Yiddish rialto in America.

In his last years, Abraham Goldfaden was an outsider to the art he had created.[22] Early in the 1880s, his own highly successful theater enterprise in eastern Europe had been curtailed and then forbidden in Russian areas by tsarist edicts. Though he constantly wrote new songs and plays, Goldfaden over the rest of his life drifted economically and spiritually. A first trip to New York in 1887 was brief and a bitter disappointment because he was unable to start a theatrical group. At the time, two impresario-writers, Moshe Horowitz (ca.1850–1910) and Joseph Lateiner (1853–1935), were flourishing with their Americanized versions of Goldfaden's materials. Boris Thomashefsky had begun to adapt the styles and formulas of uptown New York shows and performers, and the versatile Sigmund Mogulesco was enjoying a highly successful career based upon his own elaborations of earlier Goldfaden roles. Moreover, a number of younger composers and lyricists had embarked upon shaping a new form of Jewish popular songs, which would reflect the sentiments of American audiences and be sung at the parlor pianos in their homes. Goldfaden went back to Europe by way of London and Paris, where he was also unable to start theater companies. Though no longer the protagonist in the Yiddish theatrical world, he was deeply respected as the father of that art. In 1902, he returned to New York, remaining there to the end of his life. A month before his death, Goldfaden's final work, *Ben Ami* (Son of my people) was staged by Thomashefsky and Mogulesco, with additional songs composed by Mogulesco and Louis Friedsell (1950–1923). Abraham Goldfaden died in January 1908, and a large funeral procession escorted his body to the Washington Cemetery in Brooklyn. Over the following six months, that production of Goldfaden's *Ben Ami* played to a record full house.

Later that year, in July 1908, at the annual meeting of the Central Conference of American (Reform) Rabbis (CCAR), a motion was presented by their Committee on Contemporaneous Jewish History and later published in its annual report (Cincinnati: CCAR, 1909). The Reform rabbis recorded their sorrow at the death of Abraham Goldfaden, the popular playwright and composer in New York in January 1908. They acknowledged Goldfaden's personal achievements as well as the significance of an emerging Yiddish theatrical enterprise in America and its positive values for the advancement of Jewish educational and cultural life. Clearly, Abraham Goldfaden had created a distinctive art form, setting in motion theatrical and popular musical ideas that were to flourish in the free atmosphere of twentieth-century American society.

Many of Goldfaden's songs have entered into the folk culture of Jewish life, most notably the lovely lullaby *Rozhinkes mit Mandlen* (Raisins and almonds). A favorite encore performed by Cantor Yossele Rosenblatt at his concerts was

Goldfaden's *Di Yiddishe Hofnung, oder Shofar Shel Moshiakh* (The Jewish hope, or ram's horn of the Messiah). In more recent times, the cantor and operatic tenor Richard (Reuben) Tucker (1912–1975) recorded an album of songs from Goldfaden's operettas for Columbia Records. The style of those selections, their sweet, simple melodies and poignant, moving lyrics were the models by which a next generation of American Yiddish minstrels fashioned their songs.

American society provided an extraordinary environment for the great development of Yiddish minstrelsy. There was freedom of expression, with unlimited exposure to a diversity of styles, to forms and modes of entertainment that crossed ethnic and racial lines. Opportunities for adaptation and innovation grew with each new presentation to an intensely loyal Jewish patronage. Most surprising was the acclaim from other Americans, who increasingly joined those audiences.[23] Early on, Jewish entertainers had learned to create Yiddish lyrics for such favorites as "Sweet Rosie O'Grady," "A Bird in a Gilded Cage," "In the Good Old Summertime," "The Banks of the Wabash," and "Meet Me in St. Louis." Those versions performed at vaudeville revues provided the Jewish parodists with valuable training in the shaping of American popular tunes and lyrics.

By 1895, copyrights had begun to appear for Yiddish songs, commencing with selections by Goldfaden, Mogulesco, and Zunser. The earliest Yiddish song publishing house in America was Katzenelenbogen and Rabinowitz, a combined enterprise of two Jewish book printers. In rapid order, others appeared on the scene, some also as book and music stores: Theodore Lohr, Meyer Levin, Hebrew Publishing, S. Goldberg, S. Schenker, and Albert Teres. The Hebrew Publishing Company and another company, Jos. P. Katz, soon incorporated most of the other publishers and their holdings. In the late 1920s, those two companies in turn were superseded in this musical enterprise by two newer firms: Metro Music, whose owner-editor Henry Lefkowitch (1892–1959) was deeply devoted to Yiddish music, and J. and J. Kammen, founded by the twin brothers Jack and Joseph Kammen (Jacob Kamenetzky 1888–1954?, and Joseph Kamenetzky 1888–1957?), who soon moved uptown and eventually published general popular music. Both companies ceased to exist in the 1970s. By the mid-twentieth century, over three hundred publishers nationwide—including Oliver Ditson, Carl Fischer, E. B. Marks, Theodore Presser, G. Schirmer, and Summy-Burchard—had issued Yiddish selections.

The burgeoning of Yiddish song sheet publications was due not only to the great popularity of that music among immigrants and their native-born children, but also tot the surge in parlor piano ownership throughout the country starting late in the nineteenth century. Moreover, the printed appearance of Jewish sheet music replicated the general American publication practices of the time. Music covers were handsomely designed in elaborate typefaces, often with signed artistic lithography. Photographs of performers and composers and even of arrangers adorned the music. Detailed publication catalogs filled back covers and inside pages, along with brief samplings from other selections. Yiddish songs were often issued in two forms, either as piano/voice or violin/text, and those editions were color coded. Extra lyrics filled available spaces at the bottom of pages or across folds, and text inserts were sometimes sold separately as broadsheets. Often, this music was vended in the theaters as program souvenirs, and featured the show's cast roster. Yiddish lyrics were usually given in Hebrew/Yiddish print, but were also given in romanized characters under the music lines themselves. Editing of printed copy lent itself to numerous errors and inconsistencies in text material. Many of those variations in the transliterations were due to the different Yiddish dialects spoken and sung at the time by the entertainers and writer-lyricists.

Most songs were introduced in a theatrical production, and many were linked to particular performers. The early melodies were derivative, or at least reminiscent, of traditional sacred and secular music. Lyrics were filled with didactic information and ethical issues, in the age-old custom of Judaic minstrelsy. Soon, however, those tunes began to be affected by the different musical sounds of other Americans, and the texts began to articulate the special experiences and concerns of life in America. Several early figures emerged, each reflecting those changing patterns of creativity. Louis Friedsell (1850–1923) wrote and arranged selections in the style of his mentor, Abraham Goldfaden, for whose last poetics he had shaped some new melodies. Arriving with a synagogue choir background, Friedsell was a self-educated musician and became facile at music writing and violin playing. He was an able accompanist, conductor, arranger, and composer for the productions of Horowitz, Lateiner, Mogulesco, and Thomashefsky. For David Kessler's (1860–1920) acclaimed performance as the Jewish Hamlet in *Der Yeshivoh Bokhur* (The seminary student), Friedsell adapted liturgical chants, including a graveside memorial intoned for the Jewish Ophelia. In 1905, he wrote the songs for Thomashefsky's successful production of *Der Yiddishe Yankee Doodle* (The Jewish Yankee Doodle).

Sigmund Mogulesco (?1856/8–1914) had been a choir singer who was recruited by Goldfaden for his early operettas. He rapidly developed into a highly versatile star who acted, sang, danced, composed, improvised dialogue, and staged his own productions. Mogulesco had a charismatic personality, and many of his highly innovative theatrical ideas were taken over by later performers. The most famous of his own songs is one he wrote for the operetta *Blihmele* (Little blossom), a selection that has passed into folk culture without his name as the ubiquitous Jewish wedding ode, *Khosson, kallah mazel tov* (Bridegroom, bride, good luck). Mogulesco suffered from throat cancer, despite which he managed to perform publicly into the final month of his life.

David Meyerowitz (1867–1943) began as a writer of parody lyrics and specialty ditties for Jewish Bowery revues. His first successful songs were shaped for the dramatic actor Jacob P. Adler (1856–1926), and he then embarked upon the creation of many highly personalized arietta-like selections. Meyerowitz's works remained rooted in the old-style didactic minstrelsy of heritage and ethics, which he applied to the newer American ways. Though prolific, he was not skilled at musical transcription, and in 1904 he began a longtime association with Jack Kammen as his arranger and then publisher. When Goldfaden died in 1908, Meyerowitz and Kammen collaborated on the music for an elegy, *A Kaddish nokh Goldfaden* (A memorial for Goldfaden). By the 1930s, Meyerowitz himself had faded from recognition, despite the fact that many of his selections were still sung on the Yiddish stage.[24]

Henry A. (Russotta) Russotto (?1867/9–1925) was a self-taught immigrant musician who became the most well-known Yiddish music arranger of his time. His photograph adorned numerous editions of the works of other composers, including complete song albums of several of Goldfaden's operettas. Russotto's skills as a transcriber and editor were indispensable to the early publishers, especially to the Katzenelenbogen and Rabinowitz Company and the Hebrew Publishing Company. His own compositions, however, were not at all successful.

From 1903 onward, a song writing team of Arnold Perlmutter (1859–1953) and Herman Wohl (1877–1936) churned out many easily sung tunes for theatrical productions that featured well-known performers. Their most celebrated score was for an operetta, *Dos pinteleh Yid* (The essence of being a Jew). Wohl, the more musically literate, was also active as a synagogue musician. The team worked well together into the late 1920s, but when they ventured to go their separate musical ways, both faded into obscurity. For the popular Yiddish songs, there were numerous lyricists whose words articulated, often quite poetically, the great variety of experiences in immigrant adjustment to American life. Among the more noted names were: Joseph Brody (1877–1943), Rubin Doctor (1882–1960?), Louis Gilrod (1879–1956), Jacob Jacobs (1890–1970?), Isidore Lillian (1880–1960), and Anshel Schorr (1871–1942).

Of all, Solomon Smulewitz (Sol Small) (1868–1943) was the most innovatively gifted and left behind a significant legacy. Like the traditional eastern European Jewish minstrel, he was a masterful performer of his own songs. Along with Meyerowitz, he started out in America by adapting Yiddish lyrics to English popular songs. Unlike most other melodists, he could also pen fine lyrics, and wrote many texts for the tunes of Meyerowitz, Mogulesco, Perlmutter and Wohl, among others. In 1904, Smulewitz first achieved recognition when he collaborated with Louis Friedsell on a Passover song for the noted soubrette Sophie Karp (1861–1906). Three years later, he composed the poignant song, *A briveleh der mamen* (A little letter to mother), and began a remarkable period of creativity. Smulewitz caught on to the different spirit of the times, and personalized American immigrant life. Over the next decades, he fashioned wedding odes and *bar mitzvah* tunes, melodic tributes to laboring workers, songs about parents and children, ballads for Sabbath and holidays, ariettas about Bible, Jewish history and religious observances. When the scourge of tuberculosis threatened tenement Jews, his song described it as *Menshen fresser* (Man eater), and when the ocean liner *Titanic* sank in 1912, his Yiddish song about it was sung on the general American stage.

In 1914, Smulewitz wrote a Yiddish song *Oh, Ellis Island,* the song that forever clarifies the immigrant experience for every generation and for all people: "We struggled to get here, and arrived with our hopes and prayers. Now, at the very threshold of this golden land, we wait to know whether we will be admitted." In 1917, he parodied Goldfaden's *Rozhinkes mit Mandlen* (Raisins and almonds) with a new title, *Di nayeh Rusland* (The new Russia), and his lyrics expressed a fervent hope for happier times ahead in that distressed country. Always a performer, Smulewitz toured to the end of his life throughout America, and in the mid-1930s traveled across Canada to entertain the Jewish communities in Calgary, Saskatoon, Winnipeg, Toronto, Montreal, and Halifax. In 1934, several of his best known songs were issued with English lyrics by E. B. Marks Company, including *A briveleh der mamen,* which in that newer version was recorded by several non-Jewish entertainers. Late in life, he offered an artistic bow to his two musical role models, Eliakum Zunser and Abraham Goldfaden, with the song, *Man shpilt teater* (One plays at theater): "We behave as if we were all on the stage, acting out our little lives according to a script written and directed by Almighty God."[25]

Twentieth Century: Between the Two World Wars

When America entered into World War I, the Yiddish musicals sang more than 200,000 Jewish soldiers into uniform, and American patriotic hymns resounded on those stages. The 1920s remained productive, and during that decade those theatricals moved to lower Second Avenue in New York City. Troupes toured around the country, introducing their unique performing styles and highlighting the different sounds of their music. A great mainstreaming of Jewish talent was now under way, with an increasing mobility of creativity entering into all of the American arts.

By that time, the artistic crossover movement had gotten into full stride, especially by entertainers and songwriters. An early example was Izzy Bailin (Irving Berlin, 1888–1989), who had sung in the New York streets for pennies and then worked as a singing waiter at downtown saloons. As a fast learner of the popular music business, he recognized the general interest in tunes from his own background. Between 1908 and 1912, Berlin's copyrighted songs still included such Jewish titles as "Yiddisha Eyes," "Yiddle on your Fiddle, Play Some Ragtime," "That Kazzatsky Dance, a Yiddisha Tune," "Yiddisha Nightingale," and "Yiddisha Professor Cohen, the Piano Teacher." Those musical sounds themselves had come into their own in America. In 1923, a popular-style arrangement of the liturgical chant *kol nidrey* appeared for nationwide sale on player piano rolls. The Tin Pan Alley songwriter Jack Yellen (1894–1991) achieved early recognition in 1925 for his song, "My Yiddisha Mama." It was published in a Yiddish text edition as well as the English version, and soon became a repertoire standard for many American performers. In 1926, the impresario Billy Rose (1899–1986) copyrighted his own dance tune, "Yiddisha Charleston."

United States government copyright catalogs for the years 1921 to 1925 listed the largest number of roster entries ever registered for the genre of Yiddish American popular songs. Afterwards, there began to be a steady decline in those numbers. Only the productivity of several gifted musicians, along with some highly talented performers, helped to sustain that creativity into and beyond the 1930s. Their talents attracted loyal audiences despite the fact that the appeal of Yiddish theatricals was fast waning, increasingly replaced by phonograph, radio, and films. Not only was that linguistic constituency diminishing in numbers, but there were rapid changes in societal demographics. There were new shifts in educational and cultural interests and an increase in general economic problems. The distinctive identity of eastern European origins was passing away with the dying of immigrant generations and with a tightening of the gates at Ellis Island.

Yet there still was a golden glow of Yiddish spirit, and by the latter part of the twentieth century, thousands of Yiddish songs had been written by hundreds of American composers and lyricists and sung throughout America. Three Jewish composers especially enriched that roster over those years: Rumshinsky, Secunda, and Ellstein. Joseph (Rumshisky) Rumshinsky (?1879/81–1956) was a prolific arranger and composer. Born in Vilna to a musical family, he was a choirboy, studied piano and music theory, and then conducted synagogue and secular choral groups in Poland. Upon his arrival in America in 1903, he began to work for publishers, preparing simplified piano selections and Russian-Slavic folk songs. He provided skillful piano and violin arrangements for numerous theatrical composers, including Meyerowitz, Mogulesco, and Smulewitz. In the early decades, his editing activities rivaled those of his friend and mentor Russotto. Unlike the latter, Rumshinsky rapidly became facile at composing show tunes. His busy career in the Yiddish theater was launched by a song, with lyrics by Smulewitz, for a 1909 Yiddish production *Natan, der khokhem* (Nathan the wise) based on Lessing's play. Subsequently, all Jewish publishing houses issued Rumshinsky's arrangements and compositions. Influenced by the works of Sigmund Romberg and Victor Herbert, he wrote scores for such operettas as *Dem rebbens nigun* (The rabbi's tune), *Di khazinteh* (The lady cantor), *Tsubrokheneh fideleh* (Broken fiddle), and, *Shir hashirim* (Song of songs). Greatly valued also as a music coach and piano accompanist, Rumshinsky assisted the leading Yiddish performers of that era: Nellie Casman (1896–1984), Jennie Goldstein (1895–1960), Aaron Lebedeff (1873–1960), Michal Michalesko (?1885/8–1957), Ludwig Satz (1891–1944), and Molly Picon (1898–1992). In the 1940s, Rumshinsky expanded his musical activities as a conductor and arranger for synagogue choirs and secular choruses, and he sustained his professional work to the end of his life.

Sholom (Samuel) Secunda (1894–1974) is probably best known for his adaptation of the Polish-Jewish folk song *Dona, dona* (Tra-la-la) and for his romantic ballad, *Bei [Bay] mir bistu sheyn* (I think you're pretty). He composed many other selections and enjoyed a long and successful career as piano accompanist, vocal coach, arranger, and conductor for religious music as well as theatricals. Over the years, he was also associated with operatic tenor Richard Tucker (1912–1975) in concerts and liturgical performances. Secunda was born in the Ukraine and came to the United States in 1908 with his parents. He started as a boy chorister at a Lower East Side synagogue and then was a music student at the Institute of Musical Art (Juilliard). For a time, he also studied composition with Ernest Bloch (1880–1959). In 1915, Secunda's first published work was the title song for a musical show, *Leybedigeh yesoymim* (Lively orphans). Like Rumshinsky, he began his career by shaping melodies for the lyrics of Smulewitz.

After serving as a music arranger for the United States Navy Band during World War I, Secunda blossomed into a highly prolific and greatly respected musician in the Yiddish theater. Widely published, he worked with most of the star entertainers in their heyday. He composed incidental music for the dramas of Maurice Schwartz (?1888/90–1960), notably for a production in 1940 of *Tevye der milkhiger* (Tevye the dairyman), based upon the writings of Sholom Aleichem (1859–1916). Late in his career, Secunda created a full opera based upon Abraham Goldfaden's Yiddish operetta *Shulamith*. He also composed serious music especially for synagogue services. Some of Secunda's selections, like *Der Yiddish lid* (The Jewish song) and his adaptations of various Sabbath *z'miroth* (table carols) with their art-song qualities, have entered into the repertoires of internationally famous concert artists. In 1932, he helped form the Society of Jewish Composers, Publishers, and Songwriters (SJCPS), following the pattern of ASCAP (American Society of Composers, Authors, and Publishers). However, the SJCPS organization proved unsuccessful and was disbanded after several years.

Sholom Secunda wrote *Bei mir bistu sheyn* in 1933, with lyrics by Jacob Jacobs (1890–1977). Then in 1937, two popular songwriters, Sammy Cahn and Saul Chaplin, adapted its melody and added English lyrics for performance in a Hollywood film called *Love, Honor and Behave*. That newer version, as published by T. B. Harms Company, achieved great success, and still continues to be popular. During those years, there were a number of easily recognized crossover Yiddish-Yinglish-English songs, including the adaptation of a Hasidic *freylakhs* (happy dance tune) in 1939 by Ziggy Elman (1914–1968) which, with new lyrics by Johnny Mercer (1909–1976), was retitled "And the Angels Sing." Yiddish comedienne Nellie Casman's (1896–1984) specialty song, *Yosl, Yosl* (male name), was revised into "Joseph, Joseph, Won't You Make Your Mind Up," and rapidly became a general favorite. Long before Sholom Secunda died in 1974, the great epoch of the Yiddish musicals had passed, and its distinctive qualities lingered on only as nostalgic echoes in ethnic entertainment.[26]

Abraham Ellstein (1907–1963) was a latecomer to Yiddish American musicals. Born in New York City, he was a synagogue chorister and choir conductor, and studied piano and composition. From 1926 to 1932, he toured the country as arranger and accompanist for Cantor Yossele Rosenblatt. In the 1930s, Ellstein came into the Yiddish theater, where he worked with many of its stars, most especially Molly Picon (1898–1992). He wrote the music for two films that she made in Poland in 1937 and 1938, and she introduced his four most popular songs: *Yidl mit'n fidl* (Little Jew with a fiddle), *Oy mameh bin ikh farlibt* (Oh mother, am I in love), *Abi gezunt* (Only good health), and *Mameleh* (Little mother). In addition to a number of other ballads, Ellstein modernized several traditional Jewish dance tunes, including *Der nayer sher* (The new scissors dance), whose wide popularity added new luster to the genre of Jewish folk band music. After World War II, Ellstein concentrated upon the creation of serious compositions and also assisted an array of cantorial artists as well as operatic tenor Jan Peerce (1904–1984), in concert tours and recordings.

The Great Ballad-Hymn Eili, Eili

One of Cantor Yossele Rosenblatt's special solos on his vaudeville tours across the country was *Eili [Eyli], Eili* (My God, my God), which he intoned as a liturgical selection. That song is a remarkable example of the evolution of an American theatrical ballad into a religious arietta. Moreover, this song also was the subject of important copyright litigation, resulting in a landmark federal judicial decision regarding the protection of musical works in America. Its composer, Peretz Jacob Koppel Sandler (?1853/60–1931), had been a choirsinger and choral leader in eastern Europe. Soon after arriving in New York City, he began his association with the Bowery area Jewish theaters as a pianist, coach, composer, arranger, and choral director for Mogulesco and Thomashefsky and for the operettas of impresarios Horowitz and Lateiner.

In April 1896, Moshe Horowitz planned the production of a historical drama with music, entitled *Brokhoh* (male name), or The Jewish King of Poland for a Night. Sandler prepared all the music, including an appealing lamentation for soubrette Sophie Karp (1861–1906) to sing in her role as a Jewish girl about to be martyred for her faith. Horowitz had suggested a text be adapted from verses of Psalm 22, along with poetic passages out of other Jewish supplication prayers, for which Sandler then shaped a dramatic melody incorporating elements of traditional liturgical chant. Its first words were: *Eili, Eili, Lomo Asavtoni* (My God, my God, why hast Thou forsaken me), and it was an immediate success during the several weeks' run of the play. The song then became a featured extra number at other theatricals, and was performed by a succession of female performers. The following year, one of the most famous Yiddish dramatic performers of that day, Bertha Kalish (1872–1939), took it as her special solo. Meanwhile, Sandler decided to leave theatrical work and concentrate upon other musical activities, assisting cantors and training choirs as well as arranging wedding music and teaching piano. It was not until twenty years later that he briefly returned to the Yiddish theater as a composer and conductor.

Over the decades following its introduction on the Bowery stage, the song *Eili, Eili* was printed and sold by many publishers in a multitude of different arrangements. Widely performed, it rapidly moved into national and then international recognition, noted either as a folk tune or a liturgical chant and treated as an anonymous creation. There was no mention of Sandler's name. As early as ten years after the initial performance, the song began to be accorded the same respect as a cantorial selection, and was known to the general public as "the Jewish lament." Its first known publication, prepared in 1906 by Joseph Rumshinsky for S. Goldberg Company, was dedicated to the memory of Sophie Karp. By 1912, the song had traveled to Europe and was even printed in St. Petersburg, Russia. Then in 1917, publishers G. Schirmer and Carl Fischer issued edited choral concert-style arrangements. Because *Eili, Eili* was being featured by so many Jewish entertainers, it also reached Tin Pan Alley in several forms. Sandler himself heard it sung by Sophie Braslau (1892–1935) in 1919 on the stage of the Metropolitan Opera House and again in a melodic arrangement performed at Carnegie Hall by violinist Mischa Elman (1891–1967). However, it was Cantor Yossele Rosenblatt's nationwide renditions that gave *Eili, Eili* its serious liturgical anchor. Finally, urged by members of his family, Sandler began years of legal proceedings to have that song recognized as his own.

Sandler started that long process by publishing the song himself in 1919, printing the details of his authorship on the sheet music. In 1923, he sued Jos. P. Katz Company, that company standing in for all other publishers. The case, on appeal, finally reached the United States Federal Court, Southern District of New York. Testifying for Sandler were members of the Jewish Ministers Cantors Association, who stated that the song was not in the ritual music of the synagogue, not part of traditional Jewish folk song, nor ever known in eastern Europe or America prior to its creation in 1896. A final judicial ruling was published in full detail on the front page of the *New York Law Journal* of September 22, 1925. The decision was that "long delay in asserting authorship to a song, which is meanwhile being openly published and sold by others, constitutes fatal acquiescence and *laches*." In essence, it was a matter of personal negligence, for which there could be no remedy. Sandler's role as composer-creator was acknowledged, but he and his heirs could never claim copyright ownership. To the end of his life, Sandler labored for further verification, while the song itself grew in general popularity. This particular case has become a textbook case study on music copyright law in America.

Throughout the following decades and into the difficult years of World War II, *Eili, Eili* was featured on records, radio, and the stage. There were copyrighted versions for orchestra, military band, and a great variety of solo instruments, including guitar and ukulele. Increasingly, it was rendered by cantorial artists as a prayerful selection. Lacking formal structure in verse and chorus and without rhythmic pattern, this song would seem to be a strange work to receive such general appreciation. Indeed, it was the epitome of difference, of melodic sounds as yet unintegrated into American music. Appealingly different in its form, tone, content, and mode of presentation, it offered a challenge for change in popular song creativity, much as did the growing influence of Afro-American music. All of these unusual new musical strains evoked reactions of misunderstanding, even of bigotry. A Michigan periodical, *The Dearborn Independent*, in its circulated editions of August and September 1921, concentrated upon such topics as "*Eli* [*sic*] *Eli*, explained, or the Jewish religious propaganda on the vaudeville stage," and "Congo, ragtime and jazz, how they make you sing the stuff."

Slavic-Jewish Resonances

Nevertheless, those newer sounds were fast becoming part of the American domestic musical scene. By the late 1920s, catchy recordings by Jewish folk bands featuring Hasidic tunes, wedding ballads, folk songs, and Slavic dances, were being played on home phonographs. At all types of theatricals and public functions, versatile musicians played piano and violin and led ensembles in their own arrangements of those ethnic melodies. The earliest Jewish music publishers had employed Louis Friedsell, Henry Russotto, and Joseph Rumshinsky to arrange Polish, Romanian, Russian, and Ukrainian folk selections into simplified form. This music was issued either as single pieces or in albums. The published song sheets provided texts printed in Cyrillic characters and romanized along with any Yiddish lyrics. Performers on the Jewish stage carried forward the Slavic multimusical and multilingual customs brought over from eastern Europe, and that music became a staple in the repertoires of Yiddish singers and instrumentalists. No wonder that a certain blend of Judaic-Slavic elements soon came to be identified by the American public as part and parcel of Yiddish music.

The nineteenth-century eastern European Jewish folk band ensembles (variously called *klezmer*, *musikanter*, or *kapelyeh*) consisted of strings, (fiddle and bass) and woodwinds (wood or metal), often with a hammered dulcimer. In America, there were gradual changes, such as more violins and the prominence of the clarinet. A piano or an accordion displaced the dulcimer, and the beat was sustained by some form of percussion. As in the Old Country, instrumental parts were usually improvised, based upon melody lines supplied for voice, piano, or violin. The performance duration was set by the lead musician. Many players could not read music, and few groups used any sort of prepared orchestration. Those American Jewish bandmasters were modern versions of the eastern European dance leaders, moving their ballroom groups along from the traditional folk steps to the newer ragtime and jazz, fox-trot and tango. There were three types of old-style dances: Jewish—*freylakhs, sher,* and *husid'l*; Slavic-Jewish—*bulgar, hora, kozatska*; and Slavic—*doina, hopak, mazurka/polka.* Jewish bands were engaged by non-Jews, who also bought their recordings. In a matter of time, those Slavic elements became integral aspects of Jewish entertainment, blurring any melodic distinctions.

One of the leading Jewish bandmasters was Abe Schwartz (d. 1963). By 1919, his photograph, violin in hand, began to appear on sheet music covers. He arranged all kinds of dance tunes, and even launched into the writing of Yiddish songs. His most successful was *Di grineh kuzineh* (The green/naïve female cousin), which he based upon the tune of a Hasidic dance. For a while, the authorship was a matter of public dispute between Abe Schwartz and a vaude-villian named Yankele Brisker (1893–1965). The issue was settled with the copyrighted publication by J. and J. Kammen Company of Schwartz's melodic version with lyrics by an entertainer named Hyman Prizant, in an arrangement by Jack Kammen. Rosters of ethnic recording companies were filled with Jewish band selections by more than a dozen different "name" band groups, and their music became the hallmark of Yiddish-style performances.

In 1927, Irving Berlin's (1888–1989) song "Russian Lullaby" utilized some of those Slavic-Judaic elements, incorporating the major-minor ambiguity into a folklike tune somewhat suggestive of the *Hatikvah* melodic motif. However, the quintessential mainstreaming of Slavic-Judaic materials happened in quite another way. In the late 1920s, Chaim (Tauber) Towber (1901–1972) was known on the Yiddish American stage as "the singing poet," a performer who wrote his own lyrics. Born in Russia, he first appeared in Romanian theatricals, soon emigrated to Montreal, and then came to New York City. He collaborated with theater composers, supplying them with song lyrics that were sentimental and nostalgic and had Russian words. Towber's texts were tailored to his own lyric tenor and stage persona. Among his highly popular lyrics were: *Sheyn vi di levoneh* (Pretty as the moon), to music by Rumshinsky, and *Skripeh, klezmer'l, skripeh* (Scrape musician, scrape away), to music by Secunda. Often Towber's presentations had dramatic story lines for the songs that he adapted from Slavic tunes. In one of his most celebrated performances, he related the tragedy of a worker who died on the picket line, *Mot'l der operator* (Mot'l, the sewing ma-chine worker). Towber shaped Ivan Ivanovici's (1845–1902) melody of *Valurile dundrei* (Waves of the Danube) into a romantic serenade, *Di khasseneh valts* (The wedding waltz). Within several years, that song acquired English lyrics, and it has since become a perennial general favorite as "The Anniversary Waltz" or "Oh, How We Danced on the Night We Were Wed." Chaim Towber made two other highly successful adaptations. The melody of Emil Waldteufel's (1837–1915) "Delores Waltz" became his song *Nokh eyn tants* (One more dance, or oh my love), and a Russian waltz, *Ozidanie* (Expectation) became *Der ershter valts*

(The first waltz). For a time, he toured throughout the country and was a Yiddish radio personality.

Also derived from Slavic culture were the numerous amateur mandolin ensembles and secular choruses, as activities carried over from eastern European life. In America, such groups were formed by Jewish social organizations and labor unions. The mandolin players used violin parts printed on song sheets, and many arrangements of various folk songs were printed and published in simple choral form. The popularity of those musical diversions diminished with the passing of the immigrant generation. However, many choral associations continued to flourish late into the twentieth century, under the leadership of a roster of dedicated musicians. The earliest was Platon Brounoff (?1859/63–1924), who was a prototype for later Jewish music directors in America. Born in Russia, he studied piano and composition at the St. Petersburg Conservatory. In New York City, he formed the Poale Zion Singing Society, modeled after similar groups in Warsaw and Vilna. Especially for his singers, Brounoff arranged Yiddish, Hebrew, Russian, and Polish folk songs, and presented his chorus at gala concerts. In 1911, Charles K. Harris Company published a collection by Brounoff of fifty Jewish folk songs, together with his detailed introduction treating the background of that music.

Brounoff's successor as choral conductor was his protégé, Henry Lefkowitch (1892–1959), who also founded Metro Music Company. Over the next decades, the leadership of singing societies passed among a network of Jewish musicians: Jacob Beimel (?1875/80–1944), Abraham W. Binder (1895–1966),[27] Samuel Bugatch (1898–1984), Isadore Freed (1900–1960),[28] Michl Gelbart (1889–1962), Vladimir Heifetz (1893–1970), Max Helfman (1901–1963),[29] Leo Low (1878–1960), Meyer Posner (1890–1931), Lazare Saminsky (1882–1959),[30] Nicholas Saslavsky (1885–1965), Jacob Schaefer (1888–1936), Jacob Weinberg (1879–1956), Lazar Weiner (1897–1982),[31] and Zavel Zilberts (1880/1–1949). Under their direction, the repertoires of folk choruses encompassed a wide range of European and American materials. Impetus also was provided in America for the collection, arrangement, public performance, and publication of Yiddish, Hebrew, Ladino, and English Jewish folk songs, and for the broader general recognition of that music.[32]

Worker Songs

Some of those choral groups were associated with the rising trade union labor movement throughout the country.[33] Songs helped to rally workers at union meetings and on the picket lines. Well into recent times, that type of music found its way into Broadway shows and public entertainment programs. From the beginning, Yiddish American popular songs and theatricals addressed the problems of earning a livelihood; of sweatshop factories and home-bundle workers; of laboring men, women, and children. There were songs about the rise of an organized labor movement, viewed as a uniquely American phenomenon. After all, as early as 1888 there was a fledgling union of Jewish theatrical choristers, and by 1902 a Hebrew Actors Union had been constituted.

In 1911, the Yiddish and general stages echoed with elegiac songs about the 146 Jewish and Italian girls who had perished in the Triangle Shirtwaist Company factory loft fire on the Lower East Side of New York City. The actress Jennie Goldstein (1895–1960) became a particular favorite of working people; in dramatic performances she mirrored the world of lonely women struggling to survive despite great adversity. In one role, she gave away her baby, singing the song *Ikh bin a mameh, un vu Iz mayn kind* (I am a mother, and where is my child). In another, she portrayed an ailing seamstress, singing *Nem mikh tsi fun dem machine* (Take me away from the sewing machine). Her heroines were forced to work because no one would provide for them and were fired from jobs because they grew sick or too old. For many decades, Jewish workers were especially associated with the needle trades, and Yiddish songs reflected poetically upon those labors. The Yiddish folksinger Sidor Belarsky (1900–1975) toured widely throughout North America, featuring an encore selection that was the creation of worker-poet Morris Rosenfeld (1861–1923), titled *Mayn rueh plats* (My quiet place): "Do not seek to find me, my beloved, in cool green gardens where there are flowers, birds, breezes, and streams of clear water. Seek me, rather, among the bundles and machines in the hot crowded darkness of a sweatshop. Not under a tree am I, but bent over bound to the work. Here is where you will find me. This is my quiet place."[34]

Cantorial Developments

As early as the late nineteenth century, attempts had been made by cantorial artists to establish some form of group protection, in a sense, to unionize. From 1924 to 1931, a Board of American *Hazzan* Ministers (also known as the Modern Reform Cantors Association) had tried to define the economic terms of their employment and to mediate in congregational disputes. The board issued and circulated a pamphlet, "The Ministerial Status of the Cantor." Some cantors from the rising Conservative branch of American Judaism also joined with that group. Meanwhile, the Jewish Ministers Cantors Association continued as the organization of the strictly traditional, or Orthodox. Neither group was effective in monitoring the working conditions for its membership.

By the decade of the 1920s, there were three distinctively defined branches of American Judaism: Orthodox, Conservative, and Reform. When rabbinical scholar Solomon Schechter (1850–1915) emigrated to America from England in 1902, he took over the direction of the New York training school for rabbis, soon known as the Jewish Theological Seminary of America. The school had been established before the turn of the century by two rabbis, Sabato Morais (1823–1897) and Alexander Kohut (1842–1894). Rabbi Schechter and his colleagues at the seminary began to encourage evolving changes in American synagogue services, allowing for the introduction of some moderate reforming ideas within the purview of traditional observances. This was to be a form of centrist Judaism that would be conservative in outlook. American cantorial practices went along, accommodating liturgical music to those three directions: strictly observant, moderately changed, and reformist.[35]

The Union Hymnal

Many congregants, especially those of eastern European origins, were becoming increasingly mobile in their affiliations; attendance particularly swung between the Reform and Conservative services. As a result, the music of Reform Judaism found itself much in need of adaptive adjustment. As early as 1924, there were proposals for a completely revised third edition of the official Reform Union Hymnal that would "ring true to the Jewish spirit." It was to be a resource for congregational singing and suitable for educational use in the religious schools. Five years later, the Central Conference of American Rabbis asked Abraham W. Binder (1895–1966) to serve on the hymnal revision committee as music editor. He was uniquely prepared to take on that task.

Abraham W. Binder was born in New York City into a cantorial family. He was a boy chorister, and studied piano and music theory. In 1911, he began a music career as organist and choir director at a Brooklyn temple and continued his formal musical studies. Binder soon became associated with a congregation in the Bronx, and in 1916 also took on the leadership of the Hadassah Choral Union, for which he began to arrange and compose selections. In 1917, he was invited to organize a music department at the 92nd Street YM-YWHA in New York, where he commenced a lifelong association as educator. About the same time, he began to teach at the religious school of Temple Emanu-El and to write hymns for that Reform congregation, including his "Come, oh Sabbath Day" for the Sabbath eve services. In 1921, Rabbi Stephen S. Wise (1874–1949), a charismatic leader in Reform Judaism, invited Binder to join the faculty of a newly organized Jewish Institute of Religion in New York, as teacher of Jewish liturgical music to the rabbinical students. The following year, he became choirmaster at the Stephen Wise Free Synagogue. Eventually, the Jewish Institute of Religion merged with the Cincinnati-based Hebrew Union College as its New York branch, and was housed next door to the Wise Synagogue. Binder remained associated with both institutions to the end of his life.

With the encouragement of his mentor, Rabbi Stephen S. Wise, Binder reintroduced many of the traditional liturgical melodies and restored biblical cantillations at those Reform services. It was Rabbi Wise who urged the appointment of Binder as music editor to prepare the revised third Reform Union Hymnal. For that edition, published in 1932, Binder added and rearranged materials from the earlier editions of 1897 and 1914.[36] He also contributed new settings for some liturgical texts, included more European traditional chants, and invited several American Jewish composers to write hymns based upon the synagogue melodic motifs. As editor, Binder divided the music materials into three sections, each of which was also published as a separate volume: Hymns: *Songs and Prayers for Jewish Worship*, with 266 selections; *Musical Services for Sabbath, Festivals, and Special Occasions*, with 74 selections; and *Services for the Religious School*, with 114 congregational chants. This vastly expanded edition of the Reform Union Hymnal was fully reprinted numerous times, and in 1957 was issued with only some minor changes, remaining the standard musical resource for Reform congregations. In 1960, its third section was fully revised and published for youth as the official Reform Union Songster. Although several other collections of hymns and responses have been prepared for Reform services in recent years, the work edited by Abraham W. Binder remains a significant American Jewish musical achievement. The hymnals compiled for the United States Armed Forces have included selections from that volume.

Over those years, liturgical songbooks were issued by congregations of the Conservative branch of Judaism, also influenced by the strong predilection among Americans for service hymnody. As early as 1915, Max (Halper) Halpern, reverend-cantor at a Boston traditional synagogue, prepared a book of chants for Sabbath and year-round services and religious schools. It was published by both Boston Music Company and G. Schirmer Company, with a brief preface citing consultation with Orthodox and Conservative rabbis and stating that "congregational singing alone combines the decorum and impressiveness of a modern house of worship with the enthusiasms and religious fervor of the olden synagogues." (unpaginated text) Other collections of traditional music appeared over the next decades, including a hymnal compiled by Philadelphia educator and anthologist Rabbi Abraham Millgram (1901–1988), published in 1937. Rabbi Millgram acknowledged his inclusion of several hymns from the Reform Union Hymnal edited by Abraham W. Binder.

Jewish Education and Music

After World War I, three types of formal Jewish religious schooling emerged in America: all-day parochial institutions, combining general with Jewish studies; afternoon and evening supplementary classes; and Sunday school sessions. However, for some youngsters, there was still private Hebrew tutoring. Well into recent times, there also have been Yiddish language educational groups for children as well as adults. In 1910, a Bureau of Jewish Education was organized in New York City by an educator and physician, Dr. Samson Benderly (1876–1944), and other American cities soon followed suit. Although association with those bureaus, or boards, of Jewish education was a voluntary matter, their pedagogical recommendations were taken up by communities throughout the country. As Judaism's language of religious devotions, Hebrew was a prominent part of Jewish studies. In America, it was fast becoming the modern special vernacular, increasingly displacing Yiddish and Ladino. Hebrew defined the source of Judaic concepts bound up in Bible, history, and tradition. Moreover, it was the literary voice of Zionism, a growing movement centered upon the Holyland and Jerusalem. Jewish music became an important tool in the teaching of the Hebrew language. As a result, educational songsters were prepared for use in Jewish classrooms along with the religious service hymnals, and many congregational cantors assumed the additional role of music teacher.

At that time in many eastern European cities, especially in Warsaw, Lodz, and Vilna, there was a rising sentiment for renascent Jewish cultural life. The leaders in this movement advocated a progressive outlook on Jewish education. They espoused modernized studies of Yiddish and Hebrew and sought to establish formal credentials for certification of rabbis and cantors. They encouraged new Jewish scholarship, notably of literature and music, and supported the collection of age-old folklore, folk songs, and liturgical chants. All those objectives were to reach fruition in America with achievements in Jewish music.

The rapid growth in America of organized Jewish education resulted in the publication of numerous songsters and folk song collections with Hebrew, Yiddish, Ladino, and English texts.[37] That music was selected and compiled, arranged and composed, taught and performed by dedicated educators and musicians. Among those early leaders were Rabbi Israel Goldfarb (1879–1956) and his brother Samuel Goldfarb (1884–1967). Commencing during the second decade of the twentieth century, they collaborated upon a series of music pamphlets that were later published as children's songsters. They consisted of traditional Sabbath hymns in single vocal lines or simple choral arrangements, with easy piano accompaniments. All the materials were intended for practical pedagogical purposes. Over the next years, the brothers issued other collections of religious holiday music, and of Yiddish and Hebrew folk songs. Samuel Goldfarb was also a highly active director of adult choral groups, and Rabbi Israel Goldfarb served at Congregation Beth Elohim in Brooklyn and was *bar mitzvah* instructor to the young Aaron Copland (1900–1990).

Another formative figure among those Jewish music educators was Harry Coopersmith (1902–1975), who started his career in Chicago before joining the Bureau of Jewish Education in New York City as its director for music. Under his leadership, credentials were set for the guidance and selection of music teachers serving religious schools, and a wide variety of musical resources were introduced. Other communities throughout the country adopted those training guidelines and certification criteria, and used the educational materials. Between 1928 and 1971, Coopersmith prepared and published eighteen volumes of collected Jewish songs and hymns. A notable roster of other educator-collectors included Shalom Altman (1910–1986), Samuel Bugatch (1898–1984), Yehudah Leyb Cahan (1881–1937), Gershon Ephros (1890–1978), Michl Gelbart (1889–1962), Abraham Z. Idelsohn (1882–1938), Moshe Nathanson (1899–1981),

Richard Neumann (1915–1984), and Lazar Weiner (1897–1982). Among others in the later 20th century years have been Judith Kaplan Eisenstein, Tsipora Jochsberger, Eleanor Gordon Mlotek, Velvel Pasternak, and Ruth Rubin.

Shalom Altman formed the Department of Jewish Music at the Gratz College for Jewish Studies, which serves also as the central agency for Jewish education in the Greater Philadelphia area. Under his direction, academic courses were developed for the formal study of Jewish music, and a Jewish music library was established as a major national repository of written literature, musical scores, assorted collections, manuscripts, recorded performances, and media materials. In 1970, that library acquired the significant music holdings that had been assembled in Europe by scholar Arno Nadel (1878–1943), as well as the balance of a major collection of *musica Judaica* assembled by the American synagogue musician Eric Mandell (1902–1986).[38]

The folk song compilations by Samuel Bugatch, Michl Gelbart, Eleanor Gordon Mlotek, and Ruth Rubin concentrated upon the Yiddish genre, notably the preservation in modern arrangements of older European creations. Their work followed in the pioneer footsteps of the anthologist Yehudah Leyb Cahan, who began to assemble his monumental treasury of Yiddish folklore, poetry, and tunes before emigrating to America in 1904. A volume of Cahan's materials was posthumously issued in 1957 by the YIVO Institute for Jewish Research in New York City, under the editorship of scholar Max Weinreich (1894–1969). Judith Kaplan Eisenstein, Tzipora Jochsberger, and Lazar Weiner have been composers as well as educators. Richard Neumann ably succeeded Harry Coopersmith as director of music at the Bureau of Jewish Education. Velvel Pasternak formed the Tara Music Publishing Company in 1960, for which he has developed a substantial catalog of liturgical-cantorial, Hasidic, Hebrew, Ladino, and Yiddish songbooks as well as music teaching and performance manuals and literature on music.

Cantors Gershon Ephros and Moshe Nathanson had been apprenticed protégés of the father of modern Jewish musical scholarship, Abraham Z. Idelsohn (1882–1938), at the time that they were all in Jerusalem, during the years before World War I. Upon emigrating to New York City, both Ephros and Nathanson briefly served as music directors for the Bureau of Jewish Education before assuming cantorial duties at congregations. In Jerusalem, Cantor Ephros had assisted Idelsohn in his musical research and collection of liturgical materials, and he followed in that scholarly direction himself after settling in America in 1911. Between 1929 and 1975, Ephros published six volumes of a cantorial anthology, covering materials from the twelfth to the twentieth centuries. A brief preface to the first volume was contributed by Idelsohn.[39]

In America, Cantor Moshe Nathanson helped popularize a song originally shaped by Idelsohn for his students at a Jerusalem academy. Adapting a folk tune sung by Hasidic Jews in the eastern European town of Sadigora, Idelsohn added some Hebrew words, and it became *Hava Nagilah* (Let us be merry).

That song was not copyrighted and is in the public domain. It is doubtful, however, that Idelsohn cared much about such matters. He concentrated rather upon the completion and publication of his ten-volume *Thesaurus of Oriental-Hebrew Melodies*, which consisted of edited and annotated liturgical and folk materials collected from all traditions of Judaism—Oriental, Sephardic, and Ashkenazic. Those volumes were issued from 1922 to 1933, and remain uniquely valuable for their musical scope and contents.[40] Cantor Idelsohn had come to America in 1922, and three years later joined the faculty of Hebrew Union College in Cincinnati as teacher of liturgical music to its students. He also served as curator for that rabbinical library's substantial and invaluable collection of Jewish music materials acquired from the estate of European cantor and scholar Eduard Birnbaum (1855–1920). In 1929, Idelsohn's musicological study of the history of Jewish music, painstakingly begun while he was still teaching in Jerusalem, was translated from the original Hebrew and published in America.[41]

Scholars and Organizations

The tragedy of the Holocaust has underscored the significance of the manifold Jewish music activities in America over the decades of the twentieth century—research and scholarly studies, collection and edited publications, youth and adult education institutions, secular and religious organizations. In 1931, Jewish musicians and scholars formed the American Palestine Music Association (*Mailamm*) in order to support music research in Palestine and America.[42] Its West Coast branch was led by Joseph Achron (1886–1943), who had come to America in 1922 from Russia. In 1934, Achron went to Los Angeles, where he was associated with Arnold Schoenberg (1874–1951) and other German émigré musicians who settled out there. It was at a 1934 meeting of the *Mailamm* society in New York that Schoenberg, very soon after his arrival in America, delivered an impassioned address. His topic surprised the audience because it focused upon the necessity for a Jewish refuge homeland in Palestine rather than upon his twelve-tone system of musical composition.[43] In 1939, *Mailamm* reconstituted itself as the Jewish Music Forum, and flourished until 1962 with a membership roster that included many well-known musicians. The forum was established as a "society for the advancement of Jewish music culture" and, over a number of years, ably served that leadership function. This writer studied with several of those members and felt privileged to be invited to attend some of the forum's final meetings.[44]

The impetus to organize on behalf of the scholarly study and serious performance of Jewish music actually had begun in Russia.[45] In 1908, a group that included Joel Engel (1868–1927), Solomon Rosowsky (1878–1962), Lazare Saminsky (1882–1959), and Jacob Weinberg (1879–1956) secured permission from Russian authorities in St. Petersburg to form the Society for Jewish Folk Music. The idea itself had been initiated by Joel Engel, then a music critic for

Russian newspapers. He wanted to concentrate upon the historic musical creativity of the Jewish people, much as the Russian nationalists of the time were
doing for Russian folk music. By 1913, the St. Petersburg group had also established a branch in Moscow. Soon after the Russian Revolution, however, Engel
went to Palestine, and many of the others left for America. Lazare Saminsky
became the music director at Temple Emanu-El in New York City. Also eventually settling in New York, Solomon Rosowsky and Jacob Weinberg devoted
themselves to teaching, composing, and scholarly writing. Essentially, the work
launched in St. Petersburg had been transferred to America, and it continued
with the subsequent activities of the Jewish Music Forum.

For over twenty-five years, those associated with the Jewish Music Forum
constituted a distinguished roster of composers, performers, scholar-writers,
educators, and synagogue musicians. That notable list included Leonard Bernstein (1918–1990), Abraham W. Binder (1895–1966), Ernest Bloch (1880–1959),
Nathan Broder (1905–1967), Mario Castelnuovo-Tedesco (1895–1968), Harry
Coopersmith (1902–1975), Paul Dessau (1895–1979), Gershon Ephros (1890–
1978), David Ewen (1907–1985), Isadore Freed (1900–1960), Max Helfman
(1901–1963), Artur Holde (1885–1962),[46] Frederick Jacobi (1891–1952), Paul
Nettl (1889–1972), Karol Rathaus (1895–1962), Curt Sachs (1881–1959), Lazare
Saminsky (1882–1959), Sholom Secunda (1894–1974), Alfred Sendrey (1884–
1976), Albert Weisser (1918–1982), Eric Werner (1901–1988), Stefan Wolpe
(1902–1972), and Joseph Yasser (1893–1981).

Records of the meetings of the New York Jewish Music Forum indicated that
there were wide-ranging lectures on a great variety of topics as well as numerous
music performances. Nettl, Rosowsky, Sachs, Sendrey, Werner, and Yasser presented progress reports on their own important musicological studies.
Composers discussed and performed their own works. Dessau analyzed Arnold
Schoenberg's composition titled *Kol Nidrey*. Freed reviewed the creativity of his
teacher, Ernest Bloch. Bernstein spoke about the cantillation elements in his
Jeremiah Symphony. Secunda outlined a history of the Yiddish musical theater
in America. Josef Freudenthal (1903–1964) announced his formation of the
Transcontinental Music Company for the express purpose of publishing Jewish
liturgical and secular music.[47] Coopersmith discussed his recommendations for
the formal training and certification of Jewish music teachers. When the forum
disbanded in 1962, it was succeeded by the Jewish Liturgical Music Society of
America, organized by Binder. That group was superseded in 1973 by the
American Society for Jewish Music, which has concentrated upon the presentation of concert programs in the New York City area and the publication of a
periodical, *Musica Judaica*.

In 1944, a Jewish Community Center (JCC) director and social worker, Bernard Carp, enlisted the active support of the Jewish Music Forum to work with a
group of communal leaders in forming the National Jewish Music Council.
Housed as a department of the Jewish Welfare Board (the umbrella organization

of Jewish Ys, community centers, and Jewish military service chaplains), the council was established as a North American service agency. Its tasks were to create and distribute Jewish music resources, offer program aid information, and oversee the annual observance of Jewish Music Week (later expanded to a festival month and then a spring season).[48]

Schools for Cantorial Study

Because many of its members were liturgical musicians, the Jewish Music Forum held a conference in 1941 on the status of synagogue music in America. The sessions were held in association with the Central Conference of American Rabbis and the Rabbinical Assembly of America. Led by liturgists Jacob Beimel (1880–1944), Pinchos Jassinowsky (1886–1954), and David Putterman (1901–1979), along with the distinguished members of the forum, discussions ranged from the preservation of traditional liturgical music to the matter of guidelines for the creation of new devotional selections. Also considered were proposals to introduce formal courses of cantorial study at American rabbinical institutions. At a subsequent meeting held by the same group in 1944, consideration was given to the formation of an academy of Jewish music education for the training of cantors as well as music teachers in the religious schools. However, it was not until 1948 that Eric Werner, successor to Abraham Z. Idelsohn at Hebrew Union College (HUC), and Abraham W. Binder, on the faculty of the Jewish Institute of Religion (JIR), could report to the forum members concerning plans for a school of Jewish sacred music at the newly combined HUC-JIR in New York City.

Several factors influenced that decision. Since 1924, the admission of immigrants from eastern Europe had shrunk, and thereby diminished that source of traditionally trained cantors. During the 1930s, growing peril for European Jewish life brought an increasing desire on the part of American Jews to gather and preserve their historic liturgy and religious culture. Moreover, Jewish congregants had begun to recognize the necessity for stricter professional standards among synagogue musicians. The customary oral apprenticeship for cantors could no longer provide skills for those who would have to serve also as religious-school teachers and arbiters of Jewish music programming in their communities.

Contributing to the July 1934 issue of the short-lived (two editions) *Journal of Jewish Music* (edited and published by Jacob Beimel), Abraham W. Binder wrote that modern cantors must reclaim their important role by understanding the full range of synagogue music and by strengthening their dedication to that sacred office. Over the next decade, other writers in many Jewish periodicals also underscored the issues of cantorial competence and liturgical fidelity. Especially after 1939, there were urgent recommendations for a conservatory of Jewish music in America, and rabbinical schools were petitioned to set up courses for cantorial training. At the fiftieth anniversary celebration in 1947 of the Jewish Ministers Cantors Association of American (*Hazzanim Farband*), that organization firmly endorsed the idea of a cantorial seminary.[49] Then in January of 1948, Binder and Werner convinced the Board of Governors of the combined HUC-JIR in New York City to bring into being the School of Sacred Music. Courses commenced that fall in Jewish music history, biblical cantillation, cantorial chant, sacred and secular folk traditions, synagogue repertoire, and music pedagogy, along with general instruction in theory, conducting, and the organ.

At first, it was hoped that this school would serve the educational needs of traditional as well as Reform congregational musicians. However, the other branches soon developed separate academies. In 1952, the Jewish Theological Seminary of America (JTSA) inaugurated its own Cantors Institute and College of Liturgical Music on behalf of Conservative Judaism. Two years later, Yeshiva University (YU) added courses of musical study, culminating in 1964 with the establishment of the Cantorial Training Institute to serve Orthodox synagogues.

Along with those schools, three professional cantorial groups, with memberships and annual conventions, were also developed: for the Reform branch, the American Conference of Cantors (ACC); for the Conservative branch, the Cantors Assembly of America (CAA); and for the Orthodox branch, the Cantorial Council of America (CCA). Although there has been active interchange of publication materials and cantorial activities, the three schools have maintained discretely different criteria for admission, training, and placement. More recently, with the entrance of women into cantorial roles, those differences have sharpened. Orthodoxy retains its strictly male distinction, while the Reform temples welcome female cantors. For the Conservative branch, women have been admitted, but the issue remains polemical. While they may be instructed and certified, matters of employment and details of professional association are still hotly contested within the ranks of traditionally minded cantors and congregations. Two organizations also presently involved with the roles of women in synagogue music are the American Guild of Temple Organists and the Women Cantors Network.

The formation of three cantorial schools has led to the publication of valuable scores and literature in the field. Each school has prepared educational resources, issued edited collections, and supported a professional journal featuring articles on secular as well as sacred music. In particular, the Sacred Music Press of HUC-JIR has reproduced the original European editions of cantorial classics by Abraham Baer (1834–1894), Abraham Ber Birnbaum (1865–1922), Eliezer Gerovitsch (1844–1913), Louis Lewandowski (1821–1894), Samuel Naumbourg (1815–1880), Salomon Sulzer (1804–1890), and Hirsch Weintraub (1811–1882).[50]

Each of the cantorial schools has encouraged research and music creativity on the part of their faculty members. The scholarly contributions of Eric Werner have been of exceptional value to the entire range of musicology.[51] Indeed, such interaction of studies and publications has proved productive for the general music and Judaica faculties at universities throughout North America and Europe. Contacts have also been highly fruitful with academic institutions and scholars in the State of Israel. Another positive consequence has been the growth of Jewish music materials at Christian seminaries, together with a concurrent strengthening of that subject in the catalogs of all academic and public libraries.

As the twentieth century draws to a close, across the American continent, bureaus of Jewish education and branch schools of Judaic studies offer courses to adults as well as children on all types of Jewish music. A profusion of Jewish songbooks and recordings provide a variety of selections for education and entertainment. Of particular interest has been the resurgent interest in Yiddish tunes, folk bands, and ethnic dances. Moreover, attention also has been drawn to the musical heritage of Sephardic Jews, who have come to North America from the Mediterranean areas (Turkey, Greece, Balkans, and North Africa). Youth groups in particular have begun to seek out newer musical styles of Judaic expression, and that quest is somewhat akin to that of the earlier innovative poet-singers and minstrel bards in Jewish music history.

Commissioning of Jewish Music in America

An intriguing development in American Jewish music has been the commissioning of new liturgical compositions. One of the earliest and most significant commissions was tendered in 1930 by Temple Emanu-El of San Francisco to Ernest Bloch, for creation of a musical work based upon the liturgical order of the Sabbath day service. Swiss-born Ernest Bloch (1880–1959) had settled in America in 1916 and become a citizen in 1923. He had been residing and teaching in the Oakland area, and that grant from Temple Emanu-El enabled him to return to Switzerland for several years. In 1933, Bloch's "Sacred Service for the Sabbath" (*Avodath Hakodesh*) was completed, and was introduced at the Temple in San Francisco, under the direction of Cantor Reuben Rinder (1887–1966). Soon afterwards, the work was performed in New York City, and subsequently entered into concert repertoires as a Jewish oratorio. Beyond its musical qualities, Bloch's sacred service constitutes an artistic verification of the Reform movement's *minhag* (established custom) as it has evolved in America. The work reflects a distinctive conciliation between tradition and modern change in terms of the treatment and presentation of liturgical motifs, cantorial chants, mixed choir parts, and instrumental configurations.[52]

That setting of the sacred service was a landmark achievement by Bloch, whose Judaic works were first introduced to the American public in 1917 at Carnegie Hall by conductor Artur Bodansky (1877–1939). In the audience at the time were many Jewish liturgical musicians and composers, among them Abraham W. Binder, who wrote afterwards that the event had inspired him and his colleagues to write concert music based upon liturgical motifs. Indeed, over the decades, Bloch's music has stimulated much consideration of the special nature of Jewish music itself, beyond its liturgical and folk materials. The issue of what constitutes Jewish music has become the basis for a particularly American debate. Late in his life, Bloch himself sought an answer to that question, writing:

In all those compositions of mine which have been termed Jewish, I have not approached the problem from without, by employing more or less authentic themes... or more or less sacred oriental formulas, rhythms, or intervals... I have hearkened to an inner voice, deep, secret, insistent, burning, an instinct rather than any cold dry reasoning process, a voice which seemed to come from far beyond, beyond myself and my parents, a voice which surged up in me on reading certain passages in the Bible... It was this Jewish heritage as a whole which stirred me, and music was the result. To what extent such music is Jewish, to what extent it is just Ernest Bloch, of that I know nothing. The future alone will decide.[53]

Because Jewish music may be defined most readily in terms of liturgy, that has been the more congenial area for the encouragement of new creativity. In twentieth-century America, the commissioning of Jewish liturgical music has resulted in some significant compositions. Arnold Schoenberg (1874–1951), after emigrating to America late in 1933, composed two of those commissioned Judaic works. His distinctive text and musical interpretation for the *kol nidrey* prayer was requested in 1938 by Rabbi Jacob Sonderling for a Los Angeles Reform congregation, and his powerful Holocaust musical statement, "A Survivor from Warsaw," was written in 1947 upon a grant of the Serge Koussevitsky Music Foundation. In both works, Schoenberg did not utilize actual chant motifs, but preferred to enlarge upon the essence of that material. Particularly in the latter work, his all-male choral setting of the age-old Jewish proclamation of faith (*Shema Yisrael*—Hear, Israel) goes well beyond a simple melodic setting and becomes an impassioned outcry. Darius Milhaud (1892–1974), while residing in Oakland, California, composed the "Sabbath Morning Sacred Service" (*Service Sacré*) in 1948 for Temple Emanu-El of San Francisco. He drew upon liturgical chants from his Comtadin Provençal Jewish background, motifs that, though unfamiliar to that American Reform congregation, were warmly appreciated as spiritual inspiration. In 1954, for celebration of the American Jewish Tercentenary, a great variety of selections for the religious services were commissioned from among a number of American composers and performed throughout the country.

Although commissioning can never guarantee artistic achievement, it has always constituted a significant means of cultural endorsement and economic support, and as such remains a worthy enterprise. One of the best examples of such dedication to new liturgical creativity in America was a project of the Park Avenue (Conservative) Synagogue in New York City. Over the years 1943 to 1978, under the guiding leadership of Cantor David Putterman (1901–1979), that congregation commissioned (and performed) selections for the ritual services by seventy-three composers, Jews and non-Jews. Among them were Leonard Bernstein (1918–1990) and Kurt Weill (1900–1950). In 1950 G. Schirmer Company, in association with the synagogue, published an anthology of thirty-eight of those works for the Friday evening service. Then in 1979, shortly before his death, Cantor Putterman oversaw an expanded new edition of 125 selections.[54] One of the contributions was a setting of the *Kiddush* (prayer over sacramental wine) written in 1946 by Kurt Weill, who dedicated the piece to his father, who had been a cantor in Germany. Interestingly, both Weill and songwriter Harold Arlen (1905–1986) were the sons of practicing professional cantors. Inasmuch as many Jewish American popular composers have had such musical roots, or at least have been personally familiar with that Jewish liturgical background, one may consider what influences such elements of musical memory have had in their own melodic inspiration.

Early in this century, the songwriter and critic Monroe Rosenfeld (1861–1918) coined the name Tin Pan Alley for the location in New York City of a rapidly rising commercial music industry in America. Since then, there have been legions of tunesmiths and lyricists, many of whom were of Jewish descent. Rather than any in-depth analysis of that song genre, one may merely reflect upon some particular Judaic elements that, along with other ethnic influences and the significant Afro-American qualities, have shaped twentieth-century American popular music. Among those salient characteristics are major-minor ambiguity, asymmetrical melodic shaping, motival Judeo-Slavicisms, textual focus, and actual adaptation of Jewish themes. The American song styles that prevailed during the first half of the twentieth century have been largely displaced in the latter decades by materials that are more culturally varied and musically daring. These newer sounds and forms manifest a unique spirit of integration, acculturation, self-expression, and melodic synthesis. They are, in a sense, the musical statements of human freedom.

Canada

What about Jewish music elsewhere in North America? Jews had lived in the Canadian Dominions since 1759, emigrating from western and middle European countries. The Act of 1832 specifically granted the Jews of Canada the same rights as all other subjects. By the late nineteenth century, Yiddish-speaking immigrants from eastern Europe began to arrive, settling in Halifax, Montreal, Quebec City, and Toronto. Responding to opportunities for homesteading on farmland tracts in the western areas, they came to Winnipeg, Saskatoon, Regina, Edmonton, Calgary, and then Vancouver, British Columbia.[55]

By the early twentieth century, the Abraham and Samuel Nordheimer Music Publishing Company was a leading printer and seller of Jewish as well as general sheet music, along with pianos and violins, at its branches in Montreal and

Toronto. From the start, strong ties of cultural heritage and religious practices bridged the geographical borders for American and Canadian Jewry. Traveling cantorial artistes and stars of Yiddish American theatricals have always entertained widely in Canada. When the folk-composer Solomon Smulewitz toured across that country during the 1930s, he performed before Yiddish groups in cities and farming communities and sang with such lively singing societies as the Winnipeg Jewish Folk Chorus, a musical group that had been established there in 1910.

Inasmuch as over the years leading figures in American Jewish music have lectured and performed in Canada, most of the newer developments in liturgical and secular creativity have appeared in both countries. Yet this has not simply been a matter of repetition or imitation. The synagogue in Canada, whether Spaniolic-Sephardic or Yiddish-Ashkenazic, has maintained a more traditional form of congregational services and order of ritual presentation. There is less difference between Canadian Reform and Conservative formulations than in the United States. The old repertoire of European Jewish folk songs has been greatly sustained by an abiding interest among Canadian Jews in amateur choruses and mandolin or other string ensembles. Late in the twentieth century, the range of trained Jewish musicians functioning there, in Jewish as well as general areas, includes singers, instrumentalists, conductors, composers, educators, and scholars. Academic institutions and public libraries include materials related to Jewish music, and CBC (Canadian Broadcasting Company) radio and television programs regularly feature all types of Jewish selections and performers.

Although Jews have resided for several centuries in Mexico and in the other countries of Central and South America, an influx during the twentieth century of Yiddish-speaking Jews to those areas has created a group of modern Hispanic Jews. They speak Spanish, but their musical traditions mostly reflect those of Ashkenazic and Yiddish eastern Europe rather than historic Spaniolic Jewry. Generally, Mexican and other Hispanic synagogue practices do not include many of the modernized innovations prevalent among Jewish congregations in the United States. Their indigenous folk songs relate to the holidays and life-cycle customs and are sung in Yiddish or else in modern Spanish, not in Ladino (Judeo-Español).[56]

All Jewish groups in the areas of the western hemisphere, North and South America, have welcomed music from the State of Israel, a country whose melodies represent the ethnic ingatherings of Jews, Christians, Muslims, Druse, and Samaritans, and a wide range of sacred liturgy as well as secular light and serious works.

The modern renaissance of Jewish music has truly been an American achievement. Although the idea arose among Europeans, it was brought over by immigrants who sought an environment in which to find fulfillment. In America, Jewish musicality developed in an atmosphere receptive to self-expression, adaptation, and innovation. Here, also, Jewish musicians of all types have managed to flourish in every facet of the music world, well beyond their own double root-stock of liturgical tradition and folk heritage.

However, the claim that whatever has filtered through a Jewish mind may be termed a Jewish experience and its product a Judaic expression is an oversimplification of an extremely complex matter. Instead, the issue should be considered in terms of three shaping forces: specific Jewish attributes, shared qualities with other Americans, and the unique confluence of cultural ingredients and opportunities gathered together in American society. There are those who have chosen to concentrate their energies upon Jewish music itself. However, very many others have successfully joined the general American musical mainstream.

To examine only the formal qualities of a musical expression and overlook its historical and geographical contexts is to diminish that artistry. Music defines both time and place, and then transcends them. For Jews, music has always and everywhere illuminated and documented Jewish life. Consequently, their extensive, multifaceted participation in American music goes to the very heart of what it means for Jews to be Americans.

NOTES

Much of the material presented in this chapter originally was prepared as an essay "Jewish Music in North America" for inclusion in *Music in North America*, ed. Charles Hamm, (tenth volume of a series, *The Universe of Music: A History*, project of the UNESCO-International Music Council, Barry S. Brook, editorial director [Washington, D.C.: Smithsonian Institution Press, as of 1994 still in publication preparation]). Additional information on many topical aspects has been added, along with the appended reference notes.

1. An excellent chronicle of the three centuries in America of the Shearith Israel Congregation has been provided in David de Sola Pool and Tamar de Sola Pool, *An Old Faith in the New World* (New York: Columbia University Press, 1955).

2. In his poem "The Jewish Cemetery at Newport" written in 1858, Henry Wadsworth Longfellow eulogized those early settlers.

3. A Jew, Mordecai Sheftall, who for a time had been captured and held prisoner by the British, sent a letter in 1783 to his son, then flag master of the sloop Carolina Packett at base in the Charleston harbor. His letter, informing of the conclusion of the war, ended with this sentence: "An entire new scene will open itself, and we have the world to begin again." Quoted in Jacob Rader Marcus, *The Jew and the American Revolution* (Cincinnati: American Jewish Archives-Hebrew Union College, 1974–1976), p. 17.

4. For further details on early American Jewish history, see:

Max Margolis and Alexander Marx, *A History of the Jewish People* (Philadelphia: Jewish Publication Society of America, 1941).

Jacob Rader Marcus, *United States Jewry: 1776–1785*, 3 vols. (Detroit: Wayne State University Press, 1989).

5. See: H. Wiley Hitchcock, *Music in the United States: A Historical Introduction* (Englewood Cliffs, N.J.: Prentice Hall, 1969), chaps. 1 and 2.

6. A detailed description of hazzanic duties at that time and a roster of rabbis, ministers, and precentors serving congregations in New York City may be found in Hyman B. Grinstein, *The Rise of the Jewish Community of New York, 1654–1860* (Philadelphia: Jewish Publication Society of America, 1945), pp. 484–87.

7. For this information and other interesting items concerning synagogue music in early America, I am indebted to material in Irving H. Cohen, "Synagogue Music in the Early American Republic," *The Gratz College Annual of Jewish Studies*, vol. 5 (Philadelphia: Gratz College, 1976), pp. 17–23.

8. Bertram Korn, *American Jewry and the Civil War* (New York: Atheneum, 1970), pp. 77–78.

9. Copies of this music, as well as most of the other nineteenth- and early twentieth-century hymnals and songbooks cited and quoted in this chapter, may be found and examined from among the substantial collection of Jewish music scores and literature presently housed at the library of Gratz College in Philadelphia.

10. A fuller description of the career of Kitziger is presented in John H. Baron, "Frederick Emil Kitziger of New Orleans: A Nineteenth Century Composer of Synagogue Music," *Musica Judaica*, vol. 5, no. 1 (American Society for Jewish Music, 1982–83), pp. 21–33.

11. For discussion of traditional Ashkenazic liturgical music and contributions of such leaders as Sulzer, Lewandowski, and Naumbourg, refer to Chapter 6 (The Golden Age of the Cantorial Art), and to Chapter 7 (Melodies of Prayer: The Jewish Liturgical Calendar).

12. Excerpted from the preface in Moritz Goldstein, *The Temple Service: Containing All the Music Required for the Union Prayer-Book for Jewish Worship* (Cincinnati: Bloch Publishing, 1895), unpaginated text.

13. Isaac S. Moses, *The Sabbath-School Hymnal: A Collection of Songs, Services, and Responsive Readings for the School, Synagogue and Home* (New York: privately issued, 1894). All the numerous subsequent editions were prepared and published by the Bloch Publishing Company in Cincinnati and in New York.

14. A fuller treatment of the life and career of Edward Stark may be found in Jeffrey S. Zucker, "Edward Stark: American Cantor-Composer at the Turn of the Century," *The Journal of Synagogue Music*, vol. 8, no. 1 (Cantors Assembly, 1983), pp. 14–28.

15. For full discussion of the development of Jewish liturgical music, especially that of the Ashkenazic tradition, see Part II (Bible, Liturgy, and the Cantorial Art).

16. Extensive biographical details (along with salient musical examples) concerning a number of those immigrant cantors, "golden age artistes" from eastern Europe, is provided in Velvel Pasternak, Noah Schall, and Irene Heskes, comps. and eds., *The*

Golden Age of Cantors: Musical Masterpieces of the Synagogue (Cedarhurst, N.Y.: Tara Publications, 1991).

17. For fuller discussions of United States immigration policies, see the following publications:

Samuel Joseph, *Jewish Immigration to the United States, 1881–1910* (orig., Ph.D. thesis, Columbia University, 1914) (New York: Arno Press, 1969).

Marion Bennett, *American Immigration Policies: A History* (Washington, D.C.: Public Affairs Press, 1963). "The objections were many and from diverse sources against what President Woodrow Wilson called this coarse crew that comes crowding in every year at the eastern ports" (p. 32).

Oscar Handlin and Mary Flug Handlin, "A Century of Jewish Immigration to the United States," *The American Yearbook*, vol. 50 (Philadelphia: Jewish Publication Society of America, 1948), pp. 1–84.

18. See Samuel Rosenblatt, *Yossele Rosenblatt: The Story of His Life as Told by His Son* (New York: Farrar, Straus and Young, 1954).

19. A fuller discussion of this topic is given in Chapter 14 (The Music of Hasidism: Melodies of Spiritual Ecstasy), and in Chapter 15 (Collections of Hasidic Music).

20. For a comprehensive treatment of the American phenomenon of Yiddish popular song and an annotated listing of that musical genre, see Irene Heskes, *Yiddish American Popular Songs, 1895 to 1950: A Catalog Based on the Lawrence Marwick Roster of Copyright Entries* (Washington, D.C.: The Library of Congress, 1992).

21. A fuller discussion of the rise of Yiddish theater is provided in Chapter 17 (Yiddish Musical Theater: Its Origins in Europe).

22. For further biographical information on Abraham Goldfaden and his relationships to much of the rising artistry and many of the artists of the Yiddish theater in America, and for a music score collection of his operetta songs, see Irene Heskes, *The Music of Abraham Goldfaden* (Cedarhurst, N.Y.: Tara Publications, 1991).

23. Early twentieth-century Yiddish American theatricals were viewed and written about by a number of journalists of that period, most notably:

Hutchins Hapgood, *Spirit of the Ghetto: Studies of the Jewish Quarter of New York* (orig. pub. New York, 1902; reprint ed., New York: Schocken Books, 1966).

Edward James, *The Immigrant Jew in America* (New York: B. F. Buck, 1906).

24. There are two extensive indexes in Heskes, *Yiddish American Popular Songs*: (1) composers, arrangers, and lyricists, and (2) song titles. Those listings afford access to an entire body of materials, including annotated information on the songs, their creators and performers, and the theatrical productions.

25. A good source of information about the life and times of New York tenement Jews is Moses Rischin, *The Promised City: New York's Jews, 1870–1914* (Cambridge, Mass.: Harvard University Press, 1962). There is an extended discussion by Rischin (pp. 74–138) treating the influence of the Yiddish theater—its stories, songs and performers—upon the lives of Jewish immigrants.

26. See Victoria Secunda, *Bei Mir Bistu Schoen: The Life of Shalom Secunda* (Weston, Conn.: Magic Circle Press, 1982).

27. Abraham W. Binder was a highly versatile and active musician. For biographical background and a collection of his articles, see Irene Heskes, *Studies in Jewish Music: The Collected Writings of A. W. Binder* (New York: Bloch Publishing, 1971).

28. See Leah Jaffa, *A Jewish Composer by Choice, Isadore Freed: His Life and Work* (New York: National Jewish Music Council, 1961).

29. See the following:

Philip Moddel, *Max Helfman: A Biographical Sketch* (Berkeley, Calif.: Magnes Museum, 1974).

Leah Jaffa, *The Music of Abraham Ellstein and Max Helfman* (New York: National Jewish Music Council, 1964).

30. Composer and conductor Lazare Saminsky also wrote extensively on Jewish music topics. Two of his books are:

Music of Our Day: Essentials and Prophecies (New York: Crowell, 1932).

Music of the Ghetto and Bible (New York: Bloch Publishing, 1934).

Also, biographical background on Saminsky may be found in Albert Weisser, *The Modern Renaissance of Jewish Music* (New York: Bloch Publishing, 1954).

31. For a biography of Lazar Weiner, see Irene Heskes, *The Historic Contribution of Russian Jewry to Jewish Music: Supplement* (New York: National Jewish Music Council, 1968).

32. An annotated listing of Jewish music score collections has been included in Irene Heskes, *The Resource Book of Jewish Music: A Bibliographical and Topical Guide to the Book and Journal Literature and Program Materials* (Westport, Conn.: Greenwood Press, 1985), pp. 171–262.

33. A good account of a typical Jewish folk chorus is Robert Snyder, "The Paterson Jewish Folk Chorus: Politics, Ethnicity and Music Culture," *Journal of Synagogue Music*, vol. 18, no. 1 (Cantors Assembly, 1988), pp. 11–28.

34. Details concerning this song and others of the era may be found in Heskes, *Yiddish American Popular Songs.*

35. For additional information about the evolving changes in Jewish liturgical services and cantorial professional duties, see W. Belskin Ginsburg, "Some Preliminary Notes for a Future History of *Hazzanut* in America," *Journal of Synagogue Music*, vol. 7, no. 2 (Cantors Assembly, 1977), pp. 23–42.

36. In addition to the second edition of the *Union Hymnal for Jewish Worship* issued by the Central Conference of American Rabbis (CCAR) in 1914, there were these earlier hymnals:

James Waterman Wise, ed., *Synagogue Songs: Personal, Social, and National* (New York: Bloch Publishing, 1924).

Max D. Klein, ed., *Hymns of Praise and Prayer* (Philadelphia: Congregation Adath Jeshurun, 1926).

37. An annotated list of those Jewish songsters is included in Heskes, *Resource Book*, pp. 208–55.

38. A description of the library at Gratz College, as well as the collections of Nadel and Mandell, is given in Chapter 1 (A Duty of Preservation and Continuity: Collectors and Collections of Jewish Music in America).

39. Gershon Ephros, comp. and ed., *The Cantorial Anthology: Traditional and Modern Synagogue Music*, 6 vols. (New York: Bloch Publishing, 1929–1975). For an account of the warm relationship between Ephros and Idelsohn, see Chapter 2 (Abraham Z. Idelsohn and Gershon Ephros: Creative Connection).

40. Abraham Z. Idelsohn, comp. and ed., *Hebraeish-Orientalisher Melodienschatz—Thesaurus of Oriental Hebrew Melodies*, 10 vols. (Berlin, Leipzig, Vienna, Jerusalem: Breitkopt u. Haertel and Benjamin Harz, 1922–1933).

41. Abraham Z. Idelsohn, *Jewish Music in Its Historical Development* (New York: Henry Holt, 1929, original edition).

42. In 1941, the *Mailamm* collection of scores and literature was presented to the music section of the New York Public Library (NYPL), where it was classified and kept together as noncirculating materials. The collection was transferred in 1965 to the Music Reference Division at the Lincoln Center Library of the Performing Arts. There, it has been recatalogued and placed in the special collections stacks.

43. Fuller consideration of the Judaic aspects of the career of Arnold Schoenberg is given in Chapter 25 (Reflections on Creativity and Heritage).

44. A bound collection of issues (1940–1957) of the *Jewish Music Forum Bulletin* may be examined at the Lincoln Center Library for the Performing Arts, Music Reference Section, New York Public Library.

45. For a discussion of other aspects of Jewish music in Russia, see Chapter 18 (Russian Nationalism and Jewish Music).

46. Biographical information about many members of the Jewish Music Forum may be found in Artur Holde, *Jews in Music: From the Age of Enlightenment to the Mid-Twentieth Century*, rev. edition prepared by Irene Heskes (New York: Bloch Publishing, 1974).

47. In 1980, Transcontinental Music Company was taken over by the Union of American Hebrew Congregations (UAHC), and has continued to publish and market Jewish musical works.

48. The formation committee included Shalom Altman, Abraham W. Binder, Harry Coopersmith, Judith Kaplan Eisenstein, Gershon Ephros, Israel Goldfarb, Max Helfman, David Putterman, Eric Werner, and Lazar Weiner. The first "Jewish Music Festival" week was held May 20–30, 1945. In 1946, the week was February 24 to March 3. The following year, the festival became a month-long event, commencing with *Shabbat Shirah* (Sabbath of song), the Sabbath at which the biblical portion includes the Song of Moses. The council had two professional music directors: Leah Jaffa (Rosenbluth), from 1948 to 1964, and Irene Heskes, from 1968 to 1980.

49. At that gala concert event, held in the old Metropolitan Opera House, Joseph Rumshinsky led a chorus of notable synagogue musicians, and the roster of liturgical soloists included Cantor (Reuben) Richard Tucker (1912–1975). The full program and

photographs of the members may be found in Pasternak, Schall, and Heskes, comps. and eds., *The Golden Age of Cantors.*

50. An annotated list of liturgical collections is given in Heskes, *Resource Book,* pp. 184–208.

51. Of Eric Werner's prodigious scholarly output, among the most notable publications are:

The Sacred Bridge: The Interdependence of Liturgy and Music in Synagogue and Church during the First Millennium (New York: Columbia University Press, 1959).

A Voice Still Heard: The Sacred Songs of the Ashkenazic Jews (University Park: Pennsylvania State University Press, 1976).

Three Ages of Musical Thought: Essays on Ethics and Aesthetics (New York: Da Capo Press, 1981).

52. For a detailed discussion of the sacred service, along with program notes for all the works of Ernest Bloch, and biographical information on the composer, see Suzanne Bloch and Irene Heskes, comps. and eds., *Ernest Bloch: Creative Spirit* (New York: National Jewish Music Council, 1976).

53. Ibid., p. 38.

54. Those two published collections of the commissioned liturgical selections are

David Putterman, comp. and ed., *Synagogue Music by Contemporary Composers: An Anthology of Compositions for Sabbath Eve Service* (New York: G. Schirmer, 1951).

David Putterman, comp. and ed., *Mizmor L'David: An Anthology of Synagogue Music* (New York: Cantors Assembly of America, 1979).

55. For further historical information, see:

Benjamin G. Sack, *History of the Jews in Canada,* trans. from the original 1945 Yiddish edition by Ralph Novek (Montreal: Harvest House, 1965).

Joseph Kage, *With Faith and Thanksgiving: The Story of Two Hundred Years of Jewish Immigration and Immigrant Aid Effort in Canada, 1760–1960* (Montreal: Eagle Publishing, 1962).

56. A good source of details concerning the Jews in Hispanic America may be found under entries by the various countries in: Cecil Roth and Geoffrey Wigoder, eds., *Encyclopadeia Judaica,* 16 vols. (Jerusalem and New York: Keter and Macmillan, 1971–1972).

Part VIII

The Music of Zion and Israel

21

Hope and the Man: *Hatikvah* and Naphtali Herz Imber

At the first Zionist Congress held in Basle, Switzerland, August 1897, Theodor Herzl delivered his famous opening address to the assembled delegates. At that time, a Jewish flag was formed when David Wolffsohn held up a *tallis/tallith* (Jewish prayer shawl) and said: "These are our national colors."[1] That blue and white banner with the Star of David is now the official flag of the State of Israel. It flies over consulates throughout the world and is universally recognized. During those momentous three days of meetings in Basle with Theodor Herzl, two particular songs were enthusiastically sung: the Yiddish *Dort vu di tseyder* (There, where the cedars blossom), and the Hebrew *Hatikvah* (The hope). By 1907, at a later Zionist Congress held at The Hague, it was *Hatikvah* that became the adopted national anthem of Zionism. That hymn of hope has become a paean of triumph for Jewish people in the twentieth century. Its text was the inspiration of a vagabond poet, Naphtali Herz Imber (1856–1909).

Originally titled *Tikvateynu* (Our hope), its nine stanzas were written in late 1877 or early 1878, while Imber, having embarked upon his travels throughout Europe, was temporarily residing in Iasi, Romania. The Hebrew poem later appeared among a collection of his poetry and other writings in a volume called *Barkai* (Morning star), which was published in 1886 in Jerusalem and dedicated to Imber's then patron, Lawrence Oliphant (1829–1888). Subsequently, the poem acquired a musical setting, and it was first sung during celebration of the first wine season at a place called Rishon-le-Zion (First-to-Zion), one of the earliest of the modern pioneer Jewish settlements in Palestine. Rapidly taken up by the colonists, *Hatikvah* was already generally popular before it made its eventful way to Basle in 1897. Its poetics provided fitting sensitive expression to Jewish diasporic aspirations for the modern return to Zion.

The melody to which *Hatikvah* was set was quite simple and easy to sing, and it proved to be a fortuitous union of words and music. One of the early pioneer settlers at Rishon-le-Zion was Samuel Cohen, to whom is generally attributed credit for that musical setting. Newly arrived from Europe, Cohen is said to have copied a Czech folk song that he had heard in his youth. This could explain its striking thematic similarity to the second section, *Vltava/Moldau*, of the orchestral suite *Ma Vlast* (My country) by Czech composer Bedrich Smetana (1824–1884), who had adapted some Bohemian folk melodies for his work.[2]

Yet there are obvious parallels between the *Hatikvah* music and other melodies, notably the so-called Leoni *Yigdal* (Praise) tune,[3] which includes an old folk motif indigenous to Jewish and Slavic as well as Spanish-Basque songs. This was likely a nomadic tune, whose widespread dissemination was accomplished not only by various Jewish wanderings but also by the traveling troubadours of medieval Europe. The melody is reminiscent of the *tal* (dew) chant in the *Sukkoth* liturgy of the Portuguese Jews and also of an ancient Sephardic *Hallel* (Psalm 117) prayer intonation. That *Hallel* melody, with a new English text, appeared in American Jewish hymnals of the nineteenth century as "For Still in Rev'rent Tones" or "There Is a Mystic Tie." The tune appears to have migrated northeastward in Europe among the Ashkenazic Jews, who used the theme in various ways: as a hymn tune for the Sabbath *z'miroth* (table carols), as a melody at the *Havdalah* (Sabbath conclusion) in prayers for coming of the Messiah, and as a chant for the grace blessing after meals *Shir Hama-aloth* (Song of ascents, "Return us as in days of yore"). Imber himself may likely have been familiar with this melody in one of those forms as a result of his wide travels. He may have actually thought of his poem in terms of the meter of that tune or have suggested its use to Samuel Cohen. The significance of *Hatikvah*, however, lies with the implications of its poetry rather than the melody to which it is sung. One could somehow wish for more spirited music, but never more inspiring and elevated poetic concepts.

Biographical information about Naphtali Herz Imber indicates that he led a highly creative yet restless life, suffused with great personal difficulties and the struggles of a dysfunctional life. The enigma is that this incandescent inspiration arose from such an individual. How could he write the Hebrew poem which so stirred the spirit of a people, which epitomized a worldwide movement, and which implanted itself within the conscience of modern Diaspora society?

Imber was born into an orthodox Hasidic family in Zloczow, Galicia, in 1856. He was a prodigious student, especially of Hebrew, and was deeply interested in the *Zohar* and *Kabbalah*. A remarkably facile linguist, he became a wanderer from early youth, briefly visiting many Jewish communities in Europe.[4] While in Constantinople, he met a charismatic Englishman, Lawrence Oliphant. Then, as Oliphant's private secretary, Imber accompanied him and his wife, Alice Oliphant, to Palestine in 1882. Oliphant was a Christian Zionist as well as a devoted student of mysticism, and he found an apt companion in the young Jewish poet. They sailed to Beirut and then went on to Haifa, settling among the Druse of Daliya, a place in the Mount Carmel area. Mrs. Oliphant, who had assumed the biblical name of Lilith, sickened and died in 1886, and was buried in Haifa. Oliphant left for England in 1888, where he soon died.

From 1882 to 1888, Imber had lived in Palestine, assisting Oliphant and writing poetry and articles. His Zionist poems, including *Mishmar ha-Yardeyn* (Watch on the Jordan) became widely known among the Jewish colonists. Almost as portentous as Imber's *Hatikvah* poetic was his zeal on behalf of the Hebrew language, and while in Palestine, he began to make many literary translations of the English classics. This was during an era when Hebrew was still only the language of scholars, of Bible and prayer, and when Hebrew had not yet emerged as a living conversational tongue. At a later time, Imber also translated the *Rubaiyat of Omar Khayyam* into poetic Hebrew.[5]

In 1888, Imber went to England, where he contributed articles to *The Jewish Standard*, among other publications, and lectured on various Judaic subjects.[6] In London, he made the acquaintance of the writer Israel Zangwill (1864–1926), to whom he taught Hebrew. Imber is acknowledged to have been a subject of caricature for the character of the beggar poet Melchitsedek Pinchas in Zangwill's novel *Children of the Ghetto* as well as the model for Zangwill's later book *King of the Schnorrers*. That "fictional" *schnorrer* lived on charity, but courted prestige. Wandering from ghetto to ghetto, he would exploit his personality and scholarship, disdaining money and playing the role of the conscience of Jewish society; he was an impudent yet romantic literary character. Imber himself may have been the master *schnorrer* of his day, but he was much more than that; he was a gifted poetic voice of his people.

In 1892, Imber came to the United States, traveling throughout the country and writing articles for various publications on a wide variety of topics, including *Talmud, Kabbalah*, religious education, and Jewish music. Along the way, there was a very short-lived marriage to a convert to Judaism, Amanda Kate Davidson. In Boston in 1895, Imber briefly edited a monthly magazine, *Uriel*, devoted to mysticism and its interpretations in literature. A second volume of his poetry had been published in 1900 by his family in Zloczow, and in 1904 a third edition of poems appeared in New York. In America, Imber wrote: "I am a rolling stone, which means, in ordinary language, a citizen of the world. This dignity invests me with an ability to judge bricks and human beings—I mean cities and their populations."[7]

By that time, Imber had made the acquaintance of New York journalist Hutchins Hapgood (1869–1944). The two met often during the last years of Imber's life; they shared an interest in the growth of the Yiddish stage and its significance to the Jewish immigrants in America. Imber wrote about the contributions of Abraham Goldfaden, Sigmund Mogulesco, and Sophie Karp, noting that music played a significant role in all the Jewish theatricals. He also wrote several articles on the nature and substance of Jewish music for *Music*, a monthly magazine published in Chicago. His extended essay "Music of the Ghetto" was intended as a historical sweep, and, though simplistic in approach, remains viable for its sensitive insights into the topic.[8] That article was dedicated to Judge Mayer Sulzberger (1843–1923) of Philadelphia.

Sulzberger, a nationally respected legal leader, was one of the poet's most devoted American patrons. Israel Zangwill had introduced Imber to him, and Sulzberger grew to respect the poet's scholarship, permitting him to play the part of a court jester. Inevitably, Imber's impudence and general misbehavior became untenable. Nevertheless, Judge Sulzberger endeavored to assist Imber with a monthly allowance, though the poet continued to be entirely improvident and hopelessly alcoholic. Finally disenchanted, Sulzberger asked Abraham Solomon Freidus (1867–1923), then chief of the Jewish Division of the New York Public Library, to be official custodian of funds for the care of Imber. Freidus limited Imber to a dollar at a time. Not wanting to offend the sensibilities of the man, he would place the dollar bill in a special book on the library shelf, to which Imber always would refer for the money upon entering the room.

Rebekah Kohut (1864–1951), in her personal sketchbook of Jewish personalities she had known, commented upon the unusual relationship of these three extraordinary men: "Judge Sulzberger, Freidus, and Imber made a curiously contrasting trio of intellectual types of thirty years ago; the judge, serving the world and gaining a rich share of its honors; the bookman, scorning the world and gaining his own soul; the poet, courting the world and gaining more than his share of dishonor, but living today after death, in ever increasing glory, because his literary genius expressed the soul of his people."[9]

The qualities of Imber's gifts were indeed timeless, but he also had a lifelong compulsion to be restless and alone. Utterly devoid of warm personal connections and contemptuous of material things, he preferred to live on friendly assistance, and died in abject poverty. During his final months, he was hospitalized in New York City for a variety of serious ailments, and he finally expired on a Lower East Side street on October 9, 1909. The following day, Imber's funeral service was held at the Educational Alliance, with burial at Mount Zion Cemetery in Maspeth, Queens. On April 24, 1953, Naphtali Herz Imber was reinterred in Jerusalem at Har Menuhat Cemetery, with a memorial ceremony attended by leaders of the State of Israel. There is no doubt that Imber realized the significance of his work, calling himself *Ba'al Hatikvah* (Master of the hope). As to why he conceived of that poem while still wandering in Europe, he wrote: "At that time, it was a foregone conclusion that every Jew who went to Jerusalem, came there to die; but I wanted to go there to live."[10]

To the many who sing *Hatikvah* as a prayer and indeed as a credo, the life-size figure of Naphtali Herz Imber poses an enigma as to the strange nature of the man who could create such an anthem. Yet was Imber a prophet? Or was it really the spirit of ageless Jewish idealism that gave the soul of fulfillment to the simple text of a Hebrew poem? Without the actual heroes of the Zionist cause, would *Hatikvah* be just another lovely, simple fragment of Hebrew verse?

NOTES

1. Some sources cite the originator of the Jewish national banner as being a man named Jacob Baruch Askowith of Boston, who designed it especially for the Basle congress. Shortly after the formation of the State of Israel, his son, Charles Askowith, sent on that "original design" to be placed in Israel's government archives.

2. Gustav Mahler (1864–1911), who was born in Kalischt, Bohemia, quoted this particular thematic motif in one of his four *Lieder eines fahrenden Gesellen* (Songs of the wayfarer), composed ca. 1884.

3. A religiously observant singer, Meir/Meyer Leoni (Singer) (ca. 1740–1800) was *hazzan* at the Duke's Place Synagogue in London commencing in 1766. In 1772, he left that pulpit to become a stage performer, and subsequently acted and sang at the Covent Garden in 1775 in Richard Brinsley Sheridan's play *The Duenna*. He later returned to cantorial officiating, and in 1787 went overseas to serve as the *hazzan* at an Ashkenazic synagogue in Kingston, Jamaica, where he died. That *Yigdal* tune attributed to him (or at least popularized by him), was adapted in England in 1772 by a Wesleyan minister named Thomas Olivers for the Christian hymn "God of Abraham, Praise."

4. An interesting anecdotal biography of Imber was written by the granddaughter of one of Imber's sisters: Ethel Lithman, *The Man Who Wrote Hatikvah: A Biography of Naphtali Herz Imber* (London: Cazenova, 1979).

5. That work was published as *The Rubaiyat of Omar Kayyam (Rendered into English Verse)* by Edward FitzGerald, with Hebrew translation by Naphtali Herz Imber (New York: S. Levine Printer, 1905). This slender volume provides English verses alongside Hebrew versification, and has the following additional text matter (unpaginated):

(1) A dedication "to my beloved patron and benefactor his honor Judge Mayer Sulzberger" with the following dated May 1, 1905: "I was thinking all my life in what way I can be grateful to you for the goodness and kindness you have shown to me which I do not deserve; neither did I earn it. I know, money and honor you have. At last an idea struck me that you are a lover of ancient Hebrew songs, so I took the pains and my spirit got wings to capture that beautiful Bulbul which thrilled out the sweetest songs in the Plains of Shirah. I have been successful in capturing that song bird known as Omar. I bring it to you in a Hebrew cage. May its sweet songs brighten your days; whenever you hear its song, remember the hunter who gave it to you."

(2) There is a rather pompous, joyless "introduction" by a Joseph Jacobs (fl. 19th–20th cent.), and then a delightful brief set of poetic verses dedicated to Imber, written by his patron for this publication, George Alexander Kohut (1874–1933).

(3) However, of special poignant interest is an additional prefatory poetic by Imber, which he presented in both Hebrew and English:

I drink, don't know why?
  With this habit I cannot cope;
I thrill out the rythmic [*sic*] of my Lay

Each thought is in harmony with each drop.
I drink and my mind goes up
   To other spheres of delight and hope.
What a magic power lies in the cup?
   What a vital strength in each drop?
Perhaps this cup or bowl
   From which the wine I drain
Was once, poet, the abode of they soul
   The skull wherein was kept thy brain.
That skull was turned into pottery
   By the great potter yet unknown,
But could not change the poetry
   Which is now world wide renown.
Therefore, when I the cups kiss,
   My lips are pressing the bowl,
I feel a heavenly bliss
   As once felt the soul.
Perhaps, when wings will take my soul,
   When my body to dust will return,
The potter will then make another bowl
   From the dust kept in my urn.
Then I pray that another poet
   Shall drink form my bony bowl
Like I did, he shall not me forget
   And feel like I, the pains of my soul.

As to his translation of that literary classic, Imber honored FitzGerald's original English verses with his own graceful Hebrew poetics.

6. For a collection of Imber's writings in English, the literary products of his years in England and America, see Jacob Kabakoff, ed., *Master of Hope: Selected Writings of Naphtali Herz Imber* (Rutherford, N.J.: Fairleigh Dickinson University Press, 1985).

7. Ibid., p. 165.

8. Ibid., pp. 293–302.

9. Rebekah Kohut, *As I Knew them: Some Jews and a Few Gentiles* (Garden City, N.Y.: Doubleday, Doran, 1929), p. 199.

10. Ibid., Kabakoff, *Master of Hope*, p. 20.

22

Song and the Modern Return to Zion

Commencing in the last decade of the nineteenth century, a new and distinctively rich genre of Jewish folk song was created and sung, reflecting the emergence of a modern Zionist movement. It became the ad hoc artistry of ideology and vitality, of spiritual renewal and practical purpose. It underscored the concept of Jews as a people of the written word wedded to melody. Age-old heritages of both Bible and music had always constituted essences of Judaic civilization, the active companions, as it were, of Jewish history. Though based upon melodic and poetic continuity, those newer songs of Zionist return, *yishuv mizug ha-galuyoth* (ingathering from the Diasporas), arose as a unique form of folk music expression that fueled the movement. Its origins were motifs from the religious chants, holiday hymns, and secular diasporic tunes. Its earliest languages were in prayer book Hebrew, along with the vernaculars of Ladino and most especially Yiddish. Carried forward were qualities from the centuries of Jewish folklore—intense expression and melodic inventiveness. It was finally shaped by issues and events, and ultimately by the land itself.

Remember Jerusalem! Psalm 137 asks: "How shall we sing the Lord's song in strange lands?" Exiled and captive, by the rivers of Babylon the psalmist vows: "If I forget thee, O Jerusalem, may my right hand forget its cunning." That sentiment pervaded the Jewish religious experience everywhere for more than two thousand years. Small wonder that an early anthem of nineteenth-century Zionists was *Tsiyon tomosi* (Zion beloved). Though melodically resonant with eastern European Slavic strains, it affirmed the ancient pledge: "Zion, how I long for thee from afar. May my right hand forget its cunning, if I ever forget thee." This song, attributed to a man named Dolitzsky, characterized the first *aliyah* (going up) of settlers to work on the land. Those Jews who had always lived in the area of Palestine generally were either religious scholars and zealous pilgrims or else members of centuries-old enclaves of Oriental/Near Eastern Jewish groups. Starting in 1882, modern Zionists came to work on the land itself, fired with the zeal of rebuilding the Jewish homeland. They were Russian-Jewish intellectuals who called their movement *Bilu*, the Hebrew acronym for "House of Jacob, arise and go up to Zion." Between 1882 and 1904, under the sponsorship of *Bilu*, about 25,000 members emigrated to Zion, and sent delegates to the Zionist Congresses. Some of them were also known as *Chovevei Tsiyon* (Lovers of Zion). They all sang the Yiddish anthem *Dort vo di tseyder* (There where the cedars blossom) and *Hatikvah* (The hope).

It was for idealistic settlers on their way to the Holyland, that the *badkh'n* (folk bard) Eliakum Zunser (1836–1913), then still residing in eastern Europe, wrote two special songs. In 1882, he wrote *Shivas Tsiyon* (Return to Zion): "The world will bless these youths who are dedicating themselves to building a path for the return to Zion. As in Ezra's time, our people are resettling in their homeland." In 1887, *Di sokhe* (The plow) appeared: "In the plow have I found fulfillment, creating food for my body and nourishment for my soul. I am a farmer on my own land."[1] At that time, Abraham Goldfaden (1840–1908), also inspired by the *Bilu* movement, wrote operettas celebrating Jewish history as well as the new return to Zion. In his operetta *Bar Kokhba* (Son of the star), the chorus sings *Gekumen iz di tsayt* (The time has come): "We are ready to reclaim our land, and rebuild the Holy Temple."[2] Mark Warshawsky (1845–1907), another popular eastern European *badkh'n*, celebrated the reports of a first harvest by young settlers in Zion with his song *Dos lid fun broyt* (The song of bread): "Almighty God, we sing our songs to you, as we gather in the sheaves of wheat from which we will make our daily bread. May our children know the blessings of such a life, that the bread they eat will come from their labors on their own soil." Earlier, he had composed a lamentation, *Di milners trehren* (The miller's tears) about Jews oppressed in vicious Russian pogroms and driven away from places where they had lived, farmed, and labored for generations. Warshawsky also wrote a great melodic tribute to the Hebrew language, *Oyf'n pripitchok* (By the fireside): "Learn the letters of your holy tongue, little one, and remember them well all the days of your life. It is the language of our people, our faith and history, our joys and sorrows."[3]

During the early decades of the twentieth century, each of several different groups settling in Palestine had particular songs written by folk composers. The melodies and lyrics were crafted for the most part by untrained musicians and amateur poets; they were intended for their own groups, to strengthen their spirits in often trying conditions. The best of those songs and poems, however, were shared from place to place, and many found their way to back to Europe and then to America. As a result, the songs helped develop general interest in the settlers and build support for their work. Indeed, for many people, a first contact with Zionism was through those songs. *Na-aleh le-artseynu* (We will go up to our land), an adaptation of a Hasidic *nigun* (tune), was sung eagerly by those who had no intention of resettling, but who took hold of the idea of a viable Jewish life anew in the Holyland.[4]

From 1904 until the outbreak of World War I in 1914, there was a second *aliyah*, this time of socialists who called themselves *po'aley Tsiyon* (laborers of Zion) and founded *kibbutsim* (collective farms). More than 35,000 Jews migrated to Palestine in reaction to the severity of Russian pogroms in those years. Those settlers called themselves *khalutsim* (pioneers). Their songs were fashioned with Yiddish or Hebrew lyrics shaped to adapted Slavic march tunes, as for example, *Niyeh kulanu khalutsim v'khalutsoth* (We will all be pioneers, men and women). By that time, many Jewish educational institutions were being established in Jerusalem, Haifa, and Jaffa (near the developing town of Tel Aviv). There, Eliezer Ben Yehuda (1858–1922), father of modern Hebrew development, was urging that a Jewish nation must have its own true language, a revitalized Hebrew spoken every day in every way. At the same time, his colleague Abraham Z. Idelsohn (1882–1938) was assiduously collecting sacred and secular melodies from among the Near Eastern Oriental Jews then residing in Jerusalem and other areas of Palestine. Encouraged by Ben Yehudah, he was teaching Hebrew songs to his students, and for them he adapted a Hasidic *nigun* (tune) into the now ubiquitous Hebrew popular ditty *Hava Nagilah* (Let's be merry). At the time, Idelsohn also fashioned a melody for the well-known poem by Naphtali Herz Imber, *Hala Yardeyn* (Flow on, Jordan).[5]

November of 1917 was a watershed time: World War I ended, revolution broke out in Russia, and there was the Balfour Declaration in England, which stated that Jews had a right to settle and develop the land of Palestine. Between 1918 and 1923, there was a third *aliyah* of another 35,000 arrivals from Poland and Russia. Those Jews established farming *k'vutsoth* (collectives) and also began to settle into urban community life, notably in the fast-growing Tel Aviv. Their songs were still melodically rooted in eastern European Hasidic and Yiddish melodies, but more of them had Hebrew lyrics, for example, *Na'aleh l'artseynu b'rina* (Let us go up to our land with song) and *Artsa alinu* (We go up to the land): "We have plowed and sown, but not yet reaped the harvest." Among the visionary settlers, there was an increasing diversion of spirited dancing. The dancers adapted known eastern European Slavic dances in combination with those observed among the Arabs and Oriental/Near Eastern Jews; and there were new tunes to go along with the dancing. One such hybrid was the vigorous group circle dance known as the *hora* (also the Romanian name for a similar formula of steps), which rapidly caught the popular Jewish fancy.[6]

A fourth *aliyah* movement from 1924 to 1932 brought almost 100,000 to Palestine, fleeing economic troubles throughout Europe and resumption of pogroms in areas of the Soviet Union. In America, the Reed-Johnson Immigration Act of 1924 had severely limited further entry to that country. As a result, most of these newer Palestinian settlers sought refuge haven rather than fulfillment of ideology. Many had been urban business and professional people, and they began in earnest to build up the cities, especially Tel Aviv, which had been founded in 1909 on sand dunes north of the town of Jaffa. Their cultural life began to replicate that of urban Europe. Soon, there were a variety of public musical performances of all types, ranging from concerts and opera to folk choral and amateur instrumental ensembles, activities spurred not only by Zionist fervor but a rise of academic and cultural educational institutions in rural settlements and growing towns. In 1925, Hebrew University was established on Mount Scopus in Jerusalem, and building commenced for a new section of housing outside of the walls of the Old City. A favorite song was an old Yiddish-Slavic melody setting of a poem by an anonymous folk poet who took as a literary name the Hebrew word *Ha-meiri* (From my city), *Me-al pisgat har ha-tsofim* (From atop Mount Scopus): "I greet you, Jerusalem. For generations, I have dreamed of this return, and I shall never leave again."

Ironically, the more people urbanized in Palestine, the more their newly created favorite songs extolled the beauty of the landscape and sentimentalized the virtues of the countryside. It was likely an era of the richest natural folk music development, a time when songs were freely crafted out of idealistic struggle and emotional need. Those songs easily carried over to the Diaspora, where Jews began to sing them as the heartfelt expression, the very essence, of the modern Zionist movement. There began to be Palestinian *badkhonim* (poet- bards) recognized for their particular poetics and tunes. Most had little or no professional training, and they wrote easily and often beautifully. One of their works reached the level of art-song. Their roster included such names as: Shertok-Sharett, Weiner-Shelem, Samburksy, and Ze'ira.

Yehudah Shertok-Sharett (b. 1901) was a member of the communal settlement of Yagur in the north near Haifa, where he formed a choral group for which he devised song sheets and eventually published the first Zionist songster. He set the lovely tribute to Lake Kinereth (Tiberias) written by poet Rachel Blaustein (1890–1931), *V'ulai* (Perhaps): "O my lovely Kinereth, were you indeed real, or have I merely been dreaming?" Matityahu Weiner-Shelem (b. 1904), a settler at Ramat Yokhanan in the north, helped establish special harvest festivals at the settlements. For those celebrations, he organized songfests and wrote tunes, among them, *Hazorim b'dima* (Who sows in tears shall reap in joy). Daniel Samburksy (b. 1909), who worked in the malarial hula swamp area of Emek Jezreel, set a poem by another worker, Natan Alterman (1910–1970), *Ba-a menukha* (Evening comes): "Night hushes the *emek* (valley) as dew covers the soil. Sleep restfully, oh lovely valley, glorious land which we are preserving." Mordecai Ze'ira (1905–1968), settled on an agricultural commune, Kibbuts Afikim, where he taught the children of the settlement. Subsequently a hero of the Jewish Brigade during World War II, Ze'ira over the years was a prolific writer of Zionist songs, the earliest of which was *Pakad Adonay* (God commanded): "We have been bidden to rebuild the land." In 1960, a collection of 112 of his songs was published by the Education and Culture Department of Histadruth, a governmental agency of the State of Israel.[7]

Among those who arrived about that time was Joel Engel (1868–1927), a preeminent formative figure in the emergence of the modern era in Jewish music. In Russia, his prodigious activities as collector and arranger, lecturer and writer had spurred the rise of interest in Jewish folk song, inspiring others to follow along in that musical interest.[8] Settled in Palestine from 1923 onward, Engel was to make other significant contributions in the brief time until his death in Tel Aviv. For a time after he left Russia after the revolution, Engel lived in Berlin. While there, he established a Jewish music publishing company, Yibne Verlag, which issued works by Jewish composers and arrangers. He also published some of his own compositions, including his setting, with both Hebrew and German text, of a Zionist poem by Saul Tchernikowsky (1875–1943), *Omrim Yeshnah Erets* (They say there is a land). Engel had known Tchernikowsky, a physician, while both were in St. Petersburg and then in Berlin. Tchernikowsky briefly visited Palestine in 1925 to help establish the medical relief group *Magen David Adom* (Red Shield of David), a Jewish equivalent of the Christian Red Cross. He finally settled there in 1931, and until his death, he served as a doctor for the schoolchildren. He wrote Hebrew poetry as well as numerous articles and books on medicine, Zionism, and world affairs.

Among other poets whose Yiddish and Hebrew texts were set to music by Joel Engel was Chayim Nachman Bialik (1873–1934). Considered the father of modern Hebrew poetry, Bialik's texts have been set to music by many composers. Russian-born, early in life he formed a strong emotional tie with modern Zionism and the Hebrew language. In 1894, Bialik wrote *Tekhezaknah* (Be strong): "Strengthen the hands of our brethren who are striving shoulder to shoulder to rebuild our land of Zion." First known as *Birkath ha-am* (Blessing of the people), its eight verses compared those on their way to Palestine with priests going to rebuild the Holy Temple. Sung to a Slavic-type march tune, it became an anthem for the *Chovevei Zion* (Lovers of Zion) movement itself. Bialik was a teacher in the Ukraine until 1921, and a writer in Yiddish and Hebrew on all aspects of Jewish life as well as on Zionism. His range of topics included the translation into Yiddish of works by the Judeo-Español poets Yehudah Halevi, Solomon ibn Gabirol, and Moses ibn Ezra, thereby sparking a renewal of interest in medieval Jewish literature. Ever an educator, many of Bialik's original Hebrew poetics were for the education of little children, and especially for teaching the modern Hebrew language. He translated a number of European literary classics, including *Don Quixote*, into Hebrew. His Zionist resolve was set by the terrible afflictions upon Jews in Russia. In reaction to the infamous Kishinev pogroms, he bitterly lamented: "The sun shone, the acacia blossomed, and the slaughterer slaughtered."

Joel Engel first knew of Bialik by way of his poetry, and he encouraged Jewish composers to set those poems as art-songs. Engel published some of those settings, for example, *El ha-tsipor* (To the bird), by Moses Milner (1886–1953), and *Minhag khodosh* (New ways), by Engel himself. The lengthy list of twentieth-century composers worldwide who have set Bialik's poetry includes two of particular interest: Abraham Z. Idelsohn and Gershon Ephros,[9] both of whom became deeply attracted to those poetics early in their lives while they were residing in Jerusalem. While on a visit to Germany in 1921 in connection with the European publication of his *Thesaurus*, Idelsohn attended the Zionist Congress in Carlsbad. There, he was introduced to Bialik, and showed him parts of his unique collection of Jewish liturgical and folk music materials as well as the draft of a Hebrew manuscript outlining a full history of Jewish music. Bialik urged Idelsohn to complete that historical survey, and it eventually appeared in the United States in an English text.[10] During the course of a brief visit to the United States in 1925, Bialik met with Ephros, encouraging him to complete his project of a cantorial anthology and to compose art songs as well as liturgical works. Ephros later set sixteen children's poems by Bialik as a serious song cycle.[11]

In 1922, Bialik translated Shlomo Ansky's (1863–1920) Yiddish play *Di dybbuk* (The spirit) into Hebrew for a presentation at the Habimah Theater in Warsaw. In addition, some incidental music for that stage production was written by Joel Engel. Shortly afterwards in Palestine, the two were able to develop a warm personal relationship. Engel had reconstituted his publishing company in Jerusalem as Yibneh/Yuval, and reissued several musical settings of Bialik's poems in a salute to the poet upon his fiftieth birthday. Bialik had become an enormously popular literary figure there and abroad, his writings having helped shape the spirit of modern Zionism. Palestinian settlers dedicated to him the dance song *Nigun Bialik* (Bialik's tune), a lively melody sung without words in Hasidic style.

At that time, Bialik began to formulate the idea of an *Oneg Shabbat* (Pleasure of the Sabbath) as a special celebration. Initially held in Bialik's home, it was intended as a Jewish cultural as well as religious observance, a festive gathering for study, discussion, readings, and songs, preceding the chanting of *Havdalah*, concluding liturgy of the Sabbath day. Bialik believed that the Sabbath embodied the very essence of Judaism, reflecting sustained trust in a Messianic Era to come and affording a brief sample of that promised ideal time to Jews living in the mundane difficult world of the present. He felt that this was the true motivation for a modern Zionist movement, the goals of renewal and promise, faith and hope, identity and history. Among his lovely Sabbath poetics, Bialik's *Kabbalat Shabbat* (Welcome the Sabbath), set to a melody by Pinchos Minkowsky (1859–1924), has become a significant Sabbath hymn in Israel and abroad: "The sun has disappeared from the tops of the trees. Come, let us go out to meet the Sabbath Queen... and with her angels, a host of peace and rest." Soon after Bialik initiated the idea of *Oneg Shabbat*, it grew rapidly into a communal festivity celebrated on agricultural settlements as well as in synagogues. By the late 1920s, it was being held at public halls in Jerusalem, Tel Aviv, and Haifa. The concept took hold in the Diaspora as well, becoming a part of Sabbath afternoon

observances for all branches of Judaism, and indeed even among those not ri-
tually observant. Before his death in 1934, while in Europe for medical treatment,
Bialik had been named poet laureate of the *yishuv* (return). Beyond his literary
legacy, he typified the vigorous idealism of the third *aliyah*. He personally
spurred significant activities in the settlements and growing urban areas of that
period: modern Hebrew linguistics, a structured educational system, and new
forms of intellectual and artistic expression. In Tel Aviv, the house once occupied by Bialik and his wife has since become a municipal museum and library, to
which has been built an addition known as the Manya Bialik Cultural House for
Women.

During the early decades of the twentieth century, new Zionist folk songs
were being fashioned out of old folk songs from Europe, including Hasidic
tunes, Yiddish ballads, Slavic melodies, and the liturgical chants. By the 1920s,
however, there was an increasing appreciation of the songs and folklore of other
Diaspora vernacular cultures, such as the Sephardic and Oriental-Near Eastern.
An especially significant influence was the array of artistry of Yemenite Jews,
many of whom had resided in the Holyland for generations. Moreover, there
were other Jewish groups from the Mediterranean region and North Africa who
had resettled in Palestine prior to World War I. They were the groups from
whom Idelsohn had collected music materials for several volumes of his *Thesaurus*. Their melodies and poetics, as well as those of the Arabs, Druse, and
Bedouins and of Near Eastern Christian sects, began to shape the later Zionist
folk songs. There was a rise of self-conscious creativity and of particular folk
composers who were known by name and associated with particular songs. They
were a genre of Zionist Hebrew *badkh'n* (minstrel bard), and constituted a substantial roster of talented men and women, of whom the most typical was
Nahum Nardi (1901–1977).

Nahum (Narudetzky) Nardi was born in Kiev in 1901. Showing early musical
ability, he studied piano in Warsaw and Vienna. He emigrated to Palestine in
1923 and began to work as a piano accompanist for vocalists and choral groups,
also arranging old Jewish folk songs for performers and various theatricals. Nardi
soon took on the music teaching of children, for whom he wrote very many Hebrew songs that used melodic motifs from the Oriental-Near Eastern groups.
Though intended for youngsters, the appealing qualities of poetry and music
made his songs popular among adults. As a folk composer, someone with professional training but with charming simplicity of expression, Nardi was able to
reflect the essence of a time and place, of the full range of Zionist life on rural
settlements and urban areas, at seasides and in desert places. Nardi was a particularly capable pianist, and held concerts over the years with several well-known
singers, especially Yemenite folksinger Bracha Zefira (1911–1990). In association
with Zefira, he arranged many Yemenite and other Oriental Jewish songs, helping to popularize that style of music abroad in the Diaspora. He also borrowed
heavily from those melodies to write his settings of many Hebrew poems,

including those of Bialik. Unusually prolific in composition and arrangement, Nardi wrote songs that easily became recognized and considered "folk" in origin, especially the children's songs for Jewish holidays. His last years were spent in attempting to reclaim the author's rights to some of his popular songs.[12]

The period from 1933 to 1939, ending with the outbreak of World War II, is known as the fifth *aliyah*. For a short time, Palestine became the haven for refugees fleeing the advance of the Nazis in Germany and then throughout Europe. At that time, the immigration laws limiting admission to the United States and Canada denied very many of those desperately seeking sanctuary. Awareness of this sad fact solidified the support for Zionism among North American Jews. Philosophical idealism had been displaced by physical necessity. In all, about 210,000 managed to arrive in Palestine from Germany and central Europe. Quite a few came with professional education, and a considerable number were writers and musicians. They brought along their cosmopolitan culture, mainly Germanic in style. In 1936, the Palestine Philharmonic Orchestra was established under the leadership of Bronislaw Huberman (1882–1947), and a radio station, *Kol Yisrael* (Voice of Israel), also was put into broadcast operation that year. Soon, there was a legion of composers, performers, and educators along with publications, concerts, and music institutions.[13]

Most poignant was the so-called sixth *aliyah*, 1939–1948, from the war years to the establishment of the State of Israel. The best estimate is that there were only about 120,000 people who arrived. Most were children rescued from a variety of hard circumstances, and all who arrived were considered "illegal" immigrants. Their musical creativity was muted by frightful circumstances, and many still sang their ghetto protest and concentration camp songs. The Zionist songs created at that time reflected the growth of militant nationalism, viewed as the sole viable means for Jewish survival. The lyrics bespoke of human peril, social isolation, and spiritual determination. One song *Lo ira* (I fear not) borrowed a tune from central Europe and took its Hebrew text from the Bible: "I shall have no fear, even though I am surrounded by those who seek to annihilate me."

The seventh *aliyah*, which commenced in 1948 with the establishment of the State of Israel, goes forward into a yet undocumented future. As an independent country, Israel may admit Jewish people from anywhere, and its musical expression in the second half of the twentieth century has amply reflected that fact. Arrivals from more than sixty countries have brought their music with them. The wide diversity of those ethnic Diaspora sources has necessitated a reconsideration of Jewish music in its totality. There is the realization that Abraham Z. Idelsohn, the prodigious collector of Judaic ethnomusicology, has been surpassed and overwhelmed by an ingathering of materials from all types of sources and varieties of Jewish traditions. Moreover, time is likely running out for proper collection and evaluation of this folk music heritage, inasmuch as a process of ethnic nationalization and sociological accommodation has rapidly taken hold of a growing Israeli population. An acculturation of sameness, an aura of homogeneous life-style, has become the desirable norm. With the birth of new generations, the old traditional Diaspora folklore has parted company with the music of the bright young Israelis who now are accustomed to radio, records, and television, all presenting an admixture of modern Israeli life. The sounds of their music give voice to the nature of a people. Israelis are first and foremost Israelis, fewer and fewer of whom recall another social milieu, a different location, or any earlier vernacular dialect. This seventh *aliyah* has been a real ingathering, and, idealism aside, its multicultural nature has been absorbed, adapted, and altered by the Israeli education system and military services and even more by the country's varied types of media and whatever that technology conveys daily to the public from within Israel, as well as from the rest of the world.

Yet, during the second half of the twentieth century in Israel, there have been notable musical achievements. An influx of varied Diaspora music cultures has provided scholars with exciting opportunities to explore the ethnomusicological heritage of Jewish settlers coming from a multitude of different sociohistorical experiences. After World War II, individual researchers, following in the pioneer footsteps of Idelsohn, began to circulate among the arriving groups to collect, record, and annotate their songs, dances, and sacred chants. Over the next decades, departments of musicology were established at Israel's universities, and an Israeli Musicological Society was founded in 1964. Spurred on by scholars and musicians, there have been many national and international conferences in Israel and abroad presenting a great array of studies treating those varied ethno-Judaic musical traditions.[14]

By 1950, aware of a rich influx of ethnic heritage starting to arrive in the land, the Israeli Ministry of Culture and Education established the Ethnomusicological Institute for Jewish Music. An organized area for collections was set up in 1953 at Hebrew University in Jerusalem. In 1980, the great storehouse of those documentary materials was integrated at the university into a repository known as the National Sound Archive and Laboratory for Musical Research. The Archive had been founded in 1964 by scholars Israel Adler and Avigdor Herzog, and soon grew to incorporate not only music of Jewish origin but also music from the traditions of the Samaritans, Arabic music, and liturgies of the Near Eastern Christian sects in Israel. At that time, two other research areas were established: an electronic laboratory for the study of musical sound and a cognate electronic music notation center.

Over the years, formal departments of musicological study offering a full range of degrees were founded: in 1965, at Hebrew University; in 1966, at Tel Aviv University; and in 1970, at Bar Ilan University. Faculty members included leading scholars from Israel, Europe, and North America, among them Israel Adler, Henoch Avenary, Bathja Bayer, Bathia Churgin, Edith Gerson-Kiwi, Peter Gradenwitz, Avigdor Herzog, Alexander Ringer, Amnon Shiloah, Josef Tal, and

Eric Werner. Out of this activity, scholarly publications and regularly issued periodicals emerged, among them the following in series: *Orbis Musicae: Studies in Musicology*; *Yuval: Studies of the Jewish Music Research Centre*; and, a yearbook, *Tazlil/Chord: Forum for Music Research and Bibliography*.[15] The Israel Institute for Sacred Music has issued a Hebrew periodical, *Dukhan/Pulpit*, as well as individual monographs treating the cantorial art and various examples of Jewish cantillation, sacred chant, and holiday music. Over the decades, a roster of significant musicological studies by Israeli scholars, published and issued in English and Hebrew, have become valued music resources at educational institutions and reference libraries throughout the world. Another productive outreach consequence, particularly in North America, has been a literal explosion of songbook publications, featuring the great range of ethnic Jewish songs in Yiddish, Ladino, and Hebrew.[16]

By the 1980s, most of the *aliyah* arrivals came from eastern Europe, in particular, the Soviet political sphere. This group, however, brought their Slavic linguistics and culture, but a much less substantial Judaic ethnicity, compared to the legions of previous *aliyah* immigrants—Ashkenazic, Sephardic, and Oriental/Near East Jews—from Europe, North and South America, Asia, the Mediterranean bowl, North and South Africa, Australia, New Zealand, and the Far East. Those newer Slavic Jewish settlers brought meager Jewish folk music resources, most especially as to sacred song, and a surprisingly limited Yiddish folklore. Here, any musicological study sadly has been concerned with evidence of cultural deprivation, with an absence rather than a rich surfeit of Jewish legacy. Another group of immigrants, Falasha-Ethiopian Jews, are arriving late in the twentieth century from a quite different ethnic background. They have begun to be musically documented, and ethnomusicological studies (notably by scholar Kay Kaufman Shelemay) have begun to sort out those fascinating cultural materials.

As the twentieth century concludes, the sounds of Israeli music are more worldly and less given to ingenuous folk expression. Young people sing and dance to music not unlike that of their counterparts in other countries, and their ears are flooded with pop tunes from radio programs, television shows, theatrical presentations, recordings, and films. Serious art music presented in the concert halls and opera houses mirrors the programs in other lands, and for the most part, Israeli composers send out musical messages of creative universality. Liturgical music in Israel has remained tradition bound, and restrictive in practice, and therefore vastly less innovative than in North America.

Despite all the evolutionary cultural changes since the early days of *aliyah*, there have been certain sustained influences upon the music of Israel, whether sacred or secular, pop-folk or serious-art. They are the Jewish year of observances, the life cycle of human events, the concept of an Israeli nationhood, and, most of all, the country's geography—the landscape of Israel itself. After the Six-Day War in June 1967 and reunification of the city of Jerusalem including the

Western Wall, a folklike song written by Naomi Shemer captured the essence of that time and place, perhaps as no other Zionist song had done for many years. The song is *Yerushalayim shel zahav* (Jerusalem of gold): "Jerusalem of gold, and of bronze, and of light, am I not the harp for all your songs?"

In that landscape resides the Zionist ideal, a timeless linkage to the land, an awareness of its Biblical setting, and the special Jewish calendar year of holidays, which celebrate this land for its functional nature no less than for its special history. In abstract, that land is the address of Messianic Judaism, the core of religious belief, the "exile from" that is called Diaspora. Yet in the realistic practical nature of things, Israel is a nation among other nations, with people whose musical expression reflects their everyday lives. And after all, it is difficult enough to live history, let alone to sing about it.

NOTES

1. For biographical information about Zunser, see Sol Liptzin, *Eliakum Zunser: Poet of His People* (New York: Behrman House, 1950).

2. Chapter 17 (Yiddish Musical Theater: Its Origins in Europe) treats the life and works of Abraham Goldfaden.

3. Chapter 17 also includes a discussion of the Yiddish folk bards and their creativity in nineteenth-century eastern Europe.

4. An annotated listing of published Zionist folk song collections may be found in Irene Heskes, *The Resource Book of Jewish Music* (Westport, Conn.: Greenwood Press, 1985), pp. 208–55.

5. Chapter 2 (Abraham Z. Idelsohn and Gershon Ephros: Creative Connection) discusses the contributions of Abraham Z. Idelsohn.

6. Heskes, *Resource Book,* section on "Dance with Jewish Music," pp. 257–62.

7. A survey of that period is presented in Peter Gradenwitz, *The Music of Israel; Its Rise and Growth through 5000 Years* (New York: Norton, 1949), Chapter 12, "The Return to Zion," pp. 251–83.

Two later books, also by Gradenwitz, cover this earlier period as well as later musical developments, and introduce a distinguished roster of Israeli composers:

Music of Israel: Composers and Their Works (Jerusalem: Hechalutz/Jewish Agency, 1952).

Music and Musicians in Israel: A Comprehensive Guide to Modern Israeli Music (Tel Aviv: Israel Music Publications, 1978).

8. Chapter 18 (Russian Nationalism and Jewish Music) provides information about Engel's activities in Russia.

9. See Chapter 2 for further information.

10. Abraham Z. Idelsohn, *Jewish Music in Its Historical Development* (New York: Henry Holt, 1929, original edition).

11. Gershon Ephros:

The Cantorial Anthology, 6 Vols. (New York: Bloch Publishing, 1929–1975).

Children's Suite, for voice and piano (New York: Bloch Publishing, 1944).

12. While many of Nardi's compositions and arrangements have been included (often without proper acknowledgment) in many song collections, the following publications were actually prepared by Nahum Nardi:

An Album of Jewish Songs (New York: E.B. Marks, 1952).

Songs for Children (Tel Aviv: Negen/Schreiber, 1958).

Nardi's Collection of Children's Songs (Tel Aviv: Nardi, 1960).

13. An in-depth treatment of those émigrés from Germany and other areas of central Europe is provided in Philip V. Bohlman, *The Land Where Two Streams Flow: Music in the German Jewish Community of Israel* (Urbana: University of Illinois Press, 1989). Bohlman reviews the historical accommodations by Jews to the culture of western European, especially German society. He discusses the transplantation of that culture, notably of its music, with the refugee migrations to Palestine during the 1930s. Considered are subsequent influences upon the shaping of artistic and intellectual life there, particularly in the more urban areas of the country. Bohlman also draws attention to the songbooks of German Jewry in Europe and then Palestine, as well as to several Jewish music organizations, including the St. Petersburg Society for Jewish Folk Music. In this connection, a corollary work by this same author is also of interest: Philip V. Bohlman, *The World Centre for Jewish Music in Palestine, 1939–1940: Jewish Musical life on the Eve of World War II* (New York: Oxford University Press, 1992).

14. A good overview of that wide range of activities is provided in the following study: Amnon Shiloah and Edith Gerson-Kiwi, "Musicology in Israel, 1960–1980," *Acta Musicologica*, vol. 53 (1981), pp. 200–16.

15. For a list of the topical studies issued in those publications, see Heskes, *Resource Book*, pp. 166–70. In addition, listed with annotations are numerous books and articles by many of the scholars mentioned in this passage.

16. For additional resource information on these developments, see: Judith Kaplan Eisenstein and Irene Heskes, *Israeli Music: A Program Aid* (New York: National Jewish Music Council, 1978).

23

The Inspiration of Israeli Composers

In the main, serious musical works composed in the country of Israel should be considered within the context of worldwide creativity. After decades of statehood, the issue of Israeli cum Judaic qualities in music appears to matter less than issues of innovative style, technical form, and artistic concept. If distinctions remain that set Israel's composers apart, it is likely because of the richness of ingathered ethnic melodic resources available to them. For many, there has been a blending of eastern and western influences, a natural expression of those musicians who are of Oriental-Near East descent rather than of European origins. It has been a fashion of Israeli artistry to embrace and incorporate the varied melodic sounds of the area in a conscious effort to make musical statements about the land and its people. As a result, a great measure of the composition genre has bordered on folk expression and has consequently been critically viewed as modern Zionist music. Some composers and performers actively espoused this approach for several professional reasons. After all, the music produced was surprisingly effective in performance, and a number of those works were successfully integrated into international repertoires for concert programs and recordings.

Aside from that essence of indigenous national spirit, some other effective ingredients have increasingly been productively employed: a free-ranging ethnicity, with modes and *maqamoth* (melodic patterns) along with the use of quarter tones and Near East tone elements; the sweep of improvisation, clued to traditional Jewish liturgical styles as well as Arabo-Judaic-Oriental formulas; linkage to folklore, landscape, history, and Bible as prime sources of inspiration and of textual interpretation; and a unique and exciting combination of Western musical techniques with non-Western freer melodic expression. In Israel, the cultural atmosphere of its cosmopolitan audiences, a plethora of well-trained versatile performers, and the encouragement of commissioning projects are factors that now serve to broaden the scope of outside influences upon Israeli composers. As the nation has matured politically and socially, weathering military and economic struggles, worldwide musical ideas have taken hold: serial technique, altered instrumentation, alleatory experience, and electronic invention.[1]

Regardless of many of its unique aspects, however, Israeli music remains mainly Western in pedagogy and presentation. Its creative figures have been variously grouped into three aesthetic categories: Eastern European, an approach grounded in the musical traditions of Yiddish, Judeo-Slavic, Hasidic, and liturgical expressions; Central European, a formulation of general classical soundings and trends; and Mediterranean, a blending of ethnic music from that area.[2] Eastern European Joachim Stutchevsky (1891–1982) collected and published Hasidic music and composed in that style. In 1967, he received the Joel Engel Award for his musical contributions. German émigré Josef (Gruenthal) Tal (1910–19??) came to Palestine in 1934 and brought the concepts of serialism and extended tonality. He established a laboratory for electronic composition at Hebrew University. Although European born and educated, three leading figures shaped a newer approach: Alexander Uriah Boscovich (1907–1964), a Transylvanian who studied in Vienna and Paris and arrived in 1938; Mark Lavry (1903–1967), a Latvian trained in Germany, who arrived in 1935; and Oedoen Partos (1907–1977), a Hungarian who arrived in 1938. They were all attracted to the folk patterns and melodic elements of their adopted land, and readily found ways to integrate those sounds into their music. Boscovich, a prolific music critic and energetic educator, first termed the special musical style of his European-born colleagues the "Mediterranean School." Lavry served as music director for Israeli radio broadcasting, arranging programs featuring the many types of folksingers and their diverse instrumentations. Partos was a particularly active music conductor and teacher who arranged ethnic music and encouraged its public performance.[3]

Of all the European-born composers, Paul (Frankenburger) Ben-Haim (1897–1984) most completely fitted the role of an Israeli composer, and his works have entered into the international concert repertoires of soloists and orchestras. German by birth, he studied in Germany and was highly active as a teacher, accompanist, conductor, and composer before fleeing the Nazis in 1933. Settled in Palestine, he quickly acquired a strong interest in the folk music of the area, particularly spurred by his association over those years as piano accompanist and music arranger for Yemenite folksinger Bracha Zefira (1911–1990). He began to write compositions in a variety of forms, setting his own pattern for a Mediterranean style of music; that style of melodic treatment was soon taken up by some of his colleagues and later also emulated by a legion of younger creative figures.

Ben-Haim's prolific output included selections for all types of orchestral ensembles and instruments as well as solo and choral music of both secular and liturgical nature. Among his compositions is the brief "Fanfare to Israel," written in 1949 for the official military band of Israel. Incorporating ethnic melodic strains, the work has become a favorite musical flourish played throughout the country on Israel Independence Day. For a number of years until his death, Paul Ben-Haim served as Honorary Chairman of the League of Composers in Israel.[4]

Over the decades, along with the many gifted composers, capable performers have crowded the rapidly growing musical scene in Israel. It has become a place of concerts and operas, of theatricals and musicales, of broadcast media and recording studios. Music inhabits the land, in rural no less than urban areas. Amateurs vie easily with professionals in terms of quality, quantity, and dedication. Music making is a part of school education from earliest childhood onward, and choral or instrumental festivals fill the calendar year. Israel has busy conservatories and musicological institutions, substantial music libraries, museums, and research archives. It has become an exporter of talent to the rest of the world. Musical expression is an everyday part of life, but also can be a serious matter. Though an increasingly sophisticated and structured aspect of Israeli society, it still readily reflects the daily events and abiding concerns of the nation, often blurring differences between folk-style and serio-classic expressions. Army marches and pop ditties easily fit into programs along with old Zionist chestnuts, ethnic songs, holiday tunes, and serious works—a melodic cornucopia, eclectic and all too often shy of critical selectivity. Israel has constituted itself as a haven for all Jews, and its musical expression appears to follow along in that same all-embracing way.

A particularly strong ethnic influence has been that of the Yemenite culture of folk dances and decorative arts, as well as of music. In evolving a specific national identity, Israel has set its horizons toward Western civilization, but at the same time its geography is distinctly a part of the East. This refashioning of outlook has been most apparent among Yemenite Jews, whose mass rescue and resettlement in Israel during the 1950s was a dramatic and profoundly inspiring experience. Though some had always lived in the Holyland, the majority had been isolated for centuries, residing on the southern tip of the Arabian peninsula. Coming to modern Israel, those Yemenites represented a mode of Jewish life hitherto untouched by Western culture. They had maintained their local vernacular, traditions, customs, and arts intact through centuries upon centuries of Diaspora. As striking as their genre of folk songs tied to their life-cycle observances was the legacy of their ornamental costuming and their traditional dances, characterized by special hand, head, and body postures. The music for those dances contained melodic elements that had been preserved and passed on orally from generation to generation, along with the indigenous instrumentation of flutes, cymbals, drums, and bells. Yemenite folk music elements have provided Israeli's society with tones that flow readily into the newer sounds of contemporary music, fast growing accustomed to polytonality, multirhythmics, acoustical alterations, and electronic warps. Beyond that, the distinctive Yemenite culture, created and preserved over centuries despite human adversity, still retains innate qualities of ethnic strength, and thereby adds a vital dimension of "survival art-istry" to the music of the State of Israel.[5]

NOTES

1. For a detailed consideration of developments in Israeli musical creativity, see Zvi Keren, *Contemporary Israeli Music: Its source and Stylistic Development* (Ramat Gan, Israel: Bar Ilan University Press, 1980).

2. There are several resource publications treating the lives, and especially the var-ied creative works, of Israeli composers:

Peter Gradenwitz, *Music of Israel: Composers and Their Works* (Jerusalem: Hechalutz/Jewish Agency, 1952).

Issachar Miron, *A Profile of Israeli Music Today* (New York: National Jewish Mu-sic Council, 1964).

Menashe Ravina, comp., *Who's Who in ACUM (Society of Authors, Composers, and Music Publishers in Israel)* (Tel Aviv: ACUM, 1965/66).

Jehoash Hirshberg and others, *Aspects of Music in Israel: A Series of Articles Pub-lished on the Occasion of the International Society for Contemporary Music (ISCM) World Music Days* (Tel Aviv: Israel Composers League, 1980).

Peter Gradenwitz, *Music and Musicians in Israel: A Comprehensive Guide to Mod-ern Israeli Music* (Tel Aviv: Israel Music Publications, 1978).

Alice Tischler, *A Descriptive Bibliography of Art Music by Israeli Composers* (Warren, Mich.: Harmonie Park Press, 1988).

3. Catalogs listing works by these composers as well as those by a substantial roster of other Israelis are available from the following publishers:

Israel Music Institute (I.M.I.), established in 1961 by the Ministry of Education and Culture in association with the League of Israeli Composers, P.O.B. 11253, Tel Aviv 61112, Israel.

Israeli Music Publications Ltd. (I.M.P.), a private company, P.O.B. 7681, Jerusalem 91076, Israel.

4. For further information about this composer and his music, see

Peter Gradenwitz, *Paul Ben-Haim: His 70th Birthday Tribute* (Tel Aviv: Israel Music Publications, 1967).

Jehoash Hirshberg, *Paul Ben-Haim: His Life and Works*, trans. Nathan Friedgut and ed. Bathja Bayer (Jerusalem: Israel Music Publications, 1990).

Hadassah Guttmann, *The Music of Paul Ben-Haim: A Performance Guide* (Metuchen, N.J.: Scarecrow Press, 1992).

5. For resource publications on Yemenite music, see Paul Marks, comp., *Bibliog-raphy of Literature Concerning Yemenite-Jewish Music*, Studies in Music Bibliography, 27 (Detroit: Information Coordinators, 1973).

24

Musical Festivities in Israel

In the summer of 1963, I attended the International Music Conference held in Jerusalem from August 5 to August 12. That gathering was organized by the Israel National Council of Culture and Art in cooperation with the International Music Council of UNESCO and the international Folk Music Council, with the assistance of the Kol Israel Broadcasting Service, Hebrew University, and the America-Israel Cultural Foundation. In addition, during the course of an extended sojourn in the State of Israel, I was able to be present at numerous concerts celebrating the year's third annual Israel Music Festival and also to participate in a wide variety of musical activities.

Earlier during my stay in Israel, I rode out one evening to a new Yemenite immigrant village charmingly named *T'nuvot* (harvest fruits), then situated on the Israel-Jordan border. I sat in a small community hall and listened with much pleasure to the singing of about thirty young teenagers from the settlement. They sang and then danced to new Israeli songs, to old traditional Yemenite folk songs, and to some of their liturgical chants, which may be as old as antiquity. Over later weeks, I had opportunities to hear and see very many spirited and competent Israeli folksingers and dancers in cities and in rural areas, at formal concerts and at informal amateur gatherings. Yet none of those other fine performances quite stirred my feelings as much as did that little musicale at the Yemenite village.

Of course, I heard performances of the Israel Philharmonic Orchestra. One of those programs, conducted by Mendi Rodan at the Mann Auditorium in Tel Aviv, truly typifies the organization's professional approach—there was an eclectic array of works, performed with excellent musicianship. That particular evening, there were three contrasting compositions. The first half of the concert consisted of a specially commissioned brief overture, "Toccata," by Romanian-born Israeli composer Sergiu Natra, followed by a Mozart concerto for two pianos performed by Israeli artists Bracha Eden and Alexander Tamir. After intermission, William Walton's "Belshazzar's Feast" was presented, with a newly prepared Hebrew version of the original English text, and conducted by the composer himself. For this large work, the 140-piece orchestra was augmented with an extra brass section. The assisting artists were the 150 members of the Tel Aviv Choir and baritone soloist Mordechai Ben-Shachar. Composed by Walton in 1931, this oratorio had been performed in many languages, but never before in Hebrew, despite the fact that its text was derived by Osbert Sitwell from the biblical passages of Isaiah, Jeremiah, Daniel, Ezekiel, and the Psalms. Another time, at the Mann Auditorium, I heard a program of three Beethoven trios performed by Isaac Stern, Leonard Rose, and Eugene Istomin. It was an evening of great music presented by a superb string ensemble to a hushed and appreciative full hall.

The 1963 Israel Music Festival opened its season with an orchestral concert on July 16, and special programming throughout the country lasted for over four weeks. During that time, over fifty performances of sixteen different musical programs were highlighted in the cities of Tel Aviv, Jerusalem, Haifa, Rehovoth, Beersheba, and Ein Hod as well as at the large agricultural settlements of Ayelet Hashachar, Ein Hashofet, Givat Brenner, and Tsofit.

In Israel, there are probably more concert halls to the square mile than anywhere else in the world, and many of them are unique. On the way down through the Negev desert to Eilat, I stopped at Avdat, a small village situated at the site of some archeological excavations searching for materials from the Byzantine and earlier Nabatean eras. There, I came upon an ancient meeting hall that, although without a roof and with broken walls, still had excellent resonance and carried the human voice beautifully. In the north of the country are several outdoor amphitheaters, all in current use. A small lovely one at Ein Hod affords the audience an exquisite view of the countryside. At Natanya, a large amphitheater looks out over the bay inlet and into a fantastic sunset. Commanding a magnificent view of the Mediterranean shore at Caesarea is a partially reconstructed Roman amphitheater, originally built by King Herod about 10 B.C.E. Cellist Pablo Casals had performed there in 1961 to an audience of over 1,200, but no concerts had been scheduled at Caesarea for the 1963 festival. The capacious auditoriums at the Weizmann Institute in Rehovot and at the Technion Institute in Haifa are used frequently for performances. And of course, there are numerous *kibbutz* dining rooms that often double as concert halls.

I spent much valuable time at the Central Music Library located in the building of the Mann Auditorium in Tel Aviv. There, materials overflow the many shelves and storage archives. Staff librarians were quite helpful, and they managed to familiarize me with the range and contents of those valuable collections. This particular library serves the communal musical needs of individuals, schools, and various groups throughout the country, well beyond the city of Tel Aviv. Supported by the Ministry of Education and Culture and by privately donated funds, that library supplies books, periodicals, and scores without any charge. Recordings are also loaned to institutions and agricultural settlements. I was told that in 1962, over five hundred different types of groups borrowed materials and recordings from this library.

Among the many musicians I met was William Elias, the administrative director of the Israel Music Institute (I.M.I.). Founded in 1961, the Institute is engaged in the publication and distribution of serious musical scores and significant musicological studies. Exploring the published roster of scores at I.M.I. provided me with valuable insights into the newer ideas among emerging Israeli composers. For the 1963 International Music Conference, the institute published five scholarly monographs with photographs and musical illustrations, each treating different aspects of Jewish music.[1]

In Haifa, I visited the extremely busy Rothschild Community Center, which also houses a section for the instrumental and score cases, library collections, and research materials of the Haifa Music Library and Museum, then directed by Moshe Gorali. During the music festival weeks and for the International Conference itself, Gorali and his staff prepared an extensive display of musical instruments and printed items that was placed on special view at the Rubin Academy of Music in Jerusalem.[2] Also exhibited there at the same time were sixty musical instruments donated to the State of Israel by the estate of the late Serge Koussevitzky, along with some African folk instruments lent by the governments of Ghana and Nigeria.

During my stay in Haifa, I attended a concert presented at the Armon Theater, a local movie house. Despite the acoustical problems of that improvised concert hall, an excellent program was presented by the New York Pro Musica. Under the direction of Noah Greenberg, an ensemble of four instrumentalists and five vocalists performed selections of sixteenth century music that set biblical texts. The evening of early baroque music commenced auspiciously with a lovely setting of Psalm 137 composed by a Jewish musician at the Ducal Court of Mantua, Salomone Rossi (ca.1565–ca.1628): "How shall we sing the Lord's song in a strange land? If I forget thee, Oh Jerusalem, may my right hand forget its cunning."

Later I again heard this work by Salomone Rossi when it was performed with moving eloquence by the joint choir of the *Ihud ha-kevutsot v'ha-kibbutzim* (The organization of agricultural settlements). The occasion was the opening session of the World Jewish Youth Conference held in the *binyanei ha-uma* (convention hall) in Jerusalem. In attendance were several hundred representatives from thirty-nine countries, many international notables, and Israeli government officials. Then still incomplete, the hall would soon be a magnificent building and a much favored concert and theatrical auditorium.

On August 5, 1963 an opening reception was held at the King David Hotel in Jerusalem for delegates to the International Music Conference. On an open terrace overlooking the Old City walls then under Jordanian control were gathered 127 representatives from thirty-five countries and 130 Israeli musicians.

Delegates had come from the Far East, many African countries, and every European country except the Soviet Union. This was to be a musical encounter of many varied ideas and traditions, a world meeting of composers, performers, and scholars from five continents. Specially honored was an Hungarian folk composer, 81-year-old Zoltán Kodály, who was the president of the International Folk Music Council.[3]

That same evening, a welcoming ceremony and concert were held at the elegantly designed Wise Auditorium on the Hebrew University campus. Official greetings were extended by Foreign Minister Golda Meir and Deputy-Premier Abba Eban. Chairing was Yeshayahu Spira, director of Kol Israel Broadcasting Service and head of the organizing committee for the conference. The musical portion of that program included instrumental and vocal folk music presented by delegates from Ghana, Hungary, India, Iran, Japan, and Vietnam. In addition, there was the premiere of a commissioned work, "Four Festive Songs," by the Israeli Mordecai Seter. This composition is based upon traditional Sephardic and Ashkenazic liturgical melodies, and was performed by the Rinat Choir, a professional choral group founded and directed by Gary Bertini.

The next morning, regular conference sessions commenced in the lecture hall of the Kaplan building at the Hebrew University. The official languages for presentations—lectures and discussions—were French, English, and Hebrew. Simultaneous multitranslations were made available. It ran on an extremely full schedule. Among the sixteen papers read on that first day were some treating means of collection and preservation of traditional folk music and ways to integrate this music into modern compositions. That evening, the Kol Israel Symphony Orchestra presented a concert at the YMCA Auditorium in Jerusalem. As a salute to some of the many composers in attendance, there were performances of works by Paul Ben-Haim, Luigi Dallapiccola, Roman Haubenstock-Ramati, Andre Jolivet, Toshiro Mayuzumi, and Oedoen Partos, conducted by Gary Bertini and Mendi Rodan, with pianist Frank Pelleg and violist Oedoen Partos.

The following day, fifteen papers were read, and a sectional meeting on folk dance was held in the afternoon. Among the topics treated during the day were: polyphony in folk and art music and comparative studies of the liturgies of Occident and Orient. In this connection, by courtesy of the Ministry of Religious Affairs, a kit of liturgical materials published by the Israeli Institute for Sacred Music was presented to the attendees. This collection of ten booklets, titled *Renanot* (Exaltations), consists of twenty-nine liturgical selections edited by Avigdor Herzog. Included are chants for Sabbath and holidays in the traditions of Jews from Algeria, Iraq, Morocco, Tunisia, and Yemen as well as examples of Hasidic, Ashkenazic, and Sephardic liturgy. The music is intended for devotional service practices in Israel as well as for scholarly comparative ethnic study.[4]

In the evening, there was a concert program at the Wise Auditorium that could not have been presented anywhere else in the world. Gathered together and residing in the area of Jerusalem are congregations from all types of Jewish religious communities. In addition, nearly all of the many Christian sects have missions clustered around the Mount Zion area or just over the [pre-1967] Israel/Jordan border in the Old City. With informative introductory remarks by the ethnomusicological scholar Edith Gerson-Kiwi, the very same Bible reading of the previous Sabbath was cantillated in respectively different musical traditions by the following: Jews from Babylonia-Baghdad and Yemen, Ashkenazics from Lithuania and Central Europe, Sephardics from Morocco and Turkey, and a leader from the dissident sect of Samaritans. Then, selections from the Prophets and the Scroll of Esther were chanted in succession by Jews from Aleppo, Bukhara, Djerba, Persia, and Yemen. Readings of the Psalms were also intoned by representatives from churches of the Ethiopians, Copts, and Armenians. Finally, the week's chapter of the Koran was chanted by an Arab sheikh. It was altogether a dramatic testimony to the "sacred bridge" of liturgical music that connects all faiths. This unique program was rounded out with some lighter examples of several types of Jewish folk music, performed by singers and instrumentalists along with dancers.

The next day's sessions were given to the reading of eleven papers on such topics as ornamental music performances and origins or migrations of various types of musical instruments. That evening, a second gala concert by the Kol Israel Symphony Orchestra was presented at the YMCA auditorium. The program opened with a short composition by Bela Bartok followed by an intriguing new work—a piano concerto with electronic tape accompaniment, performed by its composer Josef Tal. The balance of the concert was devoted to a specially prepared Hebrew text performance of Zoltán Kodály's secular folk-cantata, *Szekely-fono* (Spinning-room). Under the spirited direction of Eytan Lustig, the orchestra, supplemented by six vocal soloists and the Kol Israel Choir, gave a dramatic and musically appealing performance.

On the final working day of the conference, the morning was devoted to six papers on various problems in the notation of new musical forms, such as multi-faceted acoustics, alleatory experience, and electronic music. Then, at the closing session, Peter Crossley-Holland of the United Kingdom Broadcasting Service ably recalled the many outstanding events of the entire conference and paid warm tribute to all the organizers and participants.

While I was in Israel in 1963, it was my particular honor to meet President Zalman Shazar and to sing for him while he was staying in Tel Aviv. Later, during my stay in Jerusalem, I was invited to come to the *Bet Hanassi* (presidential residence), where I sang *zemiroth* with him at his Friday evening *Oneg Shabbat*.

NOTES

This author's first stay in Israel was in 1963, and her report on the musical activities there at the time was published in the journal of the American Jewish Congress, *Congress Bi-Weekly*, vol. 30, no. 15 (1963). The article is reprinted here with some editing of the text and added footnotes.

1. Those monographs issued by the Israel Music Institute (Tel Aviv: I.M.I., 1963) were:

Hanoch Avenary, *Studies in the Hebrew, Syrian and Greek Liturgical Recitative.*

Bathja Bayer, *The Material Relics of Music in Ancient Palestine and Its Environs: An Archeological Inventory.*

Avigdor Herzog, *The Intonation of the Pentateuch in the Heder of Tunis.*

Menashe Ravina, *Organum and the Samaritans*, trans. Alan Marbe.

Michal Smoira-Roll, *Folk Song in Israel: An Analysis Attempted.*

2. A simple flyer guide for that exhibition was subsequently expanded and issued as a catalogue publication: Moshe Gorali and committee, eds., *The Old Testament in World Music: A Pictorial Catalogue* (Haifa, Israel: Haifa Music Museum and Amli Library, 1974).

3. Zoltán Kodály (1882–1967).

4. Avigdor Herzog, comp. and ed., *Renanot—Songster of Sacred Music* (Jerusalem: Institute for Sacred Music, 1962).

Part IX

Composers and Compositions

25

Reflections on Creativity and Heritage: Salomone Rossi and His Era

Over the centuries, a number of significant musicians of Judaic antecedents, composers and performers, have illumined the annals of cultural history. Many had little or no association with their Jewish antecedents, and but for incidental records would not be known as of Jewish origin. Whether their careers and artistic expressions may be termed "Jewish" remains a debatable issue. Among those who did maintain linkage to Judaism, there are aspects of their creativity that do reflect that heritage, often deliberately.

This consideration of Jewish composers commences with Salamone Rossi, Ebreo del Mantua, (ca.1565–ca.1628) because he was particularly known as a Jew. As a distinguished music master of his time and place, he occupies a niche in the history of Western music. Rossi was born in Mantua, son of the rabbinical scholar Azaria de' Rossi (d. 1578), whose family claimed to have come to Rome from Jerusalem as captives of Titus. Musically gifted from childhood, Salomone Rossi (Shelomo Me'ha-adumim) grew to be a notable string player, teacher, composer, and the conductor of instrumental ensembles. From 1589 to 1628, he flourished as court musician for two Mantuan Dukes of Gonzaga, Vicenzo (d. 1612) and Fernando (d. 1626). In 1606, Rossi's ducal patrons formally absolved him from wearing the onerous "yellow patch" designating him as a Jew and allowed him freedom of passage throughout the duchy. Those Mantuan dukes supported a number of Jews as performers—actors, dancers, singers, musicians—and also permitted (indeed protected) a synagogue within Mantua. At that time in northern Italy, it was not unusual for Jewish artists and artisans to be retained in the employ of the various ducal and affluent families.[1]

Rossi has been particularly recognized for his introduction of a monodic form in instrumental music. His general works bridged the styles of florid Renaissance with an emerging, more clarified baroque monody, and he is most noted for his development of the trio sonata for strings. A vocal as well as instrumental composer, Rossi's solo and choral madrigals and *canzonettas* were widely performed. During his lifetime, he published an unusual quantity of music, fourteen volumes composed of secular works and liturgical selections.[2] His music was printed in Venice between 1589 and 1623, with the support of benefactors. It was a Mantuan Jew, Moses Sullam (fl. 16th cent.), who paid for Rossi's publication of a collection of thirty-three settings for the prayer services. His compositions have achieved a measure of general recognition in present times, and appear on concert programs and recordings.[3]

The contributions of Rossi must be viewed within a larger context of cultural life in northern Italy during his era. At the lively court of Mantua, he came into contact and likely made music with the leading figures of the time. It was a time of great cultural achievements, of lively Italian courts in Ferrara, Florence, Milano, Modena, Rome, Turino, and Venice as well as Mantua, where composers such as Caccini, Gabrieli, Gastoldi, Giaches-de-Wert, Monteverdi, Pallavicino, and Willaert were influential shapers of the musical ideas of the late Renaissance era. Many Jewish musicians performed at feasts, weddings, coronations, theatricals, and other celebrations. They performed a great variety of works, the sounds of which they brought back into the ghettos.[4] Rossi's career constitutes a fine example of melodic interaction because he introduced some elements of the music he created and played for the court into his settings of Judaic sacred song. He was a Jewish composer well ahead of his time whose oeuvre was to inspire a movement among late nineteenth-century European cantors to modernize their liturgical musical settings.

Jewish musicians visibly performing at royal courts was not an unusual occurrence at that time, in England as well as Italy. Both Henry VIII and his daughter Elizabeth I employed them as instrumentalists, singers, dancers, and actors.[5] On the continent, such artists often publicly changed their names, and they usually hid their origins.[6]

Italian Jewry had enjoyed a long history since the Roman Empire. When southern Italy and the Italian islands came under the domain of Spain, the Jews living there began to be persecuted, and then were expelled. By the sixteenth century, only in northern and central Italy could the Jewish communities be considered historically continuous.[7] The Renaissance Popes Leo X and Clement VII of the Medici family were indulgent toward "their Jewish" artists and artisans. By 1475, there were known Jewish printing presses in Reggio di Calabria and Piavi di Sacco near Padua. A printing family, Soncino, had established its own press in 1500, and then moved on in the sixteenth century to Venice, there to flourish among several other such active Jewish enterprises. In 1516, the Venetian Republic ordered its Jews to be segregated into a special quarter, which was formerly known as *ghetto nuovo* (new foundry). Nonetheless, Jewish intellectual and artistic life there thrived, and its vitality still reached out to influence other places in Europe. By 1592, however, Pope Clement VIII had severely restricted activities of Jews residing within papal territories and had ordered the idea of their residency restriction, or "ghetto," to be strictly enforced. By the seventeenth century, only in the areas of Tuscany, Pisa, and Leghorn were there no openly defined ghettos.

The Mantuan duchy fell to Austrian invaders in 1630, thereby not only winding down its communal intellectual and artistic vigor but also seriously threatening the very existence of its Jewish population. Yet the Jews of other northern Italian centers flourished well into modern times, a period only ending with the Nazi Holocaust. Well into the end of the eighteenth century, Venice remained a great center of Judaic cultural activity. Its busy printers issued a wide selection of significant Judaica, including prayer books and translations of the Bible and Hebrew scholarly literature into Latin, Italian, Spanish, and French. Venice was the location of two age-old Jewish traditions, Ashkenazic and Sephardic, each of whom supported synagogal and societal infra-structures. Music and literature were important aspects of life, and secular music included lutes, flutes, recorders, "arm" viols, "leg" gambas, and clavichord keyboards along with singing and dancing. Jewish musicians, many of whom performed and taught also to non-Jews, were known by such derivative names as: Bellina, Civita, Faresol, Finzi, de Fano, Leone, Massarano, Porto, Rossi, and Sonatore. For many years, there was a formal music academy supported by the Sephardic Spanish synagogue. Antiphonal singing and instrumental ensembles highlighted communal celebrations, especially for the *Purim* holiday. George Frideric Handel (1685–1759), while studying in Italy, visited the Venetian ghetto in 1710 to attend *Purim* festivities and was inspired to write an opera, later revised as an oratorio, based upon the biblical Scroll of Esther.[8]

For the original publication in Venice in 1623 of Salomone Rossi's collection of liturgical music, a special introduction was written by Leone (Judah Aryeh) da Modena (1571–1648), who was a rabbi and precentor-cantor. Earlier, in 1605, while serving a congregation in Ferrara, Modena urged that special music be composed for synagogue services and defended choral liturgical music as consistent with Talmudic laws. He even tried to write some music manuscripts with the notes reading from right to left, so as to accord with the Hebrew characters, and advocated a structured order of chanting by leader and congregants. Da Modena contributed his preface for Rossi's collection shortly after his own young son had been murdered outside the ghetto walls. The essence of his message in the Rossi publication underscored those earlier arguments. He favored choral singing and composed music for Jewish worship as long as it was entirely sacred in nature and of devotional intent in performance. At the time, the Rabbinical Assembly of Venice endorsed Modena's ideas, and that rabbinical opinion was subsequently cited by such nineteenth- century liturgical music leaders as Sulzer, Lewandowski, and Naumbourg. In 1629, Leone da Modena established an academy of liturgical music in the Venetian ghetto, to which he invited Christian as well as Jewish musicians and scholars.

Finally, attention must be drawn to two Italian Christian composers, Monteverdi and Marcello. Claudio Monteverdi (1567–1643) came to the Ducal court of Mantua in 1590, where he remained until leaving in 1613 to serve as musician at St. Marks in Venice. During those years in Mantua, he composed music and performed on the viola da gamba. Monteverdi was especially innovative in his vocal selections, particularly in the development of extended dramatic song forms. Among those formative works was an early opera, *Arianna*, with a now famous aria, *Lasciatemi morire* (Let death claim me). It was first performed in 1608 for the Duke of Mantua and his guests by Rossi's instrumental ensemble, and the soloist was soprano Madama Europa (her theatrical name), a relative of Salomone Rossi.

Benedetto Marcello (1686–1739) was a Venetian nobleman and musician for whom the music of the Jews of northern Italy held great interest. Between the years 1724 and 1727, he composed and arranged melodic settings for fifty Psalms in Hebrew text, using chant motifs derived from the Sephardic and Ashkenazic musical traditions of that region. When his collection, *Estro Poetico-Armonico*, was published in Venice, the notation of the music was adapted to fit the Hebrew print, right to left. Marcello's selections soon became part of Venetian Jewish musical tradition, and since then, that music has been reprinted in various editions in England and France as well as Italy.[9]

NOTES

1. Biographical studies of Salamone Rossi have been included in many publications on Jewish and general music history. Of special content are the following sources:

Eduard Birnbaum, *Jewish Musicians at the Court of the Dukes of Mantua (1542–1628)*, originally issued in Germany by the author in 1891 or 1895; reprint trans. from German, edited, and annotated by Judith Cohen (Tel Aviv: Tel Aviv University Press, 1975).

Shlomo Simonsohn, *History of the Jews of the Duchy of Mantua* (Jerusalem: Kiryath Sepher, 1977).

Iain Fenlon, *Music and Patronage in 16th Century Mantua*, Vols. 1 and 2 (Cambridge, England: Cambridge University Press, 1980–82). This is a substantial scholarly work that offers an extended view of music activities at the Gonzaga court as well as the range of artistic life throughout Mantua and its surrounding areas during the sixteenth century.

2. For sources treating Rossi's secular works, see:

Alfred Einstein, "Salomone Rossi as Composer of Madrigals," *Hebrew Union College (H.U.C.) Annual*, vol. 23, no. 2 (1950–1951), pp. 383–96.

Hanoch Avenary, comp. and ed., *Il Primo Libro Delle Canzonette a tre Voci: Di Salomone Rossi, Venezia 1589* (*The First Book of Canzonettas for Three Voices: by Salomone Rossi, Venice 1589*), reprint ed. (Tel Aviv: Israel Music Institute, 1975).

3. For liturgical music by Salomone Rossi, see:

Samuel Naumbourg and Vincent D'Indy comps. and eds., *Hashirim Asher Lish'lomo: Salomone Rossi*, originally issued in French text, Paris, 1877; reprint ed. (New York: Sacred Music Press, 1954).

Isadore Freed, comp. and ed., *Liturgical Works: Salomone Rossi* (New York: Transcontinental Music Publications, 1954).

Fritz Rikko and Joel Newman, comps. and eds., *Hashirim Asher Lish'lomo [The Songs of Solomon]: Salomone Rossi*, Vols. 1 and 2, an annotated edition of the music (New York: Mercury Music Corp./Jewish Theological Seminary, 1966–67).

Fritz Rikko and Joel Newman, comps. and eds., *Thematic Index of Works of Salomone Rossi* (New York: Mercury Music Corp./Cantors Assembly of America, 1973).

4. A good discussion of that influential musical exchange is Israel Adler, "The Rise of Art Music in the Italian Ghetto" in *Jewish Medieval and Renaissance Studies,* ed. Alexander Altmann, Cambridge, Mass.: Harvard University Press, 1967), pp. 321–64.

5. See Roger Prior, "Jewish Musicians at the Tudor Court," *The Musical Quarterly,* vol. 69, no. 2 (1983), pp. 253–65.

6. See the following:

H. Colin Slim, "Gian and Gian Maria: Some Fifteenth- and Sixteenth-Century Namesakes," *The Musical Quarterly,* vol. 57, no. 4 (1971), pp. 562–74.

Otto Kinkeldey, "A Jewish Dancing Master of the Renaissance" [William the Jew/Guglielmo Ebreo, fl. 15th cent.], in *Studies in Jewish Bibliography* (New York: Kohut Memorial Foundation, 1929), pp. 329–72.

7. Further historical perspectives are provided in:

Jacob Rader Marcus, *The Jew in the Medieval World: A Source Book, 315-1791* (Philadelphia: Jewish Publication Society of America, 1938).

Cecil Roth, *The Jews in the Renaissance* (Philadelphia: Jewish Publication Society of America, 1959).

8. See: Alexander L. Ringer, "Handel and the Jews," *Music and Letters,* vol. 42, no. 1 (1981), pp. 17–29.

9. Abraham Z. Idelsohn has cited those works by Benedetto Marcello in Section 3 of his *Synagogue Songs of German Jews in the 18th Century,* Vol. 6 of the *Thesaurus of Oriental Hebrew Melodies,* reprint ed. (New York: Ktav, 1973). Various published editions of that music may also be found among collections at the Music Reference Division of the New York Public Library.

26

Meyerbeer, Halévy, and Offenbach: The Nineteenth Century

In the nineteenth century, there were some practical issues to be considered by musically gifted Jews in Europe: opportunities for education outside of the ghettos, performances with and for non-Jews, observances of Jewish religious duties and customs, attitudes among Christians, exposures to different societal circumstances, and self-doubts about commitments to former traditions and lifestyles. The idea of Jewish auto-emancipation was intoxicating, but a treacherous deceit for those who concluded that disappearance from Judaism constituted the viable means. Then, as throughout Jewish history, there were three types of Judeo-identification: born into and living within its orbit, a badge thrust upon one by outsiders and worn in various ways, and a personal cause taken up and integrated into one's life. Theodor Herzl (1860–1904) best typified all three: he was born as a Jew; in spite of his cosmopolitan education and professional success, he was known and treated as the outsider Jew; and finally, he devoted the last years of his life to a mission of modern Zionism as the means of Jewish survival.

There were a number of Jews who achieved recognition in nineteenth-century musical life. Some continue to hold a place in music history, and three typify that genre of Jewish musician: Meyerbeer, Halévy, and Offenbach. All were born Jewish and identified as Jews, but each adapted differently to his Judaic roots in ways that affected his creativity as well as personal life.

Giacomo Meyerbeer (1791–1864) is considered a pivotal figure in modern French opera. Born Jakob Liebmann Beer, he showed early musical talent. Subsidized by relatives, he studied piano with Muzio Clementi, and then composition with Mendelssohn and Carl Maria Von Weber. Embarked upon a concertizing career, he changed his name to Jacob Meyerbeer, in honor of a favorite uncle, Meyer Beer. In 1815, upon the advice of Antonio Salieri, whom he had met while in Vienna, he went to Italy for further musical studies, and there he began to write vocal works. While musically active in Venice, he became known as Giacomo (Italian for Jacob) Meyerbeer. Over the next ten years, he wrote six operas as well as a number of individual vocal selections, mastering the Italian style of composition. In 1826, Meyerbeer went to Paris, where he remained for the rest of his life. There, he came under the influences of Luigi Cherubini and Jacques Halévy. Although he also wrote ballet music and various types of instrumental works, opera became Meyerbeer's special musical domain, and he crafted theatrical music that captured the attention and appreciation of European audiences. His operas, now considered "extinct volcanos" because they are so rarely performed in full on twentieth-century stages, were large-scale dramatic works with extravagant melodic ideas for soli and choruses and technically extended orchestrations. Concert programs still feature excerpts of Meyerbeer's music—arias and overtures, and students of composition still pore over details of his scores.

Meyerbeer's texts were by Eugène Scribe (1791–1861), the most sought after librettist of his day. It must be noted that not until 1890 could biblical subjects be staged at the Paris Opera House. Scribe and Meyerbeer, nevertheless, took on a number of ethical topics that were advanced for that day: *Robert L'Diable* (1831), temptation of the devil and the power of superstitious belief; *Les Huguenots* (1836), religious persecution of Protestants by Catholics; *Le Prophete* (1849), struggle against tyranny by Anabaptists. Meyerbeer's last opera, *L'Africaine,* was posthumously presented in 1865. He had considered it to be his masterpiece, and was especially pleased with its story about sixteenth-century Portuguese explorer Vasco da Gama, the Africans, and the inquisition. In this libretto, da Gama has returned to Lisbon from sailing around the Cape of Good Hope, claiming that the world is round and that there exist other equally viable races and lands. He is denounced as a heretic by the Grand Inquisitor.

Many of Meyerbeer's musical ideas were innovative for their time. Beethoven admired his writing for choral groups; Berlioz modeled his opera *Les Troyens* upon elements from *Les Huguenots*; Bizet copied his stage groupings; Puccini admired his vocal duet writing; Verdi is said to have thought of the coronation march from *Le Prophete* when he composed the triumphal march in *Aida*. Meyerbeer aided the young Richard Wagner, who at the time dedicated his early operatic efforts to his mentor. Although personally befriended and helped financially by Meyerbeer, Wagner soon turned on him in vicious anti-Semitic attacks.[1]

Meyerbeer's personal life was difficult. There was an incompatible marriage, and his children died tragically. Often depressed, he poured his energies into musical activities. Even there, he encountered much to make him unhappy. His librettist, Scribe, was a temperamental and unsteady creative partner. Singers and instrumentalists battled over the operatic scores. An earlier warm association with Gioacchino Rossini (1792–1868) soured, and that composer, by then musically inactive, ceaselessly campaigned to prevent any performances in Italy of Meyerbeer's operas. Critics who envied his popularity wrote that he pandered to public interest. He felt socially isolated throughout his life, despite the fact that he was quite famous and prosperously successful.[2]

During Meyerbeer's youth, his father, Herz Beer, had a synagogue for the new reformist ideas in his Berlin home, and the talented young son arranged some liturgical music for the services. In 1860, the composer set passages of Psalm 91 as a motet for double choir, a cappella: "The Lord is my refuge and my fortress, my God, in whom I trust." He was a member of religious congregations in Berlin as well as Paris. Late in his life, Meyerbeer traveled to Vienna, where he attended services at the congregation of Cantor Salomon Sulzer, who asked him to compose a religious anthem. Meyerbeer, then already gravely ill, was unable to complete that music. In 1864, his Jewish ritual funeral in Berlin was attended by the royal family of Prussia.

Jacques-François Fromental-Elie Halévy (1799–1862) was born in Paris into a distinguished literary and musical family. His father, Elie Halphan Halévy, a cantor, also compiled the first Hebrew-French dictionary and edited a weekly journal, *L'Israelite Français* (The French Israelite). Among other noted members of that family was Leon Ludovic Halévy (1834–1908), who was librettist not only for cousin Jacques but also for composers Offenbach and Bizet.

By the age of ten, Jacques Halévy was studying music at the Paris Conservatory, and in 1819 won the Grand Prix de Rome, the first Jew to do so. That year, he composed for his father a setting for Psalm 118: *Min ha-metsar*: "Out of the depths, I called upon the Lord." His father first intoned it at High Holy Day services, and it became a regularly performed anthem at Paris congregations. Cantor Samuel Naumbourg (1815–1880) included the selection in his liturgical collection, *Zemiroth Israel* (Chants of Israel), vol. 1, p. 74.[3] Halévy studied in Rome from 1820 to 1822. Returning to Paris, he taught at the Paris Conservatory, and in 1829 became conductor at the Grand Opera. Over the years, he was a highly valued teacher whose pupils included Bizet, Gounod, and Massenet. In 1835, Halévy gave Jacques Offenbach free music lessons.

Jacques Halévy composed more than twenty operas, the most successful of which was *La Juive* (The Jewess), with a libretto by Scribe. It was premiered at the Paris Opera House in 1835. The plot had been inspired by a somewhat similar story, that of *Nathan der Weise* (Nathan the Wise), by Gotthold Lessing (1729–1781). Set in Constance, France, early in the fifteenth century, it is about the religious conflicts of that time. The opera opens with a celebration of Catholic military victory over Protestant Hussites, and the cardinal is searching for his long lost daughter. The second act features a secret Jewish celebration of the Passover *seder* by the Jew Eleazar, at which the student suitor of his daughter Rachel admits that he is really a Christian, Prince Leopold. In the third act, all are brought together at an imperial banquet, and the cardinal pronounces the damnation of the church upon them. Imprisoned in a dungeon in the fourth act, Rachel "the Jewess" and Eleazar refuse all offers to convert to Christianity. The last scene presents an *auto-da-fé*, a public inquisitional burning, where Eleazar pleads with Rachel to save herself by announcing she is in reality the cardinal's daughter. She refuses, and dies with Eleazar. As the final chorus sings an anthem, "Fire and sword, glory to the Lord," the cardinal falls to the ground, prostrate with parental anguish.

This opera is dramatic in presentation, and often vocally compelling. Eleazar's magnificent aria, *Rachel, quand du seigneur*, has been a concert selection for famous tenors, notably Enrico Caruso, whose 1920 Victor label recording remains a collector's favorite. At that time, the role of Rachel was sung by Jewish soprano Rosa Raissa, and it was also recorded by opera diva Rosa Ponselle. Shortly before his death, Richard Tucker (1912–1975) sang the role of Eleazar for a Barcelona performance of the opera. He had planned to appear in the work at the Metropolitan Opera House the following season. *La Juive* had not been performed by that company since 1936, and even then was presented in a heavily cut version eliminating the processionals, a ballet, and some of the choral selections.

In 1857, Halévy was appointed Secretary of the Paris Académie de Beaux Arts, a highly honored position. Over his final years, Halévy worked on an opera inspired by the age-old legend of "The wandering Jew." His personal life was difficult. A late marriage in 1842 to Sephardic Jewess Leonie Rodriques was disastrous. She was emotionally unstable, and her family ruined him financially. Moreover, professional success made him uneasy and anxious, and seems to have blunted his creative energies. He greatly admired Meyerbeer for his prodigious musical productivity. Halévy, however, led a busy life of teaching and social contacts, and was known to be unfailingly kind to students and cordial with colleagues. Even Richard Wagner, whom he had helped, appears to have had a good word to say of him. Possessed of a restless intellect and an academic frame of mind, Halévy was deeply interested a wide range of literature and the fine arts. Also active in Jewish communal affairs, he supported Naumbourg and other liturgical musicians in their efforts to enrich the music of the Parisian synagogues. At his funeral, in 1862, there was a personal tribute from Napoleon III. Two years later, a statue of Halévy was erected in the Jewish Cemetery in Montmarte.[4]

Jacques (Jacob Levy von) Offenbach (1819–1880) was born in Cologne, son of a cantor and liturgical composer, Isaac Judah Eberst von Offenbach.[5] By the time of his death in Paris, Offenbach, though not baptized, had assimilated away from his original background. He was considered then a foremost composer of light opera whose many works epitomized Parisian musicality of that Second Empire epoch. His notable roster of operas included: *Orphée aux Ensfers, La Belle Hélène, La Perichole, La Vie Parisienne, La Grande Duchesse de Gerolstein*, and of course *Les Contes d'Hoffmann*.

A gifted pianist and cellist, in 1834 he went to Paris with his brother, violinist Jules (Joel von) Offenbach (1815–1880), to study music. Jacques Offenbach soon achieved success, first as a performer and then, more significantly, as a composer. By 1855, he had taken over the operetta theater in Paris, and had married into a wealthy Christian family. Extremely prolific, Offenbach composed over a hundred stage works. His favorite librettist was Ludovic (Leon) Halévy (1834–1908), a relative of his friend and colleague Jacques Halévy. At Halévy's urging, he also assisted Georges Bizet (1838–1875), who later married a stepdaughter of Halévy. Offenbach enjoyed an elaborate and rather extravagant life-style, and to recoup failing finances, visited the United States in 1875, conducting a series of concerts in New York and Philadelphia. When he returned to France, Offenbach wrote his memoirs about that trip, *Notes d'un musicien en voyage* (Notes of a traveling musician). In it, there is no mention of any Jewish matters.

Ailing and unable to complete the orchestration of his last opera, *Les Contes d'Hoffmann* (The Tales of Hoffmann), Jacques Offenbach died in 1880, a year before its highly successful premiere on February 10, 1881, at the Paris Opera Comique. This work was his most ambitious creation, intended to be a truly serious and "grand" opera, and it has maintained a place in the repertoires of the world's opera houses. Ironically, although little, if indeed any, Jewish melodic resemblance may be discerned in his operatic creative works, Offenbach's music was attacked throughout his career by anti-Semitic critics as a Judaic invasion of opera. However, Rossini grudgingly publicly admired his facility as a composer and the charm of his productions. Saint-Saëns (1835–1921), of distant Jewish ancestry himself, admired his gifts. Other French musicians borrowed Offenbach's ideas over the rest of the nineteenth century. Indeed, music history has placed him as a significant formulator of light opera, and certainly as a guiding influence upon prolific operetta composers Johann Strauss, Franz Lehár, and Victor Herbert.[6]

Two other nineteenth-century musicians of Jewish ancestry merit some attention. Charles-Valentin Morhange Alkan (1813–1888) came from a musical Parisian family. As a child prodigy, he won prizes for piano and organ performances, and by the age of fourteen began to include his own compositions. Alkan had a close association with Frédéric Chopin, and often performed his works in concerts. A recognized virtuoso pianist, Alkan advocated a particular style of pedal-piano playing which was soon followed by others. He was erudite and cultured, but of extremely unstable nature, and considered of enigmatic character. Obviously in modern terms a manic-depressive, he withdrew periodically from public life. However, whenever he returned to the public, his concerts were very well received. Those emotional qualities were reflected in his compositions, which show the influences of Chopin as well as of Felix Mendelssohn, both of whom he deeply admired. His works, written for piano, and a few for other instruments, and for voice, require much technical skill, and his music notation style and tonal concepts seem advanced for his time. In fact, both Franz Liszt and Ferrucio Busoni admired his works. Gustav Mahler (1860–1911) knew of him and valued his musical ideas.

Alkan, always a strict member of the Jewish faith, was deeply interest in historical Judaica. A French-English pianist, Elie Delaborde, claimed to be his illegitimate son. There are unsubstantiated stories that Alkan died as a result of a collapsed bookcase or an accidental blow on the head from a volume of the Talmud! Only a few of his works were formally published, and his body of works remains in manuscript form in French music libraries. Alkan did write some liturgical selections for his own pleasure, among them a lovely setting of Psalm 150, composed in 1857 as a tribute to the art of music.[7]

Ferdinand Hiller (1811–1885) was born in Frankfurt, son of a Jewish merchant, Isaac Hildesheim (Justus Hiller), who encouraged his early musical gifts. Hiller went on to study in Weimar and Vienna, and as a recognized piano virtuoso, spent seven successful years in Paris. While there, he associated with Frédéric Chopin, Luigi Cherubini, and Giacomo Meyerbeer. As a composer, Ferdinand Hiller took Felix Mendelssohn (1809–1847), whom he had met in Weimar, as his musical model. Hiller wrote works for orchestra, chamber groups, and solo instruments as well as vocal selections, including some oratorios based upon biblical themes and the Psalms. In 1850, Hiller established the Music Conservatory of Cologne, which he directed until his death.

Hiller was also a prolific writer and music critic, advocating the operas of Meyerbeer and Halévy, especially *La Juive*. Among his publications were studies on the lives and works of Mendelssohn and Meyerbeer, and a commemorative monograph on Beethoven, whom he had met in Vienna in 1827. A pedagogical volume on music theory by Hiller was widely used at German music conservatories in the nineteenth century. In 1845, he contributed some choral settings for the hymnal of the Hamburg Reform Temple, including music for Psalm 137, "By the Waters of Babylon." However, it appears that by the end of his life, Hiller had distanced himself from his Judaic origins.

Does the fact of Jewish parentage fasten one's creativity to Judaism, despite a life of Christian affiliation? If so, can the following be considered Jewish composers: Felix Mendelssohn (1809–1847), Ignaz Moscheles (1794–1870), Stephen Heller (1813–1888), Anton Rubinstein (1830–1894), Karl Goldmark (1830–1915), and Paul Dukas (1865–1935)? Is it the poverty of numbers rather than specific ethnic inspiration that prompts some Jewish writers to include these composers among their Judaic listings? This question begs to be answered: What would the works of those composers have been like had they remained truly within the fold of Judaism?

Gustav Mahler (1860–1911) typified this haunting shadow of a Jewish heritage.[8] His life and career straddled two centuries of European musical culture and reflected that period of time. He was born in Kalischt, Bohemia, into a Jewish merchant family of modest means, who moved during his childhood to the more cosmopolitan city of Iglau in Moravia. There, a loosening of restrictions within the Habsburg Empire allowed somewhat more freedom for Jews to acquire general education. Mahler's father, Bernhard, sought these opportunities for his family. Early on, Gustav Mahler showed great musical talent. A generous patron sent him in 1875 to study at the Vienna Conservatory, where among his teachers was Hans von Buelow. While there, he also attended the Gymnasium, upon the insistence of his father, thus acquiring accreditation in 1881 from both institutions. Over those years in Vienna, Mahler came into active association with a number of modernists and cultural populists.[9]

Highly ambitious in his musical pursuits, Mahler soon assumed posts as music director in Leipzig, Budapest, and then in Hamburg with von Buelow. Meanwhile, he had embarked upon the dual music careers of composer as well as conductor. As his works evolved, the symphonic music and individual song settings became reflections of his artistic searchings, emotionally infused narratives. Increasingly distanced from Judaism, though not estranged from his Jewish friends, by 1895 he had joined the Catholic Church. In 1897, at the age of thirty-seven, he was appointed director of the Vienna Court Opera and also elected the conductor of the Vienna Philharmonic Orchestra. In 1901, he resigned as conductor of that orchestra under distressful circumstances. He remained as opera director until 1907. A trip to the United States to conduct the New York Philharmonic Orchestra for the season of 1908 to 1909 appeared to hasten his physical decline. In addition to several song cycles, Mahler composed nine symphonies, and before his death in Vienna in 1911, he had begun sketches for a tenth. Those large-canvas orchestral compositions remain fascinating for their intensity of subjective expression and melodic richness. They abound in folklike themes and varied rhythmic patterns, with multilayered textures of instrumental parts. Some musicians claim there are Jewish tunes in their substance. In essence theatrical works, their performances yield readily to the interpretative skills of conductors. Largely through the programming of such leading twentieth-century conductors as Serge Koussevitzky, Bruno Walter, and most especially Leonard Bernstein, Mahler's music has passed into the repertoires of the world's major orchestras.[10]

During his life, Mahler's renown rested upon his success as conductor rather than composer, but it was as a composer that he truly desired recognition. In 1901, he married Alma Schindler, and she drew him closer to her non-Jewish circle of painters and cultural activists. They had two daughters, one of whom died in early childhood. By his own admission, Mahler was ever a restless artist, a wanderer, who in his own words was "thrice homeless, as a native of Bohemia among Austrians, as an Austrian among Germans, and as a Jew throughout the world."[11]

NOTES

1. The following publications address that particular issue:

Max Brod, "Some Comments on the Relationship between Wagner and Meyerbeer," in *Leo Baeck Institute Yearbook*, Vol. 9 (London: East and West Library, 1964), pp. 202–5.

Joan Thomson, "Giacomo Meyerbeer: The Jew and His Relationship with Richard Wagner," *Musica Judaica*, vol. 1 (1975–1976), pp. 54–86.

2. For additional biographical information on Giacomo Meyerbeer, see:

Martin Cooper, "Giacomo Meyerbeer (1791–1864)," in *Annual of the Royal Music Association*, Vol. 90 (London: R.M.A., 1964), pp. 97–129.

Heinz Becker, "Giacomo Meyerbeer: On the Centenary of his Death," in *Leo Baeck Institute Yearbook*, Vol. 9 (London: East and West Library, 1964), pp. 178–201.

Heinz Becker and Gudrun Becker, comps. and eds., *Giacomo Meyerbeer: A Life in Letters* [selections from the composer's correspondence], trans. from German by Mark Violette, (Portland, Oreg.: Amadeus Press, 1989).

3. In 1961, two liturgical works, with additional piano or organ accompaniment by Isadore Freed, were issued in octavo editions by the Sacred Music Press of Hebrew Union College-Jewish Institute of Religion, New York: *U'vnucho Yomar*, for five-part mixed voices, by Giacomo Meyerbeer, and *Yigdal*, for cantor and three-part mixed choir, by Jacques Halévy.

4. Biographical information on Jacques Halévy may be found in most general music books, as well as in those specifically treating Jewish music. The following book provides sketches of these and other Jewish composers of the nineteenth and twentieth centuries:

Artur Holde, *Jews in Music: From the Age of Enlightenment to the Mid-Twentieth Century*, orig. pub. 1959; revised edition by Irene Heskes; New York: Bloch Publishing, 1974. Holde cast a wide biographical net in his book, treating a great many Jewish musicians in a general manner. It is, nevertheless, a good source of information, for which the best means of access is its index of names.

5. See Abraham W. Binder, "Isaac Offenbach (1779–1850)," in *Leo Baeck Institute Yearbook*, Vol. 14 (London: East and West Institute, 1969), pp. 215–23.

6. Offenbach has been the subject of several recent publications:

Alexander Faris, *Jacques Offenbach*, (London: Faber and Faber, 1980).

Peter Gammond, *Offenbach: His Life and Times* (Kent, England: Midas Books, 1980).

James Harding, *Jacques Offenbach: A Biography* (London: J. Calder, 1980).

7. An author and music editor, Raymond Lewenthal, has concentrated on the life and music of Charles Alkan, editing for publication a music score collection: *The Piano Music of Alkan*, (New York: G. Schirmer). Lewenthal has also recorded some of Alkan's piano music for RCA Victor and Columbia recording labels.

8. An interesting discussion of the entire matter of Judaism cum creativity is presented in Eric Werner, "Felix Mendelssohn-Gustav Mahler: Two Borderline Cases of German-Jewish Assimilation," in *Yuval*, Vol. 4 (Jerusalem: Hebrew University and Magnes Press, 1982), pp. 240–64.

9. I am indebted to the following fine article for some insightful analysis on Mahler's life and career within the context of his time: Carl Schorske, "Gustav Mahler: Formation and Transformation," issued as *Leo Baeck Memorial Lecture, 35* (New York: Leo Baeck Institute, 1991).

10. For an overview of Mahler's works, see Burnett James, *The Music of Gustav Mahler* (Rutherford, N.J.: Fairleigh Dickinson University Press, 1985).

11. Quoted from Alma Mahler, *Gustav Mahler: Memories and Letters,* trans. from German by Basil Creighton (Seattle: University of Washington Press, 1968), p. 109.

27

Arnold Schoenberg: Shaper of Twentieth-Century Music Creativity

No other composer of the twentieth century bears a closer relationship to Gustav Mahler. Arnold Schoenberg was his creative son.[1]

Arnold Schoenberg (1874–1951) reflected in his life and creativity the many dynamic changes of his era. In many respects, the man himself looms as large in history as his compositional ideas. He was born in Vienna into a middle-class Jewish family. He studied music there and then in Berlin, concentrating upon string playing and composition. His musical influences at that time were tied to a then-raging Wagner-Brahms controversy. Schoenberg wavered in his reverence for the music of Brahms, and eventually took up with the Wagnerites because so many of Wagner's newer musical ideas fascinated him.

In 1899, Schoenberg's early string ensemble composition *Verklaerte Nacht* first brought him to the attention of the general musical public. It led to a lasting friendship with Gustav Mahler, who had conducted a performance of that work. In 1912, already an established composer, arranger, and teacher, Schoenberg made his irrevocable break with the established musical traditions with a public performance of his *Pierre Lunaire*, a suite for speaker and five instruments. Subsequently, he evolved the serial technique of the twelve-tone system of music, and thereafter continued its development in his search for further advanced musical sounds. Arnold Schoenberg had taken a stand against all artistic repetition, and maintained that outlook for the rest of his life. In 1913, he began sketches for a biblically inspired composition that remained uncompleted, *Die Jakobsleiter* (The Jacob's ladder). His opera, *Moses und Aron*, composed from 1925 to 1930, also was never completed by the composer. The text he wrote for its third act was never set to notes, and is performed without any musical finale.[2]

A great measure of Schoenberg's musical significance rests upon his roster of notable pupils during the 1920s, which included Darius Milhaud (1892–1974), and Egon Wellesz (1885–1974).[3] By that time, a Schoenberg-Stravinsky controversy had displaced that of Brahms-Wagner among the young musicians of

Europe. With the rise of Hitler to power in 1933, Schoenberg lost his academic positions and fled to Paris, where he formally reconverted to Judaism in a rite attended by Marc Chagall. Late that year he emigrated to the United States, and he obtained his citizenship in 1940. He settled in Los Angeles, living there among many other German émigrés, and led a busy life of writing, composing, and painting. He taught composition both privately and at the University of Southern California.

Over those years, Schoenberg wrote several selections of particular Judaic intent. His work, *Kol Nidrey* (1938) for speaker-rabbi, mixed chorus, and small orchestra was set to an English text based upon the old prayer. Composed in ten days, in extended tonality the work introduces thematic elements well beyond the traditional Ashkenazic chant that usually opens liturgical services for *Yom Kippur* (Day of Atonement). It is a composition of very deep religious inspiration. Schoenberg's brief work, "Prologue to the Book of Genesis" (1945) for orchestra and chorus refocussed his attention upon biblical ideas. The composition, "A Survivor from Warsaw" (1947), also rapidly composed in a matter of two weeks, was scored for speaker, male chorus, and chamber orchestra. That work concludes with a dynamic proclamation of the Jewish affirmation of faith, *Sh'ma Yisrael* (Hear, Israel). Here again, he took a different melodic approach, in contrast to the traditionally sung anthemlike chant tune of that important prayer text. Among his final works were some Psalm settings (1950), including a setting of text from Psalm 118, "Out of the Depths," for mixed chorus, a cappella.

Of the many books about Arnold Schoenberg published over the decades since his death, some were written by individuals who had known him personally and thus add a dimension of understanding about the composer.[4] In 1949, Schoenberg graciously if somewhat coldly acknowledged by letter the designation tendered to him as "honorary citizen of Vienna." This was the city from which he had departed in 1925 under humiliating and discouraging circumstances, and city that had banned his music during the Nazi era.[5]

Schoenberg appears to have been a Jewish artist groping his way toward creative fulfillment. Much as the Patriarch Jacob wrestled with the Angel of God and as interpreted in Schoenberg's *Die Jacobsleiter*, so, it seems, did that composer wrestle with his own ideas throughout his life. Despite accusations by his critics that he intellectualized music, he was clearly an emotionally expressive creative figure. In matter of fact, early in his life he professed the credo that artistic inspiration arises out of personal conviction. Especially in his music conveying a Judaic connection, Schoenberg communicated that state of absolute self-expression.

It is possible that Arnold Schoenberg remains a modern composer more often written about than performed.[6] Despite the fact that he applied and was rejected three times for a Guggenheim financial grant, hardly a year passes but that one of those awards goes to someone working on aspects of the Schoenberg legacy. A man of wide-ranging intelligence and professional dedication, of energetic and ethical outlook, his life and works continue to generate worldwide interest. Three recently issued books are significant additions to the great storehouse of Schoenbergiana.

The significance of Schoenberg's contributions to twentieth-century culture does not rest solely upon his formulations for a twelve-tone system of composition, but also upon his special approach to the music for which he crafted textual concepts. Dramatic intent was inherent in the entire body of his work, and therefore he may also be considered a literary figure.

The catalogue of "neglected items" assembled by Jean Christensen and Jesper Christensen from among Schoenberg's writings provides a good addition to earlier listings. Moreover, this collection has been shaped to afford easy access to the items and to reestablish Schoenberg's own organization of his materials. While in transit from Europe, the composer began to collect and preserve his papers and scores, likely as some means of achieving personal control in the midst of chaotic circumstances. After 1933, Schoenberg added a specific category for his ideas on Jewish issues. The cataloguers have compiled an array of descriptively annotated entries, including notations for a planned autobiography as well as brief aphorisms on many topics. There is a description by Schoenberg of his 1946 heart attack and documentation of his first meeting in 1950 with Mario Castelnuovo-Tedesco, who had long been an admirer. There are drafts of letters to conductors and newspapers, both in the United States and in other countries, "thanking" them for their neglect of his works over the fifteen years of his residence in America. Much here underscores the fact that Schoenberg felt himself to be in double exile during those last years, as an observer rather than a participant in the world musical scene. An introduction and the supplementary reference listings add further substance to a book that has been dedicated to the late Clara Steuermann, devoted archivist of the Arnold Schoenberg Institute.

In 1988, the composer's daughter, Nuria Schoenberg Nono, edited a souvenir book specifically for a festival entitled *The Reluctant Revolutionary: Arnold Schoenberg, His Works and His World*, held at the South Bank Music Centre in London, England. Subsequently issued by Belmont Music Publishers, this attractive folio volume constitutes an interesting companion work to the Christensens' catalogue. Some of the materials presented in Nuria Schoenberg Nono's collection had never previously been published. Included are excerpts from letters to a number of colleagues, texts for lectures and radio talks, and program notes written by Schoenberg for performances of his music. All of the contents highlight the composer's unique attitude toward his work as well as his life experiences.

In Berlin, in 1932, Schoenberg mentioned that he had begun to collect and sort out his literary works, adding: "You'd be amazed to see how much there is."[7] In a commentary for his work *Pierre Lunaire*, Schoenberg explained his intentions for solo voice as "the kind of speaking involved in a music form."[8] Again and again, he linked drama with music. Of special interest are his remarks regarding his composition, *Kol Nidrey*, notably reflections upon examination of the traditional melodic motifs for this *Yom Kippur* eve prayer, with indications that he had become deeply interested in the text itself as "the very idea of atonement."[9] A later letter of 1941 to Paul Dessau enlarged upon those feelings. In subsequent letters in 1948 to René Leibowitz and Kurt List, Schoenberg discussed preparation of his composition "A Survivor from Warsaw," and noted that the concluding *Sh'ma Yisrael* "has special meaning to me."[10]

In 1958, when that work was performed in Warsaw by an East German chorus with the orchestra of Radio Leipzig, it was repeated in its entirety to great audience reception. Alexander Ringer reminds readers of that incident in his book treating the Jewish aspects of Arnold Schoenberg's life and work, a subject to which Ringer has devoted years of scholarly attention. This book, which incorporates a number of Ringer's previously published articles, advances the thesis that Schoenberg maintained a lifelong Jewish identity to which he passionately applied himself. Though one might argue that the composer wavered in that fidelity during his youth, as did so many of his contemporaries, it appears more likely that Schoenberg assumed the three distinct types of Jewish identification: born into it, had it thrust upon him, and took it up unto himself. Nevertheless, the broad approach and wide range of information that Alexander Ringer has brought to his collective volume provide fresh, important perspectives concerning the composer's era and his personal circumstances.

Inasmuch as Ringer's incorporated articles first appeared in German and English periodicals, each admits of separate consideration. In all, his book contains an introduction, eleven chapters, a postscript, and some illustrations. Although the content at times overlaps, the compilation provides different views of the milieu in which Schoenberg endeavored to function. An appended section includes the following original texts: a letter by Alfred Heuss protesting Schoenberg's appointment as teacher of composition at the Prussian Academy of Arts in Berlin (1925); the speech of Max Aruns, concluding the first act of the work *Der biblische Weg* (The biblical way, 1926/27)); the text of Schoenberg's "A Four-Point Program for Jewry" (1938); and his letter to Oedoen Partos accepting appointment as honorary president of the Israel Academy of Music (1951).

Ringer's introductory "Composer and Jew" begins by describing the social milieu of Germany and Austria from the late nineteenth century to the Weimar era. Ringer borrows from cultural historians, such as Peter Gay, who have explored the critical influences of societal, economic, and political conditions upon cultural life during that period, and he applies those ideas to the particular circumstances of Schoenberg and his colleagues.[11] I must, however, take issue here with Ringer, for he overstates the impact of nineteenth-century Vienna's leading *hazzan* (cantor) Salomon Sulzer as well as the status of that city as the world's leading center for Jewish liturgical music. At that time, there were other influential synagogue musicians, such as Louis Lewandowski of Berlin and Samuel Naumbourg of Paris. It was also an era of dynamic musical changes

among the liturgical reformers in Hamburg and other German cities, of flourishing cantorial artists in eastern Europe, and of notable Jewish music anthologists
like Abraham Baer of Gothenburg and Eduard Birnbaum of Koenigsberg. It is
unlikely that Schoenberg in his early years was mindful of synagogue musical
traditions, although he was known to have attended services to recite the memorial *kaddish* prayer for his father.

An opening chapter, "Prophecy and Solitude," considers the qualities of
creative inspiration and the prophetic nature of artists. Was musical art the true
faith of Arnold Schoenberg? A closer view of the composer's search for his own
literal expression of faith may be found in Ringer's next essay, "The Quest of
Language: O Word that I Lack," which examines Schoenberg's word-centered
works. Here, Ringer reflects upon the linkage of Judaic literature with music, of
words bound to melody. In point of fact, each of three Jewish languages—
Hebrew, Ladino, and Yiddish—has but one word that applies equally to poem
and song (respectively, *shir*, *canto*, and *lid*). Ringer further develops this theme
with the following study, "Idea and Realization: The Path of the Bible," and
notes that the composer had begun to espouse a Jewish national homeland early
in the 1920s, after his bitter personal encounters with anti-Semitism.

Necessarily, there are lapses in chronology throughout this book, and they
become particularly awkward in the fourth essay, "Creation, Unity, and Law,"
which addresses Schoenberg's composition of his *Kol Nidrey*. Ringer does provide interesting background on the nature of that prayer and its significance at
the beginning of the evening service for *Yom Kippur*. He cites the Jewish ethno-
musicologist Abraham Z. Idelsohn as having noted that the prayer's well-known
melodic pattern is of Rhineland origin but neglects other thematic variants that
have been documented by later scholars, especially Eric Werner and Alfred Sendrey.[12] The liturgical text itself dates from the eighth century, and in the
Sephardic Jewish tradition the prayer is usually recited without formal chant.
Schoenberg did not merely adapt the recognized Ashkenazic motifs for intoning
that prayer. He enlarged upon those elements to construct a distinctively spiritual
expression, in a composition of musical intensity and textual power.

The fifth chapter, "Relevance and the Future of Opera: Arnold Schoenberg
and Kurt Weill," presents Ringer's intriguing comparison of those two émigrés
from the Weimar cultural flowering. Weill had been an early admirer of Schoenberg, but wrote a veiled parody on him in 1928 that caused a permanent rift
between them. Both composers were text grounded and theater oriented. Indeed,
Ringer makes a strong and convincing argument that they each shaped twentieth-century opera. Beyond such seminal significance, those two creative figures
are fascinating for their similarities and contrasts. Both recognized early on the
peril for Jewish life in post-World War I Europe. In the 1930s, Schoenberg actively sought establishment of a Jewish national homeland, and Weill at the time
settled his parents and other family members in Palestine. Though each went his
distinctively different professional way in America, both responded to the times

in some works of Jewish content. In the United States, Weill's creative environment was outwardly directed, whereas Schoenberg's source of inspiration was internalized and inner-focused. Residing on the East Coast, Weill wrote successfully for Broadway and the popular sphere. Schoenberg spent many years in southern California, but he never wrote anything for the film industry.

There is much here that invites further comparative consideration. Ringer tempts us with such possibilities in his chapter "Dance on a Volcano: Von Heute auf Morgen (From today until tomorrow)," wherein he discusses the politics of music during the Weimar era. It was a time when cabarets and singing actors popularized musical satire and African-American jazz and when music, along with the other arts, flourished at the very threshold of political and economic collapse.

In the book's most extended essay, "Unity and Strength: The Politics of Jewish Survival," Alexander Ringer focuses upon the genesis and growth of Schoenberg's convictions concerning Judaism and Zionism. The composer left Berlin for Paris in May 1933, and that July formally reconverted to the Jewish faith. By the following October, he had departed for America, and while in New York in December, finished the first draft of his "Four-Point Program for Jewry," advocating the establishment of a Jewish state. Schoenberg's steps toward redefining himself as a Jew are movingly described. Then, Ringer follows with a brief exposition, "The Composer and the Rabbi," namely Stephen S. Wise (1874–1949), who was a charismatic figure in American Reform Judaism and a prominent leader of the Zionist movement. Schoenberg met Rabbi Wise in Paris in 1933, but beyond some brief communication, Ringer has found no further documentary connection between them.

In this regard I can supply some relevant information that I learned initially from Abraham W. Binder (1895–1966), who had been music director of the Stephen Wise Free Synagogue in New York City and the instructor of liturgical cantillation at Rabbi Wise's Jewish Institute of Religion (subsequently merged with Hebrew Union College). It is testimony that adds a dimension to the relationship between Wise and Schoenberg and also enlarges upon the circumstances of Schoenberg's appearance at a special meeting of *Mailamm* (American-Palestine Institute of Musical Sciences), held on April 29, 1934, at a Manhattan hall on West 73rd Street. That event was arranged by Binder upon the recommendation of Wise, who was well aware of Schoenberg's desire to present publicly his views on political Zionism.

The *Mailamm* society had been formed in 1931 to support research on Jewish music, and subsequently in 1939 was reorganized as the Jewish Music Forum. An original letter of invitation for that 1934 *Mailamm* meeting was given to me some years ago by Cantor Gershon Ephros (1890–1978), who at the time also recounted to me his recollections of the details of that evening. Listed on the *Mailamm* stationery were the following special members: Joseph Achron, Abraham W. Binder, Ernest Bloch, Mischa Elman, Ossip Gabrilowitsch, George

Gershwin, Rubin Goldmark, Louis Gruenberg, Lazare Saminsky, and Joseph Yasser. According to Cantor Ephros, the session was chaired by Saminsky, who used the opportunity to "debunk" (Ephros's word) the music of Igor Stravinsky. The preliminary musical selections were Palestinian folk songs arranged for soprano and piano and spirituals performed by the Hall Johnson Singers. Joseph Achron then introduced Schoenberg, who spoke for the most part in English. He greeted the large audience, and then read the text of his proposal, "Forward to a Jewish Unity Party." Though many were surprised at its contents, there was warm response to the composer's strong opinions, and especially to the appealing nature of his presentation. Gershon Ephros, who before World War I had studied in Jerusalem as a protégé of Abraham Z. Idelsohn,[13] felt the paper was "a revised Jabotinsky activist position" and remained deeply impressed by the entire experience. He also recalled that Achron and Schoenberg spoke together at length after the meeting. Achron soon left for Los Angeles, where he helped form a California branch of the *Mailamm* group and arranged a program on March 26, 1935, welcoming Schoenberg to the West Coast.

Alexander Ringer rounds out his book on Arnold Schoenberg with three topical pieces. In "Prague and Jerusalem," he discusses the programs of the Prague branch of Schoenberg's group, the Vienna Music Society for Performance, and indicates that many materials relating to its activities are presently held at the Jewish National and University Library in Jerusalem. Mysticism is the subject of "Faith and Symbol," treating Schoenberg's attitude toward such matters, including numerology.

Of more general scope is the concluding "Jewish Music and a Jew's Music." Here, Ringer attempts too much, and certainly the issue of a particular definition for Jewish music remains moot. He mentions the St. Petersburg (Russia) Society for Jewish Folk Music established in 1908. However, it was not Rimsky-Korsakov who influenced that society's founders, (as Ringer alleges), but rather, Vladimir Stasov who challenged Joel Engel and other Jewish musicians to collect and preserve the songs of their heritage.[14] Moreover, well before World War I had ended, there was a dispersal of many European "prime movers" in the modern renascence of Jewish music, with a significant shift of musicians and scholars to North America. Schoenberg played no role in these efforts on either continent and, for some unknown reason, declined to participate in a special Jewish music project launched in Palestine.

Ringer's references to Ernest Bloch (1880–1959) also merit some additional commentary. Bloch did not use traditional liturgical music for his setting of a Jewish sacred service, but rather extrapolated from its motifs. He was greatly influenced by the Reform liturgy of Temple Emanu-El of San Francisco, which commissioned the work. Under the musical leadership of Cantor Reuben Rinder (1887–1966), that congregation still performed the music of his predecessor, the gifted Cantor Edward Stark (1856–1918). Bloch himself was Swiss-French and not German, and thus his familial liturgy was likely northern Italian-southern

French Ashkenazic, a tradition whose European adherents were all but decimated in the Holocaust.

In a postscript, "Music, Race, and Purity," Ringer draws attention to the impact of racial politics upon music. He traces some of the early stages in which the German Fascist ideology took over, noting the effect upon such figures as Paul Hindemith and Richard Strauss, as well as Hitler favorites Hans Joachim Moser, Hans Pfitzner, and Wilhelm Furtwängler.[15] Parallels are sought between Mussolini in Italy, and Stalin in the Soviet Union. As Ringer applies those influences to Schoenberg's situation, he introduces a number of intriguing issues of broad interest and considerable substance, regarding music during the Nazi era, all of which warrant further documentary study.

Arnold Schoenberg remains a significant twentieth-century musical figure, one who appears to have drawn inspiration for his art out of intense personal necessity. He was an artist deeply shaped by society, yet alienated and iconoclastic. Alexander Ringer's book helps us to understand this important composer as an individual whose creativity was generated both within human conflict and beyond it, as someone who held fast to his beliefs and integrated those ideas into the very substance of his works. While creative artists have always been deeply affected by human events, they rarely have been able to shape history. Nevertheless, Arnold Schoenberg tried, and those efforts appear to have been heroic.[16]

NOTES

1. Several authors have linked Mahler and Schoenberg together in studies of their respective careers, in particular:

Peter Gradenwitz, "Gustav Mahler and Arnold Schoenberg," in *Leo Baeck Institute Yearbook*, Vol. 5 (London: East and West Library, 1960), pp. 262–84.

Dika Newlin, *Bruckner, Mahler, Schoenberg* (New York: Norton, 1978).

Carl E. Schorske, *Fin-de-Siècle Vienna: Politics and Culture* (New York: Knopf, 1980).

2. A monograph on Schoenberg's unfinished opera provides a helpful guide to that complex dramatic work: Karl H. Woerner, *Schoenberg's Moses and Aaron*, trans. from German by Paul Hamburger (London: Faber and Faber, 1965). Included is some consideration of the Judeo-religious implications of that opera, along with a complete libretto text as written by Schoenberg. See also Karl H. Woerner, "Arnold Schoenberg and the Theater," trans. from German by Willis Wager, *The Musical Quarterly*, vol. 48 (1962), pp. 444–60. This article treats Schoenberg's religious ideas as reflected in his work *Die Jacobsleiter*.

3. See Egon Wellesz, *Arnold Schoenberg: The Formative Years*, orig. published in Vienna, 1921; revised and trans. from German (London: Clarendon, 1925).

4. Among those works are:

Hans Heinz Stuckenschmidt, *Arnold Schoenberg*, trans. from German by Edith T. Roberts and Roy Carter (London: John Calder, 1959).

Hans Heinz Stuckenschmidt, *Arnold Schoenberg: His Life, World, and Work*, an expansion of the earlier volume, trans. from German by Humphrey Searle (New York: Schirmer Books, 1978). That author had been a music associate of Schoenberg in Germany during the 1920s.

Erwin Stein, comp. and ed., *Arnold Schoenberg Letters*, trans. from German by Eithne Wilkins and Ernst Kaiser (New York: St. Martin's Press, 1965). Stein was a close friend over many years.

Willi Reich, *Schoenberg: A Critical Biography*, trans. from German by Leo Black (London: Longman, 1971). Reich, who had corresponded with Schoenberg during the dark days of the Hitler era, also discusses the composer's particular ideas about Zionism.

Dika Newlin, "Self-Revelation and the Law: Arnold Schoenberg in his Religious Works" in *Yuval*, Vol. 1 (Jerusalem: Hebrew University and Magnes Press, 1968), pp. 204–20. Newlin studied composition with Schoenberg in California.

5. For materials from the literary output of Arnold Schoenberg, see Leonard Stein, comp. and ed., *Style and Idea: The Selected Writings of Arnold Schoenberg*, trans. from German by Leo Black and Dika Newlin (New York: St. Martin's Press, 1975).

6. This next section on Arnold Schoenberg was adapted from the author's review of three books, which was originally published in the Music Library Association quarterly journal *Notes*, vol. 48, no. 2, (1991). The three books reviewed were:

Jean Christensen and Jesper Christensen, comps. and eds., *From Arnold Schoenberg's Literary Legacy: A Catalog of Neglected Items*, Detroit Series in Music Bibliography, 59 (Warren, Mich.: Harmonie Park Press, 1988).

Nuria Schoenberg Nono, comp. and ed., *Arnold Schoenberg Self-Portrait: A Collection of Articles, Program Notes and Letters by the Composer about His Own Works*, Special Festival Edition (Pacific Palisades, Calif.: Belmont Music Publishers, 1988).

Alexander Ringer, *Arnold Schoenberg: The Composer as Jew* (Oxford, England: Oxford University Press, 1990).

7. Nono, *Arnold Schoenberg Self-Portrait*, p. 67.

8. Ibid., p. 14.

9. Ibid., p. 94.

10. Ibid., p. 105.

11. For expositions of that viewpoint, see

Peter Gay, *Freud, Jews, and Other Germans* (New York: Oxford University Press, 1978).

Carl Schorske, *Fin-de-Siècle Vienna: Politics and Culture* (New York: Knopf, 1980).

12. Regarding this matter, consult the indexes of the following:

Alfred Sendrey, *The Music of the Jews in the Diaspora, Up to 1800* (Cranbury, N.J.: Thomas Yoseloff/A. S. Barnes, 1970).

Eric Werner, *A Voice Still Heard: The Sacred Songs of the Ashkenazic Jews* (University Park: Pennsylvania State University Press, 1976).

13. See Chapter 2 (Abraham Z. Idelsohn and Gershon Ephros: Creative Connection).

14. See Chapter 18 (Russian Nationalism and Jewish Music).

15. See Chapter 19 (The Musical Legacy of the Holocaust).

16. The Arnold Schoenberg Institute houses an extensive archival collection, and is located on the campus of the University of Southern California in Los Angeles.

28

Bloch, Milhaud, and Castelnuovo-Tedesco

In many of his compositions, Ernest Bloch (1880–1959) appears to have achieved a synthesis of traditional and modern Jewish elements. To the extent that he self-consciously pursued this creative direction, his works stand in sharp contrast to those of Gustav Mahler, for whom any use of Jewish folk motifs was incidental to the music itself. Bloch was a cosmopolitan universalist of highly personal individuality, and it was neither any use of specific melodies nor a particular style that shaped those works of Judaic substance. He simply viewed musical composition as an act of faith, beyond doctrine or ritual.

Bloch was born in Geneva, Switzerland, to a Jewish merchant family, and early showed musical talent. When he was ten, he began violin studies, and soon after he determined to become a composer. Four years later, he started his composition studies, writing a symphony based upon themes he had heard his father hum. At the age of seventeen, he went to Brussels to study composition as well as violin, going on to Frankfurt, Munich, and then to Paris, where he performed publicly as well as studied. Returning in 1904 to Geneva, Bloch worked in his father's watch business, all the while also composing, teaching, and lecturing on music.[1]

Between 1912 and 1916, he composed several works of particular Judaic substance: Psalms 114, 137, 22 (1912–1914), for solo voice and orchestra, set to the French text by Edmond Fleg (1874–1963); *Trois Poèmes Juifs* (Three Jewish Poems) (1913), for orchestra; "Israel Symphony" (1912–1916), for orchestra; and, "*Schelomo*, Hebrew Rhapsody" (1915–1916), for violoncello and orchestra. At that time married and with children, he and his entire Swiss family were in bad financial trouble because of the war. He also had become deeply discouraged at the lack of interest in his music, despite staunch public support by Fleg and the novelist Romain Rolland (1866–1944). His *Schelomo* appears to reflect Bloch's feelings at that time, inspired as it was from passages in the biblical Book of Ecclesiastes. Bloch later wrote: "Vanity of vanities, all is vanity. Even the darkest of my works end with hope. This work alone concludes in a complete negation. But the subject demanded it! The only passage of light falls after the meditation of *Schelomo*. I found the meaning of this fragment, fifteen years later, when I used it in the Sacred Service; the words are words of hope, an ardent prayer that one day men will know their brotherhood, and live in harmony and peace."[2]

In 1916, Ernest Bloch came to the United States to conduct, teach, and lecture. The following year, a concert of his works was presented in New York by the Society of Friends of Music. Over the next years, in order to support his family while he continued to compose, Bloch taught privately and at music conservatories. From 1917 to 1920, he taught in New York at the David Mannes School of Music, and from 1920 to 1925 he was associated with the Cleveland Institute of Music. Then from 1925 to 1930, he was the director of the Music Conservatory of San Francisco. In 1924, Bloch became a citizen of the United States. His compositions over those years included: *"Ba'al Shem* Suite" (*Viddui, Nigun,* and *Simkhas Torah*) (1923), for violin; "From Jewish Life: Three Sketches—Prayer, Supplication, and Jewish Song" (1924), for violoncello and piano; *Meditation Hebraique* (1924), for violoncello and piano; and *Abodah* (1929), "a prayer" for violin and piano. The latter work was written expressly for the then seven-year-old violin prodigy Yehudi Menuhin.

A philanthropic endowment along with the commission to compose a setting of the Jewish Sabbath service enabled Bloch to return to Switzerland in 1930, where he remained for several years. In letters to friends, he wrote of that work: "It has become a private affair between God and me."[3] The commissioning of *Avodath ha-Kodesh* (Sacred Service) (1930–1933), for baritone, mixed chorus, and organ or orchestra, had been arranged by Cantor Reuben Rinder (1887–1966) of Temple Emanu-El in San Francisco, and the service was premiered at that congregation in 1934. That same year, the service was also performed in New York at Temple Emanu-El, under the direction of Lazare Saminsky (1882–1959). It has since been performed at synagogues and in concert halls and recorded under several labels.

When Bloch came back to the United States, he resumed teaching and lecturing on the West Coast. In 1941, he settled in Oregon at Agate Beach, where he remained until his death in 1959. Among his works in those later years were: "Voice in the Wilderness" (1936), for violoncello and orchestra, a piano excerpt from which was "Visions and Prophecies" (1936); "Six Preludes and Four Wedding Marches" (1949–1951), for organ; and, *Suite Hebraique* (1951), for viola or violin, and piano or orchestra. He was a prolific composer, and his entire output numbers over sixty major selections, including an opera ("Macbeth") three symphonies ("Israel," "Helvetia," and "America"), and a variety of works for chamber orchestra, string quartet, solo strings, piano, organ, and voice. A recipient of numerous honors during his final years, in 1951 Bloch happily accepted the Stephen Wise Award for "advancing Jewish culture."[4]

As a teacher, Ernest Bloch had a number of outstanding pupils, including George Antheil, Howard Hanson, Frederick Jacobi, Leon Kirchner, Quincy Porter, Bernard Rogers, and Roger Sessions. Though never personally associated with Bloch, Leonard Bernstein appears to have been influenced by Bloch's music in the writing of his own "Jeremiah Symphony." Gustav Mahler's works had influenced Bloch's early compositions for orchestra, and so there seems to be an interesting connection between Bernstein, Bloch, and Mahler to be pondered. Some years after his death, Bloch's family established the Ernest Bloch Society to provide a source of information on the composer and to oversee performances, publications, and recordings of his works. The society has issued a *Bulletin/Newsletter* periodically.[5]

Although many of his works were not directly of Judaic expression, much of Bloch's notable creativity reflected that heritage. He was familiar with the Ashkenazic liturgical traditions of mid-Europe and northern Italy, with their improvisational qualities and melismatic voice leadings. He knew the Hebrew language of Bible and prayer and its textual cadences. He favored musical expression of a programmatic nature, of power and passion, of rhapsodic lyricism. Though he often denied the intensity of his Jewish nature in his music and he made every effort not to directly quote folk and liturgical elements, Bloch wrote about his sources of inspiration as a Jew:

I am a Jew. I aspire to write Jewish music because racial feeling is a quality of all great music which must be an essential expression of the people as well as the individual. Does anyone think he is only himself? Far from it. He is thousands of his ancestors. If he writes as he feels, no matter how exceptional his point of view, his expression will be basically that of his forefathers... In all those compositions of mine which have been termed Jewish, I have not approached the problem from without, i.e. by employing more or less authentic melodies, or more or less sacred oriental formulas, rhythms, or intervals! No! I have hearkened to an inner voice, deep, sacred, insistent, burning, an instinct rather than any cold, dry reasoning process, a voice which seemed to come from far beyond, beyond myself and my parents, a voice which surged up in me on reading certain passages in the Bible... It was this Jewish heritage as a whole which stirred me, and music was the result. To what extent such music is Jewish, to what extent it is just Ernest Bloch—of that I know nothing. The future alone will decide.[6]

Arnold Schoenberg, Ernest Bloch, and Darius Milhaud (1892–1974) knew one another and were highly familiar with each other's music. For a time, they were all residing and teaching in southern California. In 1913, when young Milhaud first visited Bloch in Geneva, Bloch played for him his newly composed *Poémes Juifs* (Jewish Poems). Three years later, Milhaud completed his own *Poémes Juifs,* for voice and piano. For a brief time, Milhaud studied composition with Schoenberg, and then dedicated a quartet to him. In 1921, he conducted the first Paris performance of Schoenberg's *Pierre Lunaire*, and later also conducted that work in London and Brussels, to Schoenberg's great satisfaction.

In his autobiography, *Notes without Music*,[7] Darius Milhaud devoted the first two chapters to the history and traditions of his Judaic background. The first paragraphs of that opening narrative warrant inclusion here.[8]

I am a Frenchman from Provence, and by religion a Jew. The establishment of the Jews in the South of France dates back to remote antiquity. Six hundred years before Christ, when the city of Marseilles was founded, the Phoenicians, the Greeks, and the Jews set up their counting-houses on the shores of the Mediterranean in France, and so came there not as emigrants, but as traders. There are tombstones showing that there were Jews in the Rhone Valley before the Christian Era. At that time, the Jewish religion was the only one that was monotheistic, and conversion among the Gauls were very numerous. After the second destruction of the Temple, Jews emigrated from Palestine to Italy, Spain, and Provence. In Provence, they amalgamated with the Jewish colony living there under comparatively peaceful conditions. Nevertheless, early in the twelfth century King René, Count of Provence, threatened them with exile unless they all became converted to Christianity. According to the archives of the Museum of Old Aix, two noble families of Aix, who pride themselves on never having allowed a Jew to cross the threshold of their house, would seem to be by a charming irony of fate, the descendants of Jews forced to embrace the Christian faith. And yet a large number of Israelites refused to forswear their faith, and preferred exile at Avignon or elsewhere in the county of Venaissin. This country belonged to the popes after 1274, and the Jews under their jurisdiction were admirably treated.

The Jews used to speak a jargon consisting of a mixture of Hebrew and Provençal. A little Jewish-Provençal dictionary containing a fairly complete list of these expressions, which are still used in the South of France by a few persons respectful of tradition, was published in Paris about 1860 in a Jewish almanac. My good friend and librettist Armand Lunel (1892–1977) found several folklore texts written in Hebrew-Provençal dialect, very humorous and outspoken in style: carols in the form of dialogues, with one strophe in Provençal favoring conversion of the Jews, and another in Hebrew refuting arguments of the Christians; some *pioutims*, circumcision songs;[9] a little eighteenth century comedy describing a visit paid by two Jews to a bishop; and, a Tragedy of Queen Esther [*Purim* playlet].[10]

Like most of their co-religionists, the Mediterranean Jews bore the names of towns: Lunel, Milhaud, Bedarrides. Monteux, Valabregue. The county was the only place where their names were entered in the official archives, and their genealogy can be traced down to the Middle Ages. The library at Carpentras and the Calvet Museum at Avignon possess some interesting documents of this kind. I have seen there a sixteenth century picture representing a view of Carpentras, with its ramparts, belfries, and low-built houses, and its *carriere* (quarry) [French name for the Jewish quarter, like the Italian word *ghetto*], where the houses were sometimes fifteen stories high because there was not enough space for the growing population. Each tenant in the *carriere* became the owner of the floor he lived on, looked upon the pope as the head of state, and hung his portrait on the wall opposite the traditional print representing Moses and the Tablets of the Law. Prayers were also said for the pope in the synagogues.

The Provençal rite resembles, in its pronunciation of liturgical Hebrew, that of the *Sephardim* or Latin Jews, but the services are slightly different. There are only two synagogues in France which date from before the Revolution: one at Cavaillon in Louis XV style, and the other at Carpentras, whose foundations as well as the women's ritual bathing pool date from the Middle Ages. This one was rebuilt under Louis XVI, and is decorated with finely worked wood paneling and enchanting chandeliers more suggestive of an elegant salon than of a sacred edifice. Thanks to the generosity of Mme. Fernand Halphen and the Fine Arts Administration [of France], these two temples have been restored [ca.1949] and classified as historical monuments. The temple at Aix-en-Provence was founded in 1840. The speech at the inauguration was delivered by my great grandfather, at that time president of the consistory and administrator for the temple, who was succeeded in this position by his sons and grandsons. I intended to celebrate with my father the centenary of this little synagogue, and composed a cantata on three texts by Gabirol, the great Jewish poet of the Renaissance, and three texts taken from the Comtadin Provençal liturgy, translated by Armand Lunel [prayers for the pope, the victims of persecution, and for the Day of Atonement]. Unfortunately, the sad events of 1940 [World War II] prevented us from carrying out our project.

My paternal ancestors came from the Vernaissin Comtat. I found among the family archives some old papers, stamped with the pontifical arms dating from the fifteenth century, in which mention is made of a Milhaud from Carpentras in connection with some lawsuit... My mother, Sophie Allatini, was born at Marseilles. Her parents, who came from Modena [northern Italy], were descendants of the Sephardic Jews who have been established in Italy for centuries, and one of her ancestors in the fifteenth century was medical adviser to the pope.

Darius Milhaud early showed musical aptitude, teaching himself to play the piano. At the age of seven, he began serious violin studies, and progressed to playing publicly in string ensembles. After completing general schooling locally, he went to Paris to continue his musical studies. He also began to compose, and embarked on a highly active musical career of writing, teaching, and performing as a string player and conductor. A catalogue listing of his vast number of compositions includes works for voice (solo and chorus), piano and organ, strings and winds (solo and ensemble), and orchestra (chamber and full) as well as ballet music, cantatas, and operas.

In 1940, Milhaud fled to the United States with his wife and son. His elderly parents remained in hiding in the South of France, and died during the war. Milhaud often told interviewers that he had lost twenty close relatives in the Holocaust. As early as the 1930s, he had arranged Zionist folk songs as well as other Jewish selections for instruments and voice. In 1947, as previously done with Ernest Bloch, Temple Emanu-El of San Francisco, under the direction of

Cantor Reuben Rinder, commissioned Darius Milhaud to write a *Service Sacré* (Sacred Service) for the Sabbath, scored for baritone, mixed chorus, and organ or orchestra. The composer viewed this work as an important expression of his Jewish faith, and it emerged as a fluent melodic composition of great technical skill, incorporating some thematic motifs from his own Provençal liturgical traditions. It was premiered at a temple service in 1949, and since then has been recorded and widely performed in its concert version.

Milhaud made his first trip to the State of Israel in 1952 for a music festival, at which his *Candelabre à Sept Branches* (Seven branched candelabra), for piano, was premiered. That same year, he composed a cantata, *Les Miracles de la Foi* (The miracles of faith), as well as a five-act opera ("David"), which premiered in 1954 in Jerusalem and then was performed in 1955 at La Scala in Milan. In 1960, he conducted a performance of his *Service Sacré* at a newly erected synagogue in Strasbourg, France. The following year, a cantata, *Bar Mitzvah* commissioned for the occasion, was presented in Israel during celebration of Israel's thirteenth anniversary year of independence. For that text, Milhaud used his own "coming of age" portion of the *haftarah*, which was coincidentally the pertinent passage for the opening Sabbath of that Israeli festival. Illness prevented him from attending to conduct the work. Interestingly, at that same concert in 1961, another premiere performance was of Oedoen Partos's Second String Quartet, subtitled *Hommage à Schoenberg*, dedicated in posthumous musical tribute to Arnold Schoenberg and reminiscent in qualities to elements of Schoenberg's Fourth String Quartet.

During the years 1940 to 1971, when Darius Milhaud taught at Mills College in California, he was a notable musical presence with a legion of pupils. Many of his compositions were performed throughout the United States. Late in life, he returned to France, where he died.[11]

In 1948, Mario Castelnuovo-Tedesco (1895–1968) wrote to Gdal Saleski in response to a request for biographical information:

I am often asked about the second part of my family name. Tedesco was added only two generations ago through an alliance. Our family name was originally simply Castelnuovo, and so I was generally called in Italy. As you know, among the several groups of Jews of different origins who lived and still live in Italy, two were outstanding. One lived around Rome and in the former States of the Church, probably since the times of the Roman Empire, and to this the family of my mother belongs, called Senigaglia from a little town of that region. Another group came from Spain about four hundred years ago, landed in the port of Livorno, and settled down especially in Tuscany. To this group the family of father belongs. I was told once that the name Castelnuovo is perhaps a simple translation of *Castilla Nueva*, the province of Spain where my ancestors came from. However, my family lived peacefully not only in Italy, but in Tuscany, through those four hundred years.[12]

His background is likely more mixed with Ashkenazic ancestry, as the name Tedesco implies. He was born in Florence, Italy, and his mother, who was very musical, was his first piano teacher. Castelnuovo-Tedesco rapidly advanced in music studies with private instructors, and then studied at the Cherubini Institute of Music in Florence. As a young music student in 1918, he had been impressed with a performance of Ernest Bloch's *Schelomo*, though the two did not actually meet until 1930. The death of a beloved grandfather brought the composer closer to his religious identity. Some years later, in 1925, he discovered musical settings of Hebrew prayers among his grandfather's papers, and viewed those genetic roots of his own musical creativity as symbolic of his destiny. It was at that time that he wrote his first distinctively Jewish work based upon those musical jottings. It was a piano selection, *Le Danze del Re David* (The dances of King David). Again, in 1926 a Jewish inspiration led him to write three choral selections based on Hebrew melodies, but fashioned after the style of Bach-Busoni.

Castelnuovo-Tedesco incorporated elements of Hebrew prayer motifs into several other works: a piano suite (1925) and a vocal work, "Three Hebrew Chants" (1928). For a commission in 1928 from the Paris Conservatory of Music, he composed a *vocalise* for solo voice, using melodic elements of Jewish folk song from his own background. Subsequently, he refashioned that work as a *Chant Hebraique*, for stringed instruments, in which form it has become a standard in concert repertoires. Another commission, this one in 1931 from violinist Jascha Heifetz (1901–1987), who had often performed the composer's first major violin work, *Concerto Italiano*, resulted in a violin concerto, *Il Profiti* (The prophets). In his letter to Gdal Saleski, the composer wrote:

When he [Heifetz] asked me to my great pleasure to write a new concerto for him, I felt I wanted to express another aspect of my origin, of my personality, the Jewish one. It was also the time when the anti-Semitic movements started and became harder in Middle Europe, and by reaction, I felt proud of belonging to a race so unjustly persecuted. I wanted to express this pride in some large work glorifying the splendor of the past days, and the burning inspiration in which inflamed the envoys of God, the Prophets. The violin seemed to me particularly adapted to personify, as a protagonist, the free and vivid eloquence of the Prophets; the orchestra in the multiform aspects of the symphonic texture could evoke all the voices of the surrounding world, voices of people, voices of nature, voice of God. An ambitious plan, I acknowledge; preparing myself for such a task, I wished to base my attempt on some foundation, more reliable than the oral tradition which helped form the former works. The only work I was able to find of historic kind on the Jewish Italian melodies was a collection printed in Florence about 1870 by Federico Consolo,[13] an Italian violinist, which I also discovered in the bookcases of my grandfather.[14]

The premiere performance of that concerto was at Carnegie Hall in April 1933, with Heifetz as soloist and the New York Philharmonic Orchestra conducted by Arturo Toscanini. In 1936, Castelnuovo-Tedesco wrote a setting of the Sabbath Eve hymn text, *L'cha dodi*, for cantor, choir, and organ, for the services of the Amsterdam Sephardic synagogue. Castelnuovo-Tedesco emigrated to America in 1939 and became a United States citizen. He spent the last years of his life in the Los Angeles area where he taught, composed, and wrote some film music. Among his later works were: a "Sacred Service for Sabbath Eve," for cantor, mixed choir, and organ (commissioned privately in 1943); some organ selections for the Jewish wedding (in 1951, for the Cantors Assembly of America); an arrangement of the traditional chant of *kol nidrey*; a biblical oratorio ("Naomi and Ruth"), and an opera ("The Merchant of Venice"), which premiered in Florence, Italy, in 1961.

NOTES

1. For additional biographical information on Ernest Bloch by several individuals, a bibliography, discography, a catalog of works, and program notes for all of Bloch's compositions (written by Suzanne Bloch, the composer's daughter), see Suzanne Bloch and Irene Heskes, comps. and eds., *Ernest Bloch, Creative Spirit: A Program Source Book* (New York: National Jewish Music Council, 1976).

2. Ibid., p. 51.

3. Ibid., p. 74.

4. Other sources on the life and works of Ernest Bloch are:

David Z. Kushner, comp., *Ernest Bloch: A Guide to Research* (New York: Garland, 1988).

Robert Strassburg, *Ernest Bloch: Voice in the Wilderness, A Biographical Study* (Los Angeles: Trident Shop and California State University, 1977).

5. The address of the Ernest Bloch Society is Star Route 2, Gualala, California 95445.

6. Bloch and Heskes, *Ernest Bloch*, p. 38.

7. Darius Milhaud, *Notes without Music: An Autobiography*, trans. from French by Donald Evans and Arthur Ogden, eds. Rollo H. Meyers and Herbert Weinstock (New York: Knopf, 1953). The book includes an annotated listing, prepared by Elena Fels Noth, of Milhaud's compositions (complete to the date of publication), pp. 325–55.

8. Ibid., pp. 3–7.

9. Sometime around 1700, the Jewish communities of Avignon and Venaissin appear to have commissioned a musician named Ludovico Saladin to arrange some of their poetics and chants for circumcision ceremony celebrations, and those settings were often performed in the communities over several generations. In more recent times, that music was rediscovered, and has been arranged as *Canticum Hebraicum*, for voice and strings, by the Israeli music scholar Israel Adler (Hebrew University in Jerusalem).

10. In 1925. Darius Milhaud composed a two-act opera, *Esther de Carpentras*, with a libretto by Armand Lunel, incorporating the following qualities: elements of the biblical story, *Purim* celebration customs, Carpentras folklore, and Judeo-Provençal melos. The work was first publicly performed in 1938 at the Opera Comique in Paris.

11. A good source of information on Schoenberg, Bloch, and Milhaud, considered together within the sweep of twentieth-century music creativity, is Paul Collaer, *A History of Modern Music,* trans. from French by Sally Abeles (Cleveland, Ohio: World Publishing, 1961).

12. Quoted in Gdal Saleski, *Famous Musicians of Jewish Origin* (New York: Bloch Publishing, 1949), p. 31.

13. Federico (Federigo) Consolo (1841–1906) was born in Ancona and died in Florence. A noted violinist of his time, he was a protégé of Vieuxtemps, and studied composition with Fetis and Liszt. Consolo collected and arranged a volume of synagogue music based upon the traditions of northern Italy: *Libro dei Canti d'Israele: Antichi Canti Liturgici del Rito degli Ebrei Spagnoli* (Florence: Bratti, 1892).

14. Quoted in Saleski, *Famous Musicians,* p. 33.

29

An Emigré Sampler: Toch, Zeisl, Wolpe, and Weill

This brief consideration of several composers who fled to America during the 1930s presents a range of Judaic self-awareness reflected in their music. Examples of cultural displacement and adaptation more than of revision of creative outlook, each apparently sought an "American" way of reaching professional fruition, despite often difficult circumstances.

Ernst Toch (1887–1964) was born in Vienna to a family of modest means. Early on, he taught himself to play the piano and then learned music notation on his own, studying scores especially of Mozartian works and copying them off. By the age of seventeen, he had begun to compose, particularly string music. In 1905, one of those works was performed publicly by the Rose Quartet. After completing his general education, Toch enrolled at the University of Vienna for a medical degree. In 1909, however, he won a coveted music competition award, the Mozart Prize, which included a four-year stipend along with a one-year fellowship to the Frankfurt Conservatory. Resettled in Germany, he subsequently secured a position as teacher of composition at the Mannheim School of Music, thereby embarking upon an active career.

Drafted into the Austrian army during World War I, Ernst Toch resumed his musical activities following the armistice, and by the 1920s had joined the ranks of the modernist *neue musik* (new music) composers in Europe. His creativity in that period (works for piano, strings, winds, orchestra, and opera) reflected a general outlook without any relevance to Jewish inspiration. By 1928, he had an established reputation in Berlin, and in 1932 he toured the United States by invitation as a noted German composer. He returned to Berlin just as Hitler came into power. Soon dismissed from his positions, his music banned by the Nazis, Toch fled to Paris, then London, and finally to New York, in 1935. Through the influence of George Gershwin (1898–1937), Toch was engaged to write music for films, and in 1937 moved to southern California. There, he wrote many movie scores, in particular for horror, chase, and tension scenes, for which he could apply his special style of composition. Some of his scores won coveted Academy Awards. Toch also taught music privately, and in 1940 he joined the music faculty of the University of California at Los Angeles. A prolific writer of articles and personal correspondence, he also wrote two musical pedagogy books for students: *Melodielehre* (1923) and *The Shaping Forces in Music* (1948).

Many of Toch's relatives had been trapped in Europe, and he devoted much of his resources to rescuing some of them. His mother died in Vienna in 1937, and at that time he was moved to create a work in her memory. He composed "Cantata of the Bitter Herbs," drawing upon elements of the Passover *seder* meal order of service (*haggadah*) to underscore the theme of biblical Exodus as universal liberation from oppression. Essentially it is a work of philosophical rather than religious outlook, and is without Jewish melodic elements. During the years of World War II and its aftermath, Toch felt that economic necessity compelled his energies to be directed to film music rather than to more serious compositions. Despite his laments, he did manage a great burst of creativity over the final ten years of his life. Three symphonies, intended as spiritual reflections after a serious illness, offer mixed autobiographical information: the first was inspired by the writings of Martin Luther; the second, dedicated to Albert Schweitzer, included biblical references to Jacob wrestling with the Angel; and the third bears upon Goethe's *Werther*, and the matter of unhappy wanderings. Another symphony, "Jephtha," was intended as a musical interpretation of that tragic biblical story. In 1964, Toch died in Los Angeles.[1]

Eric Zeisl (1905–1959) was born in Vienna to a family who owned a coffeehouse. In early childhood he felt committed to music, and at the age of fourteen began formal studies at the Vienna State Academy of Music. Only two years later, three of his songs were published. From 1920 to 1938, Zeisl struggled to earn a livelihood as a teacher while composing music, especially songs and choral works. Essentially a lyric, vocal composer, he regarded art songs as little dramatic works, for which he set poetic texts by the leading German writers. He also began to write larger works for various instruments and ensembles. It was just as Hitler entered Austria that Zeisl appeared at last to be embarked upon a highly successful career. He had won the Austrian State Music Prize, was negotiating a long-term publishing contract, and had been invited to join the faculty of the Vienna Conservatory of Music. All was lost, and Zeisl escaped to Paris in November 1938. While there, he met Darius Milhaud, and they began a warm friendship.

At that time, in the depths of his despair, Zeisl compared the sharp turn in his life with that of the biblical Job, and began to seek Hebraic elements for his musical expression. Arriving in New York in 1939, he embarked upon a regeneration of his musical career and began work on a major operatic work, "Job." Economic need led him to relocate in Hollywood, where there were opportunities to write music for films. He became a citizen in 1945, and began to teach at Southern California School of Music and then at Los Angeles City College. Zeisl was actively associated with Jewish organizations. For several years, he served as the composer-in-residence at the Brandeis Arts Institute for Jewish Culture in California. The institute then was headed by composer and liturgist Max Helfman (1901–1963), for whom Zeisl arranged several Zionist folk songs.

In America, however, Eric Zeisl felt displaced geographically as well as creatively, and his music reflected a backward inspiration. He appears to have strived to overcome that overwhelming sense of artistic exile by turning to his Jewish roots. In the 1950s, with the assistance of commissions and fellowships, his economic burdens eased, and over the final years of his life, Zeisl was able to resume composing. Among the works he produced was *Requiem Ebraico* (Hebrew Requiem), using text from Psalm 92, the Sabbath hymn: "It is good to give thanks unto the Lord, and to sing His praises." The work was written in 1945 and dedicated to the memory of his father. In 1948, inspired by the sad biblical story of Jephtha's daughter, he wrote "Four Songs for Wordless Chorus," for female voices and orchestra. In 1952, he composed a cantata, "From the Book of Psalms," using texts from Psalms 55 and 57, "Give ear, God, to my prayer... Be gracious unto me, God," and scored for tenor, male chorus, and orchestra. Zeisl also created music for two biblical ballets, "Naboth's Vineyard" (1953), and "Jacob and Rachel" (1954). At the time of his death in 1959, he had only completed two of the planned four acts of an opera, "Job, Mendel Singer," for whose music he had adapted motival elements of Jewish cantillation and liturgical chant.[2]

The music library at the University of California at Los Angeles (UCLA) houses the archival collections (manuscripts, scores, writings, and memorabilia) of both Ernst Toch and Eric Zeisl who met in 1942 in Los Angeles, and became close friends over the next years.[3] Moreover, there appears to have been lively social connection between both Toch and Zeisl and composers Schoenberg, Milhaud, and Castelnuovo-Tedesco, in additional to other émigré musicians and writers who had resettled in the California area.

Stefan Wolpe (1902–1972) was born in Berlin and began music studies at the age of fourteen. He attended the Berlin Academy of Music, where his teachers were Busoni and Webern. During the 1920s, Wolpe wrote music (as did Kurt Weill) for the theatricals of Bertoldt Brecht. Fleeing from the Nazis in 1934, Wolpe emigrated by way of Russia, Romania, and Austria to Palestine, where he taught composition at the Jerusalem Conservatory. There, he wrote arrangements of Hebrew folk songs for solo voice and chorus, and music for a stage production, "The Man from Midian," based upon the life of Moses. In 1939, Wolpe came to the United States and became an American citizen. To honor establishment of the State of Israel in 1948, he composed a cantata, "Israel and Its Land," and then a setting of the liturgical hymn *Yigdal* (Praise).

Settled in the New York City area, Wolpe had a number of notable students, and enjoyed friendships with colleagues in literature and art as well as music.

The economic problems that plagued him throughout those years were further complicated by a disastrous fire depriving him of precious manuscripts and art works, just at the time when debilitating illness had severely limited his activities. Of his American works, which included a symphony and chamber works, his "Songs from the Hebrew," for voice and piano, remains a creative contribution that has assumed a deserved place in concert repertoires. Wolpe's style of composition, which sought frontiers of tonal expression, was difficult and presented technical problems for performers. As a result, most of his other music has slipped away from inclusion in concerts and recordings.[4]

An active member of the Jewish Music Forum, Stefan Wolpe presented a lecture at a forum meeting in February 1946, held at the YM-YWHA of 92nd Street in New York City. His topic was "Folk Elements in Cultivated Music," and he concluded with the following remarks:

The composer's imagination, naturally, must not go beyond the point where variation distorts and destroys the basic features of the original. On the other hand, there is always a danger of endowing the folklore material with the power of a fetish, the slavish yielding which may stifle and sterilize the creative inventiveness of the composer. It is up to the composer alone, however, to decide to what extent he should comply with the apparent features of the folklore material, or go beyond the restricted boundary of a limited variation, for his creative instinct has the ability of carrying over these features even to an extreme transcendental plane, and yet to remain basically within their orbit. One must well consider all these conditions when striving to identify any musical characteristics based upon a national heritage; and this, of course, is true with regard to Jewish music as well. In short, Jewish musical material may sometimes preserve its basic identity, despite some very drastic transformations applied to it by the composer in the course of his creative process.[5]

Kurt Weill (1900–1950) appears to have been two composers, or rather a compositional form of Siamese twins, the European and the American, joined forever physically yet proceeding along separate intellectual planes of endeavor. Weill was born in Dessau, Germany, the son of a cantor, who was his first music teacher and trained him to sing in his choir. He soon advanced in more formal musical studies, and decided to concentrate upon composition. Among his earliest works was a religious anthem, *Lobgesang* (Prayer song), for his sister's confirmation. By the end of the 1920s, he had mastered the creation of various serious forms and had assumed an important place in the musical avant-garde of the Weimar era. His works were published and widely performed in Austria as well as Germany, and he wrote numerous articles for various journals about his own music and the works of his contemporaries. Always attracted to the dramatic genre, Weill set libretti of Georg Kaiser, and then from 1927 onward, the political and social plays by Bertoldt Brecht, which included *Mahagonny* and

Die Dreigroschenoper (The three- penny opera), ariettas of which rapidly became popular favorites throughout Europe.[6]

In 1933, Kurt Weill's works were banned, and, personally hounded by the Nazis, he fled to Paris. Through the efforts of the impresario Max Reinhardt, he was able to emigrate to America in 1935. Resettled in New York, he composed incidental music for Reinhardt's production of "The Eternal Road," a timely Jewish drama by Franz Werfel (1890–1945). Weill then embarked upon a career of writing music for theatricals, achieving great success on Broadway and in the popular song field. In the last years of his short life, Weill wrote three works of specific Jewish relevance. For a commission from Cantor David Putterman (1901–1979) of the Park Avenue Synagogue in 1946, he composed a setting of the Sabbath eve *Kiddush* (Blessing over wine), and dedicated it to his cantor father.

In 1947, Weill arranged the Palestinian folk song *Havu l'venim* (Give us building bricks) for voice and piano.[7] Before the outbreak of World War II, he had managed to settle his parents and some other family members in Palestine, and in 1947 visited them there. While in that country, he met Chaim Weizmann (soon to be the first president of the State of Israel), attended performances of the Palestine Philharmonic Orchestra, visited at Hebrew University, and toured several agricultural settlements. Then in 1948, Weill made a full orchestral arrangement of the Israeli national anthem, *Hatikvah* (The hope), for Serge Koussevitzky (1874–1951) and the Boston Symphony Orchestra. That arrangement remains in the performance repertoire of the Israel Philharmonic Orchestra. Weill died in New York in 1950.[8]

NOTES

1. To commemorate the tenth anniversary of Ernst Toch's death, several programs devoted to his works were presented in Los Angeles during the concert season of 1974–75. At that time, a biographical pamphlet was prepared by Toch's grandson for distribution at an exhibit of Toch's music scores, manuscripts, publications, and various memorabilia: Lawrence Weschler, *Ernst Toch: A Biographical Essay* (Los Angeles: UCLA Music Library, 1974).

2. Eric Zeisl's inspiration for the libretto of his work "Job," appears to have been a German novel by Joseph Roth, *Hiob, Roman eines einfachen Mannes* (Job, the story of a simple man) (Berlin: G. Kiepenheuer, 1930). For a rather sensitive analysis of "Job" and other works by Zeisl, see Malcolm S. Cole, "Eric Zeisl: The Rediscovery of an Émigré Composer," *The Musical Quarterly*, vol. 64, no. 2 (1978), pp. 237–44.

3. A particularly good discussion of both collections, viewed in the broad context of time and place, is Barbara Barclay and Malcolm S. Cole, "The Toch and Zeisl Archives at UCLA: Samples of Southern California Activity to Preserve the Heritage of

Its Émigré Composers," *Music Library Association Notes*, vol. 35, no. 3 (1979), pp. 556–77.

4. The Stefan Wolpe Archive is housed at the music library of York University in Toronto, Ontario, Canada. To highlight the acquisition of that archive, a Stefan Wolpe International Festival and Symposium was held there in 1993.

5. *Jewish Music Forum Bulletin*, vols. 7 and 8 (1946–47), p. 6.

6. For a scholarly treatment of the musical career of Kurt Weill before he emigrated to America in 1935, see Kim H. Kowalke, *Kurt Weill in Europe* (Ann Arbor, Mich.: UMI Research Press, 1979).

7. Kurt Weill's *Kiddush* may be found in David Putterman, comp., *Synagogue Music by Contemporary Composers* (New York: G. Schirmer, 1951). The arrangement by Weill of that Palestinian folk song may be found in Harry Coopersmith, comp., *The Songs We Sing* (Philadelphia: Jewish Publication Society of America, 1950). Incidentally, both of those published collections also include some music by Darius Milhaud.

8. Among the books treating the life and works of Kurt Weill are:

Ronald Sanders, *The Days Grow Short: Life and Music of Kurt Weill* (New York: Holt, Rinehart and Winston, 1980).

Douglas Jarman, *Kurt Weill: An Illustrated Biography* (Bloomington: Indiana University Press, 1982).

Mario R. Mercado, *Kurt Weill: A Guide to His Works* (New York: Kurt Weill Foundation, 1989).

Ronald Taylor, *Kurt Weill: Composer in a Divided World* (New York: Simon and Schuster, 1991).

Kurt Weill's archival materials are presently housed at the music library of Yale University in New Haven, Connecticut, and in New York City at the Kurt Weill Foundation for Music, which issues a newsletter twice a year.

30

Leonard Bernstein

A good comparison may be made between Kurt Weill and Leonard Bernstein, in that each appear to have had two distinctively creative natures housed within one singularly gifted human being. Both bridged the pop song genre with the serious music of concerts and classics. Bernstein lived longer and enjoyed much more personal success in his highly active, dual-dimensional career.

Leonard Bernstein (1918–1990) was born in Lawrence, Massachusetts to a middle-class Jewish family and spent his early years in the Boston area. His first lessons were at the piano, and he then went on to study music at Harvard University. Already a vastly capable pianist, he added studies in conducting and composition to those of piano at Curtis Institute of Music in Philadelphia, and then trained with Serge Koussevitzky at the Tanglewood Music Center in the Berkshires. At that time, he began lifelong friendships with many other musicians, some of whom were involved in the popular entertainment world, and his double-track creative career was launched. The big career break was an opportunity to substitute for the ailing Bruno Walter, and conduct the New York Philharmonic Orchestra on Sunday afternoon, November 14, 1943. For far too many, such a chance might be the ultimate moment of a lifetime, but for Bernstein it was simply a notable beginning for his long and fruitful life of conducting, piano playing, lecturing, and composing works for stage as well as concert hall.[1]

By the time of his death, Leonard Bernstein had amassed a formidable array of honors and musical achievements.[2] A substantial number of publications have treated his life, compositions, and writings. His formidable roster of recordings includes all the symphonies of Gustav Mahler, among an array of admirable music interpretations. Clearly, he was a great musical talent whose life added a measure of stature to American musicianship. That he avowed his Judaic heritage and sought in some of his compositions to express that faith, adds further luster to his name.[3]

Leonard Bernstein: Musician and Jew[4]

Examining the photograph of Leonard Bernstein on the jacket of his book *The Joy of Music,*[5] one of his friends is supposed to have remarked that the musician looked like a twentieth century Prometheus with some sort of vulture tearing at his liver. Bernstein actually had protested the use of this particular photograph. His publishers, with commercial wisdom, argued that this was the picture that all of their office girls preferred.

As the golden boy of American music, Bernstein was extolled and adored by multitudes, but he was also the object of much envy and criticism, especially in the late fifties and early sixties. His success still bred more success at that time, much to the natural chagrin of many other musicians who toiled in relative oblivion. Bernstein's detractors openly pondered whether he was protean or protein. Having made his mark in almost every phase of musical accomplishment, he enjoyed scant group association among his professional colleagues. Conductors lauded his talents as a performer. Pianists recommended his music lectures. Musicologists praised his conducting techniques. Critics balanced his "admirable Ives" with his "flabby Mozart." To serious composers, he was a new George Gershwin. On the other hand, writers of popular music admired his academic understanding of jazz, and avoided discussion of his Broadway music.

The appearance of three books about Leonard Bernstein from 1959 to 1961 provided an opportunity for wider evaluation of him as a man and musician. While each was published under separate auspices, viewed together, these books presented a fairly consistent delineation of an enormously popular personality. Moreover, the facts of Bernstein's Jewish birth and active affiliation appear to have provided a significant background for most of his interests and endeavors. He had, indeed, become an important catalyst in Jewish musical affairs.

The earliest of these books, *The Joy of Music*, was dedicated by author Leonard Bernstein to his one-time piano teacher and his devoted secretary, Helen Coates. It is a collection of five general essays and seven television scripts of Bernstein's *Omnibus* shows of 1954 to 1958. The publication of this book fulfilled a commitment made almost a decade before for a book about music.

Among those essays, written by Bernstein during the period of 1948–1955, are some fanciful dialogues in which many of his ideas about various musical topics are treated in an amusing yet thoughtful manner. Of special interest is one discussion about George Gershwin. In 1942, Bernstein secured a much needed job as an arranger with a popular music company because he reminded someone of Gershwin. The comparison, in many respects illogical, has dogged Bernstein since then.

The television scripts included in the book recall for the reader those excellent programs whose subject matter and method of presentation were then unique. Set on a printed page, the materials are still interesting and informative, but they are not as absorbing as when they were delivered by Bernstein, with his enthusiastic showmanship and his musical understanding minus condescension. He made programs about Bach and opera outstanding broadcast entertainment for a vast American audience.

The biography of Leonard Bernstein by David Ewen was intended primarily for readers in their early teens.[6] This is an age level that was attracted to Bernstein as a hero in a modern Horatio Alger story. In his early forties when the book was published, he was still a handsome and youthful figure in a country where such attributes are valued as ends in themselves. Bernstein, moreover, was an example that parents hastened to present to young, perhaps reluctant, music students. David Ewen, who also wrote for young readers biographies of Irving Berlin, Jerome Kern, and George Gershwin, took these facts into good account in his book about Leonard Bernstein. It is a straightforward narrative about the musician from his birth on August 25, 1918, through his early years and musical beginnings and into the era of many musical triumphs. Included, of course, are some of the tribulations in Bernstein's early professional life, as well as a catalogue of subsequent successes with a variety of musical projects.

With his young readers ever in mind, author David Ewen stressed Bernstein's general academic proficiency, including his graduation in 1939 from Harvard cum laude. Due attention is paid to the traditional training that the young composer-conductor received for his *bar mitzvah*. Here, too, Bernstein's early interest in the music of the synagogue is noted as an influence upon his musical and personal outlook. Indeed, many Jewish references and expressions appear throughout the account, despite the fact that the book is directed toward young readers of all faiths. Included are some photographs and an appendix listing of Bernstein's compositions and recordings.

John Briggs was one of the New York newspaper critics who reviewed Leonard Bernstein's dramatic and triumphant substitution for Bruno Walter with the New York Philharmonic Orchestra on that fateful Sunday afternoon of November 14, 1943.[7] A prominent writer on musical subjects in the early sixties, Briggs graduated from the Curtis Institute of Music in Philadelphia in 1938, a year before Bernstein enrolled there. His biography of a fellow alumnus, Bernstein, is as candid and reasonably objective as promised on the book jacket. In this balanced review of Leonard Bernstein's life and accomplishments to 1961, much of the depth of personality and innate musical vigor of the man are also disclosed. The concise chapters are informative and pleasantly written, and the book is supplemented with fifty photographs as well as an appended discography.

The author John Briggs gathered his biographical facts from very many willing sources. To this material, he also added his own perceptive views about Bernstein's fabulous musical career. Leonard Bernstein's unwavering interest in Jewish matters is amply disclosed. Two weeks after his spectacular debut at Carnegie Hall, Bernstein chose to lead the Philharmonic in a performance of Ernest Bloch's orchestral suite, *Trois Poémes Juif* (Three Jewish poems). In

1946, he conducted an orchestral concert in postwar Munich, Germany. After a favorable reception, he proceeded to an assemblage at Dachau camp where, together with seventeen former inmates, he performed on a broken upright piano to a cheering throng. The previous year, he had fulfilled a commission from the Park Avenue Synagogue in New York for a musical setting of the traditional *Hashkivenu*, Sabbath eve prayer.

In 1947, Bernstein toured Palestine during the difficult period following the end of the British mandate. He returned the following year, and while the new State of Israel was fighting a critical war for survival, traveled throughout that country, performing and meeting with the young people whose musical idol he had become. One must realize how important music has always been to the Jewish people to understand why Bernstein was considered a hero of that war without ever carrying a gun.

In 1949, when Brandeis University was established in Waltham, Massachusetts, Bernstein was invited to assist in its opening musical programs. Brandeis University seemed a logical place for a man who had firmly allied himself with Jewish causes and the Jewish community. Bernstein returned many times to the State of Israel, and also toured Europe, Russia, Latin America, and the rest of the world, as an American Jew of tactful understanding and of artistic enthusiasm.

The influence of Leonard Bernstein has been strong in every aspect of musical activity in which he ventured. His talents were prodigious, and his energy seemingly boundless. He appeared not to be halted by the new and untried. This eclecticism probably accounted for his gift of communicating the essences of contemporary composers. Yet, like the story line in his one-act opera "Trouble in Tahiti," all was not well in an apparent modern paradise.

Not since the era of Toscanini had the New York Philharmonic, with whom Bernstein had a seven-year contract in the sixties, played such long and well-subscribed concert seasons. The musicians of this organization toured the world, and their prestige and incomes were excellent, yet there was carping about their programs among many music critics. Bernstein's personal support and performance of modern music was crucial to many composers, yet he often lamented that only Bernstein played Bernstein in the concert halls. He was able to conduct the orchestra while capably performing as his own piano soloist, yet he felt remiss at never having given a piano recital.

Bernstein's friends warned that he should limit his activities only to those commitments that really interested him and would advance the substance of his career. As a result, at that time he promised to write some serious compositions, even a piano concerto. He yearned to write an opera about Jewry in an eighteenth-century Polish ghetto, perhaps a setting of the story of *The Dybbuk*, a Jewish play by Shlomo Ansky (1863–1920). As a composer, Bernstein had found Broadway to be, up to the 1960s, his most facile medium. Despite the poor commercial response to the more classic *Candide* in 1956, his other scores, for the shows *Wonderful Town* and *West Side Story* were widely acclaimed; yet he longed to write a real hit tune, like those by George Gershwin, that ever-present specter.

As the musical hero of his age. Bernstein worried about the departure of youth and about the long middle years before venerable old age. To musical art, he brought an excellent natural ear, strong rhythmic sense, much musical skill, and an attractive personality. Bernstein could project himself vitally into everything he undertook. He had the gift of communication to audiences, to other musicians, and, it appeared, to his devoted friends. However, he was a man whose enormous talents and great versatility sent him off in many directions at the same time. He had too many exceptional capabilities to enjoy inner serenity.

Such a complex career very likely created artistic conflicts for Bernstein, personally and with his associates. As a Jew, however, he seemed to have fulfilled himself most completely. Bernstein did what others would not, or perhaps could not, have achieved. The significance of his contributions to general Jewish musical affairs can truly be evaluated only in terms of the special problems that face any Jewish musical activity in our generation.

There are some very rare Jewish artists to whom Jewish musical expression is the totality of their creative being. Jewish music awaits such geniuses. Perhaps one was Ernest Bloch. The predominant type of Jewish musician is one whose Jewish self-awareness has somehow been imposed upon him and who has reacted to it with varying degrees of response, positive or negative. The American musical scene, currently the most prolific in music history, is in particular filled with many serious musicians of Jewish birth. Among them, Jewish music must gather its musical gleanings much as did biblical Ruth in the fertile harvest fields of Boaz.

The Jewish musician of our generation who may wish to realize his creative heritage is likely to be wrestling with his art much as Jacob wrestled with the Angel. Not only must this musician master his craft for this newer, subjective inspiration, but he must also be involved in the polemics of defining Jewishness in art. Of much more significance for many marginally affiliated Jewish musicians is one recognized fact in music today. Although the contemporary Jewish writer in America has a large and receptive following for his themes on Jewish life and customs, his aesthetic counterpart, the Jewish composer, does not.

Fortunately, there are some Jewish musicians who have actually taken upon themselves the obligation to advance actively the cause of Jewish musical life wherever they find an opportunity. In relative oblivion, they encourage as well as teach and assist other Jewish musicians; they perform many of the classics of Jewish music as well as newer compositions; they collect, arrange, and republish Jewish music that would otherwise fall into neglect or be lost entirely. Leonard Bernstein showed an interest, if not a dedication, to Jewish music. He also, as a very famous musician, commanded the attention of the entire musical world. Therefore his Jewish awareness was one of his more significant attributes.

In a profession where names have been altered with the skill of a custom tailor, Bernstein chose to retain his own, despite the solicitous advice in 1941 of his mentor Serge Koussevitzky. Though Bernstein's compositions for the synagogue were few, he showed an interest in Jewish liturgy, and often expressed a desire to contribute much more to devotional music. Of his secular works, his first symphony, *Jeremiah* embodies a specifically Jewish expression. His second, "Age of Anxiety," is more generally subjective.[8] Nevertheless, Bernstein's enthusiasm as an emissary for Jewish music and musicians was unbounded. He did not blush while presenting in concerts the music of Jews with Jewish performers in this country and throughout the world as well as on radio, television, and recordings. He proved that a Jew can perform a fine *St. Matthew's Passion* by Bach, and also present a rendition of Bloch's *Sabbath Sacred Service* to the acclaim of non-Jews.

Moreover, Bernstein did not bother to explain his active involvement in the musical affairs of Israel. Indeed, as a personal champion of Israel's musicians, he was an especially gracious public figure. This, then, may have been his most complete success. As a Jewish man of much sincerity and intellectual substance, he applied the advantages of his professional good fortune toward advancement of some notable projects of Jewish musical significance.

NOTES

1. A biographical study of Bernstein that includes commentary by a number of Bernstein's music associates is Peter Gradenwitz, *Leonard Bernstein: The Infinite Variety of a Musician* (New York: St. Martin's Press, 1980).

2. For a roster of his works, see Jack Gottlieb, comp., *Leonard Bernstein: A Complete Catalogue of His Works, Celebrating His 70th Birthday* (New York: Jalni Publications, 1988). This is the expanded version of a previous listing prepared by Gottlieb in 1978.

3. See Jack Gottlieb, "Symbols of Faith in the Music of Leonard Bernstein" in *The Musical Quarterly*, vol. 66, no. 2 (1980), pp. 287–95.

4. This section is an article by the present author that originally appeared in the biweekly published by the Jewish Reconstructionist Foundation, *The Reconstructionist*, vol. 27, no. 14 (1961), pp. 26–30. Only some reference notes have been added to the original text. However, alterations have been made in tense, reflecting the time lapse between the date that this material was first written and Bernstein's death in 1990. At the time of Leonard Bernstein's death, I reread this article, and realized that I would not wish to alter or amend my earlier remarks. Indeed, I found the substance of this material even more relevant, with that passage of time, to the entire sweep of what was truly a remarkably multifaceted and successful musical career.

5. Leonard Bernstein, *The Joy of Music* (New York: Simon and Schuster, 1959).

6. David Ewen, *Leonard Bernstein: A Biography for Young Readers* (Philadelphia: Chilton Company, 1960).

7. John Briggs, *Leonard Bernstein: The Man, His Work, and His World* (Cleveland, Ohio: World Publishing, 1961).

8. Among Bernstein's works composed in his later years, his *Chichester Psalms* (with a Hebrew text) remains a singular one of Jewish liturgical expression. However, he did include elements of Judaic expression in his *Kaddish Symphony*, and even in his composition, *Mass*.

31

Commissioning of Jewish Music

What is Jewish music? Over recent decades, this question has been addressed by a multitude of educators and scholars, no less than composers and critics, sometimes with intriguing ideas.[1] For a program resource book that this writer prepared in 1978, I included some intriguing professional reflections as to the special attributes of Jewish music.[2] Joseph Yasser described Jewishness in music as a balanced fusion of Jewish melos with a sympathetically developed technique. Isadore Freed cautioned that any use of Jewish melodic contours, especially sacred motifs, must be harmonized in a nondominant modal manner rather in the usual major-minor system. Abraham W. Binder emphasized the strong linkage of Jewish music to its textual materials. Mario Castelnuovo-Tedesco considered his own experiences in Jewish music as bound to his Sephardic family roots in Italy and to a legacy of liturgical music jottings by his grandfather.

Likely, the most readily identified Jewish music is that which is of liturgical or religious expression. A number of those works, such as the Sacred Services by Ernest Bloch and Darius Milhaud, originated as commissionings, a process quite common throughout the field of general music. Cantor David Putterman (1901–1979), who served at Park Avenue Synagogue in New York City, was a particularly active commissioner of Jewish liturgical music, all of which he performed at the devotional services. A native-born American trained by a number of leading cantorial figures, he was a founder of the Cantors Assembly, the professional organization affiliated with the Conservative branch of Judaism and the Jewish Theological Seminary of America.

A member of the Jewish Music Forum from 1942 onward, Putterman early on advocated the establishment of a school for cantorial studies. He delivered an ardent argument for a formalized educational approach to *hazzanut* (cantorial music) at the forum's day-long symposium "The Need for an Academy of Jewish Music," which was held in June 1944 at the 92nd Street YM-YWHA in New

York City. Putterman's presentation, "The Academy's Place in Jewish Life," included the following remarks:

The student may now begin his creative endeavors by emulating first the classical Jewish masters, and then the more recent contributors to synagogue music. Contemporary composers such as Ernest Bloch, Joseph Achron, Darius Milhaud, Mario Castelnuovo-Tedesco, Frederick Jacobi, David Diamond, Paul Dessau, and others, eager to profess Judaism by means of their creative art, or fired with a burning resentment toward the injustices, intolerances, and inhuman cruelties perpetrated upon our people in this world Holocaust, have recently poured out their hearts into new liturgical creations expressive of their own innermost feelings, heralding as it were, a new era in the liturgical music of the synagogue. New forms of hazzanic art are now likewise in the process of development, due to the influx and influence of modern Americans into the profession of *hazzanut*.[3]

By 1951, David Putterman had commissioned and performed liturgical works, a variety of prayer settings for the ritual services, by a notable array of composers: Arthur Berger, Leonard Bernstein, Abraham W. Binder, Henry Brant, Mario Castelnuovo-Tedesco, Julius Chajes, Paul Dessau, David Diamond, Lukas Foss, Isadore Freed, Herbert Fromm, Morton Gould, Alexander Grechaninoff, Roy Harris, Max Helfman, Frederick Jacobi, Ernst Levy, Jacques de Menasce, Darius Milhaud, Paul Pisk, Bernard Rogers, Solomon Rosowsky, Heinrich Schalit, Leo Smit, Leo Sowerby, William Grant Still, Alexander Tansman, Kurt Weill, Jacob Weinberg, and Zavel Zilberts.[4]

In all, between 1943 and 1978, Putterman had encouraged the creation of liturgical selections from seventy-two composers (non-Jews as well as Jews), and all that music was premiered in the services at Park Avenue Synagogue. Additional names were: Hugo Chaim Adler, Haim Alexander, Nahum Amir, David Amram, Jacob Avshalomoff, Nicolai Berezowsky, Herman Berlinski, Aviassof Bernstein, Ernest Bloch, Suzanne Bloch, Herbert Brun, Charles Davidson, Marvin David Levy, Jacob Druckman, Gershon Ephros, Isidor Geller, Miriam Gideon, Yedidia Gorochov, Jack Gottlieb, Peter Gradenwitz, Joseph Tal, Paul Ben-Haim, Gershon Kingsley, Reuven Kosakoff, Siegfried Landau, Mark Lavry, Moshe Lustig, Jan Meyerowitz, Douglas Moore, Nahum Nardi, Eda Rapaport, Neil Robinson, Laurence Rosenthal, Karl Salomon, Jakob Schonberg, Sholom Secunda, Robert Starer, Lazar Weiner, Yehudah Wohl, Stefan Wolpe, Yehudi Wyner, and Hugo Weisgall.[5]

As a pedagogical tool for the teaching of Jewish music in religious schools during the 1940s, musician and educator Harry Coopersmith (1902–1975) commissioned arrangements of Hebrew and Yiddish Jewish folk songs from many composers, including: Leonard Bernstein, Abraham W. Binder, Gershon Ephros, Isadore Freed, Herbert Fromm, Frederick Jacobi, Darius Milhaud,

Heinrich Schalit, and Kurt Weill. A collection of 265 selections was subsequently published.[6]

For his compilation of religious music, the liturgist and scholar Chemjo Vinaver (1900–1973) commissioned Arnold Schoenberg to write a devotional selection, and Schoenberg obliged with what was to be his final completed composition, a choral setting of Psalm 150.[7]

In 1974, in honor of its one hundredth anniversary, Congregation Anshe Emet of Chicago commissioned special Sabbath liturgical music from many composers: Samuel Adler, Charles Davidson, Herbert Fromm, Maurice Goldman, Shalom Katib, Frederick Piket, Heinrich Schalit, Sholom Secunda, and Lazar Weiner.

Among those receiving commissions for music celebrating the American Bicentennial were the following Jewish composers: David Diamond, Jacob Druckman, David Epstein, Morton Feldman, Lukas Foss, Morton Gould, Leon Kirchner, and George Rochberg. The works created were later published independently by the various composers.

Over the years, a number of other commissioning projects on behalf of Jewish music, for the liturgy as well as general performance, have been fulfilled in the United States, Canada, and abroad, especially in the State of Israel. In 1978, to assist Jewish communal centers, schools, organizations, temples, and synagogues, the National Jewish Music Council issued a guidance resource on the commissioning process, along with models and samplings of such activities and programs.[8] It described commissioning as follows:

Historically, some of the greatest music works were created because of direct commission patronage. Alive by miracle! Commissioning is the approaching of a composer by an individual, group, or organization, with a definite assignment, time limit, and specified payment. Any commission project ought to have a ready medium for performance of the work... The composer thus is given an important function to perform... Does every commission guarantee a masterpiece? Nevertheless, the project is worthwhile in and of itself.[9]

NOTES

1. Some consideration of the issue of the commissioning of Jewish music may be found among concluding text matter of Chapter 20 (Jewish Music in America). It was discussed there because of a particular topical application to the range of musical achievements in American life.

2. Irene Heskes, comp. and ed., *Jewish Music Programs: Concerts, Liturgical Services, and Multi-Arts Events; and How to Commission New Works: Guidelines, Procedures, and Examples* (New York: Jewish Music Council, 1978), pp. 107–24.

3. *The Jewish Music Forum Bulletin* vol. 5, no. 1 (1944), pp. 23–24.

4. Those selections were published in a volume: David Putterman, comp., *Synagogue Music by Contemporary Composers: An Anthology of Compositions for Sabbath Eve Service* (New York: G. Schirmer, 1951).

5. A compilation of 125 commissioned liturgical selections was published as David Putterman, comp., *Mizmor L'David: An Anthology of Synagogue Music* (New York: Cantors Assembly, 1979).

6. That collection was published as Harry Coopersmith, comp., *The Songs We Sing* (Philadelphia: Jewish Publication Society of America, 1950).

7. Schoenberg's choral selection is included in Chemjo Vinaver, comp., *Anthology of Jewish Music: Sacred Chant and Religious Folksong of the East European Jews* (New York: E. B. Marks, 1955).

8. Heskes, comp. and ed., *Jewish Music Programs and How to Commission.*

9. Ibid., pp. 7–8.

32

Some Thoughts on American Popular Songwriters: Berlin, Kern, Gershwin, and Arlen

The American Society of Composers, Authors, and Publishers (ASCAP) was founded in New York City in 1914 as a membership organization of, by, and for songwriters and their works. On their behalf, it licenses any performances and publications of copyrighted selections, collects the fees, and distributes that income in the form of royalty checks. Its outreach in function is national through district offices throughout the United States, and international in affiliation with performing rights societies throughout the world. One of its founders was the composer Victor Herbert (1859–1924).[1]

Scanning the roster of ASCAP members, one finds an impressive number of songwriters of Jewish background. The facts beg for examination of Judaic melodic elements in American popular songs, especially those created during the heyday of Broadway and Hollywood musicals from the 1920s into the 1970s. In particular, the influence of the songs and performers of the Yiddish American stage upon that abundant creativity might likely be a consideration for music scholars.[2] Among that multitude of twentieth-century America Jewish songwriters, four—Berlin, Kern, Gershwin, and Arlen—are briefly noted here as samplings from the rich reservoir of talent.

Irving (Izzy) Berlin (Israel Baline, 1888–1989) was born in Temun, Ukraine, the youngest of eight children of a sexton and sometime cantor. The family emigrated to America and settled on the Lower East Side of New York City in 1893. Within four years the father had died, and Izzy began to help support his family by selling newspapers and singing for pennies on the streets. At the age of sixteen, he secured a job in a Bowery saloon as a singing waiter. He was not too good as a performer, but soon realized that he could write the songs, words as well as melodies, and wisely began to copyright and publish them. Some of his earliest ones were based upon Yiddish jingles: "Yiddle on Your Fiddle, Play Some Ragtime" (1909), "Yiddisha Eyes" and "That Kazzatsky Dance" (1910), "Yiddisha Nightingale" (1911), and "Yiddisha Professor Cohen" (1912). Berlin's

first big general success was the song "Marie from Sunny Italy" (1907). It was
followed three years later by the hit tune "Alexander's Ragtime Band" (1910),
and his songwriting career was launched.

Irving Berlin was not musically trained, and he composed at the piano only in
one key signature, F-sharp major. After he became financially secure, Berlin had
a special piano constructed with a lever for shifting the mechanism so that he
could listen to his melodies in various other keys. Though not formally musically
educated, he was a diligent craftsman, and over his long life composed and published more than seven hundred songs, most of which achieved wide popularity
in America as well as abroad. Berlin had an unfailing instinct for a lyric text as
well as a melody line. In that respect, he may be considered a true American
version of the Yiddish *badkh'n* (folk bard-minstrel), because he could cast the
feelings of the public into a dynamic folk essence. Witness how brilliantly so
many of his songs have captured, indeed shaped, the spirit of people and the
nature of their circumstances. "God Bless America" is generally treated as a second American national anthem. "White Christmas" and "Easter Parade" are
extremely popular secular songs for two Christian religious holidays. Throughout his active musical career, Berlin was able to produce the proper words with
the suitable tune at the appropriate time.

Although until his death in 1989 Irving Berlin's personal papers and archives
were unavailable to scholars and authors, those materials have been ceded over
to the research collections at the Library of Congress and the Lincoln Center for
the Performing Arts of the New York Public Library. The biographies issued
early in his life were approved narratives, but some later works do afford in-
depth studies of the man and his music.[3]

To what extent did his Judaic heritage influence Berlin's creativity? Likely a
native musicality was inherited from his cantorial father, but it is unlikely that in
America he had much connection with Jewish music per se. His first wife was
Jewish and died tragically with an infant in childbirth. He waited thirteen years
before remarrying a Christian woman, with whom he had three daughters. There
do not appear to be any reflections regarding the Holocaust or the State of Israel
in his songs. During his last two decades of life, he was socially reclusive and
unproductive. Perhaps there is more to be learned about him from his papers and
memorabilia, or maybe not.

Jerome David Kern (1885–1945) was a native New Yorker born into a family
of comfortable circumstances. His grandfather had been the sexton at Temple
Emanu-El in New York City. Early a talented pianist, young Kern found employment demonstrating songs on Tin Pan Alley,[4] and by 1902 he had published
a song. In 1903, after taking courses in piano and composition at the New York
Musical College, he went to Europe for a year of advanced musical studies. Extremely prolific, most of his many songs were first shaped for a series of
Broadway (and London) theatricals, and later found their way into Hollywood
films. The greatest of those musical achievements was *Show Boat* (1927), based

upon a novel by Edna Ferber.[5] His musical creations followed the style of European operettas, with melodies that have proved equally comfortable for amateur singing and in professional repertoires.

Kern became highly successful not only as a songwriter but also as a publisher, and at one time was vice-president of T. B. Harms Company. While he always acknowledged his Jewish background, he was not associated in any way with Jewish music. There have been attempts to ferret out Judaic motifs in his melodies, especially for that perennial *Show Boat* song favorite, "Old Man River." Kern died just as World War II ended, and one may merely speculate on whether any later creativity would have reflected the Holocaust aftermath. He had led a pleasant, affluent life, and there are some interesting biographical treatments of him and his work.[6]

George (Gershovitz) Gershwin (1898–1937) greatly admired Jerome Kern's songs. Like Kern, he also began his musical career as a Tin Pan Alley publishers' pianist, which was truly a hands-on education in the art of songwriting. Gershwin was born in Brooklyn, and died in Hollywood just when he seemed to be on the threshold of more serious musical achievements. Largely self-taught, he early on was determined to have a musical career, and was a rehearsal pianist by the time he was fifteen. Al Jolson (1886–1950) gave Gershwin a first big success by putting his song "Swanee" into one of his shows, and then included it in his nationwide vaudeville performances. Soon much in demand, Gershwin wrote melodies for Broadway musicals and began to work with his brother, Ira Gershwin (1896–1983), as the lyricist for many of his songs. In 1924, he was invited by bandleader Paul Whiteman to compose a jazz-style concert selection. What emerged was Gershwin's "Rhapsody in Blue" for orchestra and piano, arranged by Ferde Grofé. Gershwin played the piano solo part for the premiere at Carnegie Hall.

Residing and composing in Hollywood during the 1930s, George Gershwin associated with a number of the émigré musicians in California, among them Arnold Schoenberg. He assisted Ernst Toch in emigrating to America and in securing music work with the film industry. Traveling abroad, Gershwin made a point of meeting and discussing music with Igor Stravinsky and Maurice Ravel, among other noted composers. A highly gifted pianist, he was serious about his music, and studied composition over the years with such teachers as Rubin Goldmark and Joseph Schillinger.

Although busy with songwriting for musicals, Gershwin was determined to write a large-scale theatrical work, much in the genre of Kern's *Show Boat*. The result was *Porgy and Bess* (1935), based upon a play by DuBose and Dorothy Hayward. In preparation for that work, George and Ira Gershwin visited the coastal Gullah area of Charleston, South Carolina, to acquaint themselves with the tunes and folklore of that African-American culture. As a result, elements of Gullah chants were incorporated into some of the music written for what has come to be considered a truly American opera.

In 1937 in New York City, Rabbi Stephen S. Wise eulogized Gershwin as a
musical genius. Speaking at a memorial for George Gershwin held in Los Angeles, Arnold Schoenberg said: "George Gershwin was one of this rare kind of
musicians [sic] to whom music is not a matter of more or less ability. Music to
him was the air he breathed, food which nourished him, drink that refreshed him.
Music was what made him feel, and music was the feeling he expressed. Direct-
ness of this kind is given only to great men, and there is no doubt that he was a
great composer. What he achieved was not only to the benefit of a national
American music, but also a contribution to the music of the whole world."[7]

Despite his brief life, George Gershwin has achieved a place among leading
creative figures of twentieth-century American music. His life and music has
inspired a number of published biographical studies.[8] He was briefly associated
with the Yiddish theater early in his life. At one time, actor-impresario Boris
Thomashefsky (1868–1939) had hoped that pairing Gershwin with Sholom Secunda (1894–1974) could produce another prolific Joseph Rumshinsky (1879–
1956) for Second Avenue. Ultimately, Secunda stayed there with the Yiddish
theaters, while Gershwin moved further uptown professionally and musically.

Harold Arlen (Hyman Arluck, 1905–198?) was born in Buffalo, New York,
into a cantorial family. A twin brother died at birth. His grandfather, Moses Arluck (Erlich), had emigrated from Vilna to serve a congregation in Louisville, and
his father, Samuel Arluck, held pulpits in Buffalo and then Syracuse. Both men
were associated with traditional services. By the age of seven, Harold Arlen was
a boy choir singer for his father. Two years later, he began piano studies, and at
sixteen was playing piano for public functions and club dates. Arlen soon organized his own band and toured the areas around upstate New York. His father
introduced him to an older Buffalo boy, Jack (Zelig) Yellen (1894–1991), who
had already gained recognition with his song "My Yiddishe Mama" (1925), and
the two songwriters remained fast friends for the rest of their lives.

Productive into the final decade of his life, Arlen wrote a great many songs,
generally lyrical ballads, for Broadway and the films. Though none actually relate
to Jewish expression, their melodic configurations nevertheless appear to echo
his liturgical background. His tunes are asymmetric, with ambiguity of major-
minor and with wandering cadences. In essence, while he labored hard at his
writing, the outcome appears improvisational, and that particular quality has
been the lasting charm and popularity of his melodies. Harold Arlen was a reserved individual, and biographically reticent during his life.[9] Interestingly, when
the road company of Gershwin's *Porgy and Bess* went to perform in the Soviet
Union in 1956, Harold Arlen accepted an invitation to go along.

At best, Arlen's music combines the popular music idiom of the blues with
older-style lyric melody. Sometimes, the Judaic liturgy comes forward recog-
nizably, and utterly as a pleasant surprise, as for example in his song, "Blues in
the Night," which shapes up as a ripe quotation of the High Holy Days *kaddish*
chant. "More than any other influence he might have had, the composer feels

that he owes his greatest debt to his father; his father's singing style, his way with melodic phrases, his ability to improvise hauntingly beautiful melodies, Arlen feels, were inherited. Or at least he lived with it long enough to have absorbed it."[10]

NOTES

1. ASCAP, from its main office in New York City, has distributed several types of public relations bulletins and information resources: a pamphlet, *ASCAP: The Facts*; a series of bulletins, *ASCAP Today*, *ASCAP News*, *ASCAP Playback*, and *ASCAP in Action*; and a roster listing that is periodically updated, *ASCAP Biographical Dictionary*.

2. For a full treatment of Yiddish popular songs, see Irene Heskes, *Yiddish American Popular Songs, 1895 to 1950* (Washington, D.C.: The Library of Congress, 1992). The book's introductory essay, "Copyrighted and Sung" (pp. xv–xxxviii), provides an overview of that genre as it developed and flourished in America during the first half of the twentieth century.

3. Among those later books are:

Michael Freedland, *Irving Berlin* (New York: Stein and Day, 1974).

Ian Whitcomb, *Irving Berlin and Ragtime America* (London: Century, 1987).

Laurence Bergreen, *As Thousands Cheer: The Life of Irving Berlin* (New York: Viking, 1990).

4. A songwriter and theater critic, Monroe Rosenfeld (1861–1918), coined the term "Tin Pan Alley" for an area of sheet music publishers first located on West 28th Street and later further uptown in New York City.

5. See Miles Kreuger, *Show Boat: The Story of a Classic American Musical* (New York: Oxford University Press, 1977).

6. For further biographical studies, see:

David Ewen, *The World of Jerome Kern: A Biography* (New York: Henry Holt, 1960).

Michael Freedland, *Jerome Kern* (London: Robson Books, 1978).

Gerald Bordman, *Jerome Kern: His Life and Music* (New York: Oxford University Press, 1980).

7. Quoted in Gdal Saleski, *Famous Musicians of Jewish Origin* (New York: Bloch Publishing, 1949), p. 65.

8. Among those publications are:

Edward Jablonski and Lawrence B. Stewart, *The Gershwin Years* (Garden City, N.Y.: Doubleday, 1958).

Robert Payne, *Gershwin* (New York: Pyramid Books, 1960).

David Ewen, *George Gershwin: His Journey to Greatness* (Englewood Cliffs, N.J.: Prentice Hall, 19700.

Charles Schwartz, *Gershwin: His Life and Music* (New York: Bobbs-Merrill, 1973).

Alan Kendall, *George Gershwin: A Biography* (London: Harrap, 1987).

Deena Rosenberg, *Fascinating Rhythm: The Collaboration of George and Ira Gershwin* (New York: Dutton, 1991).

9. There is one biographical study, written while Arlen was alive and with his approval: Edward Jablonski, *Harold Arlen: Happy with the Blues* (Garden City, N.Y.: Doubleday, 1961).

10. Ibid., p. 37.

33

Scripture as Creative Inspiration

In 1976, the Haifa Music Museum and Amli Library organized an exhibit on "The Old Testament in World Music," and in 1982 a smaller display featured "The Old Testament in the Works of George Frideric Handel." In connection with both showings at the museum, catalogue pamphlets were prepared, adding to a roster of other bibliographic booklets published by that museum and library under the rubric of the "Bible in music."[1] It appears that an essence of Judaic spirit appears to have infused much musical creativity by non-Jews, not a few of whom were associated with Jewish colleagues in the course of their careers.[2]

Of the many composers who derived inspiration from biblical texts, George Frideric Handel (1685–1759) remains the most fascinating. Along with Johann Sebastian Bach (1685–1750), he brought eighteenth-century baroque style to musical fruition. Both of those composers were deeply religious Lutheran Protestants. Bach turned for his inspiration to the charismatic leadership and otherworldly outlook of the New Testament. Handel, likely influenced by his Pietist background, looked to the prophetic qualities and humanism of the Old Testament. Bach never traveled beyond his native Saxony. Handel, after studying music in Italy, settled in England in 1810, where he remained for the rest of his life. His many works, especially the oratorios based upon Bible narratives, display the unique qualities of musical inspiration afforded to him by those texts.

"It was only in Handel's music, Nietzsche stated once in his categorical manner, that the best in Luther and in those like him found its voice, the Judeo-heroic trait which gave the Reformation a touch of greatness, the Old Testament, not the New, become music."[3] Small wonder that Felix Mendelssohn (1809–1847) greatly admired Handel's oratorios, modeling his own *Elijah* after those works. Indeed, Mendelssohn oversaw German text versions, edited the music, and performed those Handel oratorios, among which his avowed favorite was the dramatic exposition of the Exodus, *Israel in Egypt*.[4] The characters in Handel's oratorios were heroic Jewish figures, the most significant of which was

Judas Maccabaeus. That hero sings: "Sound an alarm, your silver trumpets sound; and call the brave and only brave around. Who listens follow to the field again; justice with courage is a thousand men." Handel also celebrated biblical women, Deborah and Esther. Over half the text of his Christological oratorio *Messiah* was derived from the following portions of the Old Testament: Isaiah, Malachi, Zechariah, Job, and Psalms. In 1866, at the formal dedication of the Great London Synagogue, Handel's music was played and sung.

From the tenth century onward, music as well as the visual art forms infused the churches of a rapidly developing European Christianity. Along with the use of paintings and sculptures depicting biblical events and personalities, music began to delineate Holy Writ for the multitudes. Medieval music dramas with Latin texts were performed in the churches, especially on festival days between services, generally matins (afternoon) and lauds (eventide Psalms). They were intended as scriptural lessons, performed in simple style without instrumentation, by male singers and priest narrators. That practice was analogous in Judaism to the Sabbath and holidays synagogue study hours between *minkha* (afternoon) and *ma-ariv/arvit* (evening). Extended versions of the church lessons were known as mystery plays, and in them full biblical stories would be recounted in the local vernaculars as well as church Latin. During the Renaissance, holiday pageants and entertainments often adapted biblical stories as allegories and morality tales.

By the sixteenth century, a newer sacred musical form had arisen to great popularity—the oratorio, named for the oratory chapel in which it was initially performed. Elements of the mystery plays and biblical lessons were merged with an extended dramatic musical exposition. Presented without costumes or scenery, the oratorio was more elaborate textually and melodically, featuring vocal soloists and choruses and, increasingly, performed with an organ or instrumental ensemble. The spread of the Reformation movement and Protestantism spurred interest in the Old Testament, as did a rise in the eighteenth century of classicism, which turned to the ancient Greeks, antiquity, and the biblical era for artistic inspiration. Untheatrical and often austerely spiritual, the oratorio emerged as a religious counterpart to secularly staged opera, upon which any representation from the Bible was not approved, especially in Catholic communities. A biblical subject was not performed at the Paris Opera House until 1890.

The most religiously contemplative of oratorio compositions were the Christian concert-masses and passions. For Judaism, the concert presentation of religious services or of works setting biblical (Old Testament) and liturgical texts might also be considered oratorios. A shorter form of nonstaged dramatic work, the cantata, unlike the oratorio, could be based upon secular as well as spiritual themes and texts.

There is no intention here of presenting examples of biblically inspired music as "Jewish." However, a selected roster of such works by both Christians and Jews is ample evidence of the cultural linkage to Holy Scripture and its abiding influence upon melodic creativity over the centuries. Biographical dates are given at the first mention of each composer and only where a necrology has been verified.

Torah/Pentateuch—Five Books of Moses (Genesis, Exodus, Leviticus, Numbers, and Deuteronomy):

Franz Joseph Haydn (1732–1809)—*The Creation*, oratorio.

Aaron Copland (1900–1990)—*In the Beginning*, choral work.

Darius Milhaud (1892–1974)—*La Creation du Monde* (The creation of the world), instrumental ensemble, with narration, also as ballet music.

Gunter Bialos—*Im Anfang* (In the beginning), oratorio.

Anton Rubenstein (?1829/30–1894)—*Tower of Babel*, oratorio.

Igor Stravinsky (1882–1971)—*Noah and the Flood*, ballet music.

Giovanni Carissimi (1604–1674)—*Abraham and Isaac*, oratorio.

Alessandro Scarlatti (?1659/60–1725)—*Abraham's Sacrifice*, oratorio.

Igor Stravinsky—*Abraham and Isaac*, oratorio

César Franck (1822–1890)—*Rebecca*, operatic scene

Arnold Schoenberg (1874–1951)—*Jakobsleiter* (Jacob's ladder), oratorio.

Johann Kuhnau (1660–1722)—*Jacob's Marriage*, piano sonata.

Lazare Saminsky (1882–1959)—*Rachel's Lament*, ballet music.

Nathaniel Shilkret (1889–1982)—commissioned a biblical suite, *Genesis*, composed of the following instrumental selections: "Creation," by Shilkret; "Adam and Eve," by Alexander Tansman; "Cain and Abel," by Darius Milhaud; "Noah's Ark," by Mario Castelnuovo-Tedesco (1895–1968); "Babel," by Igor Stravinsky; "Covenant," by Ernst Toch (1887–1964); and "Postlude to Genesis," by Arnold Schoenberg.

G. F. Handel—*Joseph and His Brothers*, oratorio.

Robert Starer—*Joseph and His Brothers*, cantata.

Andrew Lloyd Webber—*Joseph and His Amazing Technicolor Dreamcoat*, a children's operetta.

David Diamond—*Young Joseph*, a choral work.

Richard Strauss (1864–1949)—*The Legend of Joseph*, ballet music.

Marc Lavry (1903–1967)—*Amnon and Tamar*, opera.

G. F. Handel—*Israel in Egypt*, oratorio.

Carl Philipp Emanuel Bach (1714–1788)—*Israelites in the Wilderness*, oratorio.

Gioacchino Rossini (1792–1868)—*Moses in Egypt*, oratorio/opera.

Arnold Schoenberg—*Moses und Aron* (Moses and Aaron), opera.

Franz Schubert (1797–1828)—*Song of Miriam*, choral work.

Stefan Wolpe (1902–1972)—*The Man from Midian*, ballet music.

Felicien David (1810–1876)—*Moses on Sinai*, oratorio.

Anton Rubinstein—*Moses*, oratorio/opera.

Joseph Tal—*Exodus*, orchestra and electronic instrumentation.

Jacob Weinberg (1879–1956)—*The Life of Moses*, oratorio.
Darius Milhaud—*Moses*, ballet music.

Haftarah—Earlier Prophets (Joshua, Judges, Samuel, Kings [Saul, David, Solomon]):
G. F. Handel—*Joshua*, oratorio.
Modest Mussorgsky (1839–1881)—*The Fall of Jericho*, cantata.
G. F. Handel—*Deborah*, oratorio.
Ildebrando Pizzetti (1880–1968)—*Deborah and Jael*, opera.
  Antonio Vivaldi (1678–1741)—*Juditha Triumphans* (Judith triumphant), oratorio.
George Chadwick (1854–1931)—*Judith*, opera.
Arthur Honegger (1892–1955)—*Judith*, opera.
William Schuman (1910–1992)—*Judith*, ballet music.
Giacomo Carissimi—*Jephthah*, musical tableaux
G. F. Handel—*Jephthah*, oratorio.
  Giacomo Meyerbeer (1791–1864)—*The Vow of Jephthah*, an uncompleted opera.
Lazare Saminsky—*Jephthah*, opera.
Ernst Toch—*Jephthah*, symphonic work.
G. F. Handel—*Samson*, oratorio.
Camille Saint-Saëns (1835–1921)—*Samson and Delilah*, opera.
Rubin Goldmark (1872–1936)—*Samson*, orchestral work.
Isadore Freed (1900–1960)—*Prophecy of Micah*, oratorio.
  Abraham W. Binder (1895–1966)—*The Birth of Samuel* (Eli and Hannah), cantata.
G. F. Handel—*Saul*, oratorio.
Charles H. H. Parry (1848–1918)—*King Saul*, oratorio.
Arthur Honegger—*Saul*, incidental music for a drama.
Joseph Tal—*Saul at Endor*, opera.
Giacomo Carissimi—*David and Goliath*, narrator and instruments.
Wolfgang Amadeus Mozart (1756–1791)—*Davide Penitente*, oratorio.
Darius Milhaud—*David*, opera.
Mario Castelnuovo-Tedesco—*David*, piano solo
Richard Strauss—*King David*, symphonic work.
  Arthur Honegger—*King David*, narrator and singers, with an instrumental ensemble.
  Paul Ben-Haim (1897–1984)—*Sweet Psalmist of Israel* (King David), symphonic work.
Karl Salomon (1897–1974)—*David and Goliath*, cantata.
G. F. Handel—*King Solomon*, oratorio.
  Ernest Bloch (1880–1959)—*Schelomo: Hebrew Rhapsody*, for the cello and orchestra.

Charles Gounod (1818–1893)—*The Queen of Sheba*, opera.
Karl Goldmark (1830–1915)—*Queen of Sheba*, opera.
Darius Milhaud—*Le Reine de Saba* (The Queen of Sheba), string quartet.

Haftarah—Later Prophets (Elijah, Isaiah, Jeremiah, Ezekiel):
Note: Many works inspired by the Prophets also include passages from other portions of the Bible.
Felix Mendelssohn (1809–1847)—*Elijah*, oratorio.[5]
Paul Ben-Haim—*Isaiah*, choral work.
Lukas Foss—*Song of Anguish* (Isaiah), cantata.
Julius Chajes (1910–1985)—*Zion, Rise and Shine* (Isaiah), cantata.
Frederick Converse (1871–1940)—*Prophecy* (Isaiah), voice and orchestra.
Randall Thompson (1899–1984)—*The Peaceable Kingdom* (Isaiah), choral work.
Robert Starer—*Ariel: Visions of Isaiah*, cantata.

Note: Excerpts from the Book of Lamentations usually are included in texts for Jeremiah.
Mario Castelnuovo-Tedesco—*The Prophets* (Isaiah, Jeremiah, Elijah), violin concerto.
Ernst Krenek (1900–1991)—*Lamentatis Jeremiah Prophetae*, male chorus.
Leonard Bernstein (1918–1990)—*Jeremiah*, symphony.
Herman Berlinski—*Symphonic Visions: Jeremiah*, instrumental work.
Alberto Ginastera—*Lamentations of Jeremiah*, male chorus.
Verdina Shlonsky—*Jeremiah*, symphonic work.
Ralph Vaughan Williams (1872–1958)—*Ezekiel*, choral work.
G. F. Handel—*Athalia*, oratorio.

Haftarah—Minor Prophets (Hosea, Joel, Amos, Obadiah, Jonah, Micah, Nahum, Habakkuk, Zephaniah, Haggai, Zechariah, Malachi):
Note: A great many vocal and choral texts include selected passages from those prophetic portions.

K'tuvim/Hagiographa—Sacred Writings and Scrolls (Psalms, Proverbs, Job, Song of Songs, Ruth, Lamentations, Ecclesiastes, Esther, Daniel, Ezra, Nehemiah, and Chronicles):
Note: There is likely no composer in the recorded history of Western society who has not set to music some passages from the Book of Psalms. It is the bedrock of highly personal religious expression for Christians as well as Jews. Handel and Mendelssohn set individual Psalms and also included them in their oratorios. Jewish liturgists and musicians have ceaselessly reflected upon those texts, for all sacred devotions as well as in a wide range of secular works, and their poetics pervade the folk song literature in every Judaic vernacular.

Ben-Haim, Bloch, Milhaud, Schoenberg, and Castelnuovo-Tedesco have set the Psalms.

Of particular interest are these settings:

Paul Ben-Haim—*Sweet Psalmist of Israel,* orchestral work

Leonard Bernstein—*Chichester Psalms,* choral with orchestra. Texts are intended to be sung in biblical Hebrew, and conclude with the excerpt from Psalm 33: "Behold how good and how pleasant it is, for brethren to dwell together in unity."

Igor Stravinsky—*Symphony of Psalms,* choral with orchestra. Its third movement is a magnificent instrumental and vocal rendition of that great hymn to music, Psalm 150.

Zoltán Kodály (1882–1967)—*Psalm Hungaricus,* choral with orchestra. In this work Hungarian folk motifs set text from Psalm 137: "By the waters of Babylon."

Charles Ives (1874–1954)—*Psalms,* voices and instruments. There are individual settings of about two dozen Psalms, including Psalm 14: "Oh that the salvation of Israel were come out of Zion! When the Lord bringeth back the captivity of his people, Jacob shall rejoice, and Israel shall be glad."

Darius Milhaud—*Cantate des Proverbes* (Cantata from Proverbs), female voices and instrumental ensemble.

Ralph Vaughan Williams—*The Voice Out of the Whirlwind* (from Job and Proverbs), choral work.

Luigi Dallapiccola (1904–1975)—*Job,* choral work.

Charles H. H. Parry—*Job,* choral work.

Frederick Jacobi (1891–1952)—*Hagiographa* (Job, Ruth, Joshua), string quartet with piano.

As with the Book of Psalms, over the centuries many musical works also have been inspired by the Songs of Songs: The Song of Solomon. Obviously, its lyrical poetry has been particularly favored in love songs and wedding odes. Those Hebrew texts are widely used by Israeli popular composers. Rabbinical tradition, on the other hand, has allegorically interpreted its biblical message as reflecting a great bond between the Jewish people and *Torah*.

Darius Milhaud—*Cante Nuptiale* (Wedding Songs), cantata. Texts from the Song of Songs were used for a work celebrating the fiftieth wedding anniversary in 1937 of the composer's parents.

Lukas Foss—*Song of Songs,* cantata.

Note: Another biblical text favored for wedding odes has been that of the passage from the Book of Ruth: "Entreat me not to leave thee."

Michael Ippolitov-Ivanov (1859–1935)—*Ruth,* opera.

Frederic H. Cowen (1852–1935)—*Ruth,* opera.

Mario Castelnuovo-Tedesco—*Naomi and Ruth,* cantata for female voices.

Miklos Rozsa—*A Time to Plant* (from Ecclesiastes), choral work.

Norman Dello Joio—*Meditations on Ecclesiastes*, string ensemble.
Robert Starer—*Koheleth* (Ecclesiastes), choral work.

G. F. Handel—*Esther*, oratorio. This is a true *Purim* celebration work because it gives an exposition of the Scroll of Esther.
Darius Milhaud—*Esther of Carpentras*, opera. It is a narrative with reflections upon the biblical story.
Abraham W. Binder—*Esther, Queen of Persia*, cantata.
Gioacchino Rossini—*Cyrus in Babylonia*, opera.
Giuseppe Verdi (1813–1901)—*Nabucco* (Nebuchadnezzar), opera.
Darius Milhaud—*Miracles of Faith* (from Daniel), cantata.
G. F. Handel—*Belshazzar* (Daniel), oratorio. Includes the text: "*Mene, mene, tekel upharsin*. Thou art weighed in the balance and found wanting."
Henry Hadley (1871–1937)—*Belshazzar*, oratorio
William Walton (1902–1983)—*Belshazzar's Feast*, oratorio.

Apochrypha—Additional Writings (Ecclesiasticus, Maccabees):
G. F. Handel—*Judas Maccabaeus*, oratorio.
Anton Rubinstein—*Maccabees*, opera.

NOTES

1. The Haifa Music Museum and Amli Library, located in Haifa and at a branch in Tel Aviv, Israel, issued the following catalogue resource publications:
Claude Abravanel and Betty Hirshowitz, comps., *The Bible in English Music: William Byrd (1543–1623) and Henry Purcell (1659–1695)*, English text, 1972.
Moshe Gorali and Betty Hirshowitz, comps., *The Old Testament in World Music*, Hebrew and English texts, 1976.
Moshe Gorali and Betty Hirshowitz, comps., *The Old Testament in the Works of Johann Sebastian Bach (1685–1750)*, Hebrew text, 1979.
Moshe Gorali and Rivka Watson, comps., *The Old Testament in the Works of George Frideric Handel (1685–1759)*, Hebrew and English texts, 1982.
2. Two articles treat the subject of relationships between Jews and non-Jewish composers:
Alexander Ringer, "Handel and the Jews," *Music and Letters*, vol. 42, no. 1 (1961), pp. 17–29.
Paul Nettl, "Jewish Connections of Some Classical Composers: Bach's Sons, Mozart, and Beethoven," *Music and Letters*, vol. 45, no. 4 (1964), pp. 337–44.
3. Quoted in Ringer, "Handel and the Jews," p. 17. Alexander Ringer's own citation for this statement appears as "Nietzsche Contra Wagner," in *Complete Works*, Vol. 8, ed. by Oscar Levy (London, 1924), pp. 63–64.

4. A good study of that musical relationship is Hellmuth Christian Wolff, trans. from German by Ernest Sanders and Luise Eitel, "Mendelssohn and Handel," *The Musical Quarterly*, vol. 45, no. 2 (1959), pp. 175–90.

5. In his review of a book about Felix Mendelssohn (R. Larry Todd, ed., *Mendelssohn and His World* [Princeton, N.J.: Princeton University Press, 1991]), the reviewer, Greg Vitercik, concludes with these remarks:

The problem of locating Mendelssohn in the complex landscape of Judaism, Christianity, and conversion, is clearly central to a fuller understanding of his life, his music, and his world; but it presses far beyond the rather comfortably parochial domains of music history and biography, and a coherent view of the larger social and historical contexts in which that understanding must itself be located continues to elude us. In this, too, it would appear Mendelssohn remains, as Donald Tovey put it, one of the strangest, and perhaps most illuminating, problems in European music history.

This review appeared in *Music Library Association Notes*, vol. 49, no. 3 (1993), p. 1005.

Part X

Women

34

Miriam's Sisters: Jewish Women and Liturgical Music

Over the centuries, Jewish and Christian women expressed their faiths through music, either in private or among groups of other devout women. Otherwise, the mainstream of communal and general society usually relegated women to the background in liturgical music. To view women's music making in terms of biblical legacy and early theological traditions raises significant issues about the historic role of women in religious ritual and in melodic creativity. Reconsidering the venerable tradition banning *vox feminae* (woman's voice; in Hebrew, *kol ishah*) from liturgical services is particularly important for our contemporary society. Evolving changes in religious perceptions among leaders in the Reform and Conservative branches of Judaism currently permit opportunities for the training and placement of women as cantors to lead synagogue prayers. In Christian congregations as well, women are becoming more visible, serving as music directors of services and as performers and composers.[1]

From Exodus 15:20 we learn that Miriam, tambourine in hand, led the Hebrew women to a location outside the desert encampment. There they sang and danced, intoning what appears to have been a refrain or responsive musical text for Moses' hymn of triumph after crossing the Red Sea. Those women at their celebration site may have been expressing music that went beyond a mere echoing of the men's chorus. While this particular biblical passage indicates a separation of male and female musical performances, further along the biblical narrative, in Judges 5, the prophet and leader Deborah and her military adjutant Barak together sing her battle hymn of praise and thanksgiving. Later, in Judges 11:34, we learn that Jephthah's daughter came out to meet him in Mizpah, accompanied by *mevaseroth*—women who celebrated Hebrew victories with songs and dances. After David slew Goliath and defeated the Philistines (1 Samuel 18:6–7), multitudes of *mevaseroth* sang his praises, much to the consternation of King Saul. Clearly the activities of those women musicians served a significant communal ritual function.

In later biblical sections, the role of female musicians becomes increasingly obscure and then all but disappears in descriptions of liturgical practices. This trend might reflect alterations made by subsequent compilers of the biblical texts, who sought to cleanse the sacred writings of any paganlike ceremonies. By the time the Holy Scriptures were codified, early religious leaders in both rabbinic Judaism and formative Christianity had displaced women from any leadership role in the ritual functions.[2] Such revisionism is apparent in Talmudic writings, as, for example, in the biblical exegesis *Bamidbar rabbah*, chapter 10, which includes the following passage: "How was Solomon, the wisest man in the world, misled by his wives to the worship of idols? By means of music. The daughter of Pharaoh, Solomon's favorite wife, brought with her a thousand different kinds of musical instruments, and ordered that they be played for Solomon, saying, 'thus do we play for Osiris and thus for Ophais.' Solomon was charmed and his senses were beguiled."[3]

Yet Bible texts continue to note women's participation in music and dance at secular celebrations (as, for example, in 2 Samuel 19:35, Jeremiah 31:4, and Ecclesiastes 2:8) and as wailing mourners (in Jeremiah 9:19). Women's musical popularity away from the religious sanctuary persisted. Following upon the successful siege of Jerusalem by the Assyrians (ca.701 B.C.E.), Hezekiah, king of Judah, sent men and women singers to Nineveh as part of a ransom tribute.[4] Women were likely also among the musicians "singing songs of Zion" (Psalm 137) who were taken into captivity after the Babylonian conquest.

During the pre-Temple era, women had been assigned the eastern end of the ritual tent, where maidens and widowed women, generally of Levite families, would sing at services. The First Temple appears to have had an auxiliary "court of women," probably with its own women's choir. Especially during the festival pilgrimages, women dancers and musicians participated in celebrations held outside the inner Temple area. Secular female singers, called *sharoth* in biblical texts, performed at the courts of Judean kings. At least for a time, groups of male and female singers, noted by both Ezra and Nehemiah as "the children of Asaph," participated in communal festivities during the Second Commonwealth Temple Era.[5]

It was during the Judean Commonwealth Era that women professional singers, possibly wives and daughters of Levites, appear to have participated in the life-cycle rites of marriage and death, but with increasing restrictions on such music making, in negative religious reaction to pagan Egyptian, Hellenist, and Roman influences. According to descriptions of the services conducted in the Temple of Solomon, the devotional music detailed the duties of the Levites and featured their basic musical texts, the psalmody. The Book of Psalms was attributed to King David, who was celebrated as the epitome of a great musician, someone who also danced before the Ark of the Lord. By the early Diaspora era, that musical tradition was preserved as a legacy from the ancient Holy Temple. Men had domain of sacred ritual music with its liturgical texts, melodies, and instrumentation. Women focused upon the secular music of domestic celebrations and folk expressions. Though informally participating at home in "sacred bridge" songs for Sabbath and holiday observances, women performed under the stricture of *kol isha be-lakhash* (woman's voice in veiled intonation). For diasporic Judaism, those distinctions took firm hold and prevailed: sacred music was performed by men, secular music by women as well as men.

Only a scattered number of historical references remain as clues to the music made by women in antiquity. By the time that the Alexandrian Jewish philosopher Philo Judaeus (ca.30 B.C.E.–40 C.E.) and the Roman Jewish historian Josephus (ca.37 C.E.–ca.95 C.E.) were writing, women musicians no longer played any distinctive part in public music. According to Philo's *Antiquitates Judaicae*, women during Herod's time had been entirely displaced at festivals by singing boys, and women who publicly sang or played the flute, harp, and tambour were considered harlots. Philo, however, described liturgical services in Alexandria among the Therapeutae, a dissident sect, whose adherents chanted the hymns and Psalms in two choirs, male and female, each led by a precentor. Their religious music was sung in three ways—alternately, responsively, or in unison—and was accompanied by rhythmic hand signs along with some dance motions.

In the early Christian Era, serious ecclesiastical strictures were placed on women musicians at liturgical ceremonies, not only by rabbinical leaders but also quite firmly by the Church Fathers. This parallel in religious practice proved highly significant in the developing rules governing gender and religious expression. Early on, in both synagogue and church, instruments were abandoned and only males were allowed to chant the ritual services. The melodic artistry of women and, indeed, their types of instrumentation had become associated with pagan customs, with lapses from the true virtues of Judaic and Christian observances, and with manifestations of immoral conduct.[6]

When Paul of Tarsus (St. Paul) instructed that women be silent in the assemblies (1 Corinthians 14:33–36), his ruling conformed strictly with that of the Pharisees and with the synagogue practices of his time. Yet, over the next centuries, Talmudic scholars and church theologians wavered in their attitudes. St. Ambrose championed the Psalm singing of Christian women, though never in unison with men. Talmudic literature showed appreciation for the singing of women as a divine gift. The pressures of pagan European cultures, however, gradually stiffened the positions of rabbis and church leaders. The *Mishnah* (the body of traditional Judaic doctrines redacted by the end of the third century) explicitly excluded women from participating in the liturgy. A passage in a later Talmudic *Midrash* (the homiletic commentary) warned women against attending theatricals and circuses, despite indications that those events included notable Jewish performers during the heyday of the Roman Empire. A Roman catacomb dating from the second century contains the sarcophagus of a prominent actress-singer named Faustina, identified as a practicing Jew by special symbols and Hebrew letters.

According to fourth-century rabbinical dicta, female responses to Psalms chanted by male voices were permitted, but not in the context of prayer services. A leading rabbinical scholar of the time, the Amora Rav Joseph, permitted responsive choral singing for women but denied them any leadership role.[7] Particularly in Asia Minor, attitudes were more relaxed, and women chanted prayers well into the fifth century. Within emergent Christianity, Gnostic religious ideas, along with the presence in heartland Europe of a substantial number of converts, reinforced the aversion to heretical—particularly female—songs and musical customs. Many Christian synods forbade parents to teach their daughters worldly music of any kind, and some even excommunicated women who made music at grave vigils. Eventually, the music of Christian women retreated into the convents, where nuns were carefully schooled to chant Psalms and hymns in a subdued manner (*kol ishah le-lakhash,* as it were). One remarkably creative figure from convent life was the Abbess Hildegard of Bingen (1098–1179) at the Benedictine monastery of Disilbodenberg, a prolific composer of music for the liturgy and a fine poet of her faith.

Among Jews there remained certain professional female musicians whose music was actively sought by their communities. Well into the later Middle Ages, especially among the Hispanic-Sephardic and Oriental-Near Eastern Jewish traditions, there were women whose singing and instrumentation prevailed at funerals and serious processions. Moreover, weddings and feasts were enhanced by female musicians, who were, however, usually relegated solely to female groupings. Since biblical times, there had been the wailing women (*mekonenoth*), whose lamentations (*inui*) were intoned individually and in chorus. As documented in Talmudic tracts, those artists performed prescribed threnodies. Especially in the Mediterranean area, women could be engaged to sing threnodies (*midrashe*) at burials. Well into the fourteenth century, Moorish wailing women (*endicheras*), and often also Jewish women, were hired by Christians in various Iberian communities to perform the lamentations at funerals and to provide general entertainment for special occasions.

The Crusades (ca.1040–ca.1230), along with the political conflicts and the general human distress at the time, threw Europe into social and religious upheaval. Men and women publicly sang, danced, and played all varieties of instruments. During that period, the Catholic Church began to consolidate its rulings concerning liturgical music. As in the strict synagogue tradition, instruments had been totally banned from the services along with the female voice. Jewish and Christian women were required to chant their prayers quietly at home or among groups of women. Church services soon began utilizing *castrati,* or adult eunuchs, whose singing together with young boy choristers carried to a morbid extreme an aesthetic desire for high voices in liturgical musical performance. The terms "soprano" and "alto" presumed male definition.

Nevertheless, people could not be prevented from developing and enjoying mundane music, such as folk songs and a range of ethnic cultural expression. Set apart from the religious domain, troubadours and minstrels traveled throughout Europe, disseminating varied melodies, spreading musical styles from one community to another, and even influencing the ritual music of the faiths.

Sensitive to the dynamics of their host societies, Jewish communities in Europe reflected all those cultural changes and strengthened their own codes of religious and social behavior. The male domain of synagogue music nourished the development of a distinctive liturgical music elaborated for the professional precentor-cantor (*hazzan*) and the male choir (*meshorerim*), which was composed of boys and adult men. Other male liturgical officiants included a scriptural reader-chanter (*ba'al korey*) and the generally nonprofessional prayer-leader (*ba'al tefiloh*). Women were physically separated during the services, curtained off or confined in upper galleries. The musical expression of Jewish women then turned to vernacular music. Wherever Jews settled in the Diaspora, they became bilingual. The liturgy and its cognate theological expressions remained in Hebrew and continued being the domain of men. At the same time, there arose various adaptive Jewish languages of diasporic life: Aramaic; Judaic Old French and Romans (*me-oz lo'am*); Judeo-Spanish, or Ladino; the German-Hebraic-Slavic Yiddish; and a variant Arabic. Inasmuch as those vernaculars were spoken at home and in the wayfare of everyday communal life, women took on the local tongues as their special societal and cultural expression and used them for their songs.

The influences of wandering Jewish and non-Jewish minstrels, with their secularized poetry and music, spurred the growth of such folk music. Jewish troubadours helped fashion special holiday and Sabbath songs, distinctive table carols (*zemirot*) that the entire family could sing at home. Maimonides (1135–1204), the towering rabbinical scholar and codifier of Jewish law, disapproved of women's singing, and indeed of secular music in general. The impact of his opinions affected traditional Jewish practices and even influenced the thinking among Christian and Moslem theologians.[8] Nevertheless, Jews of those medieval times sang the songs of the troubadours, which they changed into Judeo-vernaculars. Music iconography from that era shows Jewish marriage ceremonies with female musicians entertaining female guests, playing such instruments as the hurdy-gurdy while singing.[9]

In central Europe, not only were there women's music entertainments among themselves, but there are indications that there were liturgical services conducted entirely apart from the men.[10] In some of the Rhineland congregations, female worshippers had separate buildings (likely serving also as ritual women's baths) for their own services, connected with the main houses of worship by a gallery. In such cases, it was the custom to have specially trained female precentors conduct the independent services, as well as other ceremonies, for the women of the community. Records from the thirteenth-century annals of Worms and

Nuremberg refer to female precentors with picturesque names such as Urania and Richenza. Those professional liturgists were called (in Old Rhenish German) *saegerin* and later (in Yiddish), *sogern*.

Jewish children were generally taught the rudiments of music. In preparation for their active roles as members of congregations, boys learned to intone biblical cantillations and prayer chants. Girls often learned to play instruments, perhaps viol or keyboard, as part of their education for proper adult womanhood and marriage. Wherever Jews achieved some measure of social stability and economic opportunity, they sought to enhance their cultural levels of expression. Of course, the stresses of survival and the pressures of uprootedness often curtailed such opportunities and limited the range of creative expression in the arts. Consequently, the most consistent form of musical continuity may be found in religious devotions and in expressions of folk identity.

As secular performers, and probably as creators or adapters of music, Jewish women became notable outside the Jewish community during the Renaissance in Italy.[11] The gifted poet and musician Sarah Coppio Sullam (ca.1590–1641) organized salon concerts in her home in Venice, to which she invited the leading musical and literary figures of her time.[12] In the mid-sixteenth century, Madonna Bellina Hebrea (fl. 16th cent.) was a celebrated musician who sang, played various instruments, and composed music. In the seventeenth century, the Jewess Rachel Hebrea (fl. 16th–17th cent.) was frequently permitted to leave the confines of the Venetian ghetto in order to sing and play her music for the gentry of Venice and surrounding communities. A better-known name in music history is that of Madama Europa (fl. 16th–17th cent.), a member of the Jewish Rossi family of noted musicians. As a renowned singer of her time and place, she performed the innovative "Lamento" aria by Claudio Monteverdi at the Mantuan court of the Gonzagas in 1608. Somewhat later, another Jewish woman from Mantua, Hanna Norsa (fl. 17th cent.) found her way to London and in 1732 created the role of Polly Peachum in the *Beggar's Opera*.[13]

European Jewish homes became the private locations for increasingly elaborate *Purim* (Feast of Lots) musicales and socials, at which men and women danced, sang, and played musical instruments. Women taught each other songs and, in the process of making music together, often picked up tunes from non-Jewish neighbors, adapting them to their own milieu. In turn, they passed along Jewish melodies to gentile women with whom they had contact. Most women appeared to prefer the lute or clavichord as accompaniment for versified ballads. The Jewish diarist Glueckel of Hameln (1645–1724) wrote in her memoirs that her stepsister, while playing the spinet-clavicembalom at home, happened to hear a conversation between two visitors and thus was able to foil a blackmail attempt upon their father.[14]

Throughout those centuries, there were non-Jewish women balladeers and minstrels (*juglars* and *minnersinger*). Likewise, there were Jewish women musicians, usually wives and daughters of balladeers (*badkhonim*) and instrumentalists (*klezmorim*), all traveling together to earn a modest livelihood. Such entertainer families would perform at weddings and would especially enliven the Jewish communal festivity of *Purim* as holiday players (*purimshpiler*) with playlets, songs, dances, costumes, and pageantry. During the seventeenth and eighteenth centuries, the Jewish delegates to the Polish Council of the Four Lands regulated liturgical music and secular entertainments by obliging their own religious officiants and other types of musicians to apply for special licenses. Rabbinical authorities often made legal arrangements to ensure proper music for special occasions, and women generally were restricted as performers in those eastern European areas.

By the nineteenth century, Jewish secular entertainers had begun to achieve a measure of social acceptance, hastened undoubtedly by the spread of a modernist, or enlightenment (*haskalah*), movement in Jewish life and its advocacy of cultural enrichment. With that gradual rise in status, musically talented Jewish women ventured increasingly into the arts. Overwhelmingly, however, routes to public performance remained marriage to a Jewish entertainer or, more likely, moving out into the general world of artistic opportunities.

Particularly from 1876 onward, the Yiddish theatrical innovations of Abraham Goldfaden (1840–1908) and his performing troupes, traveling to Jewish communities in Russia, Romania, Austria, and Poland, gave rise to formalized performances with bands of singers and instrumentalists in operettas.[15] Those productions represented a Jewish genre, that featured women (rather than young boys) in the female roles, and even had special set pieces for the female performers. Eventually this theatrical art and its artists crossed the European continent and, by the late nineteenth century, emigrated to America, where those male and female entertainers rapidly adopted the qualities and societal patterns of their American counterparts. No longer considered social outsiders, the male actors became matinee idols and the actresses, role models for their audiences.

More significantly, Jewish women in America took on music leadership roles on the stage and performed all kinds of songs, including even chants of liturgical significance. For example, Sophie Karp (1861–1906), who had been discovered and trained for the stage by Goldfaden, became the toast of Yiddish theatricals, which were then flourishing in the Bowery theaters on the Lower East Side of New York City. In 1896, Karp introduced a Yiddish ballad written especially for her by the composer and music conductor Peretz Sandler (1853–1931). That selection was *Eili (Eyli), Eili*, a dramatic arietta with text material derived from Psalm 22: "My God, why hast Thou forsaken me." The song became an immediate favorite, and was taken on as a featured solo by other popular female performers of the day. However, within two decades of its introduction, it had become the special encore of Cantor Yossele Rosenblatt (1882–1933) in his nationwide vaudeville and synagogue tours. As a result, what had been the Bowery tune of women singers rapidly evolved into a Jewish hymn of liturgical qualities, assuming a form of religious status in the domain of male singers. Meanwhile, female entertainers on the Yiddish stage continued to perform sacred as well as secular selections for their appreciative audiences. In 1918, the actor-impresario Boris Thomashefsky (?1864/8–1939) produced a musical entitled *Di khazinte* (The lady cantor) starring Regina Prager (1874–1949)), a popular actress who had been the leading lady in Goldfaden's pioneer Jewish operettas.

The second half of the twentieth century has been an era of growth in self-awareness among ethnic and racial groups the world over, as well as a time of quest on the part of women for their own identity and dynamic role in society. One result has been a plethora of biographies and bibliographies devoted to women of achievement. Moreover, there is a recognition of women's current roles in the entire spectrum of the arts, and some women are emerging as important figures in the field of music. Yet the perspectives on that particular artistic expression are problematic. Did twentieth-century woman spring suddenly to life full-grown in her musical abilities, or has she been creative throughout the centuries, her voice veiled as *kol ishah be-lahash*? Should her contemporary creativity be treated as a remarkable new and vital trend, or should it be viewed rather as an opportunity for modern scholars to correct what had previously been overlooked or written out of cultural history? Clearly, there is now at least a mandate for investigating women's musical history in both its sacred and secular expressions, and several publications have begun to address that matter effectively.[16] Moreover, women today are taking advantage of the wider range of opportunities open to them in all aspects of music, even in the liturgy, though the essence of "woman's voice" still remains suspect or "veiled" in many churches and synagogues.

NOTES

This article originally appeared in *Music Library Association Notes*, vol. 48, no. 4 (1992), pp. 1193–1202.

1. For an excellent comparative study, see Denise L. Carmody, *Women and World Religions* (Englewood Cliffs, N.J.: Prentice Hall, 1989).

2. Source materials and citations in this article from the writings of the early Church Fathers are drawn from Johannes Quasten, "The Liturgical Singing of Women in Christian Antiquity," *The Catholic Historical Review*, vol. 27 (1941), pp. 149–65.

3. Louis I. Newman and Samuel Spitz, eds., *The Talmudic Anthology* (New York: Behrman House, 1947), p. 296. The *Talmud* (literally meaning "teachings") is the *corpus juris* of Judaism. Its numerous volumes are a compendium of rabbinical writings dating from the first thousand years of the Christian Era. In addition to interpretations and commentaries based upon the *Mishnah* (body of traditional doctrine), its wide range of subject matter also includes theology, philosophy, science, ethics, civil and secular issues, and sacred and secular literature.

4. Carl Heinrich Cornill, *Music in the Old Testament*, trans. from German by Lydia G. Robinson (Chicago: Open Court Publishing, 1909), p. 4.

5. For some intriguing theories about women musicians among the Levites, see the sections titled "Women in the Music of Ancient Israel" in two books by Alfred Sendrey:

Music in Ancient Israel (New York: Philosophical Library, 1969).

Music in the Social and Religious Life of Antiquity (Rutherford, N.J.: Fairleigh Dickinson University Press, 1974).

6. Interestingly, the issue of women's music is all but missing from two notable histories of Jewish music. There are only passing references in Abraham Z. Idelsohn, *Jewish Music in Its Historical Development* (New York: Holt, Rinehart and Winston, 1929). The topic is entirely absent from: Eric Werner, *A Voice Still Heard: The Sacred Songs of the Ashkenazic Jews* (University Park: Pennsylvania State University Press, 1976).

7. A good consideration of early rabbinical dicta is provided in Emily Taitz, "*Kol Isha*—The Voice of Women: Where Was It Heard in Medieval Europe?" *Conservative Judaism*, vol. 38 (1985), pp. 46–61.

8. See *The Responsum of Maimonides Concerning Music*, trans. from Hebrew by Boaz Cohen (New York: Posy-Shoulson, 1935). This translation of writings by Maimonides was also included in a subsequent work: Boaz Cohen, *Law and Tradition in Judaism* (New York: Jewish Theological Seminary of America, 1959), pp. 167–81.

9. On this topic, see Geoffrey Wigoder, ed., *Jewish Art and Civilization* (New York: Walker, 1972). The iconography of Jewish music is a topic meriting further scholarly research.

10. Alfred Sendrey, *The Music of the Jews in the Diaspora: Up to 1800* (New York: Thomas Yoseloff, 1970), p. 228.

11. Cecil Roth, *The Jews in the Renaissance* (Philadelphia: Jewish Publication Society of America, 1959), Chapter 12, "Music and Dance."

12. Cecil Roth, *History of the Jews in Venice* (New York: Schocken Books, 1975), pp. 237–40.

13. Cecil Roth, *A History of the Jews in England* (London: Clarendon Press, 1964), p. 210.

14. *Memoirs of Glueckel of Hameln*, ed. and trans. from German by Beth-Zion Abraham (New York: Thomas Yoseloff, 1963), pp. 19–20. This is a unique autobiographical report by a Jewish woman of her time and circumstances.

15. Irene Heskes, comp., *The Music of Abraham Goldfaden* (Cedarhurst, N.Y.: Tara Publications, 1990), pp. iii–ix.

16. In particular, see the following works:

Carol Neuls-Bates, ed., *Women in Music: An Anthology of Source Readings from the Middle Ages to the Present* (New York: Harper & Row, 1982).

Jane Bowers and Judith Tick, eds., *Women Making Music: The Western Art Tradition, 1150–1950* (Urbana: University of Illinois Press, 1987).

Karen Pendle, ed., *Women and Music: A History* (Bloomington: Indiana University Press, 1991).

Afterword

With Jewish music, Jews continually live their history, traditions, and culture. The religious calendar year is observed in ritual and folk melodies; the life cycle observances are interpreted in chant; the sweep of diasporic experience is reflected in manifold elements of song.

In this book I have tried to provide portal and passage into that remarkable realm of Judaic musical expression. In terms of scholarly approach, I have developed a topical summary of the field and have treated its range of creative practices and artistic achievements. These varied study essays, with their reference notes and citations as sources for further study, should contribute to the greater understanding and appreciation of a particular part of the world's melodic heritage.

Society cannot command nor demand its culture. While the arts must have their own creative ways, they serve to embellish, indeed to define, human civilization. Over the ages, artistry has documented the social and political history of mankind. And it has bound humanity together in a particular sort of unity. Some years ago, a book published by the United Nations Economic, Social, and Cultural Organization (UNESCO) underscored the significant role that music can play internationally.[1] It was a compilation of some sixty-five reports and speeches delivered at a 1953 conference of more than three hundred music leaders from many countries, including the then new State of Israel. A first meeting of its kind, the stated purpose was to consider the manifold problems connected with the encouragement of musical expression in different countries. Clearly, this was a form of world recognition for the value of musical activity, underscoring an appreciation of the role of music in sharing experiences among all peoples. That conference focused upon the melodic wealth of cultures, languages, and religions and on the unique joy in blending self-expression, first with group identification, and then through intergroup communication.

In sponsoring such a conference in 1953, UNESCO served notice that music could be a significant force for shaping the rest of the twentieth century into a more educated and enlightened era. Regardless of the past, there was optimism for the future. It appears from perusal of the published materials that the conference sessions were serious in nature and were held in a mutually respectful atmosphere. Rather than stressing any ideas of unification and assimilation, all the different musical heritages were to be preserved as a source of world cordiality and understanding. The conferees reached certain conclusions, as summarized in its final proceedings: music education is indispensable for adults as well as children, the need for musical expression is inherent in every human being and should be nurtured for the enrichment of all individuals, and the making and enjoyment of music is an integral part of community life, of cultural self-recognition, and of worldwide fellowship.

Decades later, as we enter the twenty-first century, such earlier optimism must not be clouded with disrespect. After all, music cannot be blamed for the world's problems. More likely, its potency for some good has managed to prevail.

All of this frames a cogent answer as to the why of Jewish music. It appears from those premises stated back in 1953 that there is a valid mandate to preserve this particular musical heritage and to transmit it as widely as possible on behalf of general world culture as well as for the sake of Judaic continuity. This is a concept of cultural pluralism carried into action. Reflecting upon the many viable differences in modes of self-expression extant among humanity, one earnestly seeks to negate the inevitability of a homogeneous ideal. There are strong justifications for perceiving the continuity of distinctive cultures as fully compatible with the modern way of life. Clearly, twenty-first-century world society must seek to confirm that positive view of harmonious individuality—of sustained constructive differences among races, religions, and ethnic groups—as a wellspring of strength on this planet earth. Over the ages, Jewish artistry has benefited from such symbiotic relationships in productive terms both for *Ars Judaica* and for the general cultural mainstream. This has been particularly true of the musical art.

Several days after the Yom Kippur War in 1973, then-Premier Golda Meir congratulated some musicians upon their performances at a Jerusalem concert, saying to them: "Art often both alleviates and memorializes human suffering, and thereby helps us to alleviate our pain."[2] The special art of music is a human activity continually shaped by attitudes and values, nourished by education and experience; it is the rightful domain of amateurs as well as professionals. Moreover, music is an art that is linked to all the other arts—dance, poetry, drama, literature, painting, sculpture, and, yes, the various forms of expressive electronic media. There are no boundaries between each of those creative forms. The basic enterprise of civilization is its artistic and intellectual productivity. Through the arts, we may review the past, celebrate the present, and commit ourselves to the future. The arts are both timely and timeless.

Do not disturb the musicians!
Where there is music,
Do not pour out speech,
And do not be importunate in showing thy wisdom.
Like a ruby shines in its golden setting,
So is the musicians' ensemble at a banquet.
As the precious emerald in a golden frame,
So adorn melodies of musicians at a feast.
Therefore, listen in silence
And thy modesty will be rewarded by good will.
                    Ben Sirach, Apocrypha, Ecclesiasticus 32:3–6

NOTES

1. *Music in Education: A Report on UNESCO's National Conference on the Role and Place of Music in the Education of Youth and Adults, Brussels, 1953,* comp. and ed. not indicated on publication (New York: UNESCO and Columbia University Press, 1955)

2. As told to the author by Nahum Nardi who had attended that concert, and as subsequently confirmed by several others who were also there at the time.

Index

This is a reference listing of all the individuals mentioned in the book.

About the Author

IRENE HESKES is a music historian who specializes in Jewish music. She has written numerous articles and reviews for musicological and general journal publications in America, Europe, and Israel, and has contributed to the *Encyclopedia Judaica*, as well as to *Musical Theater in America* (Greenwood, 1984), and *Handbook of Holocaust Literature* (Greenwood, 1993). Among her books are: *Studies in Jewish Music* (1971), *Jews in Music* (1974), *Ernest Bloch: Creative Spirit* (1976), *The Resource Book of Jewish Music* (Greenwood, 1985), *The Music of Abraham Goldfaden* (1990), *The Golden Age of Cantors* (1991), and *Yiddish-American Popular Songs, 1895 to 1950* (1992).

ISBN 0-313-28035-5

EAN

9 780313 280351

HARDCOVER BAR CODE